STORMING HEAVEN

STORMING HEAVEN

LSD AND THE AMERICAN DREAM

JAY STEVENS

THE ATLANTIC MONTHLY PRESS NEW YORK

For Sara

The author wishes to thank the following authors and publishers for permission to quote from the books and articles listed:

Abramson, Harold A. (ed.). *The Use of LSD in Psychotherapy*. New York: Josiah Macy, Jr., Foundation Publications, 1960. Alpert, Richard (Ram Dass). *Be Here Now*. San Cristobal, New Mexico: Lama Foundation, 1971. Ginsberg, Allen. *Howl and Other Poems*. San Francisco: City Lights, 1956. Ginsberg, Allen, and Burroughs, William. *The Yage Letters*. San Francisco: City Lights, 1956. Hesse, Herman. *The Journey to the East*. New York: Noonday, 1965. Hollingshead, Michael. *The Man Who Turned on the World*. London: Blond & Briggs, 1973. Huxley, Aldous. *The Doors of Perception* and *Heaven and Hell*. London: Penguin, 1961. Huxley, Aldous. *The Doors of Perception*. New York: Perennial Library, 1970. Huxley, Aldous. *Letters of Aldous Huxley* (ed. Grover Smith). New York: Harper & Row, 1969. Huxley, Aldous. *Moksha*. Los Angeles: Tarcher, 1982. Huxley, Julian (ed.) *Aldous Huxley: A Memorial Volume*. New York: Harper & Row, 1965. Kleps, Art. *Millbrook*. Oakland: The Bench Press, 1975. Kramer, Jane. *Allen Ginsberg in America*. New York: Random House, 1969. Leary, Timothy. *Flashbacks*. Los Angeles: Tarcher, 1983. Leary, Timothy. *High Priest*. Cleveland: World Publishing Company, 1968. Leary, Timothy. *The Politics of Ecstasy*. England: Granada Publishing, 1973. Marks, John. *The Search for the Manchurian Candidate*. New York: Times Books, 1979. McNally, Dennis. *Desolate Angel*. New York: McGraw Hill, 1980. Plummer, William. *The Holy Goof*. Englewood Cliffs, New Jersey: Prentice Hall, 1981. Rossman, Michael. *Wedding Within the War*. New York: Doubleday, 1971. Slack, Charles W. *Timothy Leary, The Madness of the Sixties, and Me*. New York: Peter H. Wyden, 1974. Solomon, David. *LSD: The Consciousness-Expanding Drug*. New York: Berkley Medallion, 1966. Thompson, Hunter. *Hells Angels*. New York: Ballantine, 1966. Von Hoffman, Nicholas. *We Are the People Our Parents Warned Us Against*. New York: Quadrangle, 1968. Watts, Alan. *In My Own Way*. New York: Vintage, 1973. Wilson, Robert Anton. *Cosmic Trigger*. New York: Pocket Books, 1977. Wolf, Leonard. *Voices from the Love Generation*. Boston: Little, Brown, 1968. Wolfe, Tom. *The Electric Kool-Aid Acid Test*. New York: Bantam, 1981.

Library of Congress Cataloging-in-Publication Data
Stevens, Jay.
    Storming heaven.
    Bibliography: p.
    1. Lysergic acid diethylamide. 2. Drug abuse—United
States. 3. Social history—1960-1970. 4. Subculture.
I. Title.
HV5822.L9S74   1987   306'.1   87-1191

Published simultaneously in Canada
Printed in the United States of America

CONTENTS

CONTENTS

PROLOGUE: AN AFTERNOON IN THE SIXTIES

During the night the rain and fog moved inland; by morning the air was sharp and clear. From the top of Nob Hill you could see the houseboats of Sausalito; Marin, in the distance, was a hazy shimmer.

It was going to be hot, going to be one of those fine winter days when the mercury suddenly climbs and for a few hours San Francisco becomes tropical, the golf links jammed with hackers, the Bay crowded with boats; the perfect sort of day to load the kids into the car and drive to San Simeon, to finally visit Randolph Hearst's baronial whim; the perfect sort of day to dig out last summer's bathing suit and catch a few rays, which was what the students at San Francisco State were doing.

It was January 14, 1967, a Saturday, and in parts of the Bay area elements from another, less integrated America, were also making plans: there was going to be a party in the park today, a curious affair with an extravagant name, *A Gathering of the Tribes for the First Human Be-In.*

The park was Golden Gate Park, one of those imperial parks built in the closing decades of the last century, with something for everyone, museums, lakes, bicycle paths, fly casting pools, a buffalo paddock with a herd of sleepy bison, a Japanese garden. On a sparkling Saturday like this, the Golden Gate should have resembled a twentieth-century version of George Seurat's epic painting, *La Grande Jatte,* but something had happened in the past few months to alter the ambiance. Just up the street, a short stroll away, was Haight-Ashbury, the home of the hippies, and the hippies, unencumbered by the Protestant work ethic, were treating the park as though it was their own special backyard.

They were everywhere, panhandling, singing, performing little existential playlets that were incomprehensible to everyone but themselves. They'd turned a nondescript slope near the tennis court into a perpetual love-in, although in these innocent days the form still lacked a name: what you saw, between serve and volley, was a shifting accumulation of—what? A European, registering the carnival costumes and the cheerful, almost dignified self-absorption of their wearers, might have credited the hippies with being another branch of the gypsy tribes of Romany. And in many of the externals they would have been correct. But in actual fact the bodies lolling on the grass next to the Golden Gate's tennis courts belonged to the educated sons and daughters of white middle-class America. They had, to use their own terminology, dropped out. In the stubborn fashion of children, they wanted nothing to do with the adult culture. That's what the Gathering of the Tribes was all about: it was a celebration of this rejection, and a partial first step toward building an alternative.

Although the possibility of the Be-In had been floating around the Haight-Ashbury for months, it was only in the last couple of weeks that the concept had jelled and notices had been sent to the local press announcing that an epochal moment was about to occur. "Would you believe Timothy Leary and Mario Savio?" enthused the hippies' favorite newspaper, the San Francisco *Oracle*.

> Allen Ginsberg and Jack Weinberg? Lao Tzu and Spartacus? Berkeley's political activists are going to join San Francisco's hippies in a love feast that will, hopefully, wipe out the last remnants of mutual skepticism and suspicion.

Which was echoed in even more ecstatic strophes by the Berkeley *Barb*, the preferred read of the activists:

> When the Berkeley political activists and the love generation of the Haight-Ashbury and thousands of young men and women from every state of the nation embrace at the gathering of the tribes for a Human Be-In at the Polo Field in Golden Gate Park, the spiritual revolution will be manifest and proven. In unity we shall shower the country with waves of ecstasy and purification. Fear will be washed away; ignorance will be exposed to sunlight; profits and empire will lie drying on deserted beaches. . . .

Added to this were thousands of posters—one showing a bearded Hindu *sadhu* gazing beatifically out at the observer, another featuring a Plains Indian cradling a guitar instead of a rifle—that blotted out the usual screeds advertising rock acts at the Fillmore.

More than a few respectable citizens must have contemplated that gnomic *a gathering of the tribes* and wondered, with a twinge of unease, what in hell was going on in their fair city.

It sounded like something the Indians might have held before riding off to massacre Custer.

What in hell . . . ? was a question a lot of Americans were asking in the first perplexing months of 1967. Unlike other periods of national crisis, the economy was healthy; the GNP, up a third in the first five years of the decade, was climbing steadily, and Wall Street was in the initial stages of what would later be called the Go Go Years. *Conglomerate* was a word on every broker's lips, as was *synergy*. Aside from some racial strife and a bit of dissension over our Indochina policy, we were also in good shape domestically. The New Frontier had segued into the Great Society without appreciable loss of momentum. In fact, LBJ, with years of legislative chits to draw on, was proving a far better salesman than JFK had ever been. Among liberal intellectuals it was generally believed that we were becoming a classless society, perhaps the first in history, material abundance having rendered the Marxist critique obsolete. In *Political Man*, Seymour Martin Lipset had magisterially declared that "the triumph of the West ends domestic politics for those intellectuals who must have ideologies or utopias to motivate them to political activities."

Yet, seemingly at the very moment of triumph—of realizing what Robert Frost, in his 1960 inaugural poem, had called an Augustan Age—the whole thrust of our national purpose was being denounced and rejected in language that had gotten Lenny Bruce jailed just five years earlier. And this critique wasn't coming from the International Communist conspiracy or the John Birch right wing or any of a dozen familiar ideological groups—it came from those adorable adolescents who spent over $10 billion a year on consumer products, and of whom Clark Kerr, the Chancellor of the University of California at Berkeley, had once said: "The employers will love this generation. . . . They are going to be easy to handle."

American Teenagers: one moment they were playing baseball and attending sock hops and the next they were racing down the Negro streets at dawn, screaming, hysterical, naked, or at least that's the way it seemed.

Even as late as 1965, had you suggested that America's well-heeled young might rise up and attempt to pull down the Republic, you would've been laughed from the room. *Time*, in January of that year, found a generation of conformists: "almost everywhere boys dress in madras shirts and chinos, or perhaps green Levis. All trim and neat. The standard for girls is sweaters and skirts dyed to match, or shirtwaists and jumpers plus blazers, Weejun loafers and knee socks or stockings." When a young Harvard psychologist named Kenneth Kenniston came to write about these kids, he painted a portrait of rudderless teens adrift in a world of material abundance and spiritual poverty. Kenniston called his book *The Uncommitted.* Three years later, his thesis in ruins, he would rush back into print with *The Young Radicals: Notes on Committed Youth.*

A lot of writers, forced to contemplate the noisy confusion that has since coalesced in the phrase *the Sixties,* turned to a poem by the Irish poet William Butler Yeats, which contained these evocative lines:

> . . . *the centre cannot hold;*
> *Mere anarchy is loosed upon the world,*
> *The blood-dimmed tide is loosed, and everywhere*
> *The ceremony of innocence is drowned;*
> *The best lack all conviction, while the worst*
> *Are full of passionate intensity.*

Yeats delivered those lines in a poem called "The Second Coming," which was ostensibly about the return of Christ, although most of the poem, the meat of it, imagined the Antichrist, bestirring itself after "twenty centuries of stony sleep," moving its slow thighs across the desert:

> *And what rough beast, its hour come round at last,*
> *Slouches towards Bethlehem to be born?*

For a lot of Americans, that image, the rough, slouching beast, captured perfectly the unease they felt whenever they contemplated their children. Indeed the only editorial change the poem needed to be completely contemporary was the location: for "Bethlehem," read "San Francisco."

What was it about America's sixth-largest city that made it, in the second half of the twentieth century, the Paris of discontent? Alan Watts, a minor but valued player in our story, thought it was the Bay Area's Mediterranean climate, which acted as a natural vaccine against the virus of Puritanism. Others attributed it to San Francisco's tradition of tolerance. Long a haven for those persecuted during America's frequent spasms of intolerance, it probably boasted more Wobblies, anarchists, communists, beatniks, mystics, and eccentric freethinkers per square mile than all the other cities put together. But of equal, if not greater, weight was the simple geographical fact that San Francisco was the Queen City of California, and California, as the magazines and sociologists never tired of pointing out, was the future impinging upon the present. Everything was bigger, newer, better, faster, shinier in California; it was the jewel in technocracy's crown. On the back of the

American dollar bill is a picture of the reverse side of the Great Seal of the United States, showing a three-quarter completed pyramid, along with the legend, *novus ordo seclorum,* a new order of the ages. California was where they were finishing the top of the pyramid. So it was only fitting that it was there that the exodus from "normalcy" began.

Allen Ginsberg appeared on Haight Street shortly before eleven, a talmudic presence with his flowing beard and bald head. He was wearing blue beach thongs and a crisp white hospital orderly's uniform, and as he strolled toward the park he was greeted with affection. Ginsberg was the closest thing the hippies had to a universally accepted hero. Others, like Tim Leary, Alan Watts, and Ken Kesey, had their partisans, but Ginsberg was adored by all. He was a link with the past, a survivor of the Beat movement, which was the most obvious cultural precursor of what was happening in the park today.

The previous evening a few of these elder statesmen had met in Michael McClure's Haight-Ashbury apartment to hammer out an agenda for today's festivities. Aside from Ginsberg, sitting cross-legged on the floor, his bald crown gleaming in the candlelight, there had been Gary Snyder, the Zen poet of Kerouac's *The Dharma Bums;* Lenore Kandel, a belly dancer and author of some lubricious lyrics called *The Love Book;* plus Lenore's boyfriend, Freewheeling Frank, the Secretary of the San Francisco chapter of the Hells Angels; plus McClure, looking professorial with his pipe; plus a local character named Buddha, who was the Be-In's official master of ceremonies.

How to juggle the assorted political speakers, poets, spiritual leaders, and rock bands into a seamless whole without destroying the Be-In's overarching purpose had been the central topic. For several years Ginsberg had been lobbying for a new form of spiritual-political theatre. Don't just march and wave placards, he had urged the New Left from the pages of the Berkeley *Barb.* Dance to the Oakland Army Terminal, sing, hand out flowers, celebrate life. The New Left would ignore him, but not the hippies. Tomorrow, America would experience its first indigenous *mela*—*mela* being Hindi for a gathering of holy seekers.

The planning had gone smoothly until they reached the topic of Tim Leary. Was Leary to be considered a poet, and therefore entitled to only seven minutes at the microphone, or was he a genuine prophet, deserving of unlimited time?

"Tim Leary's a professor," one of them had said in a tone implying that professors don't talk, they lecture.

Ginsberg had suggested that Leary get the allotted seven minutes, which, after all, was all he was going to get.

"Is Leary a prima donna?" someone else had asked.

"Man, I don't think so—after all, he's taken acid."

"Leary just needs a little of the responsibility taken off him," Ginsberg had replied. "Seven minutes, and anyway, if he gets uptight and starts to preach, Lenore can always belly dance."

"Man, I'd just as soon no one says a word tomorrow," Buddha had said. "Just beautiful silence. Just everybody sitting around smiling and digging everybody else."

Whereupon Ginsberg had started chanting *hari om nama shivaya,* which was a Hindu mantra to Shiva, god of destruction, creation, and cannabis. And his voice, "full of throbs and melodies" had lifted the others to their feet and the meeting had adjourned as everyone swayed and danced in an ecstasy that was untranslatable to someone who wasn't attuned to what was happening in the Haight-Ashbury.

"That one big street, Haight Street, running from about Masonic to Clayton, was just packed with every kind of freak you could imagine. Guys with mohawk haircuts, people walking around in commodore uniforms, you know, the hat with the fuzz all over it. Everything! You couldn't believe it. It was an incredible street scene."

That was a hippie talking. A middle-aged journalist, after spending a few exhausting months there, remembered the Haight this way: "the madness of the place, the shouts, the chasing, the gunning bikes, the chaotic, occasional screams of girls running has convinced people that the Haight is a rare species of insane disorganization."

Which is to say the Haight was one of the few genuine street scenes in America, albeit a street scene filled with what appeared to be Gilbert & Sullivan extras, pirates, and sheiks, all talking as though they had wandered out of a mystical P. G. Wodehouse novel. Dissect a typical hippie monologue and you found elements of zen, hinduism, existentialism, McLuhanism, and mysticism, mixed with equal amounts of alchemy, astrology, palm reading, a belief in auras, and a diet that consisted of rice and grains. The rational and the irrational, the scientific and the mystical rubbed shoulders with alarming intimacy.

Lining Haight Street, which ran in a flat line for several miles, were all sorts of esoteric shops, places like the I-Thou Coffee Shop or the Print Mint, with its staggering inventory of day-glo posters; places like the Psychedelic Shop with its racks of literature, its meditation room, and its enormous bronze gong, which dominated the sidewalk like a local Big Ben. Later there would be a bus tour for the curious, operated by the Gray Line, a company with a history of capitalizing on San Francisco's excesses, having run a similar excursion through the North Beach.

"We are now entering the largest hippie colony in the world," the tour guide would exclaim, urging everyone to the windows. "We are now passing down Haight Street, the very nerve center of a city within a city . . . marijuana, of course, is a household staple here, enjoyed by the natives to stimulate their senses. . . . Among the favorite pastimes of the hippies, besides taking drugs, are parading and demonstrating, seminars and group discussions about what's wrong with the status quo; malingering; plus the ever present preoccupation with the soul, reality and self-expression, such as strumming guitars, piping flutes, and banging on bongo drums."

The hippies responded by holding up mirrors so the tourists could look at themselves.

But we are getting ahead of ourselves. The tourists, including the mob of reporters who made the Haight a media port of call in the Sixties—Saigon being another—came later, after the Gathering of the Tribes for the First Human Be-In called attention to just how fast the social fabric was ripping in San Francisco. On this sparkling Saturday, the word *hippie* was barely a year old. Like beatnik, peacenik, etc., it was one of those semiderogatory diminutives that journalists love to coin. The hippies hated it. They preferred either freak or head, names illustrative of their belief that they represented an evolutionary advance, a mutation of the species, a "hopeful monster" to use one geneticist's description.

Journalists bumping into this odd notion generally discounted it as part of the cultural static that was fuzzing the lines of communication between what was becoming known as the straight world and this new configuration, which some were beginning to call a counterculture. Consequently they missed the story. To put matters bluntly: the hippies *were* an attempt to push evolution, to jump the species toward a higher integration. To exaggerate only a little: they were a laboratory experiment that had either gone awry or succeeded brilliantly—a difference of opinion that stands at the center of this story, and one that will still be standing when this book is finished.

Stop for a moment and think of the last hundred years as a symphony, a grand orchestration of crescendos and fugues, a tangle of melodies, one of which, a very faint but haunting refrain, goes like this: we are doomed unless a way can be found to speed up evolution, to consciously push the smart monkey to a higher level, to renew the assault on the gods, which was the secret purpose of all religions. But can we consciously evolve ourselves? Does a magic trigger exist that is capable of shooting the species forward a few increments? Is there a door in the mind we can pass through? And if there is, does a key exist capable of opening that door?

In the middle years of this century, out of nowhere, an answer to these questions emerged. There was a key to the door, and it was a drug, or rather a family of drugs—the psychedelics—and in particular LSD, which the hippies called acid partially on account of its usefulness in burning off that Greco-Judaic-Christian patina, and mostly because the drug's technical name was d-lysergic acid diethylamide, a mouthful even for Mary Poppins. According to the hippies, LSD was the glue that held the Haight together. It was the hippie sacrament, a mind detergent capable of washing away years of social programming, a re-imprinting device, a consciousness-expander, a tool that would push us up the evolutionary ladder. Some even claimed LSD was a gift from God, given to mankind in order to save the planet from a nuclear finale.

Not that the average hippie bothered with the metaphysics of that melody that filled his ears. Very few knew that the phrase *cosmic consciousness* had been coined as long ago as 1901 by a Canadian psychologist named Richard Bucke to describe the evolutionary stage beyond self-consciousness, the domain of Jesus and Buddha, Blake and Whitman, to name just a few of those whom Bucke believed were species forerunners of cosmic consciousness. It was gratifying but immaterial that in the January issue of *Playboy* Julian Huxley could be found speculating on what role LSD might play in man's future evolution. The hippies didn't care, because they were living within one of those revolutionary moments that seem beyond time and history, a moment that Hunter Thompson described as "a fantastic universal sense that whatever we were doing was right, that we were winning. . . . And that, I think, was the handle—that sense of inevitable victory over the forces of Old and Evil. Not in any mean or military sense; we didn't need that. Our energy would simply prevail. There was no point in fighting—on our side or theirs. We had all the momentum; we were riding the crest of a high and beautiful wave. . . ."

In a decade devoted to excess and oddity, LSD and the movement it spawned stood apart as one of the oddest and most misunderstood episodes. Which was both fitting and ironic. Had you gone to a public library on that sparkling Saturday in January 1967, and looked up *d-lysergic acid diethylamide* in the appropriate abstracts, you would have found thousands of citations. Few drugs had been studied so extensively. However, had you taken the further trouble of parsing through several dozen of these papers, you would have discovered a complete absence of formal conclusions. There were hunches and hypotheses and horror stories and glowing reports and experiments that worked for some but not for others. But there was no consensus. Every type of madness, every type of parapsychological phenomenon, every type of mystical, ecstatic illumination, Jungian archetypes, past lives, precognition, psychosis, satori-samadhi-atman, union with God—it was all there, in the scientific record.

Reading through the monographs, you could sense the confusion that LSD had created in the scientific community, when, using it as a deep probe into the unconscious, it had stirred up something that looked very much like their archenemy, the mystic religious experience! What was that doing in there? And what did it mean if all it took was 300 millionths of a gram of LSD and you could produce the most profound sort of religious epiphanies in carpet salesmen and dentists? Was the visionary core of religion—enlightenment—merely an aberration caused by a malfunction of our neural chemistry, brought on by drugs or fasting or fevers or a blow to the head? Or were the mystics correct? Was the Kingdom really inside us all the time, wired into the brain, waiting . . . ? Fascinating questions, but difficult to get a handle on. Try describing the taste of ice cream to someone who has never had any, and multiply that difficulty by a thousand, and you will get some idea of how hard it was to describe what it felt like to be one with the universe, to know that you existed on a multitude of levels, and not just on the puny one called I. So many things happened in the psychedelic state that just couldn't be expressed in language.

But all this, from the perspective of the average American, was beside the point. The real problem wasn't that the science story had turned into a religion story, it was that the religion story had somehow turned into a cultural revolt. The psychedelic experience might be as difficult to describe as the taste of ice cream, but it had still attracted an enthusiastic and dangerous bunch of salesmen. First and foremost was Dr. Timothy Leary, who had been booted out of Harvard because of these drugs. Whether the psychedelic movement would have happened without Dr. Leary is a matter of debate, but there can be no question that he defined its public style, churning out pamphlets, books, and records that equated LSD with the discovery of fire and the invention of the wheel. Dr. Leary was irrepressible. After Harvard fired him, he opened a retreat in upstate New York, where he catered to scores of young professionals eager to explore the Other World. Then, in September 1966, he founded the League for Spiritual Discovery, a sort of religion cum social movement whose purpose, he told audiences, was to "change and elevate the consciousness of every American within the next few years. Slowly, carefully, and beautifully, you can learn to drop out of American society as it is now set up." The League's slogan was the soon to be infamous "tune in, turn on, drop out."

The biography of Ken Kesey was equally spectacular. By age thirty he had published two highly praised, highly successful novels, a literary debut unmatched since the days of Hemingway and Fitzgerald. But then he had given up literature to create, using LSD, a new kind of art form, which he called the acid test. Kesey became a latter-day Johnny Appleseed, yoyoing up and down the California coast, throwing a series of multimedia drug parties. The largest of them, the Trips Festival, had occurred almost a year ago, in early 1966, when ten thousand psychedelic revelers had crowded into San Francisco's Longshoreman's Hall for a weekend of outrageous celebration.

Kesey and Leary weren't the only ones beating the psychedelic drum. On the radio the Beatles could be heard singing *"turn off the mind . . . float downstream . . ."* a phrase they had borrowed from one of Tim Leary's books, while he in turn had borrowed it from the *Tibetan Book of the Dead.* Then there was Allen Ginsberg. A few weeks earlier Ginsberg had suggested to a Boston church congregation "that everybody who hears my voice, directly or indirectly, try the chemical LSD at least once; every man, woman and child American in good health over the age of fourteen . . . that everybody including the President and his and our vast hordes of generals, executives, judges and legislators of these States go to nature, find a kindly teacher or Indian peyote chief or guru guide, and assay their consciousness with LSD."

Drop acid and change yourself, change yourself and then change the world.

It was clear to the adults that something awful was happening. LSD didn't expand your consciousness, they warned in newspapers and magazines and TV spots, it made you crazy, it probably damaged your brain cells, and it was illegal to boot. Use it and you'd either end up a vegetable or a criminal. But the kids didn't seem to be listening. If your way of life is sanity, then give me crazy, they were saying, which led a lot of people to revise their estimate of Godless communism as America's number-one enemy.

The hippies actually seemed to think they could subvert America with flowers and a few bags of the most powerful psychochemical ever discovered. How absurd! And yet they seemed so sure of themselves, they really seemed to believe that within ten years America would be a totally turned-on country, full of bodhisattvas instead of bankers. . . . It was laughable, but nobody was laughing.

Like all moments of high drama, the psychedelic movement was part tragedy, part comedy, one of those rich tapestries of coincidence and misdirection that bolster our belief that fiction is often a pale reflection of reality. What if Albert Hofmann hadn't listened to his inner voice? What if Aldous Huxley hadn't read that particular issue of the *Hibbert Journal?* What if Robert Graves hadn't passed on an obscure reference to his friend the New York banker. What if the CIA . . . you could play the what-if game for hours.

Not that the hippies bothered. They had better things to do on this beautiful Saturday in 1967. Today they were all going to be at The Human Be-In, where it was rumored Owsley acid would flow like wine.

Today they were going to party. The revolution, which was really just an evolution, could wait until Monday; give the empire another day of grace before it was dragged up onto the beach and left like the obsolete piece of flotsam it was.

What did a day or two matter when you were riding a high and beautiful wave.

BOOK ONE

THE DOOR IN THE WALL

!
A BIKE RIDE
IN BASLE

Had you asked your average hippie about beginnings, you would have discovered there were as many as there were hippies—everyone had a favorite chronology. Some preferred to begin the psychedelic story all the way back at the *Rig Veda*, the ancient Hindu text that spoke of the ecstatic visions obtainable from the plant soma; others began with the mystery cults of ancient Greece and the Middle Ages—the Rosicrucians, the Alchemists, the Illuminati. The lure of higher consciousness had exercised a fascination across the centuries, and whether it was Athenians being initiated at Eleusis, or Balzac and Baudelaire smoking hashish at the Club des Haschischins, the hippies recognized them all as parents.

But if the psychedelic story had a hundred beginnings, at some point all the plot lines converged on Basle, Switzerland, at a few minutes before five on the afternoon of Monday, April 19, 1943.

Straddling the Rhine River near the spot where the Swiss border brushes those of France and Germany, Basle was a city of spires and bridges, banks and industry, the flower of which were the three huge chemical combines that lined the river: Hoffman-La Roche, Ciba-Geigy, and Sandoz. Our story concerns this last company, Sandoz Pharmaceuticals, and in particular one of its research chemists, a Doctor Albert Hofmann.

With his cropped hair and spectacles, Albert Hofmann looked exactly like what he was: a thirty-seven-year-old bourgeois intellectual family man. He had joined Sandoz in 1927, shortly after graduating from the University of Zurich, and not too long after Sandoz had begun bolstering its traditional product line—herbicides, insecticides, and dyes—with drugs.

The pharmaceutical business in the late 1920s was an exciting place

3

for a young chemist to apprentice. Everyone in the industry was scrambling after the same clues, sifting the chemical possibilities like archeologists working adjacent digs, hoping to find a better antibiotic, a safer headache pill; hoping to discover the next sulfanimide, which was generally considered the first wonder drug. Sandoz had invested part of its research hopes in *Claviceps purpurea,* better known as ergot, a fungus that grew on diseased kernels of rye. Although it had folk medicine uses in childbirth (it speeded up uteral contractions) and abortions (same reason), ergot was principally famous as the cause of St. Anthony's Fire, one of those demiscourges that had afflicted mankind since the invention of agriculture. Swallowing ergot-contaminated rye caused one's fingers and toes to blacken, then drop off, as a prelude to a particularly nasty death. The medical men called it dry gangrene.

Hofmann, who had spent his early years at Sandoz studying the active properties of Mediterranean squill, was in charge of the ergot project. For the past eight years he had methodically synthesized one ergotomine molecule after another, shelving each synthesis as animal tests proved unpropitious and moving on to the next. Ideally he was hoping to discover a new analeptic—something for migraines perhaps—but by April 1943 he had worked his way through dozens of variations, with no sign of success. "A peculiar presentiment," is the way Hofmann later described the feeling that stole over him that spring. A premonition. Intuition. Whatever it was, Hofmann began to feel that he had missed something back in 1938, when he had synthesized the twenty-fifth compound of the lysergic acid series, the one bearing the lab notation LSD-25.

Acting upon this presentiment, Hofmann synthesized a new batch of LSD-25 on Friday, April 16. By midday he had a crystalline version that was easily soluble in water. But then he started to feel woozy. Thinking it the onset of a cold, Hofmann took the rest of the day off. And he was just climbing into bed when the hallucinations began.

In a report subsequently filed with Arthur Stoll, his immediate superior, Hofmann described these hallucinations as "an uninterrupted stream of fantastic images of extraordinary plasticity and vividness and accompanied by an intense kaleidoscopic play of colors." Suspecting that LSD-25 had caused these fireworks, Hofmann decided to test this hypothesis the following Monday, the nineteenth. At 4:20 in the afternoon, with his assistants gathered around, he dissolved what he thought was a prudently infinitesimal amount of the drug—250 millionths of a gram—in a glass of water and drank it down.

At 4:50 he noted no effect. At 5:00 he recorded a growing dizziness, some visual disturbance, and a marked desire to laugh. Forty-two words later he stopped writing altogether and asked one of his lab assistants to call a doctor before accompanying him home. Then he climbed onto

4

his bicycle—wartime gasoline shortages having made automobiles impractical—and pedaled off into a suddenly anarchic universe.

In Hofmann's mind this wasn't the familiar boulevard that led home, but a street painted by Salvador Dali, a funhouse roller coaster where the buildings yawned and rippled. But what was even stranger was the sense that although his legs were pumping steadily, he wasn't getting anywhere.

Hofmann was about to communicate this predicament to his young assistant (who later reported that they had cycled at a vigorous pace) when he discovered his voice wasn't working either. Whatever mechanism translated thoughts into speech, that too was broken.

When the doctor reached Hofmann's house, he found his patient to be physically sound, but mentally . . . mentally Hofmann was hovering near the ceiling, gazing down on what he thought was his dead body. Gone were the pleasant fireworks of the previous Friday. He had been invaded by a demon. When his neighbor arrived with milk, a liquid Hofmann hoped would neutralize the poison, she was no longer gentle Mrs. R., but a "malevolent insidious witch" wearing "a lurid mask."

Lying in bed, his thoughts moving at a thunderous clip, Hofmann wondered if he had permanently damaged his mind. Compounding his distress was the fact that his wife and children were visiting in the country. What if they returned and found not Papa, but a lunatic, a cautionary footnote in the history of psychopharmacology?

Although it took as its subject one of mankind's oldest pursuits—the use of drugs for pleasure and healing—as an accepted discipline psychopharmacology was less than a century old. The first scientific treatment of the subject was generally thought to be Von Bibra's *Die Narkotischen Genusmitteel unde der Mensch,* published in 1855, a work that identified seventeen different mind-altering plants. Von Bibra had urged others to explore this fascinating back alley of the botanical world, and his advice was followed some thirty years later by a Berlin toxicologist and artist named Louis Lewin. In 1886 Lewin had published the first pharmacological study of *kava,* a plant root indigenous to the South Seas, where the natives considered its intoxication to be far superior to that of alcohol.

A year after publishing this monograph, and probably as a result of it, Lewin received some muscale buttons from Parke, Davis, an American apothecary that would one day evolve into the multinational pharmaceutical corporation of the same name. *Muscale* and *mezcal* were the American names for the cactus buttons that the Mexicans called *peyote.* Long popular among the Indians of Mexico, peyote had spread north of the Rio Grande in the aftermath of the Civil War and had quickly achieved ritual status among tribes like the Kiowa and the Commanches. Lewin was sufficiently intrigued by the buttons to finance his own expedition to the American southwest, where he gathered numerous specimens—one of which, the dumpling cactus, was later christened *Anhalonium lewinii*. Back in his Berlin laboratory, Lewin isolated four different peyote alkaloids, but balked at self-experimentation when animal tests failed to reveal which was the psychoactive element. That risky adventure fell to Arthur Heffter, a colleague of Lewin's, who ingested each alkaloid until he isolated the important one, which he christened *mezcal*.

Just as an earlier generation of intellectuals had gathered around Diderot's Encyclopedia, men like Lewin and Heffter were also part of a great collective project, one deriving from Linnaeus, which sought to classify nature in all its variety. It was a project that transcended cultural and class boundaries, and it was carried forward largely by amateurs: the botanizing parson, the baron who financed collecting expeditions, the medical doctor who dabbled in toxicology and pharmacology. A substance like peyote, arriving in the midst of this international quest with its romantic aura of the American frontier, was bound to arouse interest. Buttons were dispatched to every important museum. Lewin himself gave them to Paul Henning at Berlin's Royal Botanical, and another German named Helmholtz mailed a sample to Harvard.

A similar dispatch, originating in Washington, D.C., ended up in the hands of Weir Mitchell, a Philadelphia physician-novelist who specialized in nervous disorders (*Injuries of the Nerves and Their Consequences,* 1872) and historical romances (*Hugh Wynne, Free Quaker,* 1896). Having read of peyote in the *Therapeutic Gazette,* Mitchell obtained a small supply of buttons from the article's author, a Doctor Prentiss. He tried them on May 24, 1896.

At first Mitchell experienced a surge of energy, closely followed by a feeling of intense mental acuity. Selecting a psychology paper that had resisted improvement all week, he sought to test this newfound brilliance. But the paper proved as resistant as ever. Next he tried a quick lyric, then a complicated math problem. Neither validated his feeling of expanded intellect. Fatigued, Mitchell retired to his bedroom for a nap. It was then that the visions came. Writing about his self-experiment in the austere pages of the *British Medical Journal,* Mitchell told how thousands of galactic suns had streamed across his vision, how a gothic tower gleaming with jewels had shot up to an immense height. It was a dreamy landscape, somewhat reminiscent of the American painter Maxfield Parrish, and it was read with interest by men like Havelock Ellis and William James.

Havelock Ellis, in many respects, was the English equivalent of Mitchell, being another medical man who preferred the literary life to the daily practice of medicine. Although he published hundreds of poems, essays, and medical treatises, Ellis is remembered today for the controversy surrounding his massive seven-volume *Psychology of Sex,* which the English courts promptly banned on the grounds of obscenity. On Good Friday, 1897, alone in his London rooms, Ellis swallowed three peyote buttons and sat down to wait. He experienced a rush of imagery similar to Mitchell's, with the distinction that his landscapes tended to be closer to Monet than Parrish.

Intrigued by these visual dramatics, Ellis thought it might be interesting to give peyote to a painter. He persuaded an artist friend to act as guinea pig, and then overdosed the poor man, causing him "hellish attacks of pain at the heart and a sense of imminent death." At one point Ellis offered the tormented fellow a biscuit. But when he touched it, the doughy lump burst into flame, tiny blue flames igniting his trousers and leaping instantly up one side of the body. And when he finally popped the biscuit into his mouth, it cast a light that was bluer than the blue of Capri's Blue Grotto, or so he told the bemused Ellis. Whereas Ellis had been captivated by peyote's transfiguration of the world, "such a silent and sudden illumination of all things around, where a moment before I had seen nothing uncommon," it had seemed a kind of madness to the painter. "Its strangeness affected me more than its beauty."

Undeterred, Ellis gave the buttons to several other artistic friends, among them the poet William Butler Yeats. *Whimsical* is the word for what Yeats experienced in the Other World: "It seems as if a series of dissolving views were carried swiftly before me, all going from right to left, none corresponding with any seen reality. For instance I saw the most delightful dragons, puffing out their breath straight in front of them like rigid lines of steam, and balancing white balls on the end of their breath."

Havelock Ellis summarized his experiments in "Mezcal: A New Artificial Paradise," an essay that appeared in the January 1898 issue of the *Contemporary Review.* Predominantly descriptive, the article did venture several generalizations, the most audacious being Ellis's assertion that an afternoon with peyote was an experience most educated gentlemen should try once or twice.

That was going too far for the editors of the *British Medical Journal,* who had published Weir Mitchell's much more conservative report on peyote. Do not be fooled by Ellis's paradise, warned the editors, it was actually a "New Inferno":

> While admiring the ripe descriptive powers of Mr. Ellis and his friends, we must venture to point out that such eulogy for any drug is a danger to the public . . . Mr. Ellis, it is true, states that in his

opinion habitual consumption of large amounts would no doubt be injurious, but he does go on to claim that "for a healthy person to be once or twice admitted to the rites of mescal is not only an unforgettable delight, but an educational influence of no mean value." Surely this is putting the temptation before the section of the public which is always in search of new sensation.

And regarding Ellis's claim that intellectuals would find peyote particularly delightful, the editors dryly noted that the Kiowa Indians of the American Plains were not "the most intellectual of the inhabitants of our sister continent."

Reading through this editorial, probably the granddaddy of all antipsychedelic editorials, two styles of argument are apparent, neither of which is particularly scientific, and both of which will reappear as our story runs its course. The first is the standard polemical technique of exchanging an opponent's term (paradise), for one of your own choosing (inferno), thereby redefining the debate to better suit your own prejudices. The second is less a stylistic device than the assumption, predominant in the Protestant West, that sensations, particularly new sensations, are necessarily bad. Drugs like peyote, argued the *BMJ* editors, will appeal to the wrong sort. Yet going by the evidence, they had so far appealed to two respected intellectuals, both of whom deemed the experience a worthy one.

By opting for the moralizing tone, the *BMJ* editors skirted a more interesting area of argument, which was just then becoming a topic of debate: what were legitimate drugs of use and what were dangerous drugs of abuse? There wasn't an issue of the *BMJ* that didn't contain a pitch for some new drug. The difference was that these were proposed cures for specific diseases, whereas peyote had no proven medical use. But did that automatically make it a drug of abuse? Was a substance used to promote nonpathological symptoms such as ecstasy, visions, even terror, a danger to the public if it wasn't a danger, physically or psychologically speaking, to the individual?

There was no simple answer then. There is no simple answer today. The fact is, the mind is constantly dulled by the inflow of everyday information, the same blue sky, the same wife and kids; it uses sensation the way we use grit to sharpen a dull blade. So to legislate against sensation seeking is to legislate against one of our strongest drives. . . .

But back to our story. Just as the editors of the *BMJ* had feared, peyote use increased, particularly among the bohemian subcultures that were emerging in London, Paris, New York. As the twentieth century moved casually toward the First World War, places like Montmartre and Greenwich Village became centers of intellectual ferment. In Greenwich Village much of this cultural flux revolved around a salon run by Mabel Dodge, a wealthy socialite with designs on becoming America's Madame de Stael. On any given evening one might find Big Bill Haywood, leader of the International Workers of the World, cheek by jowl with the anarchists Emma Goldman and Alexander Berkman, as well as freethinking Harvard boys like Walter Lippmann and John Reed. In the spring of 1914 Dodge conducted a peyote ritual (she called it, significantly, "an experiment in consciousness") that was modeled with quaint fidelity on the actual Kiowa ceremony.

> Raymond went out and found a green branch to make the arrow and he found the eagle feathers. For a fire he laid a lighted electric bulb on the floor with my Chinese Red shawl over it, and for the mountains of the moon—I forgot what he did about that—but the Peyote Path was a white sheet folded into a narrow strip running towards the east along the floor.

Raymond, Dodge wrote, swallowed his first peyote button and proceeded to howl like a dog, while she floated above it all, inviolate, filled with smug laughter for all the "facile enthrallments of humanity . . . anarchy, poetry, systems, sex, society."

Looking back on that evening from the vantage of seventy years, it is possible to discern a psychedelic epoch in miniature. In less than thirty years peyote had passed from the scientists to the intellectuals to the bohemians. Had the First World War not intervened, there is no telling how far the "dry whiskey" might have spread. After the war interest in these matters was largely confined to Germany, where in 1919 Ernst Spath succeeded in producing a synthetic version of the peyote's psychoactive alkaloid, which he called mescaline. Since it was no longer necessary to wrestle with those evil-tasting buttons—William James had managed to get only a bit of one down before succumbing to nausea; "Henceforth I'll take the visions on trust," he had written to brother Henry—research thrived. In the early twenties Karl Beringer published a massive study of mescaline, *Der Meskalinrausch,* literally "the mescaline intoxication." And in 1924 Louis Lewin produced his masterwork, *Phantastica,* in which he kept his pact with Von Bibra and catalogued most of the world's known mind-altering plants. Lewin divided this often contradictory profusion into five classes: euphorica, phantastica, inebrianta, hypnotica, and excitiantia. Seven years after its German publication, an English translation appeared, to scant notice save for an essay by Aldous Huxley that appeared in the Chicago *Herald Examiner.*

But for our purposes the unlikely encounter between Huxley and *Phantastica* is a crucial coincidence. Huxley had chanced upon the book, "dusty and neglected on one of the upper shelves" of his bookshop, in early 1931. It was a serendipitous encounter, for he had just completed a new novel, his fifth, which was a marked departure from the highbrow social satire that was his trademark. In this latest, called *Brave New World,* Huxley had designed an anti-utopia where the social glue wasn't a shared set of ethical assumptions or a national political philosophy or a conception of life's ultimate purpose, but a drug called *soma,* a name Huxley had cribbed from the mind-altering substance in the *Rig Veda.* Having designed his own mind drug out of whole cloth, as it were, Huxley was intrigued by Lewin's real-life compendium. And it elicited a prophetic pronouncement from him.

"All existing drugs," he wrote in the *Herald Examiner,* "are treacherous and harmful. The heaven into which they usher their victims soon turns into a hell of sickness and moral degradation. They kill, first the soul, then, in a few years, the body. What is the remedy? 'Prohibition,' answer all contemporary governments in chorus. But the results of prohibition are not encouraging. Men and women feel such an urgent need to take occasional holidays from reality, that they will do almost anything to procure the means of escape. . . . The way to prevent people from drinking too much alcohol, or becoming addicts to morphine and cocaine, is to give them an efficient but wholesome substitute for these delicious and (in the present imperfect world) necessary poisons. The man who invents such a substance will be counted among the greatest benefactors of suffering humanity."

Albert Hofmann did not go mad. In the morning he felt fine. More than fine, actually. Wandering into the garden after breakfast, he noticed that everything was gleaming with an extraordinary vitality. His senses were vibrating, attuned. It sounded crazy, but he felt reborn.

Equally curious was his almost perfect recall of the previous evening's turmoil. That suggested that his conscious mind had remained, well, conscious throughout the experience. Upon reaching his office, Hofmann composed a report that brought an immediate response from Arthur Stoll. "Are you certain you made no mistake in the weighing?" Stoll wanted to know. "Is the stated dose correct?"

There had been no mistake. Hofmann's incredible experience had been caused by a mere 250 millionths of a gram of LSD-25, little more than a speck, which made the stuff the most potent chemical known to man, some five thousand to ten thousand times more potent than an equivalent dose of mescaline, the substance LSD-25 most closely resembled. On subsequent experiments the dosage was lowered by two-thirds.

From Hofmann, its discoverer, LSD-25 went to Sandoz's pharmacologic department, where Ernst Rothlin tested its toxicity on a variety of animals. Cats, mice, chimpanzees, spiders, all weathered massive amounts of LSD-25 without apparent physical damage, although there was considerable behavioral oddity. Spiders, for instance, created webs of remarkable precision at low dosages, but lost all interest in weaving at higher ones. Cats exhibited a similar variability, ranging from nervous excitability to catatonia. But the most prophetic test, although no one realized this at the time, was the one with the chimps. One day Rothlin injected LSD into a lab chimp and then reintroduced the animal to its colony. Within minutes the place was in an uproar. The chimp hadn't acted crazy or strange, per se; instead it had blithely ignored all the little social niceties and regulations that govern chimp colony life.

At this point Sandoz faced a standard industry dilemma: should they continue research in hopes that a marketable use materialized, or should they go on to something else? Their decision to follow the former course was heavily influenced by the mescaline research of Beringer and others. In *Der Meskalinrausch,* Beringer had commented on the similarity between mescaline intoxication and psychosis, an observation that was echoed by more recent researchers, notably E. Guttmann and G. T. Stockings. "Mescaline intoxication," the latter had written in 1940, "is indeed a true 'schizophrenia' if we use that word in its literal sense of 'split mind,' for the characteristic effect of mescaline is a molecular fragmentation of the entire personality, exactly similar to that found in schizophrenic patients."

Besides giving it to schizophrenics, Stockings had tried mescaline himself, and had discovered that he could reproduce a whole spectrum of abnormal states: catatonia, paranoia, delusions of persecution, delusions of grandeur, hallucinations, religious ecstasy, homicidal impulses, suicidal impulses, apathy, mania. To use Freud's vocabulary, drugs like mescaline seemed to shatter the unity of the ego. It opened the Pandora's box of the unconscious.

The first human experiments, aside from the self-experimentation of the Sandoz staff, were conducted by Arthur Stoll's son Werner, who was a psychiatrist affiliated with the University of Zurich. Besides duplicating some of Stockings's work, Stoll made an additional discovery: in low dosages, LSD seemed to facilitate the psychotherapeutic process by allowing repressed material to pass easily into consciousness. Later there would be rumors that one of Stoll's patients had committed suicide after an LSD trip. In some versions of the story the patient was a female psychotic who killed herself two weeks after taking the drug in a therapeutic session; in others the woman's death occurred after the drug had been administered without her knowledge.

Stoll published his findings in 1947, and shortly thereafter Sandoz offered to supply LSD to select researchers. Trade-named *Delysid,* the accompanying literature suggested two possible uses:

Analytical: To elicit release of repressed material and provide mental relaxation, particularly in anxiety states and obsessional neuroses.

Experimental: By taking Delysid himself, the psychiatrist is able to gain an insight into the world of ideas and sensations of mental patients. Delysid also can be used to induct model psychoses of short duration in more normal subjects, thus facilitating studies on the pathogenesis of mental illness.

It arrived on American shores in 1949, which was a good year for a new mind drug to be making its debut.

2

THE CINDERELLA SCIENCE

If anything symbolized the public's newfound respect for psychological thinking, it was the pigeon. For two days in the summer of 1947, while America's psychiatrists caucused in the conference room of New York's Pennsylvania Hotel, a pigeon was trapped in the lobby, flitting from chandelier to potted palm, eluding all attempts at capture.

Had such an ornithological visitation occurred even a few years earlier, the papers would have been full of sly plays on birdbrain and the like. Back then the bearded, sex-obsessed psychiatrist had been a stock Hollywood lampoon. Back before the war, the Nazis, the concentration camps, the Bomb, back when the thesis that this was a mad mad world because we were a mad mad species had few adherents. Back, circa 1940, when there were only three thousand psychiatrists in the whole country, and even fewer psychologists.

There was no one explanation for psychology's postwar emergence as a serious discipline. Part of it was just the normal drift of science, the accumulation of theory and experiment, the attraction of capable minds to a new endeavor. But part of it was also the way war and revolution had shattered the serene rationalities of the Victorian and Edwardian eras. The fact that a hundred thousand men had died quibbling over a few yards of mud one day in 1916 had gone a long way toward popularizing the theory that our mental equilibrium was constantly being tested by what the ancients would have called inner demons, but which this new science was calling the unconscious.

A genuine period of the psyche was the way Grace Adams, writing in a 1936 *Atlantic Monthly,* described the years between 1919 and 1929; years when "literate Americans, and much of illiterate America, were more deeply interested in the whats and whys and wherefores of the human mind than they ever were before, and than, it seems likely, they ever will be again."

These were the years when the public acquired a working knowledge of such exotica as libido, IQ, conditioned reflexes, perversions, stimulus and response; when they digested Behaviorism, Freudianism, intelligence testing and gestalt psychology; when they purchased hundreds of books with titles like *The Psychology of Beauty, The Psychology of Buying, The Psychology of Bolshevism,* to peruse just the *B*s.

According to Adams, much of this enthusiasm could be traced to a single source: a battery of intelligence tests that had been administered during WWI to the almost two million recruits of the American Expeditionary Force by psychologists attached to the Surgeon General's staff. The results had been discouraging. Besides weeding out 8,646 recruits for mental insufficiency, the tests had also determined that the average mental age of these men—and by extension the nation—was thirteen years and one month. In other words, the average American was about as smart as a young teenager. What followed was an orgy of mental self-improvement, which lasted until the stock market crash, after which few had time for anything but material self-improvement.

By the mid-Thirties psychology had become a confederation of squabbling clans, which was why Grace Adams's article in the *Atlantic* had such a eulogistic tone. Within psychoanalysis there were a half dozen different schools, each headed by a charismatic thinker like Jung or Adler, who accepted the basic Freudian dynamic while differing in their interpretation of its effect on daily life. Behaviorism, which was also known as experimental psychology, was a much more unified body of dogma, and one that stood in opposition to everything psychoanalysis cherished. Through a clever bit of sophistry, the Behaviorists had decided that since many mental acts couldn't be measured they therefore didn't exist. The Freudian unconscious, to a Behaviorist, was about as scientific as a sonnet by Keats. Man was a robot conditioned by his environment, a complex of stimulus-response units! To back up these claims, the Behaviorists assembled a wealth of data derived from experiments with rats and pigeons. As an oft-told joke put it, psychology had first lost its soul, then its mind.

Behaviorism was popular in the corporate boardrooms, where its lessons were diligently applied to the American worker, whereas psychoanalysis found its audience among the wives and bohemian offspring of these same corporate managers.

Squeezed between these two massifs were several smaller duchies, principally medical psychiatry and academic psychology. Closely allied with neurology, medical psychiatry was interested in the organic rather than the psychic cause of mental illness; it favored surgery to talk therapy, and by the mid-Thirties was on the verge of two important breakthroughs. The first involved the severing of fibers in the brain's frontal lobes, a simple operation known technically as a leucotomy or lobotomy, that pacified even the most aggressive psychotics. The second discovery was less a specific surgical operation than a dawning awareness that certain drugs sometimes altered a psychosis's traditional course.

What was left, academic psychology, can best be summarized by quoting James Bruner's description of what it was like to be a psychology graduate student at Harvard in 1938: "We went together to Kurt Goldstein's seminar on brain and behavior, to Bob White's on 'Lives in Progress,' to Gordon Allport's on the life history, to Smitty Stevens on operationism, to Kohler's William James lectures, to Professor Boring's on sensation and perception, to Kurt Lewin's on topological psychology, whether we were intending eventually to be animal psychologists, social psychologists, psychophysicists, whatever." At a place like Harvard, academic psychology grouped itself into two nominal camps: the experimentalists, Bruner among them, who studied perception, memory, learning, and motivation; and the personality psychologists, who were interested in the way habits, traits, and values combined to form the individual ego. Although the experimentalists considered themselves more hard-nosed and scientific, the personality psychologists (appropriately) possessed two dynamic leaders in the patrician Harry Murray and the less flamboyant but brilliant teacher, Gordon Allport. At the Harvard Clinic, Murray was pioneering the use of diagnostic tests that purportedly provided an accurate reading of a patient's personality.

These tests had a curious background. Besides administering intelligence tests to America's doughboys, the Surgeon General's psychologists had also experimented with a questionnaire designed to weed out potential psychoneurotics. This was the Wordsworth Personal Data Sheet, named after its creator, Robert Wordsworth, a Columbia University psychologist. Using Binet's IQ test as a model, Wordsworth had come up with a 125-question inventory that was supposed to detect which personalities would crumble under fire. Unfortunately, as a practical device the Wordsworth had been a failure. Yet an odd thing had happened. Instead of shunning the Wordsworth, psychologists had been "so overjoyed at having a psychoneurotic tool—even one that didn't work—that [they] enthusiastically threw all [their] energies into its use and development."

The Wordsworth implied that human personality was quantifiable, that you could measure degrees of extroversion and neurosis, which was a godsend to psychologists caught between Behaviorism's penchant for rats, and the untestable models of psychoanalysis. By the mid-Thirties there was an abundance of these diagnostics, ranging from Hermann

Rorschach's inkblots (1921) to the Minnesota Multiphasic Personality Index and the Thematic Apperception Test, which was co-created by Harry Murray.

These tests came in two styles. The first resembled a standard school quiz, either true/false or fill in the blank, which asked things like: Do you daydream frequently? Do you prefer to associate with people younger than you? Are you troubled with the idea that people on the street are watching you? The second style favored neutral devices like inkblots or pictures. The Thematic Apperception Test, for example, used nineteen black and white illustrations, which you were asked to explain. The assumption was that the resulting fantasies would be loaded with unconscious data.

Although the predictive value of these diagnostics was questionable, their popularity was enormous. When America declared war in 1941, personality tests were an important part of its therapeutic arsenal. Fourteen million inductees were tested, with the disturbing result that 14 percent were declared unfit due to neuropsychiatric disorders. The size of this figure shocked a postwar America that already was tapping its toes to the beat of Henry Luce's American Century. Was it possible to rebuild Europe, bolster the GNP, educate the young, and thwart the communist menace, if 14 percent of our able-bodied young men were judged less than sound? Congress didn't think so, nor did the media, who made mental health, and our lack of it, a staple of postwar reportage.

In many ways it was a replay of the uproar that had greeted the army intelligence scores of the First World War. But what distinguished this second flowering of psychological enthusiasm from the first was the Depression, and in particular the philosophy of government intervention in the form of massive public works programs that had grown out of that decade's economic woes. Confronted by evidence that public sanity was more fragile than heretofore suspected, Congress responded with the National Mental Health Act, signed into law on July 3, 1946. Its first appropriation, a modest $4.2 million, was targeted for research into the cause, diagnosis, and treatment of neuropsychiatric disorders; the education of psychiatrists and psychologists; and the establishment of a nationwide network of clinics.

The numbers tell the rest of the story. In 1940 there were barely three thousand psychiatrists; a decade later, seven thousand five hundred. In 1951 the American Psychological Association counted eight thousand five hundred members, a twelvefold increase since 1940; by 1956 membership would surpass fifteen thousand. And the money curve was even more robust: by 1964 that modest $4.2 million will have jumped fortyfold to $176 million.

It was the arithmetic of twentieth-century progress. Where there had been only a handful of pioneers a decade before, now there were thousands of sophisticated intellects focused on the same problems. The result might be a little chaotic, but it worked. The Manhattan Project had proven that. And if the human mind was capable of penetrating invisible matter and releasing the energy that powered the sun, then wasn't it absurd to think that madness or maladaptation or depression could withstand a similar onslaught?

Inside the Pennsylvania Hotel, while the pigeon cavorted in the lobby, America's psychiatrists were electing the top wartime psychiatrist, Brigadier General William Menninger, as their new standard bearer. Described by the press as "neither a crackpot nor a foreigner," Menninger had occupied, by 1948, most of the top jobs within the psychiatric establishment. From this vantage he urged his colleagues, of which there were still fewer than five thousand, to forgo their traditional clientele of neurotic dowagers and wealthy bohemians, and concentrate on the man in the street, for that was where the real danger lay. The war, Menninger wrote, had taught two great lessons: (1) that there were far more maladjusted people than anyone had previously expected; and (2) that under strain even the sanest individual can break down. "Is there any hope," he asked his audience that day in the Pennsylvania Hotel, "that medicine, through its Cinderella, psychiatry, can step forward and offer its therapeutic effort to a world full of unhappiness and maladjustment?"

As is usual with crises that leap upon us unawares, a certain amount of overstatement occurred. Extrapolating from that questionable figure of 14 percent, it wasn't long before some psychiatrists were maintaining that everyone was crazy, or potentially crazy. *Time,* in the first feverish flush, quoted one psychiatrist to the effect that there were probably only one million normal people in the whole country—normal in this context meaning "no anxieties, no fears, no strong prejudices, no attractive vices."

Particular attention was paid to the children, for they were "fertile soil into which all kinds of mind-twists and deviations strike the root, grow rapidly like weeds, and crush everything that is normal." The Bureau of Census estimated that each year 840,000 kids were lost to neurosis, not to mention the disruption they caused in the smooth childhoods of their peers. According to *Newsweek,* a diligent psychiatrist could detect these weeds in children as young as one and two years old. A Doctor Leo Kanner described these problem kids as "quiet and retiring, anxiously overconscientious, almost too goody goody. Or they may be highly irritable, sensitive, and disagreeable . . . preschizophrenic children are overly moody, peevish, humorless, easily angered, taciturn, secretive, suspicious, careless, flighty, and easily fatigued."

At times it seemed no mood or activity was immune from the

psychological lexicon. Happiness became euphoria; enthusiasm, mania; creativity was a socially approved outlet for neurosis, while homosexuality and other forms of deviant bedroom behavior were an indication of psychopathology; as were "alcoholism and drug addiction . . . vagabondage, panhandling, the inability to form stable attachments." Old age became senile psychosis.

What was lost in this surge of prestige and money was the almost religious adherence to grand theories, be they Freudian or Behaviorist. Data poured in from a dozen different directions. When the first issue of the *Archives of General Psychiatry* appeared in 1956, the editor, Roy Grinker, promised to publish "contributions from all disciplines whether morphological, physiological, biochemical, endocrinological, psychosomatic, psychological, psychiatric, child psychiatric, psychoanalytical, sociological and anthropological . . . eventually a unified science of behavior may emerge," he wrote in the first editorial.

Great things in particular were expected from the marriage of psychology and neuroscience, which was just then emerging from infancy. The late Forties were the period when the various centers of the brain were discovered and mapped. Aldous Huxley paid a memorable visit to a UCLA lab that was filled with cats and monkeys, each with a forest of electrodes sticking out of its skull. The caged animals, by pressing a lever, could massage their brains' pleasure centers with little electrical shocks, an experience so wondrously ecstatic that some pressed the lever eight thousand times an hour, until they collapsed from exhaustion and lack of food. "We are obviously very close to reproducing the Moslem paradise where every orgasm lasts six hundred years," Huxley wrote to a friend.

But even more momentous than the mapping of the pleasure centers was the discovery of the chemical brain. Up until the late Forties the brain had been conceptualized as a complex electrical system, an "enchanted loom . . . where millions of flashing shuttles weave a dissolving pattern." But then, beginning with nor-adrenaline in 1946, a class of chemical messengers were discovered that served as transmission devices, carrying impulses from cell to cell. The existence of the chemical brain raised some interesting questions. Might not madness, psychosis, etc. be the result of a metabolic malfunction? Wasn't it possible that these pathological states could be caused by an overabundance or a depletion of one of these chemicals? Or did these chemicals, perhaps through some undiscovered mutation, become something else? These were interesting but as yet unanswerable questions, which were the best kind. As one researcher put it, "the man who discovers the chemical basis for madness has a Nobel in his pocket."

The fact of the chemical brain had important ramifications in a corollary and hotly debated area of psychology, namely the use of drugs in therapy. This had become an issue back in the Thirties, when a Viennese psychiatrist named Sakel began treating schizophrenics with insulin. Sakel claimed that between thirty and fifty hypoglecemia comas could arrest schizophrenia in its early stages, but was useless in more advanced cases. The psychological community had barely digested this piece of news than word came that a Hungarian doctor was successfully treating schizophrenia by inducing epileptic fits with another drug, cardiozol, a technique that he later expanded to include depressives.

Classical analysts, with their carefully articulated schemes of repression, neurosis, and abreaction, greeted this work with derision. In 1939 an English psychiatrist named William Sargant attended the American Psychiatric Association's convention in St. Louis. His description of the debates, the rancors, the partisan posturing reads like a cross between a Marxist cell meeting and the Harvard-Yale game. When a paper was read claiming 40 percent of the patients receiving cardiozol treatments had hairline fractures of their vertebrae, "the audience almost jumped on their chairs, cheering the speaker for having given what seemed the death blow to this treatment." Sargant also observed that Dr. Walter Freeman, one of the first Americans to popularize the lobotomy, was treated as a pariah. Not so much because of problems attending his procedure, as for his temerity in suggesting that madness may have a physical cause and therefore a physical treatment. "They felt so insulted by this attempt to treat otherwise incurable mental disorders with the knife that some would almost have used their own on him at the least excuse," Sargant reported.

But by the late Forties cracks were beginning to appear in this blanket refusal to accept the evidence that some drugs did alter the course of some psychopathologies. "One doesn't have to know the cause of a fire to put it out," Menninger said. Sensing a lucrative market, the pharmaceutical companies began an aggressive search for mind drugs. Thorazine, the first major tranquilizer, appeared in 1954, the sedative Miltown a year later, to be followed by Stellazine, Mellaril, Valium, Librium, Elavil, Tofranil—a miscellany that was destined to change the face of psychology by giving it a technology that could control, if not actually cure, most mental illness.

By the mid-Fifties the American Psychological Association divided its membership into eighteen different specialties—the Division of Personality and Social Psychology, the Division of Industrial and Business Psychology, etc.—and published eleven different journals just to keep its members up to date on current research. The largest division, clinical psychology, was also one of the newest. Clinical psych was a sort of psychological Frankenstein, in that it combined the scientific rigor of Behaviorism, the therapeutic insights of psychoanalysis, and the diagnostic techniques of personality psychology. The clinical psychologist was the scientist/healer par excellence.

So it was inevitable that sooner or later one side of this professional persona, the scientist, would focus on just how successful the other side, the healer, really was. In 1955 two clinical psychologists working in the Bay Area published the results of a study in which they measured the progress of a group of patients receiving psychotherapy at Oakland's Kaiser Hospital against a group of prospective patients who had applied for therapy but had been put on a waiting list. Upon testing the two groups after nine months, the psychologists were astonished to discover that both showed similar ratios of improvement: a third had gotten better, a third had gotten worse, and a third had stayed about the same.

The principal author of this study was a young psychologist named Timothy Leary.

Detractors of the Cinderella science interpreted Leary's data as proof that psychotherapy was a hoax. But this wasn't Leary's interpretation. He believed that the Kaiser study confirmed what he had long felt, that what passed for therapy was merely a collection of techniques and tricks that worked sometimes, but failed just as often. In the successful cases something else was happening, a "vitalizing transaction," as his collaborator, Frank Barron, put it: the healing moment was "ephemeral, as frail as love or blessedness . . . in almost all appearances we remain the same, even though we are different."

And the key to these vitalizing transactions lay somewhere beyond consciousness, in the depths of the unconscious mind.

It is worthwhile asking how much of psychology's outward expansion was a response to its inability to solve its own central mystery. The unconscious was a void at the center of psychology. Studying it was like studying air bubbles in the middle of the ocean and wondering what presence, moving in the depths below, was responsible. It was a walled city, a *terra incognita,* knowable only through the signals that broke against the surface of the personality. In the public mind it was like the proverbial locked room in a Victorian mansion.

Most people credited Sigmund Freud with the discovery of the unconscious, an honor the Freudians worked hard to promote. But formal debate over the mind's internal architecture predated the Viennese doctor by several decades, while informal debate stretched back beyond the Greeks. Modern discussions of the unconscious are generally dated from 1869, when the German philosopher Eduard von Hartmann published *The Philosophy of the Unconscious.* Von Hartmann portrayed the unconscious as a parallel world whose geography, while unknowable by normal methods of introspection, was not immune to study. Echoes of the unconscious were everywhere, in dreams, myths, puns, jokes, fantasies; in abnormal behavior and its opposite, supernormal behavior, which was the realm of genius and mystical experience.

Hartmann's book presaged a formidable assault upon the locked room, which was conceived as both "a rubbish heap as well as a treasure house," containing "degenerations and insanities as well as the beginning of a higher development." By 1900 psychologists had distinguished four different kinds of unconscious: the conservative, or storing mind, which was the repository of memories and perceptions dating back to the first moments of life; the dissolutive, or repressing mind, which was made up of events that over time had been either forgotten or consciously repressed; the creative unconscious, instigator of the poetic muse, the creative trance, the intuitive leap; and the mythopoetic mind, wherein elements of the other three were constantly being combined into romances and fantasies.

Keep this last quality in mind, for its workings are intrinsic to our tale. And don't be fooled by the use of romances and fantasies into believing that the mythopoetic unconscious is some kind of fairytale land. Henri Ellenberger, whose *History of the Unconscious* is probably the best text available on these matters, speaks of its "terrible power—a power that fathered epidemics of demonism, collective psychoses among witches, revelations of spiritualists, the so-called reincarnation of mediums, automatic writing, the mirages that lured generations of hypnotists, and the profuse literature of the subliminal imagination." The great psychologist Jung spent the last years of his life puzzling over the mathematics of the mythopoetic, concluding they were as cockeyed, in their own way, as those of quantum physics. Where did archetypes, those primordial images that we all carry around inside us, come from? Were they simply a byproduct of the brain's structure, were they the reflection of some sort of oversoul, or were they a symbolic residue that encoded our own evolution?

Unfortunately, history conspired to make Jung a rather conspicuous eccentric in these matters. No sooner had this rich model of the unconscious been proposed, than it fell under attack, first from the Freudians, who focused exclusively on the dissolutive unconscious, and second from the Behaviorists, who considered the whole thing unscientific poppycock. The result was a diminution, a simplification of the unconscious, so that by 1948 an anonymous *Times* man could write with an absolutely straight face: "The Id, which makes up most of the Unconscious, contains man's prehistoric, primitive, must-have-it-now, animal drives . . .

> Dr. Will Menninger has a single illustration of the Conscious v. Unconscious conflict. The mind, he says, is something like a clown act featuring a two-man fake horse. The man up front (the conscious part of the mind) tries to set the direction and make the whole animal behave; but he can never be sure what the man at the rear end of the horse (the unconscious) is going to do next. If both ends of the horse are going in the same direction, your mental health is all right. If they aren't pulling together, there's likely to be trouble.

This, then, was the problem: for the mental health movement to succeed, a way had to be found to make sure that the rear end of the horse had the right marching papers. But this was impossible so long as the unconscious remained a locked room. A way had to be found to get inside, which was why, when Sandoz Pharmaceuticals announced it had discovered a substance capable of producing powerful psychoses, a lot of psychologists assumed that the key to the door had finally been found.

But what would they discover when they used this key? Would it be the Freudian unconscious, buzzing with repressed impulses? Or would it tend more toward the Jungian? Or maybe the Behaviorists were right, and the locked room was nothing more than an accountant's ledger with conditioned reflexes lined up in neat columns? Or maybe the door would open on to something much weirder . . .

3

LABORATORY MADNESS

There is no way of determining who was the first American to take LSD. But one of the earliest was a Boston doctor named Robert Hyde, who practiced at the Massachusetts Mental Health Center. One of Hyde's colleagues, a psychiatrist named Max Rinkel, had obtained some LSD and was curious whether it really did make a normal person crazy for a few hours. Rinkel didn't phrase it quite that way, of course. What he was interested in was model psychoses, test-tube schizophrenias that might shed a little light on the etiology of madness.

Hyde was Rinkel's first guinea pig. With the others gathered around, he emptied the brown ampule of Delysid into a glass of water and sat down to wait. And wait. Growing impatient, Hyde announced he was going to do his evening rounds; the others could tag along if they wished, but it certainly didn't feel like anything much was going to happen. What followed was fascinating. Right before their eyes, Hyde, the even-keeled Vermonter, turned into a paranoiac, as a swarm of little suspicions—Why are those people smiling? Was that a door closing?—began eating away at his composure.

Rinkel reported on his LSD work at the 1951 APA Convention in Cincinnati. He had found, he said, remarkable congruence between LSD-inspired model psychoses and schizophrenia:

> We noticed, predominantly, changes similar to those seen in schizophrenic patients. The subjects exhibited preeminently difficulties in thinking, which became retarded, blocked, autistic, and disconnected. . . . Feelings of indifference and unreality with suspiciousness, hostility, and resentment also approximated schizophrenic phenomena. Hallucinations and delusional disturbances were much less prominent . . .

But these were relative conclusions, Rinkel was quick to stress. For every person who became autistic, another turned manic, making jokes and puns that were completely out of character; for every bout of hostility, there was a corresponding moment of deep ecstasy. About the only generality that could be made was that normal people did not remain normal after taking LSD: they changed, and in that sense what happened could be classed as abnormal.

But were they crazy? Were these true model psychoses? Or were the researchers projecting their own desires onto what they were seeing? These weren't easy questions to answer, but as time went on, and as more and more researchers began studying LSD, they discovered that they were creating a lot of the negative reaction. LSD made one remarkably sensitive to nuance. If the examining psychologist was cold or abrupt, then the patient often responded with hostility or hurt. Conversely a warm, gentle doctor could provoke assertions of love and well-being that went far beyond the bounds of respectability.

The tests were a particular sore spot. Just as the LSD state reached full throttle, out came the personality tests, the Rohrschach, the TAT, the Bellevue Blocks, and Draw-A-Person Test. Frequently the research subjects became angry and intractable at this point, claiming, just the way schizophrenics did, that the questions were boring, stupid, irrelevant. "In the LSD test situation," warned Rinkel, "subjects appeared more interested in their own feelings and inner experiences than in interacting with the examiner, confirming behaviorally the test results, which indicated increasing self-centeredness." Many years later, a former school psychologist named Arthur Kleps, appearing before a Congressional hearing, offered one of the better explanations for why people taking LSD found tests irritating: "If I were to give you an IQ test and during the administration one of the walls of the room opened up, giving you a vision of the blazing glories of the central galactic suns, and at the same time your childhood began to unreel before your inner eye like a three-dimension color movie, you would not do well on the intelligence test."

But a science has to use the tools available to it; besides, the tests bore out what everyone hoped, that LSD really was creating model psychoses. Researchers began referring to it not as a hallucinogen, which was its proper medical classification, but as a *psychotomimetic,* a mimicker of madness.

By the early Fifties there were a dozen pockets of LSD research around the country. Most followed Rinkel's work with model psychoses, although a few confined themselves to animal toxicology studies, and at least one was pursuing Sandoz's other suggestion and using LSD in a therapeutic setting. But all were impressed by the drug's sheer power and the astonishing effects it produced, not just in normal folks, but in crazy people as well. Startling things happened when you gave LSD to mental patients. One catatonic took the drug and three and a half hours later began bouncing around the ward, laughing uproariously. In the afternoon she played basketball. That night she danced. But the next morning she was her old catatonic self again. Or there was the case of the hebrephenic schizophrenic that usually spent her days giggling and chattering inanities about the birds and the flowers. Thirty minutes after receiving 100 micrograms of LSD she became dead serious, all the laughter gone from her voice. "This is serious business," she told her ward doctor. "We are pathetic people. Don't play with us." Later she assaulted the hospital aides and made sexual overtures to the chief nurse.

It was fascinating stuff. But what did it all mean? What happened after LSD or mescaline passed through the blood/brain barrier? Did it interfere in some fundamental way with the normal neurochemistry? And if it did, might not the brain produce its own LSD-like metabolites? This, anyway, was what a lot of researchers were asking themselves. Was there an organic basis for madness, and if there was, who was going to find it?

A number of theories were ventured, but the one that concerns us here is the adrenochrome theory of two English psychiatrists, Humphrey Osmond and John Smythies.

The first schizophrenic Humphrey Osmond ever treated was a girl who told him that whenever she looked in the mirror, what she saw was an elephant. As soon as she left, Osmond trotted off to find his superior and tell him of this very odd delusion. "Well you know she has schizophrenia," his boss had said. "What's that?" Osmond had asked. He'd heard of it, of course. What he wanted were the answers to the usual first questions—symptoms, treatment, etiology. But what he discovered was that nobody could tell him anything substantive. There were lots of theories, but no hard data that did for schizophrenia what Freud and his followers had done for the mechanism of repression, for the dynamics of neuroses. Tired of his questions, Osmond's boss finally suggested that he look up a Jungian analyst named Anthony Hampton, who in turn suggested that he read a book by Thomas Hennell called *The Witnesses*.

Alongside Clifford Beers's *The Mind That Found Itself,* Hennell's book was one of the more evocative descriptions of what it was like to suffer and recover from extreme psychosis. Hennell captured perfectly the gradual inflation of his own disease. The nocturnal noises. The odd subjectivity of objects. The contradictory feeling of great personal destiny coupled with a growing certainty that one's ego was shredding away. The symptoms were a bit like an orchestra tuning up, first the strings, then the woodwinds, last the brass. As anyone who has attended a concert knows, the tuning up is nothing compared to the full orchestral blast. For Hennell the crescendo came on a day when he decided to walk into Oxford. He noticed that the other pedestrians were giving him meaningful looks, as though they knew something he didn't. As dusk arrived, Hennell saw that the fields beyond the hedgerow were beginning to boil, a bit like a Van Gogh painting, while up in the sky the stars were wheeling about, again a bit like a Van Gogh painting. Hennell only had a second to savor these weird perceptions before a squad car of secret police roared up, clapped him into a van filled with meat, and drove him off to a secret prison.

Although Osmond reread *The Witnesses* many times, its net effect was to leave him more perplexed than ever about the nature of schizophrenia.

After his apprenticeship ended, Osmond took a job at St. George's, one of London's famous teaching hospitals. There he met a rather exotic—exotic in terms of Osmond's Scotch upbringing in the Surrey downs—junior resident named John Smythies. Smythies had grown up in India during the twilight of the Raj, where his father had been chief forestor. It was Osmond's impression that young Smythies had had numerous exotic adventures before being dispatched to Rugby and Cambridge, for the intellectual tempering all proper English gentlemen underwent. Smythies's passion was the nature of mind, and he was not at all reticent about the fact that he considered psychiatry merely a handy way to investigate what was really a philosophical problem. This, plus his habit of speaking in brisk declaratives prefaced by the phrase "it's obvious," did not endear Smythies to his superiors, most of whom were old-time clinicians with a deep distrust of theory. But Osmond thought Smythies "not much less bright than he thought he was," and they got on famously.

Smythies had a number of eccentric enthusiasms—parapsychology was one—and one day he showed up at St. George's with a book by Alexandre Rouhier, a contemporary of Beringer's, who had written a book on peyote called *Le Peyotl.* On one of its pages was a molecular formula for mescaline.

The formula reminded Smythies of something, but he couldn't put his finger on what it was. Osmond also had a feeling of vague recognition. Then they showed the picture to a former biochemist who said it looked sort of like thyroid and sort of like adrenaline, with the nod probably going to the latter. This similarity between adrenaline and mescaline suggested an intriguing hypothesis: what if, in stressful situations, adrenaline got transformed into something chemically akin to mescaline. Wouldn't that account for Hennell's boiling fields and whirling skies, for the elephant in the mirror? It was known that certain plants were capable of such a metabolic transformation, known as transmethylation, but there was no evidence that animals were capable of transmethylation.

Obtaining some mescaline from Lights Chemical, Osmond and Smythies began testing their hypothesis. Osmond took 400 milligrams of mescaline one afternoon in Smythies's rooms, which were down a back alley off Wimpole Street. A tape recorder had been borrowed to record his thoughts. Osmond found it menacing. First it glowed a deep purple, then a cherry red. Putting his hand close to it, it felt as though someone had thrown open the door to a blast furnace. For the first time Hennell made sense. Schizophrenics weren't talking in similes and metaphors—there was no *as if* involved in the mad state—they were talking about reality, and it was scientific arrogance to dismiss it as delusion.

Once his astonishment had cooled, Osmond turned to the philosophical ramifications. If what we took to be objective reality was so fragile that it could be swept away by 400 milligrams of mescaline, then perhaps the vitalists who had argued that the brain was merely a mechanism to stabilize an anarchic world were correct. Perhaps the notion of objective reality was a paradox.

Smythies and Osmond published a small essay on these matters in 1952 called "A New Approach to Schizophrenia." In it they theorized that the body, confronted with an anxious state, might react by producing an endogamous hallucinogen, in this case one derived from adrenaline. The hallucinogen would cause the perceptual world to change, leading to more stress, more adrenaline, more of the natural hallucinogen, and ever deeper levels of psychosis. The only way to break this cycle would be for the sufferer to literally turn off reality: to retreat into another world. This, paradoxically, was the body's only way, short of death, of preserving its own sanity.

What was particularly elegant about this theory, which they called the M factor theory, was the way it combined both a neurological and a psychological dynamic, thus marrying what were usually two mutually exclusive bodies of research.

Having imagined this hypothetical chemical, the M factor, the next step was either to isolate it in its natural state or to make some up in the lab. It was a dilemma not unlike that faced by the American astronomer W. H. Pickering, when he had deduced in 1919 that the solar system had to contain another planet, as yet undiscovered, which Pickering confidently named Pluto. Eleven years later Pluto was found exactly where Pickering had predicted it would be. But the tools of astronomy, as Osmond and Smythies quickly learned, were far more sophisticated than the tools of neuropharmacology. The mysteries of outer space were child's play compared to the complexities of inner space. They approached some chemists at Imperial Chemical—"the chaps who had done the original work on synthesizing penicillin"—and asked them to work on a series of compounds intermediate between adrenaline and mescaline. The chemists tried, but soon gave up: however slight the differences were on paper, they were insurmountable in the lab.

So they decided to concentrate on the amenochromes, which were formed when adrenaline decomposes naturally. One of these amenochromes, adrenochrome, seemed a likely candidate, as it had a molecular structure surprisingly similar to mescaline.

Osmond swallowed his first adrenochrome in 1952. After ten minutes the ceiling changed color, and whenever he closed his eyes he was overwhelmed by a swarm of dots, which merged and fled with the kind of shifting pointillism one finds in schools of fish. Someone pulled out a pack of Rohrschach cards, and Osmond astounded himself with the inventive shapes he was able to discover. Walking back down the corridors of the hospital, Osmond was amazed at how sinister they seemed: what did all the cracks on the floor mean? And why were there so many of them? His colleagues were delighted with his behavior—this certainly was a model psychosis—and Osmond watched them celebrating as though from behind a thick glass wall.

Osmond was no longer in England when he had his adventure with adrenochrome. In mid-1952 he had accepted a job in the Canadian province of Saskatchewan, as Clinical Director of Saskatchewan Hospital. The place was touted as the finest mental hospital on the prairies, although this was something of a joke since it was the *only* mental hospital on the prairies. Actually the place was so rank, so depressingly nineteenth-century-madhouse, that when Osmond and his colleagues received the APA's Silver Plaque award for most improved mental hospital, American customs declared the "before" pictures to be obscene and special dispensation had to be obtained before they were allowed into the country.

It was Osmond's job to clean up this mess without unduly rattling the Old Director, who was supposed to remain on as a patriarchal figurehead until retirement. But the Old Director resented this new crop of bright boys, with their talk of insulin treatments and electroshock and the search for the mysterious M factor. Whenever possible he countermanded Osmond's innovations.

Work on the M factor was proceeding slowly. In the absence of Smythies, who was scheduled to arrive in Saskatchewan in a few months, Osmond had begun working with a psychiatrist affiliated with Saskatchewan University named Abram Hoffer. Hoffer had a passing acquaintance with Heinrich Kluver, who had suggested that sometime he might want to look into mescaline as "quite the most interesting thing around." When Smythies finally arrived he brought along some notes for an essay, which, after some input from Osmond, was published under both their names in the *Hibbert Journal*. Smythies had been reading up on eighteenth-century medicine, a period of fanciful theories and bitter polemics, with little regard for the facts. It was, Smythies thought, a period with remarkable similarity to twentieth-century psychology. What was needed was a new model of scientific progress, one along the lines that Karl Popper had suggested, which saw science proceeding from Orthodoxy (the accepted theory of the known facts) to Heresy (a new ordering of the facts, often of greater inclusiveness) and thence to a New Orthodoxy, and so on through further heresies and better orthodoxies.

Mescaline was mentioned exactly twice. The first instance came in the context of an analysis of the psychobiological explanation of schizophrenia. "No one is really competent to treat schizophrenia unless he has experienced the schizophrenic world himself," they wrote. "This is possible to do quite simply by taking mescaline." The second mention was in the context of a new theory of mind, which henceforth would have to account for three new sets of facts:

A) The recent development in the study of the design and behaviour of electronic computing machines, and the study of analogous brain mechanisms.

B) The recent advances in parapsychology. We refer to the establishment of Extra-sensory perception as scientific fact.

C) The nature of the phenomena witnessed under the influence of mescaline. One would have thought that anyone, concerned in devising systems of psychology based on the concept of the unconscious mind, would have utilized such a prolific source of material as mescaline offers, but no one has yet done so, although Rouhier made this suggestion as long ago as 1922.

One day, out of the blue, a note arrived from Aldous Huxley congratulating them on their sound reasoning and inviting them to drop by and see him should they be in Los Angeles in the near future. Huxley also expressed a willingness to try mescaline.

Although Osmond and Smythies were flattered by praise from such an illustrious intellectual, the probability that either would be passing through Los Angeles in the near future was almost nil, however willing they might have been to escape the bitter Canadian winter. But then fate intervened. Tensions at the hospital had reached such a level that the politicians in charge of the Saskatchewan mental health program felt it was time to have it out with the Old Director.

For practical reasons, it was felt that Osmond should be absent during this confrontation and arrangements were made for him to attend the upcoming APA convention in Los Angeles. Which was why, in early May 1953, Osmond found himself flying south, carrying not only a rare invitation to stay at the house of Aldous Huxley, but a small vial of mescaline as well.

4

INTUITION AND INTELLECT

Aldous Huxley was fifty-eight when he dashed off that characteristically enthusiastic note to Osmond and Smythies. He had been a featured player on the literary stage for thirty-two years, his reputation secured by a quartet of satirical novels begun when both he and the century were in their twenties—exercises of such brilliance that Andre Maurois, the French belle lettrist, lauded Huxley as "the most intelligent writer of our generation," by which he meant Huxley's mind held more information in perfect equilibrium than anyone else around.

He was supposed to have read, while still in short pants, the entire *Encyclopedia Britannica,* which was certainly conceivable from the volumes of essays that flowed from his pen, and paid his rent for most of his life. He seemed to know something about everything, which might lead one to think he was either a bore or a dilettante, but he was neither. His opinions, whether the subject was molecular biology or the Renaissance painter Piero della Francesca, were so precociously sharp that art critic Kenneth Clark once groused that after a lifetime studying Piero, in the end he seemed to know "far less than Aldous had learnt in a few weeks, by some miraculous combination of intellect and intuition."

Once, vacationing in Italy, Huxley happened to stumble across the filming of *Helen of Troy,* one of those excessive Hollywood costume dramas of the 1950s. Now this production, on this particular day, had a particularly pressing problem: the script called for a *bacchanale.* But neither the director, a midwesterner, nor the assistant director, a New Yorker, were exactly sure what a *bacchanale* was. Enter Aldous Huxley. Who, as the assistant director later told the story, "went on for hours relating what he knew about bacchanales. As a result our bacchanale was so successful that the crowd people could not stop when the director cried 'cut.'"

That was the quintessential Huxley: amusing, full of exotic lore made even more exotic by his own exotic physique: six four and so thin it was as though a flagpole had animated itself. When Aldous was young most of his friends thought he looked like a grasshopper, but as he matured he was usually compared to a waterbird, a heron or egret. He had a long, wide face that was always a decade younger than his calendar age, topped first by brown, then silver hair. But his most compelling features were his blue eyes, one sightless, the other nearly so, and his conversation, which flowed with such grace it was easily the most athletic aspect of a decidedly unathletic man. Huxley would lean back in his chair, fix his myopic blue eyes above and beyond one's head and then let his thoughts unwind "without interruption until he had turned over every stone to discover the strange facts hidden beneath them, or had followed the labyrinth . . . and had unravelled the truth at the end of it." Unlike a lot of champion talkers, he was also an avid listener, with an insatiable appetite for information, for gossip, stories, books, politics, science, scandal, and facts, the more exotic the better, murmuring "most extraordinary" whenever a choice tidbit presented itself.

Had Aldous Huxley died at thirty-five, shortly after the publication of his fifth novel, *Brave New World,* his place in English literature would have been secure. Somerset Maugham might have placed him alongside himself, in the first seats of the second row; Scott Fitzgerald could have lamented the premature closing, after a rousing first act, of another promising career. But Huxley didn't die—he changed, which is sometimes worse. From the mid-Thirties on he immersed himself in mysticism and oriental philosophy. His novels, when he stirred himself to produce one (which he did at regular intervals for the simple reason that novels earned more than essays), were really philosophical essays dolled up in fictional garb, like something Voltaire or one of the other *philosophes* might have written. "Nobody since Chesterton has so squandered his gifts," wrote the critic Cyril Connolly in *Enemies of Promise,* which was, ironically, an inquiry into why he, Connolly, had squandered his own gifts.

But the feeling that something alarming had happened to Aldous was widespread. To Andre Maurois, the new incarnation was "an astonishing reversal of his thought, and disturbing to anyone as close to the earlier Aldous Huxley as I had been." Few of his early admirers dared or cared to follow him down the paths that led first to *The Perennial Philosophy,* his compilation of the mystical components underlying all religion, and thence to his suggestion to Osmond and Smythies that he was not adverse, indeed he was most eager, to try mescaline, a drug that presumably made one crazy.

The consternation over this transformation dogged Huxley until the day he died, which was the same day John Kennedy died, November

22, 1963. When the obituary writers came to summarize his life in the twenty or thirty column inches reserved for the passing of Great Men, their inability to rationalize the whole was obvious. What they didn't realize was that Huxley's life was less a career than a quest for . . . what? The perfect synthesis of science, religion, and art? The uniting of the inner man and the outer man? "My primary occupation," Huxley once wrote in one of his approximately ten thousand letters, "is the achievement of some kind of over-all understanding of the world . . . that accounts for the facts."

He was born Aldous Leonard Huxley on July 26, 1894, in the county of Surrey, England, the third son of Dr. Leonard Huxley, educator, editor, and minor literary figure, and the grandson of T. H. Huxley, eminent biologist and one of the most famous men in Victorian England. Known as "Darwin's Bulldog," T. H. was the man who had demolished Bishop Wilberforce in the famous Oxford debates over Darwin's theory of evolution. He personified the scientific rationalist, and he eloquently argued its case in newspapers and magazines, and from lecterns throughout the English-speaking world. His collected essays, filling nine volumes, began appearing in the year of his third grandson's birth, and just a few months before his own death at age seventy.

"Clear, cold logic engines," were what T. H. demanded from his son and grandsons. As Aldous's older brother, Julian, once defined it, the Huxley tradition was one of "hard but high thinking, plain but fiery living, wide intellectual interest and constant intellectual achievement."

Huxley's mother, Julia, came from equally impressive stock. She was the niece of poet Matthew Arnold and granddaughter of the moralist and educator Dr. Thomas Arnold, one of the eminent Victorians later eviscerated by Lytton Strachey in the book of that name. Julia Huxley was an educator who founded Prior's Field, a girls' school just a few meadows away from Hillside School, where young Aldous received his first education.

He was, by all accounts, a brilliant, unathletic, aloof student, whose capacity for detachment unnerved his peers. "Aldous possessed the key to an inviolable inner fortress," said his cousin Gervas, who also attended Hillside. "Never can I remember him losing his control or giving way to violent emotion as most of us did." He "possessed some innate superiority and moved on a different level from us other children," according to his older brother, Julian. He was always thinking, measuring, comparing, assessing. Once his godmother, after observing him staring fixedly out a window, asked what on earth he was thinking about and received the single word *skin* in reply.

So he was an odd child, even a little scary. Some years later the

English science fiction writer Olaf Stapledon published a book called *Odd John,* which was an attempt to imagine what an intellectual super-man, a true *Übermensch* to use Nietzsche's much debated term, would really be like. The resulting portrait bears a striking resemblance to the adolescent Aldous Huxley, with the profound qualification that Odd John was never tested by personal tragedy the way Huxley was. Beginning with his entrance to Eton, Huxley's detachment was shattered by three tragedies. When he was fourteen his mother died. When he was sixteen he contracted a streptococcus infection that destroyed the cornea in his right eye and left the other clouded to the point of blindness. The condition was so serious that Huxley was forced to learn Braille, which he shrugged off with the wry joke that now he could read with impunity after lights out. He was also forced to give up his dream of studying biology, in preparation for a medical career. Adapting a typewriter with Braille keys, he began tapping out poems and stories.

Finally, two years after his blindness lifted and a year after matriculating at Balliol College, Oxford, in the same August that saw the beginning of World War One, Huxley's middle brother, Trev, committed suicide.

"There is, apart from the sheer grief of the loss, an added pain in the cynicism of the situation," Aldous wrote to cousin Gervas. "It is just the highest and best in Trev, his ideals, which have driven him to his death, while there are thousands who shelter their weakness from the same fate by a cynical, unidealistic outlook on life. Trev was not strong, but he had the courage to face life with ideals—and his ideals were too much for him."

This was not a mistake Aldous intended to make. At Oxford he buried his idealism under a cloak of aesthetic dandyism, affecting yellow ties and white socks, and instead of the usual classical reproduction above the fireplace, installing a poster of bare-breasted bathing beauties—French of course. He moved a piano into his room and began banging out American jazz. And he started spending weekends at Garsington, a manor house some six miles from Oxford that Phillip and Ottoline Morrell maintained as a country retreat for the Bloomsbury crowd. A typical Garsington houseparty mingled the likes of Maynard Keynes, Lytton Strachey, Bertrand Russell, the Woolfs—Leonard and Virginia—with assorted other aristocrats of the artistic and intellectual beau monde. Young Huxley held his own amid this galaxy of wits, and was considered by them an intellectual comer and promising poet. When he published a chapbook of poems entitled *The Defeat of Youth* in 1918, tout Garsington joined in his praise.

Garsington was also where Huxley met his future wife, Maria Nys, a waifish Belgian war refugee who was one of Lady Ottoline's charges. Besides being more than a foot shorter than her future husband, Maria's temperament—intuitive, magical, sensuous—was the exact opposite of Aldous's clear cold logic engine. Igor Stravinsky once said of Maria: "knowing nothing, she understands everything." And one of the things she understood was people. Maria had great psychological acuity, something her husband was almost totally without. Aldous called her his "personal relationship interpreter," and he used to quiz her thoroughly about the people they met at Garsington.

Their partnership—they began living together in 1919 and were married a few months later—produced one child, a boy, Matthew, and at least eight novels. The first of these, *Chrome Yellow,* was published in 1921, and was followed at two-year intervals by *Antic Hay, Those Barren Leaves,* and *Point, Counterpoint.* Opening the boards of that first book, none of Huxley's friends could have been prepared for what they found inside. The gentle, abstracted poet of lines like

No dip and dart of swallows wakes the blank
Slumber of the canal: —a mirror dead
for lack of loveliness remembered

turned into an assassin when he wrote fiction. ("I have done an admirable short story," Huxley once wrote to his brother Julian's future wife. "So heartless and cruel that you would probably scream if you heard it: the concentrated venom of it is quite delicious.") Sure the writing sparkled and the plot unfolded with professional ease, but there was something acid and unsettling about the way the stories portrayed the emptiness, the artistic and moral pretenses of the very friends who were now reading the book. The only thing that saved Huxley from the anger that later greeted Evelyn Waugh's similar lampoons was the fact that Huxley dissected his own pretensions with equal ferocity. He never stinted on himself.

Huxley's fiction had a liberating quality that the poet Stephen Spender once described as "a kind of freedom which might be described as freedom from: freedom from all sorts of things such as conventional orthodoxies, officious humbug, sexual taboos, respect for establishments." But there was also an undercurrent of yearning beneath Huxley's mocking detachment, a yearning for a new and more fulfilling orthodoxy, and this too caught the spirit of the times. It was a thirst many quenched with Marxism or fascism or extreme aestheticism, while others turned to science and the religion of progress. But these apparently weren't options for Huxley. It would be too strong to say that he was an unhappy man, here at the height of his literary success, but he was a deeply dissatisfied one. He had become "a kind of amphibious creature, rejecting emotional contacts with skillful evasions, using his intellectual equipment as a shield."

Huxley dealt with this angst by moving frequently, living in Belgium, France, Spain, and Tunisia, and Italy, where Maria and he became friends with D. H. Lawrence. As the Twenties drew to a close they semipermanently established themselves at a villa in Sanary, France, among the mix of artists and idle rich lucky enough to live on the Côte in the years immediately preceding the Crash of '29. From Marseilles to Antibes, the Midi was an expanded version of a Garsington weekend. It was familiar fauna, and one might have expected a continuation of what the London *Times* described as "the many-toned wit . . . the learning, the thought, the richness of character."

But Huxley gave his readers instead the anti-utopian *Brave New World. Brave New World* was Huxley's first stab at themes that would occupy him for the rest of his life: the gap between technology and human wisdom; the misapplication of evolution; the failure of education to create a whole man; the increasing centralization of power, with its elevation of ends over means. It was also his most savage book, consigning the human species to the trash heap, albeit a comfortable, pleasureful trash heap. In a world in which science allows you to customize the ultimate in bread and circuses, argued Huxley, the concept of coercion becomes meaningless. One of the brilliant elements of *Brave New World,* indeed the one that made the whole vision of state-controlled euphoria plausible, was the drug *soma.* In terms of pharmacological reality, soma was a combination of three different kinds of mind drugs: on one level it was a pleasant and entertaining hallucinogen, on another a tranquilizer like Librium or Valium, on a third a sleeping pill. There was nothing coercive about soma use: diehard individualists had the option of relocating to several offshore islands.

But soma was only a symptom of Huxley's larger theme, which was the machining of human nature. The genius that had allowed the smart monkey to tame the natural world was beginning to focus on itself. And unless something was done to alter the monkey's fundamental psyche, the consequence was going to be a scientific hell that called itself paradise.

Huxley's intellectual companion during these years, and perhaps his mentor, certainly one of the fulcrums upon which his interests were shifting, was a London literary boulevardier named Henry Fitz Gerald Heard—Gerald to his friends. Five years older than Huxley, Heard was the son of an honorary canon of the Church of England. Educated at Cambridge, with a degree in history, he had spent the First World War in Ireland, helping Sir Horace Plunkett in his attempt to organize the Irish farmers into agricultural cooperatives, a scheme that foundered when a bomb placed by Irish freedom fighters destroyed Sir Horace's residence and very nearly destroyed Gerald, who had been working in the house alone. Concluding that a civil service career was uncongenial to his health and his nature, Heard decided to concentrate on writing, and in the mid-Twenties published an eccentric but erudite little tome called *Narcissus: An Anatomy of Clothes,* which traced the historical relationship between architecture and clothing.

Anyone wishing to dip into the yellowing pages of *Narcissus* will discover the donnish Gerald, the one who could stun everyone to silence with his ability to remember everything he had ever read about everything and his willingness to explain it all to you in great detail. It was a recipe for a boorish windbag, and that might have been Heard's fate had he not also been one of those classically racy English eccentrics who pen mysteries in which Anglican clerics use Arabian spells (authentic, of course) to destroy their rivals. To one segment of the reading public he was Gerald Heard, mystic and philosopher, the author of *Pain, Sex and Time, Is God Evident, A Preface to Prayer;* while to another, less exalted group of readers he was H. F. Heard, creator of such macabre entertainments as *The Black Fox,* the *Great Fog,* and *Doppelgangers,* a book which the *Saturday Review* described as "strange and terrible . . . as repellently fascinating as the discovery of a cobra in one's bed."

Perhaps it was the actor in Gerald who made the intellectual such a compelling presence, but an astonishing number of people considered Heard to be the most brilliant man they had ever met, outshining even Huxley, who himself gave Heard the compliment of "knowing more than any one I know." A typical Heard soliloquy rambled "like a river over a vast area of knowledge . . . past the shores of pre-history, anthropology, astronomy, physics, parapsychology, mythology and much else." Christopher Isherwood, who knew him slightly in London and became better acquainted after both emigrated to Los Angeles in the late Thirties, once described Gerald's life as "an artistic performance expressed in a language of metaphors and analogies."

Unfortunately, the brilliant Heard, the voluble Heard, was missing from the written Heard. His writing tended to be pedantic, "practically unreadable" according to Huxley.

Heard met Huxley in 1928, when he was working as editor of the *Realist,* a literary magazine whose contributors included H. G. Wells, Rebecca West, Arnold Bennett, and the two Huxleys, Julian and Aldous. Heard began accompanying the successful young novelist on nocturnal strolls across London, from which he deduced that his young friend was suffering from a routine literary affliction:

> The style is formed, the specific frame of reference and interpretation of life is clear, and a public has gathered to buy the wares this craftsman knows how to produce in steady supply. And then suddenly the formula seems false, the angle hopelessly inaccurate, the analyses contemptibly shallow. Huxley's family mores and his an-

cestral genii were challenging his own personal genius. Satire could entertain; it could not assure. The sardonic, to keep its edge, must sharpen on the whetstone of the full truth of man—man, the one unfinished animal; man the incomparably teachable; untaught, less than a beast; ill-taught, worse than a beast; well-taught, the one creature of infinite promise, of superhuman potential.

Those last sentences are classic Heard, and they point us toward the real significance of Huxley's affection for this potentially rival poly-math. Because what was about to happen between the two men was a form of intellectual seduction, and an ironic one at that, as T. H. Huxley's grandson was seduced by a deviant form of the evolutionary argument.

Without bogging down in a lengthy discussion of scientific politics in the late nineteenth century, it is important to understand that there were two interpretations of evolution. The first, following Darwin, believed that natural selection was directionless, the product of random mutations; man was a biological fluke. The second interpretation, deriving from Lamarck and championed by the French philosopher Henri Bergson, smuggled teleology back into the evolutionary drama. Bergson called his philosophy vitalism, and argued that evolution was not directionless but was controlled by a creative lifeforce, an *elan vital,* which sought ever higher expressions of complexity and competence. In the insect world, for example, this *elan vital* achieved its highest state with ants and bees, while among mammals it was that ever-curious, ever-experimenting species *Homo sapiens* who best expressed this upward drive.

Of course once it had been decided that there was a pot of gold at the end of the evolutionary rainbow, it was hard not to speculate about the nature of this treasure. Friedrich Nietzsche meditated on the *elan vital* and came up with the *Übermensch,* the overman, a race of supermen who, depending on the luck of the variables, would either be mystic-saints or tyrant-creators. For Bergson only the first was a possibility: the universe was "a machine for the production of gods," he wrote.

But how was man going to become like unto gods? Further physical transformation was doubtful and pretty much beside the point, but what about further mental development? The growth of psychology in the late nineteenth century, with its emphasis on the unconscious, prompted a number of intellectuals to theorize that consciousness was the probable area of emergent evolution. Just as man had gone from simple consciousness to self-consciousness, perhaps at some point he would jump from self-consciousness to . . . *cosmic consciousness?* At least that's what a Canadian psychologist named Richard Bucke proposed in 1901. From a state of "mere vitality without perception," *Homo sapiens* had evolved to simple consciousness, which was characterized by perception, and thence to self-consciousness, whose distinguishing feature was the ability to image thoughts using language, and that refinement of language, mathematics. Bucke believed that *Homo sapiens,* having attained self-consciousness some three hundred thousand years ago, was now at a point where his ability to process concepts was such that he was about to push through to a new level, to the cosmic level.

Speculating that certain members of the species would probably make the jump to each level of consciousness before the rest, Bucke compiled a list of those whom he felt exhibited cosmic consciousness: the Buddha, Jesus, Plotinus, William Blake, Honore Balzac, Walt Whitman. Using eleven criteria, Bucke attempted to prove that each of these forerunners had undergone a comparable mental experience: that each, usually in their thirties, had experienced an intense white light followed by a massive intellectual and moral illumination.

Bucke's own brush with cosmic consciousness happened late one night after an evening of philosophical debate with his friends. He was returning to his lodgings in a hansom cab when he found himself "wrapped in a flame-coloured cloud":

> For an instant I thought of fire, an immense conflagration some-where close in that great city; the next, I knew the fire was within myself. Directly afterward there came upon me a sense of exulta-tion, of immense joyousness accompanied or immediately followed by an intellectual illumination impossible to describe. Among other things, I did not merely come to believe, but I saw that the universe is not composed of dead matter, but is, on the contrary, a living Presence; I became conscious in myself of eternal life.

Bucke's book, *Cosmic Consciousness,* made a deep impression on William James, America's foremost psychologist. While the average individual was under no compulsion to accept these extraordinary mental states as superior, wrote James, a blanket denial of their existence was equally ridiculous. "No account of the universe in its totality can be final which leaves these other forms of consciousness quite disregarded. How to regard them is the question—for they are so discontinuous with ordinary consciousness. Yet they may determine attitudes though they cannot furnish formulas, and open a region though they fail to give a map. At any rate, they forbid a premature closing of our accounts with reality."

James also noted, in passing, that in India the pursuit of cosmic consciousness, of mystic moments such as Bucke's, was a well-established science.

Although it was Darwin's interpretation of evolution that triumphed in the laboratories and the classrooms of the twentieth century, the heresy of Bergson and Bucke kept resurfacing in odd configurations. After the First World War it turned up in Europe in the guise of gurus from the East, men like Krishnamurti and Georges Gurdjieff, who advertised practical techniques for tapping into the mind's higher powers. For a few years London and Paris, Berlin and Vienna, were virtual supermarkets of the esoteric, boasting dozens of semisecret schools— theosophists, Buddhists, Vedantists, dark occultists in the Alistair Crowley mold. In Germany the mysterious Thule Society gave birth to the National Socialist Party and Adolph Hitler, who had his own special interpretation of the evolutionary curve *Homo* Aryan should follow.

In England, among the Oxbridge demimonde that Heard and Huxley were part of, this evolutionary romance generally took the form of believing a way had to be found to heal the gap between *Homo faber*, man the wielder of increasingly ingenious and dangerous tools, and *Homo sapiens*, man the conceptualizer, man the smart monkey who had mastered the planet but not his own inner flaws—flaws that were now threatening to bring the whole evolutionary game to a precipitous close. It was one thing for the smart monkey to pick up clubs and spears and go about bashing craniums over questions of power, territory, and sexual prerogative. But to exhibit the same behavior when the clubs had turned to machine guns and Big Berthas was the maddest kind of folly.

Whether by accident or design, there was no shortage of gurus who seemed to speak directly to this desire. When Ouspensky, the chief disciple of the mysterious Armenian teacher Georges Gurdjieff, arrived in London, he advertised himself with a series of lectures called The Psychology of Man's Possible Evolution. Man is not a completed being, Ouspensky told his audience. "Nature develops him up to a certain point and then leaves him, to develop further, by his own efforts and devices . . . evolution of man in this case will mean the development of certain inner qualities and features which usually remain undeveloped, and cannot develop by themselves."

So this was the riddle Heard placed before Aldous Huxley: was there a mechanism that could be tripped, a sense that could be awakened, a door that could be found that led to these higher states?

Starting in the late Twenties (and ending only with their deaths) the two polymaths embarked on a grand tour of the esoteric. They chanted and meditated, they counted breaths and tried to shed their old conditioning; they studied hypnosis and the Gurdjieff technique—"too much nirvana and strawberry jam" was Aldous's airy opinion of Ouspensky, indeed of most of the gurus they met. Of course, as Robert de Ropp, a follower of Ouspensky observed, neither Heard nor Huxley were ideal students, both being rather "too fond of their own opinions to work under the direction of someone else."

They began formulating their own philosophy in the late Thirties, beginning with Heard's *Third Morality*, followed by Huxley's *Ends and*

Means and *The Perennial Philosophy*. Their system, greatly compressed, went something like this: detachment is the essence of wisdom. The wise man participates passionately in the game of life, but at the same time remains aloof, free of entangling emotional or material ties. This science of detachment forms the basis of all religion, and it reaches its culmination in those moments of brilliant illumination that the mystics speak of.

Like Bucke, Huxley was impressed with the similarities between widely divergent mystical experiences: if you filtered out the particular religious dogma, what you had left was a physiological occurrence that appeared to be universal, that appeared to be wired into the very structure of the mind itself, waiting for a moment of deep meditation, fever or death, perhaps a blow to the head, perhaps the reflection of a cloud in a stream . . . there was no rhyme nor reason to what could trigger these astonishing events.

Following Bergson, Huxley also believed that the brain and the central nervous system operated as a vast filter that reduced the flood of sensory data to a manageable trickle. This was not a difficult or even a debatable concept. We have all experienced moments, pausing in the midst of reading the newspaper or tying our shoelaces, when we become aware that a bird is singing nearby. Then, turning back to our task, the bird again disappears. The soundwaves of birdsong still enter the ear, but the brain edits them out, thus allowing us to concentrate on the task at hand. No doubt such an editing process had been vitally necessary for us to survive on a hostile planet. But by the twentieth century (felt men like Huxley and Heard) it had become a detriment to further evolution. A way had to be found to bypass the reducing valve and tap the unlimited potentials of the brain's 20 billion neurons. This was where the saints and mystics became important. Somehow, along with the occasional artist and scientist, they had chanced upon a way of circumventing the brain's central program.

Whether the answer turned out to be a form of physical therapy like that of the Indian yogis, or something entirely different, Huxley believed that a way could be found to standardize the mystical experience. As Heard described it, "His biological background made him believe it must be physiological; his metaphysical aspiration let him hope it would transform the psyche."

That the answer might come from the field of psychopharmacology was a possibility that Huxley did not rule out. In an essay written at Sanary around the time he read Lewin's *Phantastica*, Huxley had mused that should he ever become a millionaire he would "endow a band of research workers to look for the ideal intoxicant."

> If we could sniff or swallow something that would, for five or six hours each day, abolish our solitude as individuals, attune us with

our fellows in a glowing exaltation of affection and make life in all its aspects seem not only worth living, but divinely beautiful and significant . . . then, it seems to me, all our problems would be wholly solved and earth would become a paradise.

This was grand, heady stuff. But unfortunately it was only theory. At no time, despite their exertions, did Heard or Huxley find the key that unlocked the overmind. As Huxley later confided to Humphrey Osmond, "It seems the great Huxley brain is exceptionally stable."

Huxley and Heard left England for America in 1937, eventually settling in Los Angeles, where they became familiar presences on the local spiritual scene, studying Vedantic Hinduism at an ashram in Hollywood. The ashram was under the supervision of a canny, charismatic teacher, Swami Prabhavananda, who some years earlier had been ordered to Los Angeles by his teacher to fulfill the larger karma of introducing the inner disciplines of the East to the materialistic West. To leave not only his native land, but the contemplative solitude of the ashram, for Hollywood, California—it was not a task Prabhavananda had welcomed. But he had come and prospered, confirming the shrewdness of his teacher's foresight.

The ashram, in classic Southern California fashion, was shaped like a miniature Taj Mahal, and was surrounded by lemon trees and young girls meditating in saris. Prabhavananda was fond of tea parties, during which he would debate Huxley and Heard, and later Alan Watts, on various doctrinal points. The swami counseled asceticism in all things, including sex. And Gerald agreed wholeheartedly. Los Angeles represented a sea change for him, a chance to re-create himself in a more appropriate image. He grew a goatee and discarded his suits and flannels in favor of dungarees and work shirts. He became obsessed with meditation, hastily terminating conversation so he could prepare for his twelve o'clock contemplation, or his six o'clock contemplation, or whatever contemplation was impending. He was ridding himself of the three main obstacles to enlightenment, he told Huxley: addictions, possessions, and pretensions. But for his lack of personal humility, Gerald would have been an excellent monk. Indeed the one quibble he regularly had with Huxley was over the latter's sociability: Gerald felt that time was too precious to waste on those who were not on the same path, a fundamentalist perspective that was very impractical for a novelist with a limited gift for characterization to begin with. "I am some kind of essayist sufficiently ingenious to get away with writing a very limited kind of fiction," Huxley ruefully admitted in one of his letters.

Actually, writing was the one constant in both their lives. With the exception of several film scripts, Huxley kept to his routine of a novel every two years, with a book of essays in between. And H. F. Heard scored his greatest literary success in 1946, when he won the three-thousand-dollar Ellery Queen Prize for a futuristic whodunit called *The President of the United States, Detective.*

They wrote and they waited; and then in early 1953 Huxley happened to read an article by Humphrey Osmond and John Smythies in the *Hibbert Journal* . . .

5

THE DOOR IN THE WALL

"**B**ut Aldous, what if we don't like him? What if he wears a beard?" was Maria's comment when Huxley announced that he had invited an unknown chap named Osmond, a psychiatrist no less, for a visit. The offer of room and board chez Huxley was a rare ticket; even Julian, when he was in town, stayed at a local hotel.

The possibility that Osmond might be a tedious bore hadn't occurred to Huxley, and after a few moments' thought he arrived at a simple solution. "We can always be out," he said.

Osmond, some three thousand miles away, was having similar fears. What if he couldn't play in Huxley's intellectual league? What if he came off as a tedious bore? "You can always arrange to stay late at the APA," his wife said.

He need not have worried. The one thing Huxley prized most in a fellow conversationalist was intellectual breadth, and Osmond had plenty of that. Like Heard, he could turn on a conversational dime and launch into a disquisition on, say, scurvy, that was so vivid one would almost swear he had shipped with Da Gama when half of that gentleman's crew perished. Maria, watching Aldous warm to the younger man, confided to Osmond: "I knew you'd get along. You're both Englishmen."

Huxley accompanied Osmond to several APA sessions, which he found deadly dull, and amused himself by genuflecting whenever Freud's name was mentioned. The subject of mescaline didn't arise until two days before Osmond was to leave, and then it was Maria who broached the subject, having decided that the famous British reticence was going to prevent the two men from discussing what was certainly uppermost in Aldous's mind. Osmond admitted that he had brought

44

some mescaline with him; while Huxley conceded that he had borrowed a tape recorder to preserve a record of the experiment.

The next day, May 4, 1953, Osmond dissolved some mescaline crystals in a glass of water and nervously handed it to Huxley. Outside it was one of those perfect LA mornings, blue and warm, with just a trace of smog hanging over the San Bernardino valley. What if the drug worked too well, Osmond thought to himself. Although Smythies and he had begun to appreciate that there was more to the mescaline experience than simple psychosis, that didn't diminish the possibility that the next six hours might be absolutely hellish. And Osmond didn't relish the possibility that he might become infamous as the man who drove Aldous Huxley crazy.

On the other hand, what if nothing happened? It was beginning to dawn on Humphrey that Huxley had some rather idiosyncratic notions about what he hoped to achieve in the mescaline state. Nowhere was this more explicit than in the letter Osmond had received confirming his invitation to stay with the Huxleys while at the APA. After the usual pleasantries, Aldous had launched into a critique of what he called the Sears & Roebuck culture:

> Under the current dispensation the vast majority of individuals lose, in the course of education, all the openness to inspiration, all the capacity to be aware of other things than those enumerated in the Sears-Roebuck catalogue; is it too much to hope that a system of education may someday be devised which shall give results, in terms of human development, commensurate with the time, money, energy and action expended? In such a system of education it may be that mescaline or some other chemical substance may play a part by making it possible for young people to "taste and see" what they have learned at second hand, or directly but at a lower level of intensity, in the writings of the religious, or the works of poets, painters and musicians.

Osmond was using mescaline as a mimicker of madness; Huxley wanted to incorporate it into the curriculum.

The minutes passed slowly—too slowly for Huxley, who told Osmond he expected to enter what he called the Blakeian world of heroic perception. What actually happened was much more mundane. The lights danced. The insides of his eyelids dissolved into a complex of gray squares that occasionally gave birth to a blue sphere.

Then, ninety minutes into the experience, Huxley felt himself pass through a screen, at least that's what it seemed like, and suddenly he was seeing "what Adam had seen on the morning of creation." It was as though, born myopic, he had just put on his first pair of glasses. The colors, the shapes, the sensuous mysteriousness of his flannel trousers.

Later Aldous would pun that he had seen "eternity in a flower, infinity in four chair legs, and the Absolute in the folds of a pair of flannel trousers."

He kept murmuring, "This is how one ought to see."

Mescaline, Huxley decided, intensified the visual at the expense of the temporal and spatial. There was a pronounced loss of will, which gradually expanded into a loss of ego. And as the ego relinquished its grip, all sorts of useless data, biologically speaking, began to seep into the mind.

From the house, with its suddenly cubist furniture, they wandered into the garden. For the first time Huxley felt the presence of paranoia, and beyond that, madness. "If you started the wrong way," he told Osmond, "everything that happened would be proof of the conspiracy against you. It would all be self-validating. You couldn't draw a breath without knowing it was part of the plot."

"So you think you know where madness lies?" Osmond asked.

"Yes."

"And you couldn't control it?"

"No, I couldn't control it," Huxley said. "If one began with fear and hate as the major premise, one would have to go on to the conclusion."

But then the shadow passed. From the garden they moved to the street, where a large blue automobile touched off gales of laughter. Fat and self-satisfied, it seemed to Huxley that the car was a self-portrait of twentieth-century man; for the rest of the day he giggled whenever he saw one. Aldous was having a wonderful time. After years of theorizing that each of us carries a reservoir of untapped vision and inspiration, he had suddenly stumbled across it at the advanced age of fifty-eight.

It was a little like that classic moment in children's literature when the hero walks outside one morning and discovers a door, where yesterday there was only blank wall. And beyond that door, a garden of infinite dimension, infinite adventure.

6

OUT IN THE NOONDAY SUN

Huxley was jubilant.

Mescaline was "the most extraordinary and significant experience available to human beings this side of the Beatific Vision," he cabled his New York editor, Harold Raymond, adding that he was working on a long essay that would raise "all manner of questions in the fields of aesthetics, religion, theory of knowledge." He planned to call this essay *The Doors of Perception,* after Blake's observation that

> *If the doors of perception were cleansed*
> *everything will appear to man as it is, infinite.*

Destined to become the most famous volume on the psychedelic bookshelf, *Doors* took Huxley a month to write, and when he was done he had a blow-by-blow account of that afternoon with Osmond—events like the Dharma body of the Buddha manifesting itself in the garden hedge—tempered by liberal speculation as to what it all might possibly mean in terms of human psychology.

What it all meant, Huxley thought, was that Bergson and the English philosopher C. D. Broad had been correct when they suggested that the brain operated as a vast reducing valve, "shutting out most of what we should otherwise perceive or remember at any moment, and leaving only that very small and special selection which is likely to be practically useful." Like the Freudian ego, this reducing valve was constantly beset by the raging tides of Mind-At-Large, which was what Huxley called Jung's archetypal unconscious plus Freud's pathological unconscious plus Myer's treasure house plus all the other unconsciousnesses yet to be named. And like Freud's ego, this reducing valve was not watertight: its seal was susceptible to pressure.

"As Mind at Large seeps past the no longer watertight valve," he wrote, "all kinds of biologically useless things start to happen. In some cases there may be extra-sensory perceptions. Other persons discover a world of visionary beauty. To others again is revealed the glory, the infinite value and meaningfulness of naked existence. . . . In the final stage of egolessness there is an 'obscure knowledge' that All is in all—that All is actually each." Which was why bookjackets gleamed with godliness and an innocuous canvas chair in the garden "looked like the Last Judgement."

There was nothing unique about Mind at Large: the smart monkey had been vacationing there for millennia—the number of hit or miss techniques could've filled a small booklet. But suddenly, with mescaline, mankind had lucked upon a technology. For the first time a science of the Other World was possible. Perhaps.

In his excitement over all the possibilities, educational and mystical and philosophical, Huxley skated past a few rather large problems with a nod and a wink. For example, one of the things he particularly liked about mescaline was the way it undercut verbal concepts. Words became superfluous. You didn't need to intellectualize about love or sadness or death, because you felt those emotions with every cell of your body. And that was a very useful condition in a culture that was increasingly dominated by its verbal constructs. "We can easily become the victims as well as the beneficiaries of these systems," Huxley wrote in *Doors*. "We must learn how to handle words effectively; but at the same time we must preserve, and, if necessary, intensify our ability to look at the world directly and not through that half opaque medium of concepts, which distorts every given fact into the all too familiar likeness of some generic label or explanatory abstraction."

But if mescaline's ability to transport the user to an area of experience that was preverbal or antiverbal was a major plus, it was also a major drawback. You tried to pour language over it, but the words just slid away, like water off a duck's back. It was almost as if the highest tools of self-consciousness were inadequate when it came to capturing Bucke's cosmic realm. Of course part of the problem was that Huxley was pouring English, which lacked any kind of appreciation for these matters: Sanskrit, as Gerald loved to point out, was a far superior language, with over forty different words for alterations in consciousness.

How could you create a science out of something you couldn't even talk about? Huxley didn't bother to explore this central paradox, although its influence is apparent in the essay's rather tame imagery. Later, having learned the lesson of Freud and Jung that inner dynamics are best expressed through metaphors and parables, Huxley grew more bold in his descriptions of what life was like beyond the Door in the Wall. In one of his first public talks, he likened the personal ego to the Old World. Using mescaline, he said, it was possible to sail beyond the horizon, "cross a dividing ocean, and find ourselves in the world of the personal subconscious":

> . . . with its flora and fauna of repressions, conflicts, traumatic memories and the like. Traveling further, we reach a kind of Far West, inhabited by Jungian archetypes and the raw materials of human mythology. Beyond this region lies a broad Pacific. Wafted across it on the wings of mescaline . . . we reach what may be called the Antipodes of the mind. In this psychological equivalent of Australia we discover the equivalents of kangaroos, wallabies, and duck-billed platypuses—a whole host of extremely improbable animals, which nevertheless exist and can be observed.

You might note that Huxley's central conceit here is that of a trip. That's what it felt like. A trip to what the spiritualists had called the Other World, which lay just beyond the deceptive boundary of everyday consciousness.

The Doors of Perception was published in the spring of 1954 to generally perplexed reviews. Had anyone else written a book recommending mescaline as "an experience of estimable value to everyone and especially to the intellectual," declared *The Reporter*'s Marvin Barrett, it would have been dismissed "as the woolgathering of a misguided crackpot. But coming . . . from one of the current masters of English prose, a man of immense erudition and intellect who usually demonstrates a high moral seriousness, they deserve more careful scrutiny." Barrett called around until he found some Lab Madness researchers who were using mescaline as a psychotomimetic. They were "less enthusiastic than Dr. Huxley and the Indians," he reported. "In controlled experiments they have found that mescaline more often than not produces symptoms unpleasantly similar to those of schizophrenia."

The critical response to *Doors* was almost an echo of the *British Medical Journal*'s condemnation of Havelock Ellis for his enthusiastic endorsement of peyote. In effect, Huxley's knuckles were rapped, and another black mark was added to the "whatever happened to Aldous" column. "How odd it is that writers like Belloc and Chesterton may sing the praises of alcohol (which is responsible for about two-thirds of the car accidents and three-quarters of the crimes of violence) and be regarded as good Christians and noble fellows," Huxley complained, "whereas anyone who ventures to suggest that there may be other and less harmful short cuts to self transcendence is treated as a dangerous drug fiend and wicked perverter of weak-minded humanity."

But *Doors* sold, slowly but steadily. Someone was reading it.

Osmond read it and was delighted. Since that May afternoon he and Huxley had exchanged numerous letters (learn how to type! Huxley implored, "It took two days of intensive work to decipher your last letter.") concerning future mescaline experiments, but time and commitments had prevented a second rendezvous. Aldous was genuinely fond of his young friend, and he had high hopes that Humphrey would "do work of fundamental importance," provided an adequate source of funding was discovered so that the mescaline experiments could continue in proper scientific style. "Perhaps we could write a play together," Huxley joked in a letter. "And make enough to finance your research and our second childhood."

They finally got together again in December 1954. Huxley had wanted to test the effects of mescaline in the desert east of Los Angeles, away from the comical cars and the smog. But when Osmond arrived he found Aldous too ill to travel. So he contented himself with giving the drug to Gerald and photographer George Huene, another friend of Aldous. The reactions couldn't have been more different. Huene's experience was similar to Aldous's, with the mescaline enhancing all of the aesthetic tendencies that had made him a photographer. But Gerald . . . Gerald was another case altogether. Strange mediumistic voices spoke through him, and he claimed to have glimpsed the Clear Light of the Void, which was the phrase the Tibetans used for that moment of complete understanding when one comprehends the Big Picture. Years later, addressing some students, Gerald gave the following description of what usually happened to him in the Other World. First, he said, there would be a hum, a vibration spreading out from the furniture until everything in the room, Heard included, was caught in its rhythm, pulse after pulse, until the ego began to "melt like an iceberg that has gotten into tropical seas." And then, in a flash, the Door in the Wall would slide open, and wherever you were—in a room, lying on the grass, walking on the beach—would be magically transformed. "You may have to stop and linger there for a time like a child in a garden," Gerald told the kids. While lingering you would probably notice the shadows, and after that, the realization that the world was boundless. Which did not mean it was pointless. At its center was the Pure Void, which Heard described as a blazing central sun surrounded by an ocean of darkness that one crossed with respect, for it was here that the fears were most profound. "The little man meeting Pan feels panic," Gerald liked to say.

But what Heard didn't say that day was that the panic of the darkness was nothing compared to the terror of the Void. According to the *Bardo Thodol*, the Tibetan *Book of the Dead*, which was probably the most thorough guide to these regions ever written, the soul beheld unvarnished Reality at its peril: confronted with the Void, it went howling back to the wheel of life, gratefully chaining itself to another reincarnation.

That no two people found themselves in the same part of the Other World was one of the troublesome aspects of mescaline. Why did Gerald immediately find the mystic path, while Aldous and Huene couldn't, no matter how diligently they searched? And why did some people have absolutely hellish experiences? Huxley pondered, but produced no solutions to these questions in his second long mescaline essay, *Heaven and Hell.* He decided that there had to be a basic distinction between visionary experience and true mystical experience—in the first, one was aware not only of the opposition between Heaven and Hell, but of the fact that only the slenderest of gaps separated these two states. In some people, he wrote, the ego doesn't melt like an iceberg in tropical waters, but expands to the point of suffocation: "Negative emotions, the fear which is the absence of confidence, the hatred, anger or malice which exclude love [these] are the guarantee that visionary experience, if and when it comes, shall be appalling."

With mystical experience, such distinctions were meaningless.

At one point during Osmond's December visit Maria drew him aside and confessed that she would soon die of cancer. Aldous was refusing to accept the reality of her disease, she told Humphrey, please look after him when I'm gone. Osmond was so moved by her calm acceptance of her own death that he went off and wept for half an hour. How would Aldous cope? For thirty years Maria had been his surrogate eyes. She had been cook, typist, secretary, chauffeur—at Sanary she had piloted their red Bugatti with such enthusiasm that Aldous had written an essay declaring speed to be the only new sensation of the twentieth century.

Maria died in February 1955. During her last hours, "with tears streaming down his face and his quiet voice not breaking," Aldous read to her from the *Bardo Thodol,* interweaving the ancient Tibetan text with lyrical descriptions of their shared past. With Lawrence in Italy. Summers at Sanary. The weekends at Garsington when they had first met while the rest of the world was falling apart on the Somme. Their trips to the California desert. The white snowcapped mountains of the Sierras. "Go toward the light," Aldous kept murmuring. "Those last three hours were the most anguishing and moving of my life," Matthew Huxley later wrote to his wife; while for Gerald they were proof that Aldous had indeed come back through the Door a changed man; that he was able to cope with Maria's death so calmly was wholly attributable, Gerald felt, to the wisdom he had gained from mescaline.

The mescaline served Huxley in another capacity as well, filling his period of bereavement with new faces and exciting plans. Because of *Doors* and *Heaven and Hell,* which appeared in 1956, he found himself at the center of a peculiar movement, part religious, part scientific, which for the first time since the 1880s was mounting a concerted assault on

Mind at Large. "Things keep cropping up," he wrote Harold Raymond. "Work at Boston, work at Chicago, work in Buenos Aires. In connection with the last, a very able Argentinian-Italian suddenly swam into my ken a day or two ago. It turns out that he is the greatest authority on the chemistry of cactus alkaloids, including, of course, mescalin."

Huxley was invited to the American Psychoanalytic Association's annual convention, where he was the only nondoctor to participate in the panel on psychotomimetics. His reception by "the Electric Shock Boys, the Chlorpromaziners, and the 57 Varieties of Psychotherapists," was not effusive—compared to that of the Lab Madness Lobby. What might have been called Aldous's Visionary Potential Party was limited to himself, Osmond, Heard, and a small population of peripheral "crackpots" like the parapsychologist Andraj Puharich, who had already entertained Aldous at his Glen Cove, New York, headquarters. The specifics of Puharich's "strange household" are worth recording for the insight they provide into this parascientific fringe movement. Besides Puharich and his wife, who had behaved in a "conspicuously friendly way" with a girl named Alice, the menage had consisted of

> Elinor Bond, doing telepathic guessing remarkably well, but not producing anything of interest or value in the mediumistic setting she gave me; Frances Farelly, with her diagnostic machine—which Puharich's tests have shown to be merely an instrument, like a crystal ball, for concentrating ESP faculties; Harry, the Dutch sculptor, who goes into trances in the Faraday cages and produces automatic scripts in Egyptian hieroglyphics; Narodny, the cockroach man, who is preparing experiments to test the effects of human telepathy on insects.

"It was all very lively and amusing," Huxley wrote to Eileen Garrett. "And, I really think, promising; for whatever may be said against Puharich, he is certainly very intelligent, extremely well read and highly enterprising. His aim is to produce by modern pharmacological, electronic and physical methods the conditions used by the shamans for getting into a state of travelling clairvoyance and then, if he succeeds, to send people to explore systematically the Other World."

Actually, Huxley and Osmond had proposed something similar to the Ford Foundation, although they had worded it differently. What they had proposed was that mescaline be given to a hundred world-class scientists, artists, and philosophers in hopes that a definitive answer might emerge to such questions as: *Could mescaline free the mind from its habitual patterns? Did it truly allow for an expansion of sensibilities?* Although Aldous was friends with Robert Hutchins, the Ford Foundation's director, his scheme was promptly rejected, causing him to fume that "the mezozoic reptiles of the Ford Foundation are being as mezozoic as ever. The Trustees are so frightened of doing anything unconventional—for whenever the Foundation gets any adverse publicity, people go to the nearest Ford dealer and tell him that henceforth they will buy Chevvies—that the one overriding purpose is now to do nothing at all."

Other foundations were approached with equally negative results.

It is difficult to tell, judging from the polite prose of his letters, whether Huxley's frustration was beginning to erode his enthusiasm. In any case it didn't matter. Because just as things appeared at a standstill, along came a fresh explosion of interest named Al Hubbard—Captain Al Hubbard, "Cappy" to his friends.

The initial connection was made through Osmond, who one day received a mysterious invitation to lunch at the Vancouver Yacht Club with one A. M. Hubbard, flamboyant president of the locally based Uranium Corporation. Through a curious chain of events, Hubbard had learned of Osmond and Smythies's work with mescaline, had obtained a supply of the drug himself, and had experienced a mystical vision of such profundity that he had decided to devote his considerable store of personal energy to spreading the word about mescaline and the Other World.

Hubbard reappears throughout our story as a kind of peripatetic imp, so it will help to have an image of the man firmly in mind. He was small and stocky with a large round head and a razor crewcut. As he aged, he resembled nothing so much as the caricatured red-neck Southern sheriff, a resemblance that was enhanced by his eccentric habit of wearing a security officer's uniform complete with sidearm. The gun, he used to kid Osmond, fired armor-piercing bullets, the better to shoot out the engine block of any pursuing car.

Over the years bits and pieces of Hubbard's past came to light, usually through the office of Al himself, although no two of his versions were ever exactly the same. Still, it was an astonishing story. Hubbard always claimed he was just a barefoot country boy from Kentucky, and that was true, but in his first public incarnation, in December 1919, he was Seattle's boy inventor, a young Thomas Edison who had invented what the Seattle *Post-Intelligencer* claimed was a perpetual motion machine. Hubbard called it an atmospheric power generator. Whatever its name, it was small enough to fit in the hand, had no moveable parts or battery, and could power a lightbulb for days. To publicize his device, Hubbard took a boatload of journalists and future backers on a cruise of Seattle's Lake Union in a boat powered by nothing more than an electric motor and Hubbard's mysterious 11- $\times$ 14-inch box.

The Seattle community took a proprietary interest in their young genius, and in 1920 the town fathers appointed a committee of elders to shepherd the "young scientist"—Hubbard had outgrown the boy inventor label—through the labyrinth of corporate offers and patent red tape. When Al arrived in Washington to file his patent application, the local stringer for the *Post-Intelligencer* reported that he was "lodging quietly at a medium priced hotel and avoiding all publicity."

Hubbard eventually sold 50 percent of his patent rights to Radium Chemical Company of Pittsburgh, Pennsylvania, and that was the last anyone ever heard of the Hubbard Energy Transformer.

Beginning in the late Twenties the specifics of the Hubbard saga begin to blur. Around the time Huxley and Heard were embarking upon their search for the key to higher consciousness, Al was becoming involved in the charterboat business, running liquor down from Canada. In one version he is supposed to have perfected an early radar device modeled after the theories of Nicola Tesla, which he was selling to the rum runners. Whatever the truth, Seattle's boy inventor eventually went to prison. From there things get even murkier. As Hubbard told the story, he was approached in the early days of WWII by members of an unofficial intelligence unit and asked to secretly run war materials up the West Coast of America to Canada, where they were shipped overland and put aboard boats bound for England and the Battle of Britain. Whether such a program existed, and whether Hubbard was part of it, is unclear. Certainly for the rest of his life he exhibited enough familiarity with spies and spying that most of his friends believed he had once been, and perhaps still was, one. Al loved the intelligence game and he frequently boasted that his trips to Washington were not routine business jaunts: he used them to break bread with the shadow government that really ran things. By then he had become A. M. Hubbard, president of Vancouver's Uranium Corp., friend to the industrial and political elite of Western Canada, a rich entrepreneur, with his Rolls Royce, his airplane, and his island sanctuary in Vancouver Bay.

But if there was one thread that connected the barefoot boy inventor of nineteen to the spy and CEO of middle age, it was Catholicism. Hubbard was an ardent Catholic, with a lifelong interest in mysticism and the Other World.

"What Babes in the Wood we literary gents and professional men are," Aldous wrote to Osmond after his first meeting with Hubbard. "The great World occasionally requires your services, is mildly amused by mine; but its full attention and deference are paid to Uranium and Big Business. So what extraordinary luck that this representative of both these Higher Powers should (a) have become so passionately interested in mescaline and (b) be such a very nice man."

In another letter, this one to Carlyle King, a literary acquaintance of Osmond's, Huxley was even more explicit in his hopes: "Some new developments might be taking place quite soon in the mescalin field, owing to the appearance on Osmond's, Gerald's and my horizon of a remarkable personage called Captain Hubbard—a millionaire business-man—physicist, scientific director of the Uranium Corporation, who took mescalin last year, was completely bowled over by it and is now drumming up support among his influential friends (if you have any-thing to do with uranium, all doors, from the Joint Chiefs of Staff's to the Pope's, are open to you) for a commission to work on the problems of psychopharmacology in relation to religion, philosophy, ESP, artistic and scientific invention etc. Hubbard is a terrific man of action, and results of his efforts may begin appearing quite soon."

Hubbard and Huxley: the English prince and the American frog, the polished dialectician and the blunt instrument, the murmured "most interesting" contrasting with the good-old-boy bark, "I'm just a son of a bitch." They were a genuine odd couple, and naturally they were genuinely fond of each other. Al was a can-do kind of guy, with just the right amount of country-boy slyness. Little problems, like the per-petual scarcity of mescaline, disappeared almost immediately. Hubbard didn't waste time going through proper medical channels; he found out who the main suppliers were and placed an order they couldn't refuse. When he heard about LSD in early 1955, he called up Sandoz and requested forty-three cases, which Sandoz promptly shipped. And when Canadian customs seized the shipment because Hubbard's papers weren't in order, Sandoz actually supplied him with the proper forms. Later Hubbard would boast that he had stockpiled more LSD than anyone else in the world, and those who knew him tended to believe it. As far as Al was concerned this was just heads-up business: whoever controlled the supply controlled the market.

Huxley took his first LSD trip a few days before Christmas 1955, when Hubbard dropped by Los Angeles to run a session for him and Gerald. Gerald, as usual, was full of spirits and inner voices, while Al amused himself by attempting to telepathically connect with the others. It was a game he and Osmond had begun to play, but Aldous found it silly. "Certainly if future experiments should turn out to be like these last two, I should feel that such experiments were merely childish and pointless," he wrote Osmond. But if Huxley was irritated with Hub-bard, it was largely because thanks to Al he had finally broken through the visionary layers, into that realm of pure oneness that Gerald had been enjoying since day one; thanks to Al, Huxley had finally escaped from the land of platypuses and wallabies.

Everyone had assumed that Hubbard, being a businessman, would prove most useful as a financier and diplomat with the various govern-ment bureaucracies. But the truth was Hubbard had an intuitive feel for the Other World that rivaled even Gerald's; in fact it was Al who first figured out there were ways to move a person from one part of the Other

World to another. Al had a system. He always kept certain pictures handy, along with a few specific pieces of music that he would play on the stereo. And damned if it didn't work. For instance, if you found yourself caught in the shadows of the pathological unconscious and were starting to panic, Hubbard would gently show you an engraving of a cute little girl lost in a forest, and as you stared intently at this drawing you could just make out that the clouds were shaped like . . . a guardian angel! Silly, perhaps, but soothing. Which was not the case with the perfect diamond that Al would hand you at the height of a trip, and suggest you spend a few moments gazing into its depths. The perfect diamond was like entering an air-lock that shot you forward into a different part of the labyrinth. Later, at the height of his powers, Hubbard actually designed a whole experience around Death Valley, which he considered an extraordinary power spot.

Like so much in this story, Hubbard's system was not unique. Go to any library and you could find a sizeable section of anthropological monographs dealing with shamanic healing rites, in which the shaman manipulated the healing trance with a grab bag of odd cues and devices, like blowing tobacco smoke across a sick native's brow. But it was unique in terms of Western psychotherapy—unique and illegitimate. Not that Hubbard cared a whit what the scientific community thought, at least not yet. The only reason to use mescaline or LSD as far as he was concerned was to receive the Beatific Vision, which for Hubbard was primarily a Catholic experience, although he was not obnoxiously partisan. If a Methodist happened along, Al made sure they took the Methodist trip; if a Christian Scientist came by, he did his best to promote the Mary Baker Eddy experience.

Huxley initially had been skeptical of the reports coming out of Vancouver that had Al evoking the Beatific Vision in dentists and lawyers. But in October 1955, in the company of a young psychotherapist named Laura Archera who was shortly to become his second wife, he decided to give the Hubbard techniques a try. As he later wrote Osmond, "What came through the closed door was the realization . . . the direct, total awareness, from the inside, so to say, of Love as the primary and fundamental cosmic fact. The words, of course, have a kind of indecency and must necessarily ring false, seem like twaddle. But the fact remains . . ."

Huxley was overwhelmed to the point where he decided his previous experiments, the ones recorded in *Doors* and *Heaven and Hell*, had been nothing but entertaining sideshows—"temptations to escape from the central reality into false, or at least imperfect and partial Nirvanas of beauty and mere knowledge." And this raised a troublesome point. Was it better to pursue a course of careful psychological experimentation such as they had proposed to the Ford Foundation, or was Hubbard correct, was the real value of LSD and mescaline its astonishing ability to stimulate the most basic kind of religious ecstasy? Describing this dilemma to Osmond, Huxley wrote:

> My own view is that it would be important to break off experimentation from time to time and permit the participants to go, on their own, towards the Clear Light. But perhaps alteration of experimentation and mystical vision would be psychologically impossible; for who, having once come to the realization of the primordial fact of unity in love, would ever want to return to experimentation on the psychic level? . . . My point is that the opening of the door by mescalin or LSD is too precious an opportunity, too high a privilege to be neglected for the sake of experimentation. There must be experimentation, of course, but it would be wrong if there were nothing else.

Thanks to Hubbard's system, a question began to take shape in Huxley's mind. *Was it possible to use these new mind changers to stimulate a subtle but revolutionary alteration in the way the smart monkey perceived reality?* At what point, provided you selected the right mix of brilliant, influential people, and gave them LSD or mescaline in a carefully controlled setting, doing everything possible to lead them to the Clear Light, at what point would the culture begin to shift to another tack? If you initiated the best and the brightest to the Other World, and let the knowledge filter down . . . It was an appealing speculation, and the more Aldous thought about it, the more convinced he became that it was not too farfetched. If one moved cautiously, doing nothing to startle the philistines . . .

But first there was a practical matter to solve. "About a name for these drugs—what a problem!" he wrote to Osmond. One couldn't call them psychotomimetics or hallucinogens or any of the other approved synonyms. A completely new name was needed, and having perused his Liddel & Scott, Aldous felt he had a worthy candidate: *phanerothyme,* meaning to make the soul visible. He enclosed the following ditty in his letter:

> *To make this trivial world sublime*
> *Take half a gramme of phanerothyme*

But Humphrey didn't particularly like *phanerothyme,* so he created his own word, *psychedelic,* and sent Aldous an answering rhyme:

> *To fathom hell or soar angelic*
> *Just take a pinch of psychedelic.*

7

THE OTHER WORLD

Al Hubbard always operated on the theory that if you bothered to make appointments you'd never get anywhere in life. He preferred to materialize on the doorstep, and he was a sufficiently roguish charmer to get away with it.

He materialized on doorsteps all over the world, wherever a researcher was working with LSD or mescaline. Hubbard was constantly on the go, visiting with Osmond in Saskatchewan, then down to Los Angeles to see Huxley and Heard, then across the continent—New York, Boston, Bethesda, D. C.; then off to Europe to check on progress there, then back again to repeat the circuit: vetting new researchers, conducting sessions for interested professionals, brainstorming on the best way to "launch" the psychedelic movement; paying his way with the latest experimental wrinkles, the most delicious gossip, and of course his inexhaustible supply of experimental substances, which he stored in a large leather bag.

One of Al's favorite break-the-ice devices was carbogen, a mixture of carbon dioxide and oxygen, which came in a small portable tank. Carbogen was what therapists referred to as a potent abreactor: ten or fifteen lungfuls and you tended to relive your childhood traumas. And judging on how well you handled them, Al would either offer to run an LSD session for you, or he wouldn't.

Being a charge-ahead kind of guy who didn't write many letters, Hubbard hasn't left any neat synopsis of the world LSD scene, circa 1956, the year the first International Symposium was held. In general though, the trend was away from the Lab Madness boys, the psychotomimeticists, and toward therapy, which had been, after all, Sandoz's first recommendation:

To elicit release of repressed material and provide mental relaxation, particularly in anxiety states and obsessional neuroses.

To attribute this change of direction solely to Captain Hubbard's efforts
would be an overstatement; Al was more like the membrane without
which osmosis can't occur. He was a traveling symposium; it was from
Hubbard that many researchers first learned the cardinal rule of set and
setting, which stated that the LSD state was contingent on the mindset
of the person taking the drug and the setting in which the experience
occurred. To drive someone crazy with LSD was no great accomplishment, particularly if you told the person he was taking a psychotomimetic and you gave it to him in one of those pastel hospital cells with
a grim nurse standing by scribbling notes. But to use the drug for subtler
ends called for an understanding of how ambience was heightened in
the psychedelic state: how certain pieces of music—Bach, for instance—
came across under LSD as so holy it was almost as though God was
humming the tune; while others—Berlioz, say—made you sick to your
stomach with its sugary pretensions; how people under LSD liked to
sprawl around with plenty to look at, with paintings and scratchpads
that would end up filled with the most perplexing scrawls, as though
a class of kindergartners had used the room, and not one relatively
mature adult; how the most minor mood changes on the part of the
therapist (irritation, anxiety, humor) could have startlingly major effects
on the patient.

By 1956 the question "what's in the unconscious?" had fragmented into a host of subsidiary questions as therapists realized that
the Dark Room, like a grandmother's attic, was crammed with treasure. In this trunk, Jungian archetypes; in that one, lovely Freudian
neuroses that could be tracked all the way back to the moment when
the patient, standing in her cradle barely one year old, had watched
her parents making love. Instead of having to walk, the therapist
could fly. And while that presented a new set of problems—for one
thing, LSD sessions lasted a wearying three to four hours—it didn't
diminish the excited feeling that they were on the edge of Something
Big. Whenever LSD researchers got together the conversation quickly
turned anecdotal, as one eye-widening story followed another ". . .
and suddenly I found myself giving birth to myself. I could actually
feel myself floating around in the amniotic fluid, then I was flushed
down the vaginal canal, thinking 'this is it, I've died and now I'm
being reborn.' "

It was like belonging to an elite fraternity. "When you made contact," remembers Oscar Janiger, "it was like two people looking at each
other from across the room, and with a sort of nod of the head . . . like
'Welcome brother, you have now entered the Mysteries.' That's all.

That was your ticket of admission. Nothing else. That knowing look."

Oscar Janiger was a Beverly Hills psychiatrist who preferred research to analysis, although he did just enough of the latter to pay for the leisure to indulge in the former. He also taught a few courses at a local university, and it was there, in 1954, after a lecture synopsizing the Osmond/Smythies adrenochrome thesis, that he was approached by a young man named Perry Bivens. Bivens was a professional diver. He worked for Ivan Tors, the producer of *Sea Hunt,* and he had his own private decompression chamber that he had built himself. It was while perfecting the chamber that Bivens had discovered he could alter his consciousness simply by changing the mix of gases.

Bivens invited Janiger to try the chamber, which he did to rather disturbing effect. Although he could intellectualize for hours about the fragility of what man calls reality, Janiger was unprepared for just how fragile it really was. Bivens would twiddle a few knobs, and the next thing the doctor knew he was gasping with laughter or roaring with energy. Then the air would be flushed out and a new combination introduced.

After a few sessions in the chamber, Bivens casually mentioned that he knew of something much better, a drug called LSD.

Janiger, Bivens, and their wives took the LSD at Janiger's vacation home at Lake Arrowhead. A short while into the experiment Bivens's wife had disappeared into a bedroom. She returned a few minutes later wearing a purple sweater, skintight vermillion pants, yellow ballet slippers, and a long mauve scarf. And then, an intimation of things to come, she began to dance.

Driving back to Los Angeles, Janiger felt like Moses coming down from the mountain, except in his case what he lacked was the tablets—or ampules. I've got to get my hands on some more LSD, he thought. I'll go crazy if I can't figure out an experiment that will satisfy Sandoz. But what kind of an experiment? Janiger had no interest in experimental lab work, giving LSD to snails and fish and making voluminous notes on their reactions. Nor was he interested in the Lab Madness rigamorole of personality and intelligence tests. After puzzling over the problem for several weeks, he arrived at a simple solution: why not just give LSD to volunteers and let them do whatever they wanted? Provide them with paper, pencils, typewriter, tape recorder, and leave them alone—a completely naturalistic study. Much to his surprise, Sandoz agreed, and within a few weeks he had his own supply of LSD.

One of Janiger's few rules was that everyone had to have a babysitter, someone who would remain with them throughout the experience. No one could babysit unless they had already taken LSD. Other than that, the emphasis was on recording what was happening, getting it down on paper or tape before it evaporated—reams of paper, spools of tape. The volume would have been overwhelming had not Janiger been a popular lecturer with access to a willing labor pool of students who were cajoled into culling the reports and underlining salient reactions like "the room is breathing." The underlined statements were then typed onto cards, and the subjects were called back in and asked to sort them into groups ranging from statements that were "most relevant" to their own experience, to those that were "least relevant."

Except for the time one of the volunteers eluded his babysitter and got loose on Wilshire Boulevard, it was all pretty straightforward. That day the subject just flew out the door before anyone could react; he was nowhere to be found by the time Janiger reached the street. The whole office fanned out looking for him, but he had vanished. Certain his career was about to share a similar fate, Janiger was walking back to his office when he heard whistling. Glancing up, he saw the subject sitting in a tree. "Why don't you climb down from there," Janiger suggested in his most persuasive psychiatric voice. But the volunteer said, "Oh no, I'll fly right down."

Situations like this were one of the reasons why Janiger had insisted that his babysitters take LSD—because only after you had been there could you realize just how much sincerity was implied in the response, "I'll fly right down." The subject really thought he was a bird, which meant that Janiger had to convince him to climb down using logic a bird would accept. So he built a nest out of sticks and stones, and with a little persuasion coaxed the man down to sit on it.

One day a painter volunteered, and Janiger gave him an Indian kachina doll to sketch. As the LSD took hold the sketches became emotional, fiery, a mixture of cubism, fauvism, and abstract expressionism that convinced the artist he had made an artistic breakthrough. Word of the Beverly Hills shrink who had a creativity pill swept through the local bohemian art scene like a Malibu brush fire. Within days Janiger was besieged by painters and sculptors, all begging for an opportunity to expose their artistry to LSD.

At first he was reluctant. Too many artists would spoil the experiment's balance. But then the beauty of what had befallen him became apparent: art was a universal language, it was active rather than reflective, it was concrete. Instead of having to rely on posthumous statements about the room changing color and the chairs becoming the Last Judgement, he could let each artist sketch the same kachina doll: a sketch before taking LSD, a sketch in the middle of the experiment, and so on. That way he would have a simple yet elegant example of how LSD changed perception. Watching them work, Janiger realized that artists had always been the natural constituency for consciousness-changing drugs. The unconscious was their medium, and they would do anything to improve their access. One only had to think of Coleridge and opium, Balzac and hashish, Poe and laudanum—the list was endless.

Although the painters worked out fine, in the end they were insufficient: the art was expressive, the painters weren't. They had such a hard time articulating what was happening inside their heads that Janiger decided he needed a writer or two to flesh out his findings. Gil Henderson, one of the painters, suggested the novelist Anaïs Nin. This was an inspired suggestion, for not only was Nin conversant with the language of psychoanalysis, but also for two decades she had been conducting her own idiosyncratic raids on her unconscious in the form of a series of surrealistic novels.

Nin has left us a record of her LSD trips in her famous diary. She describes how, at one point, the room had dissolved into pure space, revealing the "images behind images, the walls behind the sky, the sky behind the infinite"; how she had begun to weep, copious tears flowing down her cheeks, while at the same instant she had been aware of a comic force behind the tears. And the two feelings, weeping and laughter, tragedy and comedy, had alternated at a dizzying pace. "Without being a mathematician I understand the infinite," she had told Janiger, who reminded her of a Picasso painting, an asymmetrical man with one large, prying eye. Prying into her very soul.

What part of the mind was being stimulated so that the concept of infinity could be grasped on an emotional level? Where was the place where objects suddenly became alive, where the room began to breathe? Finding the answers to these questions was the most exciting thing Oscar Janiger could imagine.

And he wasn't alone. For some reason—the presence of Huxley? Southern California in general?—the Los Angeles LSD scene was particularly fertile. One day it seemed there were only five researchers working with the drug, the next day ten, the day after that twenty, all exchanging those knowing looks.

One of Janiger's counterparts was Sidney Cohen, a psychiatrist attached to the Los Angeles Neuropsychiatric Hospital, which was part of the Veterans Administration. Cohen had obtained his first LSD fully intending to pursue the model psychoses work of Max Rinkel and the other Lab Madness researchers, but his own personal experience with the drug had caused him to change direction.

"I was taken by surprise," he recollected a few years later at an LSD symposium. "This was no confused, disoriented delirium, but something quite different. Just what it was I could not say." It refused to be Englished. Or easily psychologized. "Though we have been using the available measuring instruments, the check lists, the performance tests, the psychological batteries, and so forth, the core of the LSD situation remains in the dark, quite untouched by our activities," he confessed.

But while the core remained impenetrable, researchers like Cohen were busily building a body of data describing what happened when the typical therapy patient took LSD. Miraculous and disturbing things happened. Sometimes the patient got trapped on a paranoid merry-go-round, and went round and round until the session had to be terminated with the antipsychotic thorazine, a drug that effectively counteracted the effects of LSD. But just as often, after twisting and turning through the labyrinth of their unconscious, they suddenly stumbled onto a part of the Other World that was conflict-free, and all their pathologies vanished like startled birds. "It is as though everything that bothered them has been transcended," remarked Cohen's colleague, the psychologist Betty Eisner. Cohen made a particular study of this anomaly, which he called the "integrative experience":

> The integrative experience should be described further because it has not been a matter for scientific scrutiny and the semantic difficulties are considerable. There is usually a perceptual component which consists of looking upon beauty and light. Affectually there is a feeling of great relaxation and hyperphoria. The patients describe an insightfulness into themselves, an awareness of their place in the environment, and a sense of order in life. These are all fused into a very meaningful episode, and it is believed that this can be significantly therapeutic.

The key to the integrative experience, to the extent that one existed, was set and setting. With proper preparation and the skillful manipulation of mood enhancers, particularly music, Cohen found he could induce an integrative experience with fair regularity. But he also discovered that while enormously helpful, the integrative experience was not a miracle cure. A patient might experience that pure redemptive light one month and yet be right back where he had started from the next, nurturing the same family of neuroses that had brought him into therapy in the first place. But when Cohen mentioned these limitations to his more enthusiastic colleagues, he was usually dismissed as stuffy old Sid, middle-of-the-road Sid.

But however cautious he might have been about LSD's ultimate utility, Sidney Cohen was instrumental in turning on not only his colleagues, mostly psychiatrists and psychologists, but a few writers and scientists as well. During one stretch his office was full of analysts from the Rand Corporation, the semisecret think tank located in Santa Monica. One of them, Herman Kahn, took LSD and lay on the floor murmuring "wow" every few minutes. Later he claimed he had spent the time profitably reviewing bombing strategies against mainland China.

One of the psychologists whom Cohen introduced to LSD was a man named A. Wesley Medford. With a friend, a cancer specialist and radiologist named Mortimer Hartman, Medford began spending his weekends experimenting with the drug. Gradually others joined in, until their private weekend investigations resembled what in left political circles would have been called a cell—a cell not of the class wars, but the consciousness wars. All sorts of crazy things started happening to the Wesley group. Astral projection. Past lives. Telepathy over vast spaces. Enhanced intelligence. The sense that they could link up into a multiple mind, a Group Mind. Although all the experiments that they designed to test these newfound powers failed—remember Weir Mitchell with his poems and psychology papers—it didn't dampen the group's ardor, and the rest of the LSD research community watched in bemused fascination as the Wesley group grew in intensity and then came apart amid denunciations and recriminations. It seemed LSD also enhanced some of the negative personality traits that make it difficult for people to get along with each other.

Wesley returned to his former practice, warning that LSD was uncontrollable. But not Hartman. LSD had lit a fire under Hartman; he couldn't leave it alone. Teaming up with a psychiatrist named Arthur Chandler, who had joined the Wesley group late in the game, Hartman opened an office in Beverly Hills and launched a five-year therapeutic study that had Sandoz's blessing. Even though Chandler had the therapeutic credentials, it was Hartman who ran the office. "He was the sparkplug," remembers Oscar Janiger. "He was always needling Chandler, who was a pragmatic cookbook kind of guy, an old-line psychiatrist. But Chandler also provided a drag, otherwise Hartman would have been another Leary, getting grandiose and messianic. They were a perfect team." Although Hartman was sincerely interested in conducting a legitimate research study for Sandoz, he was also aware that LSD therapy had the potential for a healthy financial return, particularly if inroads could be made into the analysis-prone film colony.

Of all the actors, writers, musicians, and directors who passed through Chandler and Hartman's portals, the most famous was Cary Grant. Grant took LSD more than sixty times, and although he was considered one of Hollywood's most private stars, he found his enthusiasm for the drug hard to contain. It finally overflowed during the filming of the movie *Operation Petticoat.* The scene was appropriately bizarre. There was Grant sitting on the deck of the pink submarine that was *Petticoat*'s principal set. He had an aluminum sheet attached to his neck to facilitate his tan and he was chatting with two reporters, both of whom were prepared for the usual hour of teeth pulling that an interview with Grant required. But today Cary was totally relaxed, a condition he attributed to the insights he had achieved using an experimental mind drug called LSD.

"I have been born again," he told the astonished reporters. "I have

64

been through a psychiatric experience which has completely changed me. I was horrendous. I had to face things about myself which I never admitted, which I didn't know were there. Now I know that I hurt every woman I ever loved. I was an utter fake, a self-opinionated bore, a know-all who knew very little.

"I found I was hiding behind all kinds of defenses, hypocrisies and vanities. I had to get rid of them layer by layer. The moment when your conscious meets your subconscious is a hell of a wrench. With me there came a day when I saw the light."

Although Grant, his lawyers, and MGM all tried to kill the story, it appeared in print on April 20, 1959, and while it didn't alter Grant's popularity one iota, it was an enormous shot in the pocketbook for LSD therapists like Chandler and Hartman. Suddenly everyone in Hollywood wanted to be born again.

Whether it was Chandler and Hartman that Aldous Huxley had in mind when he dropped the following note to Osmond is unclear, but they certainly fit the general description. "What frightful people there are in your profession," Huxley had written. "We met two Beverly Hills psychiatrists the other day, who specialize in LSD therapy at $100 a shot—and, really, I have seldom met people of lower sensitivity, more vulgar mind! To think of people made vulnerable by LSD being exposed to such people is profoundly disturbing."

There was a lesson here, but, with the possible exception of Anaïs Nin, no one noticed.

Thanks to her sessions with Dr. Janiger, Anaïs Nin had a front-row seat as the psychedelic movement was born in a handful of fashionable Los Angeles drawing rooms, midwifed by Huxley, Heard, Hubbard, and the dozens of researchers (like Janiger) and others (like Nin) who had been drawn into the sublime quest of exploring the Other World. Attending their impassioned get-togethers, Nin was reminded of Andre Breton and his band of surrealists who had alternately shocked and delighted Paris in the Twenties and Thirties. Breton had been another believer in the revolutionary potentials of the unconscious, but lacking a tool like LSD he had been forced to rely on trances and automatic writing to make his case. Nevertheless Nin sniffed his presence in the excited speculations of Heard and Huxley, although the setting was a far cry from the noisy cafés of Montparnasse.

At first it was all talk, talk, talk, in a variety of dialects. The psychologists talked psychology, the mystics talked theology, a smattering talked parapsychology, while polymaths like Huxley and Heard danced from one vocabulary to the other, equally at home with the integrative experience or the Hindu samadhi. Misunderstandings were frequent, as was an inevitable partisanship; what kept things congenial was the bemused understanding that they were all talking about the same thing. When it came to the Other World, everyone—the psychologists, the writers, the artists, even the mystics—enjoyed amateur status. This had been a little hard for some of the medical men to swallow, as they tended to take a proprietary attitude toward drugs; some of the more hard-nosed had come in for a lot of criticism along the lines of, "My God, get it out of those sterile rooms and stop asking those stupid questions." But years of conditioning couldn't be shed overnight. Sterile rooms and questionnaires were the only scientific tools they had, and it was difficult to see how you could jettison them and still expect to solve the mystery.

From midnight discussions it was a short step to . . . *drug parties* would be the phrase used today. No one came right out and said, "Why not drop by my house tonight and we'll take LSD." The invitation was usually couched in terms like, "Why not come over and we'll conduct a modest ESP experiment." But the result was the same. Eventually a series of evening salons sprang up in some of Los Angeles's wealthier neighborhoods, bringing together the likes of Huxley, Heard, Hubbard, Nin, Oscar Janiger, Sidney Cohen, etc. "Our parties were meaningful and very special," Nin confided to her diary. "We shared our esoteric experiences. These experiences should have remained esoteric."

Nin was probably one of the first people in America to worry that LSD was getting out of hand. A couple of things bothered her. She was worried, for example, by the arrogant assumption of so many of the psychologists that in a year or two they would have the Other World neatly dissected and defanged, sterilized, objectified, another head for the trophy rooms of science. Nin had no doubt that the human spirit would elude the men in the white coats, but she did worry about the kind of unintended damage the pursuit might bring. Nevertheless, that didn't mean she endorsed the Huxley plan of introducing psychedelics to the Best and the Brightest. The more she watched the spread of LSD, the more convinced she became that there was a reason why the quest for higher consciousness had always been the province of small esoteric mystery cults: you couldn't mass produce the mystical: too many initiations, too many complex rituals were required. Sure a drug like LSD opened the Door, affording instant access to parts of the unconscious that might otherwise have taken years to achieve either through meditation or psychotherapy. But was a shortcut the best and safest way to visit the Other World? Nin didn't think so. But when she argued this point with Huxley, he responded rather irritably, "You're fortunate enough to have a natural access to your subconscious life, but other people need drugs and should have them."

It was Huxley's opinion that *Homo sapiens* didn't have the luxury to ignore any shortcuts. When he had written *Brave New World* in the early Thirties, he had imagined it taking place in the far distant future of A.D.

3500. But here it was less than a quarter of a century later, and the world was catching up to his satirical portrait. The ideal of a perfectly managed society, which was the beating heart of corporate liberalism, could have been lifted right out of the first chapter, with its insistent message— "conform, conform, conform"—murmuring from the Pavlovian television screens and from the tabloids' worshipful hagiography of the Organization Man. "Conform, or else has become something of an eleventh commandment," observed psychiatrist Robert Lindner in a little book called *Must We Conform?* Huxley explored the astonishing way life was imitating his art in a series of essays collected and published under the title *Brave New World Revisited.* Of particular interest to him was the skyrocketing popularity of tranquilizers like Miltown and Elavil. These, Huxley felt, were worthy forerunners of a true soma, in that they staunched the flow of unhappiness that was an inevitable byproduct of "conform, or else."

Given the cultural situation, Huxley felt, the rapid and efficient development of psychedelics became crucial. Gerald Heard believed much the same thing, only he tended to replace Huxley's sociological arguments with larger cosmic ones. For Heard it was the forces of light versus those of darkness, eros against thanatos, with the forces of darkness manifested in the Bomb, the proliferation of mental illness, the slide toward regimentation, while the forces of light had to make do with LSD. LSD proved once and for all that the mind contained higher powers; they should be catalogued and inventoried; and then they should be released on a wide scale. "We may be very grateful that our opponents so long have been content to be ignorant and bigoted materialists," he said.

Neither Huxley nor Heard ever sat down and drew up a formal blueprint for how the anxious present might become the psychedelic future, although Huxley was thinking of writing a reverse *Brave New World,* in which a psychedelic system of education would result in a true utopia. But that was fiction—and rather difficult fiction, he discovered, as most of his early attempts ended in the wastebasket. What Huxley and Heard seemed to be aiming for was a kind of gradual osmosis, particularly among the scientific community. If they could get science on their side, if they could map and inventory the Other World using the accepted tools of scientific truth, always careful not to alarm the philistines with grandiose claims, then there might be a chance . . . and the way to accomplish this was to recruit as many of the Lab Madness boys and the LSD researchers to their point of view as was humanly possible, and then let them turn on the Best and the Brightest under the guise of legitimate research projects.

"The man who comes back through the Door in the Wall will never be quite the same as the man who went out," Huxley had written in the last paragraph of *Doors*. "He will be wiser but less cocksure, happier but less self-satisfied, humbler in acknowledging his ignorance . . ." He will also, like Saul on the road to Tarsus, be open to a different vision.

It is important to understand that Huxley wasn't proposing a wholesale migration to the Other World. He was very selective. When the novelist Christopher Isherwood, a close friend of Heard and a disciple of the same Swami Prabhavananda who had tutored Huxley in Vedantic Hinduism back in the Forties, came to them for mescaline he was turned away as too unstable. Annoyed, Isherwood later obtained some mescaline on his own and tried it one day in London. He went to Westminster Cathedral "to see if God was there." He wasn't. In fact, his absence was so profound that Isherwood began to giggle uncontrollably and had to remove himself to a discreet nook until he could regain his composure. There wasn't a whisper of the eternal spirit in that immense, drafty space.

But if a likely candidate appeared on their horizon, he was usually accommodated. This was the case with Alan Watts, a slightly younger member of Isherwood's generation (b. 1915) and a former Anglican minister turned freelance philosopher. Watts was something of a special case, as he had spent his adolescence in the same theosophical circles that Huxley and Heard had investigated in the Thirties. He was a protégé of Christmas Humphreys, the English barrister who also ran London's Buddhist Lodge. When Watts was unable to attend Oxford, Humphreys and his friends began schooling young Alan in "every occult and far-out subject under the sun." And Watts responded by becoming a prodigy. Already at nineteen, when he published his first book, his trademark style was fully developed. Watts could take the most abstruse topics and render them as clear as a pane of glass. This was less a matter of prose than a quality of mind: about the time he was drawn into Huxley's psychedelic scenario, Watts had a radio show in San Francisco. Little old ladies would call up from Oakland and ask him the most godawful things—how Zen satori was related to the Catholic concept of grace, for instance—and Watts wouldn't even blink. He'd open his mouth (which always contained a cigarette; he amazed the engineers by being able to talk and smoke them at the same time) and perfectly formed sentences would pour out for ten, fifteen, twenty minutes, and then, just as the engineer was about to give the off-air sign, he would tie the ends of his answer up into a neat little bow and sign off. Watts's loquacity made him a great favorite of the LSD researchers; there wasn't a drug in the world, he used to boast to them, that could shut him up.

Watts wasn't an immediate convert to Huxley's high opinion of psychedelics. It struck him as "highly improbable that a true spiritual experience could follow from ingesting a particular chemical. Visions and ecstasies, yes. A taste of the mystical, like swimming with water-wings, perhaps." The first time he took LSD he had a "hilariously beautiful" but "hardly what I would call mystical" time. But then he took it again, and this time he had a full-blown mystical illumination that was as embarrassing as it was enlightening—embarrassing because that moment of cosmic Oneness was something Watts had devoted his whole adult life to finding, and now he had achieved it not through proper spiritual discipline but because he had poured an ampule of twentieth-century science into a glass of distilled water; and it was enlightening because what came through the Door wasn't Zen Buddhism, which was Watts's specialty, but something with an unmistakable Hindu cast, as though Hinduism "was a local form of some undercover wisdom, inconceivably ancient, which everyone knows in the back of his mind but will not admit."

Oscar Janiger always thought that the arrival of Alan Watts was a key moment in the psychedelic chronology, because Watts's influence lay in a different direction from that of Huxley and Heard. From his base in San Francisco he had considerable influence with the young bohemians, among them a cousin of Janiger's named Allen Ginsberg, who were beginning to look eastward for their spiritual values.

Unquestionably a momentum was developing, but its direction was a bit difficult to ascertain. Up in Canada Osmond had begun giving LSD to terminal alcoholics with promising results, but he was also doing such things as calling up his old school chum and member of Parliament, Christopher Mayhew, with the suggestion that Mayhew use his connections to entice the BBC into making a short science film about mescaline. Mayhew had offered himself as guinea pig and a BBC film crew had been dispatched to his house in Surrey to film Osmond giving him 400 milligrams of mescaline hydrochloride. What followed was by now fairly predictable: at irregular intervals Mayhew kept slipping through the door of temporal and spatial reality and arriving at a place of "pervasive pure light, like a kind of invisible sunlit snow." Although Osmond's watch indicated that these voyages lasted mere seconds, to Mayhew they seemed to go on forever.

"I'm off again for a long period," he would suddenly announce, interrupting one of Osmond's intelligence tests. "But you won't notice that I've gone away at all."

"When are you coming back?" Osmond would ask.

"I am now in your time," Mayhew would respond, to be followed a few minutes later by another "Whoops I'm off again."

Like Aldous, Mayhew also had a glimpse of the dark part of the Other World. "There were occasions when I knew with terrible vividness what being mad was like," he confided in an account of his experience that was published in the London *Observer*.

To give another illustration of how things were developing: in 1954 Gerald Heard gave a lecture in Palo Alto to an organization called the

Sequoia Seminar. Sitting in the audience was an engineer named Myron Stolaroff. Stolaroff was in charge of long-range planning at Ampex, which was one of the first of the high-technology companies to emerge in the valleys south of San Francisco. Stolaroff had heard Gerald speak several times before and considered him one of the world's outstanding mystics. So when Heard began rhapsodizing about the effects of certain mind-altering drugs, Stolaroff was predictably upset. "I thought you went to all these places anyway," he asked. "Why do you take this?" And Heard had replied, "Oh, but it just opens the doors in so many ways to so many vast dimensions."

Whether he admitted it to himself or not, Myron Stolaroff was hooked, and a few months later, in Los Angeles on business, he visited Heard and had another long discussion about these new mind drugs. At one point Hubbard's name had come up, and Heard had implied that if Stolaroff wished to try any of these substances, Al was the man to guide him through the experience. So Stolaroff had written Hubbard and one day Al had turned up on the doorstep, bounding into Myron's office with a tank of carbogen, a "fun-loving guy" who "radiated an enormous energy field." After the formal introductions were over, Hubbard had suggested that Stolaroff take a few lungfuls of the carbogen, and twenty or thirty breaths later the director of long-range planning was abreacting all over his office.

Stolaroff, who had been skeptical of a lot of Gerald's claims, was convinced. He arranged to visit Vancouver at the earliest opportunity for one of Hubbard's patented LSD sessions—by 1959 Hubbard was claiming he had conducted seventeen hundred LSD sessions.

It was a terrible experience. During those hours in Hubbard's apartment, Stolaroff relived his birth, the actual physical birth, gasping and writhing for what felt like days, until he broke through to the world, which actually smelled of ether. Although it was a torturous few hours, Myron emerged from the LSD womb convinced that many of his personal eccentricities and neuroses could be traced back to the trauma of his birth. This was not a radical possibility as far as psychoanalysis was concerned; Otto Rank, one of Freud's last disciples, had explored the effects of birth on the emerging psyche in numerous articles. But it would have taken psychoanalysis years to attain the level that LSD had reached in one climactic rush. Stolaroff returned to Ampex convinced that LSD "was the greatest discovery that man had ever made."

Over the next few years Myron and Al grew increasingly close. Stolaroff was a businessman, an engineer, a manipulator of things, not words, and he was a welcome change from the hyperintellectuality of the Heard-Huxley-Osmond circle. Gradually a fantasy took shape out of their late-night confabs: using LSD, they would turn Ampex into the most creative, successful, and lucrative corporation in the world. They would use the drug to stimulate not only creative insight, but also mental health, doing away with all that debilitating egotism and neurosis, the petty jealousies, the failures of communication. Using LSD, they would foster an environment in which individuality would flower and mesh with the budding genius of everyone else's individuality, thus creating a corporation that served the impossible task of enhancing not only the individual, but the group as well. And the bottom line would be: lots of money for everyone.

Hubbard was a perfect example of how reality can warp the best-laid fantasies. It had seemed a simple enough task back when it had first popped into Huxley's mind—just turn on enough people of sufficient caliber to tip the cultural balance—but he had forgotten that not everyone might share his Oxbridge assumptions. Huxley preferred a kind of quiet diplomacy that would spread the word "in the relative privacy of learned journals, the decent obscurity of moderately highbrow books"; American TV, with its audience of "Baptists, Methodists and nothing-but-men plus an immense lunatic fringe," should be avoided at all costs. But decent obscurity was not Al's forte. He seemed determined to sell LSD as a specifically Catholic nostrum. "Would it not be best to let Hubbard go his own way within the Church?" Huxley wrote Osmond. "It is evidently there that he feels increasingly at home. It is evident, too, that his loyalty to the Church makes him increasingly anxious to use LSD-25 as an instrument for validating Catholic doctrines and for giving new life to Catholic symbols." But the irritation lasted only until their next dinner, when Hubbard again charmed Huxley with his geniality and vigor. "Please ignore what I wrote in my last letter about him," he told Osmond, adding, "I still have doubts about the general validity of his methods."

But Hubbard's methods generally worked, and in late 1957 his campaign within Vancouver's Catholic hierarchy won a rather astounding victory in the form of a notice issued by the Cathedral of the Holy Rosary, which read, in part:

> We are aware of man's fallibility and will be protected in our studies by that understanding and recognition of the First Cause of all created things that govern them. We therefore approach the study of these psychodelics and their influence on the mind of man anxious to discover whatever attributes they possess respectfully evaluating their proper place in the Divine Economy. We humbly ask our Heavenly Mother the Virgin, help of all who call upon her to know and understand the true qualities of these psychodelics, the full capacities of man's noblest faculties and according to God's laws to use them for the benefit of mankind here and in eternity.

Today the Catholic hierarchy of western Canada, tomorrow the first psychedelic corporation—Al's aspirations certainly weren't modest.

But in this case the one precluded the other. Although Myron Stolaroff had laid the groundwork perfectly, persuading Ampex's new general manager to overlook Al's flaws and give LSD a chance, the result was disastrous. The general manager was Jewish. The last thing he wanted to do was look at pictures of Jesus Christ, but that's what Hubbard kept waving at him.

We could continue in this vein for another hundred pages, describing all the little eddies that sprang up in LSD's wake, and perhaps we should describe just one more, as it shows how far afield the psychedelic message was ranging. In 1958 Gerald and Sidney Cohen traveled to Arizona to run a session for Henry Luce, founder and president of Time-Life, Inc., and Luce's wife, the cosmopolite Clare Booth Luce. At one point during the evening the tone-deaf and unflamboyant Luce wandered out into the yard, conducting an imaginary symphony; and later on a short colloquy with God assured him all was well with the American Century.

The only problem that anyone could foresee was the possibility that somewhere down the road LSD might turn out to be physically harmful. One couldn't forget Freud, who had thought cocaine an innocuous panacea and had become addicted. But even if this happened, it wouldn't be fatal: "If the psychologists and sociologists will define the ideal," Huxley said, "the neurologists and pharmacologists can be relied upon to discover the means whereby the ideal can be realized." LSD and mescaline were just the tip of the psychedelic iceberg.

The first new psychedelic to surface was DMT, an abbreviation of dimethyltriptamine. It was introduced into the Los Angeles scene by Oscar Janiger. Besides exploring the possibilities of LSD, Janiger had been intrigued by the Osmond/Smythies thesis that psychoses might be caused by a metabolic malfunction of the adrenal system. Just as serendipity had led the two Englishmen to the molecular similarity between adrenalin and mescaline, Janiger had stumbled across a similar connection between brain tryptamines and a South American vine used in shamanic rites called *ayahuasca*. The psychoactive element in *ayahuasca* was dimethyltriptamine. Janiger searched the medical literature for any references to DMT. He found only two, both in Hungarian. Surmising that the Hungarians must have tried DMT and lived to write their monographs, Janiger had a local laboratory make a batch, and one afternoon while he was alone in his office he filled a syringe and shot it into his arm—"a dangerously stupid, idiotic thing to do."

Compared to DMT, LSD was like a lazy summer picnic. Janiger felt like he was inside a pinball machine, bombarded by flashing lights, clanging bells, infernal messages. There was no insight. He was lost, disconnected, and when he later regained consciousness (the DMT lasted only thirty minutes) he was convinced he had been "totally stark raving crazy." Which was terrific! Perhaps he had found the elusive M factor.

Janiger gave DMT to Bivens, who agreed that it was too much; then he called up Alan Watts and bet him that he had a drug that could finally shut him up. Watts took the bet and the DMT, and for thirty minutes he lay there staring at Janiger, who kept repeating, "Alan, Alan, please say something. Talk to me. Your reputation is at stake." But Watts never said a word. The next time Al Hubbard passed through town, Janiger gave him a supply of DMT for his leather bag and asked him to distribute it along the circuit. "This isn't a gift," he said. "I want reports back." Everyone who took DMT agreed that it was a hellish half hour, with absolutely no redeeming qualities.

The same couldn't be said, however, about psilocybin, which descended on the psychedelic scene like an eager debutante from a well-known society family, in this case, Sandoz Pharmaceuticals.

8

NOISES OFFSTAGE

A rather odd set of circumstances led Sandoz to psilocybin.

To begin at the beginning would be to start on a forest path in the Catskills in the summer of 1927, at the moment when Valentina Wasson spied some mushrooms growing in the woods and ran to pick them. Her new husband, for they were on their honeymoon, watched aghast as she "knelt in poses of adoration before one cluster and then another of these growths." When it became clear that no amount of argument could deter her from cooking them for dinner, Gordon Wasson began to prepare himself for the new status of widower, for there was little doubt in his mind that by morning she would be dead.

She wasn't, of course. Born in Russia, Valentina Wasson had been raised a mycophile, a lover of mushrooms, and she was knowledgeable in the specifics of their use. Gordon, an Anglo-Saxon, represented the other extreme, a mycophobe, a hater of mushrooms. Being educated sorts—Gordon was a Harvard man and financial correspondent for the New York *Herald Tribune;* Valentina a pediatrician—they began to analyze the different cultural heritages that could have produced such opposite reactions. Was it possible to imagine a similar disagreement over lichen or walnuts? In fact, once they had delved a little deeper, they discovered that whole areas of Europe could be designated either *mycophile* (the Slavic countries, with pockets in Bavaria, Austria, and Italy, and parts of southern France and Spain) or *mycophobe* (the rest of Europe). Appetites whetted, they plunged into an investigation that would continue for the rest of their lives.

In 1928 Gordon Wasson gave up journalism for banking, and took a job in the securities division of Morgan Guaranty. When an act of Congress prohibited banks from owning stock, he transferred to the regular staff of the bank, where he eventually rose to the position of vice president. During these years whatever spare time the Wassons had was devoted to their mycological quest. They tramped all over Europe, combing the language for echoes of the split that must have occurred millennia ago. They sought out uneducated peasants and interviewed them regarding the local fungi.

Gradually a thesis emerged. The Wassons began to suspect that a mushroom had played a formative role in the Ur-religion of tribal Indo-Europe. Their prime candidate was the fly amanite, considered by mycophobes to be the most poisonous mushroom of all, although there was no solid evidence that anyone had ever died from eating a fly amanite. What did occur was a species of delirium that, to quote from Cooke's *Plain and Easy Account of British Fungi* (pub. 1862), caused one to "prophesy wildly, engage in feats of prodigious physical exertion, and enjoy illusions of miraculous mobility and metamorphosis." Lewis Carroll apparently knew his Cooke—in *Alice in Wonderland* the caterpillar is puffing a hookah atop a fly amanite, which Alice promptly eats with memorable results.

Because the thesis that a narcotic mushroom lay at the heart of Indo-European culture was a trifle radical, the Wassons confided in very few people. One of their confidants was Robert Graves, the English poet who was living in balmy isolation on the island of Majorca. The Wassons had become friends with Graves when they collaborated on the historical question of which mushroom the Roman Empress Agrippina had used to poison the Emperor Claudius, the main character in Graves's most popular novel, *I, Claudius.* Marshaling the available evidence, they decided that she had probably served him a dish of his favorite mushroom, *Amanita caesarea,* a harmless and tasty fungi except when it is stewed in the juice of *Amanita phalloides,* the only lethal mushroom available to Agrippina. Because a man poisoned with *phalloides* lingers on for five or six days, they concluded that a booster poison, most likely colocynth, had to have been administered via enema; and within hours Claudius was dead, and his stepson Nero was the new emperor.

In September 1952 Graves came across a magazine story that mentioned the discovery of "mushroom stones" at various archeological excavations in Guatemala and Mexico. The archeologists speculated that the stones had been objects of worship, or at least adoration, which suggested the existence in pre-Columbian times of a mushroom cult. Although the Wassons had planned to confine their study to Eurasia, they left for Mexico at the first available opportunity.

What they found was much more tangible than their European hunt through old folklore and linguistic probabilities. A number of sixteenth-century Spanish chroniclers had actually mentioned the existence of a narcotic mushroom known in the native Nahuatl as *teonanacatl*, or "God's flesh." And the Franciscan friar Bernard de Sahagun had even gone so far as to describe the alleged effects of *teonanacatl*:

> Some saw in a vision that they would die in war. Some saw in a vision that they would be devoured by wild beasts. . . . Some saw in a vision that they would become rich, wealthy. Some saw in a vision that they would buy slaves . . .

As far as de Sahagun was concerned, this was devil's work, and the Catholic Church had moved vigorously to suppress the mushroom cult.

The Wassons were banking on the possibility that the cult had not been eradicated in the sixteenth century, but had gone underground. There was some evidence that this might be the case. In 1936 a team of American anthropologists working in the remote village of Huatla de Jimenez reported that they had been allowed to observe, but not participate in, a ceremony that involved psychotropic mushrooms.

For three years the Wassons followed rumors, cultivated sources, and learned the Indian dialects. In Huatla de Jimenez they became friends with Eunice Pike, the local missionary and someone who was rumored to know quite a bit about the mushroom cult. Only "when evening and darkness come and you are alone with a wise old man or woman whose confidence you have won, by the light of a candle held in the hand and talking in a whisper, you may bring up the subject," Wasson wrote. What they whispered was tantalizing. According to Wasson's sometimes fanciful sources, *teonanacatl* were gathered before sunrise at the time of the New Moon; they were picked in some areas only by virgins, who wrapped them in banana leaves and took them to the cathedral, where they were left on the altar to be blessed. Then they were passed from *curandero* (medicine man, healer, shaman, etc.) to *curandero*. Listening to these whispered stories, the Wassons felt like "pilgrims seeking the Grail," an apt analogy, as the mushroom cult was proving comparably elusive. Wasson described the frustration this way:

> Perhaps you will learn the names of a number of renowned *curanderos*, and your emissaries will even promise to deliver them to you, but then you wait and wait and they never come. You will brush past them in the marketplace, and they will know you but you will not know them. The judge in the town hall may be the very man you are seeking; and you may pass the time of day with him, yet never learn that he is your *curandero*.

In the summer of 1955 the Wassons hired a muleteer who knew his way around the Oaxacan mountains and set out for Huatla de Jimenez. There, as the twenty-ninth of June became the thirtieth, Gordon became the first outsider to "partake in the agape of the sacred mushrooms." He later coined the word *bemushroomed* to describe the state he passed into. Strange information flowed through his mind, visions that seemed the "very archetypes of beautiful form and color" and ideas that reminded him of the "Ideas that Plato had talked about"—ideas that impressed the banker from Morgan Guaranty not as the fantasies of an "unhinged imagination," but as a glimpse of a higher order of reality, against which our daily lives are "mere imperfect adumbrations."

The Wassons kept quiet about their discovery and returned to Huatla de Jimenez several more times. On one occasion they were accompanied by a photographer named Allan Richardson, who photographed the mushroom ceremony; on another they brought Roger Heim, a famous mycologist and the director of France's National Museum of Natural History. Heim succeeded in identifying the mushrooms as a member of the Stophariaceae family, genus *psilocybe,* but was stymied when it came to isolating the active element. That problem he passed along to Albert Hofmann at Sandoz Pharmaceuticals, who reluctantly agreed to do what he could. "I wanted to assign the investigation to one of my co-workers," Hofmann would ruefully write in his autobiography. "However, nobody showed much eagerness to take on this problem because it was known that LSD and everything connected with it were scarcely popular subjects to the top management."

In 1958 Hofmann announced that he had synthesized two new substances: psilocybin and psilocin, both of which were indole compounds with a marked similarity to the neurotransmitter serotonin; LSD now had some less potent cousins.

News of the Wassons' discovery spread slowly but steadily. Robert Graves, writing to Martin Seymour-Smith, mentioned that his "mushroom man is very elated since he actually found the mushroom oracle I sent him after in Mexico, and ate the sacred mushrooms and had them analyzed—and there's the next wonder drug to watch out for. He thinks they were what the worshippers ate at the Eleusinian mysteries to get such terrific visions." When Aldous Huxley learned of it, Wasson's office in the Morgan bank became a stopover on the psychedelic circuit. Osmond, Huxley, and Hubbard all made pilgrimages to hear about being bemushroomed (Hubbard couldn't get over the fact that Wasson had a private dining room with private waiters), but their attempt to recruit the banker failed. Wasson was too absorbed with his own theories, his own discoveries. He "likes to think that his mushrooms are somehow unique and infinitely superior to everything else," Huxley confided to Osmond after lunching with the banker at his "Temple of

Mammon." "I tried to disabuse him. But he likes to feel that he had got hold of the One and Only psychodelic—accept no substitutes, none genuine unless sold with the signature of the inventor."

That particular visit to the Temple came in June 1957 at a time when the Wassons' magnum opus about the Indo-European mushroom cult, *Mushrooms, Russia and History,* had just appeared in a limited edition of 512 copies, each costing $250. It was a prodigious work of scholarship, but for all its philological and folkloric mastery it was the Divine Mushroom of Mexico that gave the thesis its plausibility. "We have now learned," the Wassons had written, "that many species of these strange growths possess a power such as early man could only have regarded as miraculous. Indeed they may have given to him the very idea of the miraculous, and inspired many of the themes that come down to us in our heritage of folklore. . . . We have suggested that the divine mushroom played a vital part in shaking loose early man's imagination, in arousing his capacity for self-perception, for awe, wonder, and reverence. They certainly made it easier for him to entertain the idea of God."*

Had Wasson's public exposure been limited to half a thousand copies of a book costing the equivalent of two weeks' pay, our story might have been different. But one day, while recounting his Mexican adventures during lunch at the Century Club, Wasson was overheard by an editor at Time-Life, who invited him to write the experience up and submit it to *Life* magazine, which had a running feature devoted to true-life adventures. Wasson's account of the mushroom ceremony was published, along with Allan Richardson's pictures, in the July 1957 issue of *Life,* where it was read by millions, and in particular by a young psychologist named Frank Barron, who was best friends with another young psychologist named Timothy Leary.

But these are reverberations that properly belong to the future. A better question, for the present, might be: Who was James Moore, and why had he been so eager to accompany Gordon Wasson into the Mexican outback in the summer of 1956?

As far as Gordon Wasson knew, James Moore was a professor at the University of Delaware. Moore had written to him in the winter of 1956 expressing an interest in the chemistry of Mexican fungi, and upon

---

*In the course of this story we will skate past a number of rather large and heretical speculations. This is certainly one of them. Interested readers might wish to obtain the Wassons' *Mushrooms, Russia and History; Soma;* and Gordon Wasson's collaboration with Albert Hofmann and Carl Ruck, *The Road to Eleusis.*

learning that Wasson was planning another expedition to Huatla de Jimenez that summer had asked to tag along. To sweeten his unsolicited presence, Moore had mentioned a foundation that might underwrite the whole trip, the Geschickter Fund. And sure enough, the Fund had ponied up two thousand dollars to cover expenses. In retrospect, it was barely enough to cover the irritation of Moore himself.

The man was a complainer. Apparently he had thought a trip to Huatla de Jimenez would be little different from a jaunt to Acapulco; in any case he was unprepared for the diarrhea, the dirt floors, the monotonous food. "I had a terribly bad cold, we damn near starved to death, and I itched all over," was Moore's memory of the journey. To which Wasson has replied: "He was like a landlubber at sea. He got sick to his stomach and hated it all."

Moore's complaints quickly alienated him from the other members of the expedition, among them Roger Heim, the eminent French mycologist. While Moore grumbled, the others reveled in the raw primitiveness of the adventure. Moore even found the mushrooms a disappointment. While the others soared—"I had the most superb feeling, a feeling of ecstasy," reported Wasson—Moore felt nothing save a disorientation that was compounded by the droning Indian dialects, the dirt floor, and the anarchy of his bowels. Already a thin man, he discovered upon his return to Delaware that he had dropped fifteen pounds. It took him a week to regain his strength, but when he had, he notified Botner that he was ready to work on the bag of mushrooms he had brought back from Huatla de Jimenez.

Botner was Moore's case officer at the Central Intelligence Agency.

While Heard and Huxley had been searching for a substance that would open the Door to the mind's higher powers, the Central Intelligence Agency had been looking for a mind-control drug—a Manchurian candidate, to borrow the phrase popularized by Richard Condon's best-selling novel of 1959. Ironically both groups were working the same turf, looking for the answer in that class of drugs that Osmond called psychedelics.

To understand why the CIA was looking for a mind-control substance, it is necessary to backtrack to World War II and reprise what happened at Dachau, where the medical arm of the German air force had carried out some curious experiments with mescaline. As later synopsized in an intelligence report by the U.S. Navel Technical Mission, the Nazis were looking for a drug that could "eliminate the will of the person examined." Under the auspices of *SS-Hauptstürmfuhrer* Dr. Plottner (later a professor at the University of Leipzig), mescaline had been mixed with coffee or liquor and given unobtrusively to the subjects. Then the subjects were interrogated. According to the Nazi documents, while unable to impose their will upon the subjects, the doctors had been able to elicit the most intimate sort of personal details.

Although the Nazi mescaline experiments occupied only a few paragraphs in the nearly three hundred-page report—most discussed the famous ice water experiments and other tortures in the name of science—they were paragraphs that struck a responsive chord in the OSS, for the simple reason that the OSS had also been seeking a truth drug. Under the guidance of Winfred Overholser, the director of Saint Elizabeth's, Washington's famous mental hospital, an OSS drug squad had field-tested a number of compounds, including mescaline and scopalamine. Their best luck had come with concentrated liquid marijuana, of all things, which they had injected into cigarettes. They had first used this method to crack the reserve of one August Del Gracio, who was described in the files as a "notorious New York gangster," but its most rigorous test came in a program designed to cleanse the armed forces of suspected communists. Overholser's team would arrive at the interrogation room with a pack of doctored cigarettes and a big pitcher of ice water—intense thirst being a sign that the marijuana was working. Except for one nonsmoker, they broke every soldier they interrogated.

When the CIA was chartered in 1947, it revived its wartime predecessors' fascination with truth drugs like scopalamine and liquid marijuana. And it also authorized an ambitious search for new and better mind drugs. Within the Technical Services Staff, the Agency's gizmo and gadget boys, was a small semisecret subsection known as the Chemical Division. The Chemical Division was run by a Cal-Tech chemist named Sid Gottlieb, a club-footed square-dance enthusiast who rose every morning at dawn to milk his pet goats before driving to the office and a day filled with mind warfare and germ weapons. Gottlieb also had a pronounced stutter and a patron in the higher reaches of the Agency, a man named Richard Helms. Enamored with the possibilities of chemical warfare on the consciousness level, it was Helms who persuaded Allen Dulles, the then director of the CIA, to authorize the investigation of a variety of "biological and chemical materials."

On April 13, 1953, while Huxley was dashing off that enthusiastic note to Osmond concerning mescaline, the CIA formally approved MK-ULTRA, and diverted $300,000 to fund its initial investigations. Although MK-ULTRA investigated drugs as diverse as nicotine and cocaine, a large part of its interest and excitement centered on LSD. Indeed, the CIA considered LSD to be of such promise that in November 1953 they sent two men with a black bag full of cash to buy up Sandoz's entire supply, which they thought was ten kilos.

The ten-kilo figure was the result of faulty arithmetic. When the two agents arrived in Basle with their satchel containing $240,000, they learned that Sandoz's total output since 1943 was a mere forty grams—

not even two ounces. Still, a bargain was struck. The Swiss agreed not only to supply the Agency with 100 grams of LSD a week, but also keep them apprised of who else was requesting the drug.

Nevertheless, the CIA was uneasy about having to rely entirely on the neutral Swiss, and privately they began pressing the American chemical company of Eli Lilly to come up with a rival synthesis. One of the reasons LSD was so expensive and rare was because it required a supply of ergot fungus, which was notoriously difficult to cultivate. The obvious answer was to come up with a synthesis that bypassed ergot completely, using synthetic corollaries, and in October 1954 Eli Lilly announced that they had succeeded in creating an LSD made totally from available chemicals. Besides giving the CIA a domestic supplier, the Lilly synthesis meant that unlimited supplies of LSD were now available. And this, as the memo to Allen Dulles noted, meant that LSD could finally be taken seriously as a chemical warfare agent.

Because the CIA lacked the manpower to run all the complicated behavioral and physiological experiments that Gottlieb had in mind, the Agency turned to the psychological community, particularly to those Lab Madness researchers who were already investigating LSD's relation to mental illness. Most were eager to help, provided the Agency picked up the tab. They had few moral qualms: if the CIA wanted to finance basic research in an area ignored by traditional organizations like the National Institute of Mental Health, where was the problem?

Hiding itself behind two respectable fronts, the Josiah Macy Foundation and the Geschickter Fund for Medical Research, the CIA began funneling dollars to an intercontinental network that rivaled the one being forged by Huxley and Hubbard. Early on they contacted Rinkel and Hyde at Mass. Mental Health, and with Hyde as the principal contact began pouring as much as $40,000 a year into LSD work. Similar approaches were made to Harold Abramson in New York, Carl Pfieffer at the University of Illinois, and Harold Hodge at the University of Rochester. In general the money was earmarked for research that most scientists, in any other climate but that of the Cold War, would have found ethically shady. Harold Abramson, for example, received $85,000 to produce

> operationally pertinent materials along the following lines: a. Disturbance of Memory; b. Discrediting by Aberrant Behavior; c. Alteration of Sex Patterns; d. Eliciting of Information; e. Suggestibility; f. Creation of Dependence.

In another CIA-funded experiment, seven drug addicts at a Lexington, Kentucky, hospital were given LSD for seventy-seven days, with dosages doubled and quadrupled as tolerance built up.

Not all the research was done in the hinterlands, though. Within the CIA itself, Gottlieb and his associates were taking LSD regularly, tripping at the office, at Agency parties, measuring their mental equilibrium against those of their colleagues. Turn your back in the morning and some wiseacre would slip a few micrograms into your coffee. It was a game played with the most exalted of weapons, the mind, and sometimes embarrassing things happened. Case-hardened spooks would break down crying or go all gooey about the "brotherhood of man." Once or twice things went really awry, with paranoid agents escaping into the bustle of downtown Washington, their anxious colleagues in hot pursuit. After one spectacular chase the quarry was finally run to ground in Virginia, where they found him crouched under a fountain, babbling about those "terrible monster(s) with fantastic eyes" that had pursued him across Washington. Indeed every car he met had sent a jolt of terror through his body.

It was in this spirit that Gottlieb's group invited their unsuspecting opposite numbers in the Army Chemical Corps for a three-day working holiday in November 1953. Naturally there was going to be some carousing, and naturally in some cases the punch would be spiked. Although Gottlieb had been instructed to clear any outside use of LSD with his superiors, he apparently considered the Army scientists to be exempt from that ruling. They were pros and as such would be a worthy test for any mind-control drug.

The party would have been a great success if only one of the Army scientists, a Dr. Frank Olson, hadn't committed suicide two days later. Thinking he had lost his mind, Olson had jumped out of a New York hotel room window. The flap inside the Agency almost killed MK-ULTRA.

Now the CIA is nothing if not labyrinthine, and while MK-ULTRA was studying the nefarious potentials of LSD, another CIA project, ARTICHOKE, was scouring the globe for psychotropic plants. In 1952 a CIA-funded scientist had been sent to Mexico to gather samples of mind-altering plants, in particular the seeds from a shrub called the *piule*. He had returned with pounds of material and a rumor that deep in the Mexican mountains there existed a psychotropic mushroom cult that dated back to the Aztecs. The next summer, at roughly the same moment Gordon and Valentina Wasson were embarking on their quest, a CIA scientist was arriving in Mexico with a similar brief: locate the mushroom sect and acquire samples.

To be bested by a New York banker who wanted to prove a maverick historical thesis that had been nagging at him for the last twenty years must have been galling for the CIA, what with its unlimited funds and its Caligarian vision of chemical power; but to the intelligence agency's credit, it knew of Wasson's discovery almost immediately. A

Mexican botanist cabled details a few days after Wasson returned from Huatla de Jimenez. Learning that Wasson planned to return the next summer leading a team that included the noted French mycologist Roger Heim, the Agency decided to insinuate its own man into the group in the person of James Moore, a contract chemist with ARTICHOKE. It used its conduit, the Geschickter Fund, to sweeten the deal.

Moore's nasty few weeks in Mexico were immaterial to his bosses at Langley: what was important was that he had returned with plenty of the prize mushrooms. And should he succeed in isolating the psychoactive element, then it was "quite possible," memoed Sid Gottlieb, that the new drug would "remain an agency secret." So to be bested by the same Swiss chemist and the same Swiss chemical company who had once controlled the world supply of LSD must have been galling. Once again the Agency had to apply to Sandoz—this time for its supply of psilocybin.

One of the problems the CIA grappled with in its search for a mind-control drug was the problem of how to field-test the various candidates. You could run experiments on imprisoned junkies and impoverished college students, but this was a far cry from knowing whether the drug could crack open a potential double agent or a State Department communist. To address this problem the CIA converted one of its San Francisco safe houses into a behavioral field laboratory. The house, located on Telegraph Avenue, was actually a brothel equipped with two-way mirrors and a squad of prostitutes under the supervision of former narcotics agent George White, who was famous as the man who had broken August Del Gracio with liquid marijuana back during the OSS days. The idea was that the prostitutes would lure visiting businessmen back to the house, where they would then be unobtrusively dosed with LSD or psilocybin, or any of the other mind-control candidates. From a budgetary standpoint the brothel was an ingenious idea and the whole operation was dubbed, with characteristic preppie humor, Operation Midnight Climax.

We can only guess what it was like to visit the Other World under CIA auspices, but one of the first things the randy, hallucinating businessman probably focused on was the decor. The CIA decorators hadn't been able to decide whether the proper ambiance was fin de siècle decadent or Fifties chic. Swatches of African fabric and textile hangings competed with Toulouse Lautrec reproductions of Can Can girls kicking up a storm. The tables were covered with black velvet, the curtains in the bedroom were red, those in the hall plaid, with candy-striped ones in the kitchen.

The drugs were usually administered in a drink, but not always. In one series of experiments LSD was sprayed into the bathroom just before the hapless john wandered in to use it.

It was operations like Midnight Climax that the CIA's Inspector General had in mind when he raised, in a 1963 analysis of MK-ULTRA, the spectre of ethics. That an arm of the U.S. government had been testing behavior-change drugs on unsuspecting U.S. citizens didn't alarm the Inspector General so much as what might happen if the unsuspecting public ever found out. The secrecy of MK-ULTRA was vital, he warned, not only to protect the reputation of the Agency, but also its outside sources. Noting that "research in the manipulation of human behavior is considered by many authorities in medicine and related fields to be professionally unethical," he warned that loose lips could place the professional reputations of the CIA's many contract researchers in "jeopardy."

By the time the Inspector General raised these ethical issues the CIA had supposedly lost interest in LSD, although it was still testing other mind drugs, most of which would find their way into the psychedelic underground of the 1970s. Presumably the CIA's active interest in LSD ended sometime around 1958, although the Agency continued to keep tabs on the research scene, a process made infinitely easier by the fact that the Josiah Macy Foundation, an occasional Agency conduit, had begun holding regular LSD conferences in 1955—which is not to impute insincere motives to the Macy Foundation: its interest in LSD was genuine, and had been ever since its medical director, Frank Fremont-Smith, spent an afternoon in Harold Abramson's lab watching Siamese fighting fish drugged with LSD.

The Macy conferences synopsized the changing direction of LSD research. The first, in 1955, brought together most of the Lab Madness people. The second, four years later, was dominated by the therapists: the Dutchman Van Rijn, the Englishman Sandison, Hoffer from Canada, and a whole platoon from Los Angeles, including Sidney Cohen, Betty Eisner, and the psychiatric team of Chandler and Hartman. Harold Abramson of the aforementioned Siamese fighting fish was also there, and at one point, in an attempt to arrive at a limited consensus regarding LSD, he proposed six points of general agreement:

a) It is pharmacologically safe; very large doses may be given without tissue damage.

b) It is effective in small doses for therapeutic interviews in which the therapist is definitely involved.

c) The patient is conscious, cooperative, and better able to integrate material with psychodynamic significance.

d) The patient undergoes an essentially elated disturbance in ego function, which is also accompanied by integrative forces, so that it may be thought of as "hebesynthesis" rather than narcosynthesis.

e) The drug may be given repeatedly. There is no evidence of addiction. The pharmacological effects usually wear off within 12 hours.

f) Patients usually like the experience of taking LSD in the dose range stated.

This was by no means a universally accepted list. The Lab Madness researchers still had problems with the whole idea that a drug they had used to make people crazy was now being used to make them well. A number of the therapists blanched at *hebesynthesis* as an organizing title— what an awkward product of scientific language mangling that was. But they could understand the motive that had prompted Abramson to coin it. Betty Eisner mentioned how she and Cohen referred to that curious sunlit place in the mind where conflicts disappeared as the integrative experience. But she became tongue-tied as soon as she tried to expand on that: "Obviously the language is bad; I am floundering," she apologized. Then Abram Hoffer volunteered that up in Canada they were calling it the psychedelic experience. What was that, someone asked. "Psychedelic," repeated Hoffer. "I think Dr. Osmond coined it. It comes from the Greek, meaning 'mind-manifesting.' "

Besides introducing the word that would ultimately triumph in the public consciousness, Hoffer also briefed his colleagues on the startling way in which he and Osmond were now using LSD. Unlike most of the therapists at the Macy conference, they were not using small doses to "liquefy" defenses, thus speeding up the time needed for a successful treatment. Using Hubbard's curious techniques, they had begun giving their patients massive doses and then guiding them, if they could, into that part of the Other World where egos melted and something resembling a spiritual rebirth occurred. As Hoffer described it, there was scarcely any psychotherapy involved at all: "They come in one day. They know they are going to take a treatment, but they know nothing about what it is. We take a psychiatric history, to establish a diagnosis. That is on day one. On day two, they have the LSD. On day three they are discharged. We make it an absolute point not to give them psychotherapy outside of the LSD experience. We do no follow-up except to find out whether or not they are drinking. The results are that fifty percent of these people are changed."

Those were astonishing figures, particularly since Osmond and Hoffer were not working with the usual mix of neurotics and volunteers, but with chronic alcoholics, recommended by Alcoholics Anonymous, or brought in off the street by the police. Only those alcoholics who have had the transcendental experience improved, Hoffer claimed. "Those who have not had the transcendental experience are not changed. They continue to drink. The large proportion of those who have had it are changed. But this is not an invariable rule."

Of course the alcoholics didn't just stumble into the psychedelic state. They were led there using a variety of psychological and environmental tricks. We use "sound and music," Hoffer explained, "visual stimuli, such as paintings by Van Gogh; tactile stimuli, such as various smooth or rough objects for the patient to handle. We also take advantage of the heightened suggestibility of the subjects by using persuasion, suggestion, and reiterated demand, with the theme of hope and possibility of change." The results were so promising, he said, that they were thinking of introducing a businessman's special, which would take only a weekend.

Hoffer's presentation of what would become known as psychedelic therapy—as distinguished from the mainstream small dose/traditional psychotherapy that became known as psycholytic therapy—disturbed a number of therapists. They questioned the wisdom of using such large dosages in a one-shot situation. "I start the patient with small doses, increasing the dosage gradually and working through problems to get to that point," said Betty Eisner. "That is the point, I think." "Seventy-five percent of patients will get to the point if they are given enough LSD," Hoffer retorted. And they were disturbed by the mystical overtones that kept creeping into the discussion. What did the Dutchman Van Rijn mean when he talked about wanting "to change something in the totality of the person"?

Anecdotes started to rise to the surface, slicing through the murky analytical jargon. A number of therapists talked about the serendipitous side effects that they sometimes saw in their patients. They would be in the middle of a postsession interview, perhaps two or three weeks after the original LSD session, and the patient would suddenly say, "Oh and the headache is gone too." What headache? they'd ask. Why the headache I've had for ten or fifteen years, would be the answer. Betty Eisner told how she had once stayed high for three days, which was tolerable since it was a good trip. Had it been bad, who knows what she might have done to herself. Others talked about how in some people the LSD state seemed to spontaneously reoccur—the first whisper of what would later become famous as the flashback. One therapist told of an ex-patient who had re-experienced the LSD state some five years after his original session. But others questioned the whole concept of a flashback. Just because someone had a dissociative experience under LSD one month didn't mean that later dissociative experiences could be attributed to LSD. This was a case of *post hoc, ergo propter hoc* reasoning, said one.

There were a few genuine gleams of insight, however, the most important being the deepening appreciation of just how crucial set and setting really were. Most of the therapists had long ago come to terms with the way LSD magnified the environment, but they were just beginning to admit that their own personalities, and even their own professional assumptions, were somehow influencing what happened in the LSD sessions. As Arthur Chandler observed, his partner, Mortimer Hartman, was always eliciting violent sexual fantasies, while he himself never got violent sex fantasies, but rather a high proportion of paranoid delusions, something Betty Eisner said she rarely saw.

But mostly there were dozens of questions that required fresh attention. How did LSD "liquidate" a person's psychic defenses? What kind of therapeutic window did this liquidation open? And how could a therapist best exploit it? Why were some people unable to find the integrative or psychedelic state? How come roughly a quarter of those who took LSD had no reaction? On a more fundamental level, was it really wise to speed up the therapeutic process, to say nothing of reducing it to one climactic session? As the convention adjourned, Sidney Cohen stood up and announced that he was collecting data on side effects and adverse reactions, and would appreciate whatever information those assembled could give him.

The future of LSD research seemed bright, but already forces were in motion that would change what seemed a complex but ultimately solvable scientific problem into a complex and apparently insoluble social problem.

BOOK TWO

PUSHING THE ENVELOPE

"All day long you've been wantin' to dance."
—Chuck Berry—"Long Live Rock 'n' Roll."

9

SLOUCHING TOWARD
BETHLEHEM

All decades can probably lay claim to Dickens's *It was the best of times, it was the worst of times,* but in the 1950s this contradiction was tellingly apt. Economically it was an age of gadgetry and growth; spiritually it was a time of anxiety and fear, a decade when too avid an interest in Dostoevsky might be construed as sympathy for the global communist conspiracy, with all the appalling consequences that could bring. It was a decade of Richard Nixon and Marilyn Monroe, the H Bomb and Elvis, the loyalty oath, and *Playboy.* To capture its character, one must juggle contrasting statistics, balancing the few thousand careers destroyed by Eisenhower's Directive 10450 (which removed from government service not only those suspected of being soft on communism, but anyone with a history of alcoholism, drug addiction, sexual deviation, mental illness, even membership in a nudist colony) with the 4.4 million cars that Americans threw away in 1955, or the 41,000 motels that were in operation by 1957, or the 50 billion bottles of Coca Cola that, by 1959, were being consumed in an increasingly shrinking world.

In only one place do the twin themes of outward prosperity and inward dread come together, and that is in the figures for tranquilizer sales, which rose from $2.2 million in 1955, the year Miltown was introduced, to 150 million by 1957.

Politically the Fifties began with a bang. Within six months, State Department *Wunderkind* Alger Hiss had been convicted of lying and, by extension, of spying for the Soviet Union; Joe McCarthy, the junior senator from Wisconsin, had given a speech in Wheeling, West Virginia, during which he had waved a piece of paper that contained, he claimed, the names of known communists employed by the federal government; and communist troops from North Korea had swept across the 38th parallel in an attempt to overthrow the not so democratic, but certainly not communist government of South Korea. Judging from the evidence of that first half-year, it was not surprising that so many influential people concluded the communist "virus" was epidemic, that unless drastic steps were taken Henry Luce's proclamation of an "American Century" would have to be amended to "American Fortnight."

Of the many virtuosos of anti-communist fervor, Joe McCarthy was without peer. Flamboyant, intuitive, he could not possibly have known that day in Wheeling, West Virginia, that his rhetorical gesture (there was no list) would catapult him into a position of power rivaling even the presidency. For four years McCarthy was Uncle Sam's favorite nephew—"the grand inquisitor of un-American ideas," Alfred Kazin called him—rooting out the pinkos, the fellow travelers, the softheaded liberals who infected the body politic, creating an image of bullying fear that remained potent long after his censure by his Senate colleagues in 1954.

But if the hyperbolic, demagogic McCarthy set the political tone in the early years of the decade, he was soon superseded by General Dwight D. "Ike" Eisenhower, whose victory at the polls in 1952 ended a twenty-year Democratic monopoly of the White House. Ike was low key, indeed Washington hadn't seen that kind of affable disinterest in a leader since Calvin Coolidge. And although he condoned such draconian acts as Directive 10450, he was generally perceived to be a relaxed, tolerant, and even lazy chief executive. "The Eisenhower siesta," was the way writer William Manchester characterized the mid-Fifties: a long political snooze that would have been insufferable had not the American economy suddenly roared to life, for the first time since the Twenties.

Beginning in 1953, the year the Korean war ended, consumers went on a buying binge unparalleled in American history. The stock market soared, with new technologies such as aviation and electronics leading the way. In one nine-month span in 1954 the earnings of General Electric rose 68 percent, while its rival Westinghouse did even better, posting a 73 percent advance.

"The old, innate, often naive optimism of the American businessman, which went all the way back to the early nineteenth century, and which had suffered such a punishing series of setbacks during the depression that by 1939 it was practically eroded away, had come back strong," wrote John Brooks in *The Great Leap*. "The war was over, thought the men who made the corporate decisions; the country was growing again; the future was a shining promise; to hell with the pessimists! On this occasion, whether or not for the right reasons, the optimists were right."

The Pill, the TV dinner, Scotch tape, the Interstate Highway system, FM radio, washer-dryers, cars with tailfins, vinyl flooring, processed cheese—the specifics of that optimism are endless.

So robust and sudden was this economic surge that some observers decided America was living through an economic revolution as profound as the political one of 1776. One of the earliest expressions of this theme appeared in 1951 in a Sunday newspaper supplement called *This Week*. Written by the supplement's editor, William Nichols, it suggested that *capitalism* was no longer the appropriate word for the American economic system. It was too primitive, too suggestive of Dickensian sweatshops full of underpaid, illiterate proletarians to do justice to an economic system that was "imperfect, but always improving, and always capable of further improvement—where men move forward together, working together, building together, producing always more and more, and sharing together the rewards of their increased production." Should we call this system New Capitalism? wondered Nichols? Or Democratic Capitalism? Industrial Democracy? Mutualism? He asked his readers for suggestions and within a few weeks received fifteen thousand replies. Reading *This Week*, it was as though the bloody battles fought over unionization in the previous generation had never happened.

By the mid-Fifties the belief that America had solved the problem of prosperity was a governing truism, enough so that when some editors at *Fortune* published a book-length survey of the American economic scene, they called it *America: The Permanent Revolution*—a title brimming with Cold War humor since "a permanent revolution" had been Trotsky's slogan for his brand of communism. American capitalism, the editors of *Fortune* implied, was proving Marx wrong. With the standard of living rising every year, America was fast on its way to becoming a classless society, in the sense that except for a small percentage of tycoons, everyone else was middle class. The validity of this feeling received an enormous boost in 1956, when the percentage of white collar workers surpassed that of blue collar workers.

But to what did we owe this remarkable economic health? *Fortune* singled out the corporation as the single most important factor. What had once been modest-sized operations were becoming, through a combination of optimism and historical serendipity, giant behemoths whose operation called for hundreds of top-level managers with degrees from Wharton and Harvard Business School. Gone was the protean individual who had risen on wings of luck and will: the supercorporations were machines that ran regardless of who was at the helm. They were laws unto themselves, and they recognized only two variables: profit and loss.

The dramatic rise of the supercorporation was not lost on the public consciousness. In 1956 *Time* picked Harlow Curtice, GM's chief executive, as its man of the year. And it was another GM alumnus who provided the decade with one of its most quotable phrases: what's good for General Motors is good for the country. Actually, what Charles Wilson, Eisenhower's Secretary of Defense and Curtice's predecessor at GM's helm, really said was, "What's good for our country was good for General Motors, and vice versa."

Of course, with an increasing amount of the national wealth in their control—by the mid-Sixties the top 150 corporations controlled exactly half the national wealth—the distinction between the two was increasingly tenuous.

One victim of the new corporate culture was the tycoon. Although there were twenty-seven thousand millionaires in 1953, the reverence accorded an Andrew Carnegie or a John D. Rockefeller had vanished. The public imagination, fired by the romance of a perpetually rising standard of living that was going to lift everyone into the middle class, had rejected the elegant Park Avenue drawing rooms of so many Hollywood films in favor of television comedies set in the novel hinterlands of the suburbs. If the supercorporation was the most vivid expression of our national genius, then the suburbs were its corollary. They were "big, lush and uniform," exulted those same editors at *Fortune,* a marketer's dream that was growing at a rate fifteen times faster than either rural or urban America. If an image of that growth was required, all one had to do was drive out to Long Island, where Levitt and Sons were erecting standardized homes at a rate of one every fifteen minutes.

Was there a suburban ethic? As Lanford Jones observes in *Great Expectations,* his study of the Baby Boom generation, the pesky word *lifestyle* comes from this epoch, the creation of sociologists who pursued "the suburbanites like doctors after a new virus. The Baby-Boom parents were poked and prodded and examined with the kind of fascination hitherto reserved for South Sea Islanders." What the sociologists found was a race immersed to the point of worship in the fruits of corporate technology: the washer-dryers, the glossy cars that resembled rockets, the barbecue pits with their matching patio furniture, sales of which bounced from 53 million in 1950 to 145 million in 1960. It was a lifestyle rich in labor-saving devices that were affordable thanks to one of marketing's great inventions: the installment plan. The permanent revolution would not have existed without this ingenious way of extending credit. During one four-year stretch, while income increased a healthy 21 percent, consumer debt zoomed up 55 percent. In the planned communities of Levitt and Sons it was possible to buy a house for sixty dollars a month, no money down.

The image of the suburbs as colonies of consumption has become so fixed a cliché that we often overlook the reason why most people moved there: they were fine places to raise children. Starting in 1946, America had been procreating at a rate that nearly rivaled India's. At the height of the Baby Boom, from 1954 to 1964, 4 million babies were born each year—4 million new consumers! Although it may seem crass, the

connection between procreation and prosperity was widely acknowledged, and public-spirited signs like the following (which adorned New
York subway cars) were common: "Your future is great in a growing
America. Every day 11,000 babies are born in America. This means new
business, new jobs, new opportunities." Had the Baby Boom occurred
in Russia, it would have been celebrated as an army of workers; in
America it was glorified as an army of consumers.

So the kids were the true heirs of the permanent revolution. And
those that grew up in the suburbs grew up in the fattest, most carefree
age that American youth had ever known. Whether it was tennis lessons
or a personal phone, summer camp or a car on their sixteenth birthday,
the Baby Boomers lived out every material fantasy their parents, children of the Depression, had ever entertained. The kids were the true
royalty of the Fifties, both in numbers and status, and their collective
mood was monitored as closely as befit a group that was pumping 25
billion into the GNP each year.

This corporate-suburban culture was not without critics. Every few
years an Isaiah emerged from the academic wilderness with a critically
acclaimed study depicting American prosperity as a golden patina hiding a leaden, anxious psyche. The first of these was David Riesman's
The Lonely Crowd, which contrasted the "inner directed" men of America's past with the "other directed" citizens of its present. Like all
sociological constructs, these were ideal types: inner direction came
about when the child received its moral codes, its ideals and desires,
from its parents; other direction described a new phenomenon whereby
children received their identities from their peers or from society at
large. While the first character type promoted classic rugged individualism, the second fostered a kind of bland conformity.

Written for an audience of professional social scientists, *The Lonely
Crowd* was an astonishing success. Like most successful phenomena, it
spawned numerous offspring who reworked and extended its themes.
In 1951 C. Wright Mills, another sociologist, published *White Collar: The
American Middle Classes;* four years later Sloan Wilson's *The Man in the Gray
Flannel Suit* became a best-seller, and was ultimately turned into a movie
starring Gregory Peck as the frantic public relations executive who
discovers he has to barter his soul for a salary; a year after that William
Whyte's massive study of white collar managers, *The Organization Man,*
also became a best-seller by examining the kind of dues one had to pay
for success in the corporate culture.

What Whyte found was a marked desire to conform, to adjust, to be
a team player. It was a timidity that permeated all age groups. Summing
up the concept of leadership among college men, William Manchester
wrote that they believed "leadership came from the group, that progress
lay in something called problem-solving meetings, the well rounded
campus men had no use for drive and imagination. Above all they

distrusted individualism. The individual sought prestige and achievement at the expense of others. He was abrasive; he rocked the boat; he threatened the corporate One, and they wanted no part of him." Not surprisingly *nonconformist* was one of the nastiest epithets imaginable.

Perhaps it was natural that a generation weaned on depression and war should have been attracted to material success and teamwork, but this didn't explain the zeal with which they eradicated all that was distinctive or unusual from their lives. Even the sociologists who studied the suburbs were disturbed by their lack of character, their sameness. How was one to interpret the spectacle of hundreds of identically dressed businessmen being met at the train station by hundreds of blonde wives (Clairol invented its slogan, if I have but one life to live let me live it as a blonde, in the Fifties) who drove them via station wagons to the hundreds of identically decorated (shag rugs, Danish modern) houses in which they lived. Was this a symbol of stability or gross conformity?

Attempts to answer the question of why conformity had become something of an eleventh commandment resulted either in complex sociopsychological treatises that stretched for hundreds of pages, or in metaphysical invocations of forces such as the *zeitgeist.* Certainly it colored every aspect of Fifties life. What was McCarthyism but an attempt to weed out thoughts that did not conform to a rigidly defined patriotism? What was the Organization Man but a creature that had allowed itself to be compressed into a rigidly defined lifestyle? How this had come about was unclear, although implicit in the analyses of Riesman et al. was the understanding that the forces of socialization were growing increasingly sophisticated as the twentieth century progressed. Unless you lived in an Appalachian backwater beyond the reach of mass magazines and television, you were constantly bathed by reinforcing images: the happy housewife, the mature, responsible dad, the ineffectual intellectual whom Eisenhower defined as "a man who takes more words than is necessary to say more than he knows." Tapping recent advances in psychology, Madison Avenue made enormous progress in the manipulation of desires—so much so that critics began calling copywriters "stockbrokers of neuroses."

Perhaps the most blatant example of science becoming the handmaiden of the established culture was the practice of personality testing. As corporations grew in size, harried personnel directors began to cast about for some way to identify the winners from the losers; the successful organization men from the maladjusted rebels. What they turned to were those same projective tests that had served psychology so well in the Thirties and Forties—the Washburne S-A Inventory, the Thurstone Temperament Schedule, the Kahn Test of Symbol Arrangements. For as little as twenty dollars, the brain watchers promised a complete personality scan on any employee.

According to Martin Gross, who published a study of the testing industry in the early Sixties, "The psychological theory which sustains the brain watcher is that every job, from salesman to board chairman, has an ideal personality description, or type, for which he hopes to find the right mate among men. He is convinced and, more important, has convinced many others that human personality is sufficiently simple and static that it can usually be measured in minutes (or hours) and projected ahead to predict a man's behavior in any given job or professional situation." After reviewing dozens of personality tests, Gross concluded that what the psychologists, and by extension the corporations, were looking for was "the Square American: the non-neurotic, reasonably hard-driving, cooperative, anti-cultural, self-confident, loyal, conservative, healthy, employee." Any creative or cultural tendencies, any deviation from the mental health norm such as anxiety or a delight in solitude, any complicated (psychologically speaking) ties with one's past and the tester would tag you as psychologically unfit. If you were at all bright, however, you learned to lie on the dozens of little quizzes that stood between you and gainful employment.

Not surprisingly, the Baby Boomers also received considerable attention from what William Manchester called the apostles of adjustment: "Any fledgling Luther who felt inclined to cultivate his own identity was exhorted not to by the mass media, while the last layers of goodguymanship polish were zealously applied in the new suburban schools." Yet it was here, in the children of the Organization Men, that the mold began to crack.

Had the sociologists focused as much attention on the kids of the Fifties as they did on their parents, they might have pondered the significance of three interesting trends. The first was the astonishing popularity of a type of comic book which featured surreal superheroes like Plasticman, Captain Marvel, and the Human Torch. Although the culture arbiters dismissed these comics as a blight on the literary corpus—too earnest an association with these colorful bits of trash would destroy your mind!—the kids loved them. They were the new myths (the only American myths a writer named Ken Kesey would later claim), and in proper mythic form the heroes were eminently nonconformist. At a time when their parents were shrinking from the larger issues of the world, the Baby Boomers were lapping up stories about average Americans who, through a fluke of fate or an industrial accident, gained superhuman powers that they used not to improve their bank account, but to fight the forces of evil and injustice. Encoded within these lurid pamphlets was another version of the evolution myth that saw mankind transforming itself upward.

If the superhero comics were subtly subversive, *Mad* magazine was as blunt as a bathroom limerick. As Theodore Roszak observed in *The Making of the Counterculture,* for a dime, *Mad* "brought into the malt shops the same angry abuse of middle class America which comics like Mort Sahl and Lenny Bruce were to begin bringing into the night clubs of the mid-fifties." Everything was grist for the magazine's mockery— the Cold War, television, corporations, suburbia, Joe McCarthy; and if the overall impression was that the adult world was infested with pompous fools and phonies, this wasn't a vision unique to *Mad* alone. It also lay at the heart of the decade's most popular adolescent classic, J. D. Salinger's *The Catcher in the Rye*, which contained the seeds of that famous Sixties aphorism: don't trust anyone over thirty.

The second area of Baby Boom culture that offered a glimpse into a different future was the appearance in the mid-Fifties of rock 'n' roll. Although it was the inclusion of Bill Haley's "Rock Around the Clock" in a Hollywood teen picture about juvenile rebellion called *The Blackboard Jungle* that provided the first spark, the flames didn't appear until 1955, when a snake-hipped kid from Memphis named Elvis cut five gold records and set audiences to screaming from New York to Mobile. The way Elvis performed it, rock was a kinetic joy that bypassed the rational mind. You twitched, you jumped, you found the groove and rode it out. There was nothing elegant about rock music: it was simply black rhythm and blues adapted for white musicians, and although it wasn't exactly the "jungle music" that its critics claimed, when the dance floor filled the scene was as tribal and uninhibited as anything white America had ever seen. The roar of the amplifiers combined with the physical abandon of the Twist, the Watusi, the Slop, provided many teens with their first example of an altered state of consciousness that had occurred when they were, well, conscious.

Like most Baby Boom enthusiasms, rock became big business; it commanded an increasingly large slice of a record market that jumped from $182 million in retail sales in 1954 to $521 million in 1960. This economic success went a long way toward explaining why rivals like pop crooner Frank Sinatra scorned rock as "phony and false, and sung, written and played for the most part by cretinous goons."

The final area of sociological interest was probably the most obvious one. If Hollywood played a role in the popularization of rock, it was also astute enough to realize that teenage rebellion could be lucrative box office. Starting in 1953 the movie studios released dozens of variations on the theme of social deviants who preferred not to fit in. Of these, *The Wild One*, starring Marlon Brando, and *Rebel Without a Cause*, introducing James Dean, stand out as classics of the genre. In both the heroes were tuned to inner imperatives rather than socially approved codes of behavior; they were, to use Riesman's terminology, legatees of a Puritan inner direction that by the Fifties had fallen so far from favor that to exercise these tendencies in public was to risk being labeled a psychopath. An acute analysis of this process can be found in the writings of psychiatrist Robert Lindner, who spent much of the decade developing a psychological model of adolescent rebellion. In Lindner's model the Brandos and Deans of America were caught in a peculiar double bind:

> . . . forced from without to conform, and from within to rebel, he makes a compromise: he rebels within the limits set by the social order he has by now permitted to be erected around him.

Lacking a political conception of an ideal future, he reacts not by issuing manifestos or agitating for social action, but by wearing blue jeans and not shaving, by dropping out of school and mocking the pieties of the square world. In a curious case of life imitating art imitating life, Lindner's work was picked up by the Hollywood studios—*Rebel Without a Cause* was loosely based on one of his studies—and transformed into images that every rambunctious adolescent in America could identify with. Thousands of Baby Boomers began slurring their speech in imitation of Brando's inarticulate purr, wore blue jeans like James Dean, and complained that their parents didn't understand them. And if they weren't the real item—genuine psychopathic rebels—this didn't really matter, because before the Fifties was half over some genuine rebels emerged, creating in the process the noisiest literary debut since the Twenties.

They were called beatniks or hipsters or Beats or Bo's—short for bohemian—and they came from every corner of disaffected America. They were hotrodders who idolized the dead James Dean; they were young existentialists with dog-eared copies of Camus in the back pockets of their chinos; they were drug addicts and jazz buffs who wanted to live life with the careening passion of a Charlie Parker solo. Like the psychopaths Lindner specialized in, they were united by feelings of boredom and anger with the status quo; their rebellion was emotional rather than political. They dressed in black and congregated over expresso in dark cellars. They smoked marijuana and talked about satori, that flash of recognition that was a byproduct, but not the essence, of Zen. They were gluttons for experience, the more intense the better. "The only people for me are the mad ones," wrote their Flaubert, Jack Kerouac, "the ones who never yawn or say a commonplace thing, but burn, burn, burn."

Needless to say, they were not the Best and the Brightest. But they were going to get mixed up with Huxley's vision, and with LSD, in the most incongruous fashion. So it is perhaps wise to go back yet again to the early Forties, when everything seemed so clear to most Americans . . .

10

STARVING, HYSTERICAL, NAKED

Imagine one of those classic nine-teenth-century novels in which a young innocent aesthete arrives, after a rocky passage filled with eccentric sometimes sinister characters, at self-knowledge. Only in this book, the one about the Beats, there are two heroes. One is a slight, bespectacled Jewish kid from New Jersey. A bookish schoolteacher's son who dreams of literary glory and perfect love, a romantic with homosexual inclinations and a mother who is both a committed Marxist and a diagnosed schizophrenic with paranoid tendencies. The other is a working-class Catholic kid from the mill town of Lowell, Massachusetts, a college dropout turned merchant marine who ships out to places like Greenland, Dostoevsky in his kit bag, his head teeming with the novels he plans to write.

Allen Ginsberg was eighteen, a newly matriculated student at Columbia University, when he met the semilegendary Jack Kerouac. They still talked about Kerouac at Columbia, mainly as an example of wasted potential. It was a curious story, sort of a reverse Frank Merriwhether. Kerouac had arrived at Columbia on a surge of athletic fame, a brilliant and powerful running back who had torn up the eastern prep gridirons for Horace Mann, the progressive New York prep school that had plucked him out of Lowell's French Canadian tenements. He had all the earmarks of the kind of smart ethnic kid who was starting to penetrate the Wasp preserves of the Ivy League. But then, in the first game of his freshman season at Columbia, he broke his leg, and (in retrospect) something else seemed to snap as well. A month into his sophomore year, Kerouac quit football and Columbia, and took a job pumping gas in upstate Connecticut. He intended to be Thomas Wolfe, the novelist, not Frank Merriwhether, schoolboy myth. He intended to live life, not read about it in English Lit 101. By the time Ginsberg met him, he was like a character in a Jack London short story, a strapping member of the wartime merchant marine who bragged he had already written a million words.

They were introduced by an extravagantly beautiful and rather exotic young man named Lucien Carr. Carr had already been tossed out of a number of schools, among them the University of Chicago and Bowdoin. He had the kind of easy, cynical assurance that would have marked him for black-sheep status had he been a well-born Englishman, instead of an upper-middle-class American, a provincial version of the English *Sonnenkinder* of the Twenties, those idle "children of the sun" who had lived on champagne, French symbolist poetry, and witty remarks.

He was a sophisticate, something both Ginsberg and Kerouac aspired to become, although Kerouac could never completely put aside his proletarian respect for plain living and hard work ("Oh let's have more of those splendid Lowell mill-worker remarks," Carr used to sneer), and Ginsberg, when he first entered Columbia, was prelaw, the quintessence of timid practicality. Art and Spirit were Carr's preferred themes, with the one leading to an enlargement of the other. "I tell you that I repudiate your little loves," he would declaim theatrically in the dark little West Side dives where they went to drink and philosophize, "[I repudiate] your little derivative morality, your hypocritical altruism, your foolish humanity obsessions, all the loves and penalties of your expedient little modern bourgeois culture." Lucien was brimming with the kind of luminescent hatred that is the flip side of adolescent love, and it made him a compelling figure.

Besides introducing Ginsberg and Kerouac, Carr took them to meet an older bohemian named William Burroughs, who was sort of Carr's spiritual mentor. Burroughs was black-sheep material too, only of a far tougher sort. He had been born into a prominent St. Louis family connected to the Burroughs adding machine fortune. The St. Louis Burroughses were businessmen and civic leaders, and when William came of age he was packed off to Harvard to acquire the pedigreed social connections that were the principal benefit of an Ivy League education in the 1930s. But there was something about his tall, emotionless presence that communicated the message that young Burroughs was not going to be an asset; he was rebuffed by all the top social clubs that usually embraced the sons of the rich. In fact, Burroughs found it difficult to join *any* establishment. After Pearl Harbor he tried without luck to join the OSS and the American Field Service. Even the Navy spurned him. "His feet are flat, his eyesight bad, and put down that he is a very poor physical specimen," the Navy doctor had remarked. When Ginsberg and Kerouac met him, he was living on a small allowance in midtown New York, cultivating his two hobbies: heroin and the criminal mind.

In terms of physique, William Burroughs could've been Aldous

Huxley's brother: he had the same lanky lack of flesh, the same quick, nervous mind. He also had the same artistic inclinations, although he possessed an exoticness that was entirely foreign to Aldous's clear, cold logic engine. "As a child," Burroughs once said, "I wanted to be a writer because writers were rich and famous. They lounged around Singapore and Rangoon smoking opium in yellow pongee silk suits. They sniffed cocaine in Mayfair and they penetrated forbidden swamps with a faithful native boy and lived in the native quarter of Tangier smoking hashish and languidly caressing a pet gazelle."

Drugs were Burroughs's way of attaining the same state of selflessness that Huxley was seeking through meditation and religious insight. Indeed, it is not too far off the mark to say that in the early Forties the two men were on parallel paths; both were seeking access to higher states of consciousness. The difference was one of focus. While Huxley was content to build a theory about the superiority of the nonattached man, Burroughs was actively seeking a way to become nonattached, which, perhaps owing to his proximity to Madison Avenue and its corps of eager Behaviorists, he tended to conceptualize as *deconditioning.* To be free it was necessary to shed the swaddling layers of bourgeois conditioning. One way to do this was by carefully exploiting the disorienting state of drugs like heroin, speed, and the recently criminalized marijuana.

Besides drugs, our two heroes found books at Burroughs's apartment that were not included in the standard college curricula. They pored over Kafka, Cocteau's *Opium,* Celine, Rimbaud, and Spengler's *Decline of the West,* with its appealing argument that the spiritual crisis of the West would be terminal. They met marginal characters like Herbert Huncke, a junky acquaintance of Burroughs who was justifiably famous as the man who had helped pioneer sex researcher Alfred Kinsey investigate the sexual habits of New York's criminal underworld. And they started psychoanalysis. Several times a week they lay on Burroughs's couch and told him about their dreams and fantasies.

Kerouac later described that first year under Burroughs's tutelage as one of "low, evil decadence." One of his friends likened it to something out of Dostoevsky: "I knew [Burroughs] was capable of killing someone. They were all very unattractive in that way. The level of violence was high, and Kerouac liked that, and Ginsberg liked that, but it horrified me."

When they got drunk and excited, they would begin talking about something called the New Vision, which was just the old visions of Faust, Baudelaire, Rimbaud, and Nietzsche tarted up with a postwar sensibility. One of the key concepts of the New Vision was the existential *acte gratuite,* that spontaneous, usually violent act that freed one from the tyranny of bourgeois morality, or at least that's the way it worked in the novels of Andre Gide. It was Lucien Carr who provided the New

Vision with its first legitimate *acte gratuite*. Among the exotica of Carr's life was a lovesick homosexual named David Kammerer, who had been the athletic director at one of Carr's private schools, and who had been dogging his life ever since in a pantomime of unrequited infatuation. This had been going on for several years, so the consummation, when it arrived on a warm summer night in 1944, was a little unexpected, particularly for Kammerer, whose body, weighted with rocks, was later fished out of the Hudson. As befits an *acte gratuite*, Carr was never able to explain to his friends why he had stabbed Kammerer; when he came to trial he took Burroughs's advice and claimed he had been defending himself against a homosexual rape. This delighted the New York media, who promptly labeled it an "honor slaying."

Kammerer's death marked the end of Act One in our heroic tale, as Carr was charged with manslaughter and Burroughs and Kerouac were jailed as material witnesses. Burroughs, with his family connections, was out of jail within hours and on his way to St. Louis. But Kerouac languished for almost a week; he couldn't even raise a hundred dollars and his bail was five thousand. Desperate, he agreed to marry his girlfriend and in return her wealthy parents posted bond. But part of the bride price was his relocation to her hometown, Grosse Point, Michigan, where a factory job counting ball bearings awaited him. So only Ginsberg was in town for Carr's sentencing—one to twenty years in Elmira Reformatory—which occurred in early October. Writing to his brother about the disintegration of his little band of visionaries, Ginsberg drew a parallel with the decay of the West as foretold by Spengler: the "poisons of a dying culture" were to blame for their misfortunes.

It is a testament to Kerouac's self-discipline that he didn't succumb to the "low, evil decadence" that surrounded him, that he didn't disappear into the heroin haze that Burroughs lived in, or the benzedrine addiction that was steadily claiming Burroughs's wife, Joan. In fact, the emotional melodrama that climaxed with Kammerer's death only strengthened Kerouac's resolve to become a great writer. To have Jack seated in the corner, scribbling in a notebook, while assorted wild scenes ebbed and flowed around him, became a common sight. Although Kerouac burned most of his early efforts, when he did begin showing his prose to his friends they were immediately struck by the uncanny power of his memory. It was as though he could reach back into his unconscious and rummage around in the files until he located the transcript of the night Ginsberg had gotten drunk and said something so terrifically right about Dostoevsky and truth; he had the gift of total recall, and yet—the mark of the artist—the sum of the parts was completely original.

By the end of the Forties Kerouac had reworked his young life into a Proustian-Wolfian novel called *The Town and the City,* a portrait of the artist as a sincere young man seeking truth and beauty and finding, among the hustlers and dreamers of New York, a reasonable facsimile. Harcourt Brace accepted *The Town and the City* in 1949, and word went out that a promising debut was in the offing. For a season Kerouac was the new kid on the block, the new face at literary soirées. He was a literary man now. All the other roles he had ever played—jock, college dropout, sailor, bum, prisoner, faithless husband—took a back seat to this central fact. Indeed, the quality of his personal triumph was underscored by the irony that a few days after *Town and City* appeared in 1950 the real-life counterpart of one of its characters, Herbert Huncke, went to jail on a felony charge.

The Town and the City was not a best-seller. Reviews were mixed, sales modest. But that didn't dampen Kerouac's creative enthusiasm. Fueled by benzedrine and marijuana, he was racing through his second book, typing it out on a lengthy role of teletype paper that he had borrowed from UPI. The book was called *On the Road,* and it reflected the arrival in Kerouac and Ginsberg's life of their second mentor, "a sideburned hero of the snowy West" named Neal Cassady.

In Oswald Spengler's historical fantasy, *The Decline of the West,* the industrialized societies systematically destroy themselves, and the earth is inherited by the fellaheen, which is what Spengler called the teeming, unsophisticated but intelligent poor who are always on the verge of inheriting something. Neal Cassady was the closest thing to a genuine fellaheen that anyone in the Burroughs circle had ever met. Here, as Cassady's biographer, William Plummer, put it in an eminently quotable description, was "a slim hipped hedonist who could throw a football seventy yards, do fifty chinups at a clip, and masturbate six times a day every day. Here was a man who suffered a life at once blighted and intriguingly exotic and who was somehow all the more sensitive, sensual, and amorous for it. Here was a man who was as 'criminal' and 'marginal' as Huncke, but who was vastly more joyous and palatable, a man who was potentially as smart as Burroughs but who was natural, intuitive, intellectually unformed—who was, in a word, radiant."

Here was a man who didn't just sit around swapping footnoted thoughts about the New Vision, here was a man who lived it. When he wasn't stealing cars—he later estimated he stole five hundred during adolescence alone—or having sex with anyone female—for a time he slept with an imbecilic maid in order to scrounge breakfast—he was in the Denver Public Library reading the Great Books series; his favorites were Schopenhauer and Proust. And Cassady didn't just tell you this in the casual way most people impart personal anecdotes; he came rushing at you like one of the Bird's saxophone solos, riffing on the hilarious pathos of his life, scatalogical one moment, ribald the next, yet with enough pure philosophical insight so that his listeners, once they had given up trying to swim against this torrent, found themselves thinking, this kid isn't just telling stories, he's imparting wisdom. Cassady was a prodigy, with a mind as raw and as powerful as the cars he loved to steal.

Throughout Cassady's life people would attempt to harness this incredible vitality, beginning with Justin Brierly, a Denver high school teacher who saw to it that this prodigy from the local slums was introduced to "the cream of Denver youth." Inevitably a portion of this cream found its way to Columbia University, where it had a nodding acquaintance with two easterners named Ginsberg and Kerouac. Cassady blew into New York for the first time in 1946, accompanied by his fifteen-year-old bride, Luanne. He immediately seduced the tentatively homosexual Allen Ginsberg, plunging the latter into an occasionally requited infatuation that lasted years. With Kerouac the seduction was less physical but equally profound. Kerouac the novelist was fascinated both by Cassady's way of telling a story and the stories themselves. Neal's childhood, in and around Denver's skidrow district, was right out of Dickens. Together with his father, an alcoholic who sometimes worked as a barber, Cassady had grown up in a rundown flophouse called the Metropolitan, where a clientele of pimps, poolsharks, and hobo philosophers had waited out the Depression. But more than the stories, it was the philosophy of life extracted from these circumstances that appealed to Kerouac. Although he could intellectualize with the best of them, Cassady never let concepts interfere with his zest for living. "He lived right now, right at the moment," remembered one of his Denver friends. "He never planned his life in terms of goals, like a five-year goal or something, or even a two-week goal." For Cassady: if you needed a car, you borrowed one; if you needed money badly enough, it would appear; if you got into trouble, you talked your way out of it; if that failed, you paid the penalty.

Cassady's life, in many ways, was one long *acte gratuite,* although it is important not to let that fact obscure what was really a homespun set of values. Underneath the spontaneity, Cassady had worked out a detailed theory of karmic responsibility. For example, if he walked into a house and found the refrigerator full, then he would always ask for something, a meal, the loan of the car, money, whatever, on the theory that it was his host's karmic duty to be generous. But if he walked in and found only a wrinkled old apple and a carton of week-old milk, then it was his duty to offer something in return.

But in general he found more full refrigerators than empty ones, which was just as well given his craving "to consume anything and everything." At least that's the way his first wife, the teenaged Luanne, described it, and she certainly was in a position to know. One day she had been minding her own business in a Denver drugstore when Neal had waltzed in with his then girlfriend. Spotting her sitting alone, he had drawled, "That's the girl I'm going to marry." A few months later he did.

Cassady was one of the few people who made Kerouac feel square. But he never acted superior. "He had no sneer in him at all," says John Clellon Holmes, an aspiring writer who hung around with Ginsberg and Kerouac. Holmes, like everyone else, was dazzled by Neal's style, particularly his ability to "seduce endless numbers of women in literally two minutes. Walk in—boom!—into the sack!" But he was also enough of a New York intellectual to classify Cassady as "a psychopath in the traditional and most rigorous sense of the term." Later, after he had read the manuscript of *On the Road,* Holmes had marveled at Kerouac's intuitive recognition that Cassady was the perfect symbol for that species of longing that was simmering beneath the pinstriped blandness of suburban America: "Why Jack fastened on this is peculiar to him, but it's also peculiar to genius to pick out instinctively—he didn't do it cognitively—something that was going to be the next move."

On the Road was a tone poem to Cassady (who was christened Dean Moriarity to Jack's Sal Paradise) and the electrifying effect his personality had had on Kerouac and Ginsberg. "I shambled after as I've been doing all my life," Jack wrote in the opening paragraphs, shambling after anyone who was "mad to live, mad to talk, mad to be saved," shambling in this case back and forth from Denver to New York in one of those deluxe driving machines that Neal loved, with a stopover in New Orleans to visit Burroughs. *On the Road* had no plot as such. It was an extended anecdote about the ground they had covered, the cars they had stolen, the girls they had slept with, and all the fantasies and revelations they had told each other as the road slipped away under their wheels. What distinguished it was its style: sentences that came in "clickety pop word bursts" or one of Cassady's trademark monologues. In fact, it was a forty-thousand-word letter from Cassady, relating the hilarious and byzantine complications of one of his Denver love affairs, that had crystallized *On the Road* for Jack; up until then he had been trying to novelize his adventures with Neal, worrying about theme, plot line, character development; but when he read the letter something had clicked—to hell with literary convention, the way to write this book was to just let it come gushing out from that phenomenal well that was his memory. ("The writing is dewlike," Ginsberg wrote to Cassady, "everything happens as it really did, with the same juvenescent feel of spring.")

It took Kerouac twenty benzedrine-primed days in April 1951 to write *On the Road,* and when he was done his second wife tossed him out of their New York City apartment for being a bum and a bore.

(Kerouac's relationships with women are so mercurial that I won't confuse the reader by enumerating them; as Dennis McNally, whose biography of Kerouac is excellent, puts it: "One of the central myths of Jack's life was of Dostoevsky's wife and her unflagging support of her husband, of the duty of the untalented to support the creative artist." Like so many aggressive opponents of the status quo of his generation, Kerouac saw no reason to question his conditioning vis-a-vis women. They were there to fuck him, feed him, fawn over him, and then fade into the background. Unfortunately, few modern girls could put up with this for more than a few months, which shows just how far the women of the Fifties were from Madame Dostoevsky; the juices of feminism were starting to simmer.) Actually Kerouac's ejection from his (relatively) comfortable conjugal nest was an augury of what the future would bring, because no publisher would touch *On the Road*. Written on a roll of UPI teletype paper (it reminded Clellon Holmes of a big salami), it quickly acquired the reputation of being too weird, a work of genius, maybe, but unsaleable.

Kerouac was bruised in a fairly fundamental way by this rejection. And it opened up an unattractive side of his personality that was a combination of narcissistic megalomania—*why isn't the world recognizing my genius*—and paranoia—*I'm not being recognized because my friends are plotting against me, stealing my ideas, talking behind my back!* Jack lashed out at everyone, sending Ginsberg a particularly ugly letter. He thought that mediocre talents were stealing his material, and for proof he pointed to John Clellon Holmes, whose novel *Go*, published in the fall of 1952, was the kind of commercial success Harcourt Brace had hoped *The Town and the City* would be. Holmes had the effrontery (in Jack's eyes) not only to retail certain anecdotes pertaining to their little community of visionaries, but he had also appropriated certain catchy sayings of Jack's, like the night Kerouac had gotten into a long riff about his friends and had said, "We're a beat generation." Holmes had put that in *Go*, where it had caught the eye of a young editor at the New York *Times* magazine named Gilbert Millstein.

Millstein, who was always on the lookout for punchy contemporary trends, commissioned Holmes to write an article on the Beat Generation. And Holmes did, turning in a solid analysis of the post-New Visionaries. What they were seeking, he wrote, was a "nakedness of mind, ultimately of soul," i.e., a completely deconditioned state that would enable them to descend (or ascend) to "the bedrock of consciousness." That was the psychological kernel of the Beat Generation, that and the never spelled-out understanding that one of their fundamental dreams was the creation of a community of like-minded souls; a new kind of family that would be tribal rather than nuclear. And that was what most of Holmes's article was about: how to recognize a true brother, a fellow beat! "A man is beat when he wagers the sum of his resources on a single number," Holmes wrote.

Despite his anger, Kerouac was sufficiently impressed with the response to Holmes's article that he retitled his unsaleable manuscript *The Beat Generation.* Later he tried *Rock n Roll Road,* but neither change persuaded the publishers to revise their opinion.

Kerouac became manic depressive, happy one week, moody and bitter the next. When he drank he turned mean. And this made him ashamed. His best therapy was movement. Although he lacked Neal's fireball quality—he was a shambler, after all—Kerouac was almost as hyperkinetic. From 1952 to 1957 he drifted from San Francisco to Mexico City to New York, Tangier, Paris, London. He moved from job to job, woman to woman, always living in the funkiest hotels he could find, playing the role of the "skid-row wino that rambles in and out from place to place." As his friend Gary Snyder once observed, in "harking back to the hobo," Kerouac was "harking back to one of the few models—myths—of freedom and freshness and mobility and detachment . . . that were available to us at the time."

But if constant movement was Kerouac's first line of therapy, writing was a close second. His discipline was awe-inspiring. "Jack'd sit and write for hours on end," recalls Burroughs. "Longhand, longhand. He'd just sit down in a corner and say, 'I don't want to be disturbed,' and I wouldn't pay any attention to him." Between the years 1951 and 1956 Kerouac sat in the corner and produced almost a dozen manuscripts. In each he followed the formula he had perfected in *On the Road:* a stretch of earnest living followed by a benzedrine-primed bout of spontaneous remembering. He had decided to take Cassady's advice and produce a multivolumed work modeled after Proust's *Remembrance of Things Past,* except that in Jack's case it was frequently "remembrance of things that happened last month." Once, when a Greenwich Village madonna dumped him after a few weeks for poet Gregory Corso, Kerouac sat down and in three days of nonstop typing produced *The Subterraneans,* a graphic retelling of the botched affair that cost him fifteen pounds. Kerouac frequently wrote these minimemoirs in the attic of Cassady's house in San Francisco (later San Jose) where, along with Neal's wife, Carolyn, the three maintained a fragile *menage à trois.*

To the extent that his voluntary poverty personified the pursuit of private artistic genius in a culture that assigned its highest values to power and wealth, Kerouac came to symbolize—to his friends at least—the highest ideals of the Beat Generation. But he also symbolized the difficult price exacted upon anyone who tried to live out those ideals in the 1950s. As Kerouac's pile of unpublished manuscript mounted, so did his bouts of despair and black anger. He wanted the recognition of a great writer, but that wish was also an admission of how far he still had to go to purge himself completely of his social conditioning. To pursue private artistic genius was great in theory, but when it came right down to it, all the examples you could point to were people whose private artistic genius had earned them posthumous admiration; they had endured bitterness and sacrifice and been rewarded with the sinecure of fame. But where was the guarantee that if Kerouac sacrificed his life on the altars of Art, the gods would smile upon him? In December 1954 Kerouac jotted into his notebook the following self-accusation: AT THE LOWEST BEATEST EBB OF MY LIFE . . . CONSIDERED A CRIMINAL AND INSANE AND A IMBECILE, MY SELF SELF-DISAPPOINTED AND ENDLESSLY SAD BECAUSE I'M NOT DOING WHAT I KNEW SHOULD BE DONE A WHOLE YEAR AGO.

It was a dilemma they all felt in various ways. It was fine to decondition yourself, to psychologically remove yourself from the social webbing of American society, but what then? How did you live? And where? The expatriates of the Twenties had Paris, and Paris already had fifty years of bohemian experimentation under its belt by the time the Hemingways and Murphys sat down at its carefree, wine-soaked cafés. But the Beats were just starting out, they lacked a spiritual home, and you could count the number of true brothers on two hands.

So they were all gripped by the hobo habit. In the late Forties Burroughs moved to a small town north of Houston, Texas, where he bought a farm and planted a crop of marijuana between the alfalfa rows. He was a negligible farmer, perhaps because he was shooting heroin three times a day, and he managed only one trip to New York with a load of pot-filled mason jars. Eventually the local police began harassing him (whether because of his agricultural policies, or the weird characters who were always hanging around his farm, or his habit of spending a few hours every day banging away at the side of the barn with his pistol, is unclear) and he was forced to relocate to a little town up the road from New Orleans, where the pattern repeated itself. Burroughs tried Mexico after that. He was excited by a rumor he had heard that Mexican land could be had for two dollars an acre, and he moved to Mexico City with the intention of becoming a citizen. But the Mexican bureaucrats kept losing his file, and after spending nearly a thousand dollars he was still no nearer to the Mexican real estate he coveted. No doubt the Mexicans saw Burroughs as a foolish young gringo with deep pockets, but they were also aware of some of his less naive habits, particularly his love of weaponry. Several times they confiscated Burroughs's guns, although they missed the one that he used on September 7, 1951, when he accidentally shot and killed Joan. They had been playing a game of William Tell; Burroughs had missed.

Worried that the Mexican justice system might interpret this tragedy in a different light, Burroughs jumped bail and fled to Tangier, where he lived in a male brothel owned by a prominent Moroccan gangster. The next year, 1953, he went to South America to investigate the psychotropic properties of the shamanic vine *ayahuasca,* which was generally brewed into a hallucinogenic drink called yage. "Yage is space time travel," he wrote Ginsberg. "The room seems to shake and vibrate with motion. The blood and substance of many races, Negro, Polynesian, Mountain Mongol, Desert Nomad, Polyglot Near East, Indian— new races as yet unconceived and unborn, combinations not yet realized passes through your body. . . . The composite city where all human potentials are spread out in a vast silent market."

Burroughs had hoped that yage would wipe away the last webs of his social conditioning, that it would be what he characterized in a letter to Ginsberg as "the final trip." Indeed, he came back from South America a changed man. Stopping in New York on his way to Tangier, Burroughs amazed Ginsberg with his "outwardness and confidence . . . He is very personal now, and gives me the impression of suffering terribly and continuously," he confided to Cassady. In Tangier Burroughs began writing sketches and tossing them on the floor. Eventually they would be gathered up, dirty and torn, and published as *Naked Lunch.*

Burroughs's visit catalyzed Ginsberg's own restless urges, and a few weeks after Bill departed for Tangier Allen quit his job as a market researcher and moved to San Francisco where he intended to "start all over again." For a few weeks he managed to sustain an authentic hobo existence, but then his old fears about being normal reasserted themselves, and he found himself another market research job. He got an apartment on Nob Hill, and a girlfriend (yet another stab at heterosexuality), and every morning he put on his suit and tie and trolleyed down to the business section. He was trying to play the game, to be a credit to his alma mater, Columbia, he told his therapist, so why was he so bored and miserable?

One day his therapist asked him what he really wanted to do with his life and Allen replied, "Doctor, I don't think you're going to find this very healthy and clear, but I really would like to stop working forever— never work again, never do anything like the kind of work I'm doing now—and do nothing but write poetry and have leisure to spend the day outdoors and go to museums and see friends. And I'd like to keep living with someone—maybe even a man—and explore relationships that way. And cultivate my perceptions, cultivate the visionary thing in me. Just a literary and quiet city-hermit existence."

"Well why don't you?" answered the therapist.

To have a bonafide psychiatrist say, "Sure, go ahead, be as crazy as you want if it makes you happy," was like having a note from God to skip school. Ginsberg quit his marketing job; he found a male lover, Peter Orlovsky, and he began to seriously pursue his "visionary thing."

* * *

Ginsberg's visionary thing dated back to the summer of 1948, when he had been living in a tiny Harlem flat, writing poems, reading William Blake, and feeling lonely and sorry for himself because he had just received a Dear John letter from Cassady. One day he was lying there masturbating and feeling miserable when the room was suddenly filled with a sonorous voice—Blake's voice—reciting the poem he had just been reading, "Ah Sunflower":

> Ah Sunflower, weary of time
> Who countest the steps of the sun
> Seeking after that sweet golden clime
> Where the traveller's journey is done.

Accompanying this auditory hallucination was a feeling of knowing, not just knowing the ultimate meaning of the poem, but of life itself. Glancing out the window, Ginsberg found himself staring into the depths of the universe:

> I suddenly realized that this . . . was the moment I was born for. This initiation. Or this vision or this consciousness of being alive unto myself, alive myself unto the Creator. As the son of the Creator—who loved me.

It was a moment of what Richard Bucke, the turn-of-the-century Canadian psychologist who had traveled North America collecting similar epiphanies, had called cosmic consciousness.

Exalted by his vision, Ginsberg crawled out onto the fire escape and tapped on the open window of the next apartment, which was occupied by a couple of girls. "I've seen God!" he shouted, whereupon the window fell shut with a bang, leaving Ginsberg alone on the fire escape, with only the ancient cosmic sky and his racing heart for accompaniment.

The aftereffects of Ginsberg's brush with cosmic consciousness never really disappeared. In fact, this visitation marked the moment when the New Vision began to mutate into what Ginsberg called "American tenderheartedness." It didn't take a genius to see that playing at being hip, cool psychopaths had gotten them nowhere except to Kammerer's death, Huncke's imprisonment, and the silly accident that would take the life of Joan Burroughs. "The whole notion of being smarter, more psychotic, beating the world at its own game was no longer of interest," Ginsberg later explained to an interviewer. "Coolness, reserve of any kind, was the opposite of the sort of warmhearted, open, Dostoevskian Alyosha-Myshkin-Dimitri compassion that Kerouac and I were pursuing."

Although Ginsberg used a literary analogy in that example, in real life the Beats found their models of compassion in the Eastern religions, particularly Buddhism, and its variant, Zen. In the concept of the bodhisattva—the wandering Buddha—they found a rationale for the artist as cosmic bum, observing the world's follies and in return beaming a little light back into the fog of desperation. Later much would be made of the Beats' infatuation with Zen, most of it negative. Scholars of Eastern religion were quick to jump on inconsistencies and misreadings. Even Alan Watts, who was a seminal influence due to his position as director of San Francisco's Academy of Asian Studies, felt compelled to criticize the "fake-intellectual hipster" who was "name-dropping bits of Zen and jazz jargon to justify disaffiliation from society." Watts felt that Zen was "better kept to oneself as therapy," but he was sympathetic to the larger problem with which the Beats were grappling, namely the creation of a legitimate Western *sadhana*—a Sanskrit word literally meaning "the way," *sadhana* refers to the various practices used in the East to cultivate higher consciousness, enlightenment, mystical ecstasy.

The Beats set about creating their own *sadhana* from a dozen different sources. For Ginsberg, who claimed to have experienced *satori* in 1954, it was a regimen of Judaism, Zen, and Mahayana Buddhism; for Kerouac, it was all of that plus an overlay of Catholicism: he later told a television interviewer that he prayed nightly to Christ, the Virgin Mary, and the Buddha. Like Huxley and Heard before them, they experimented with yoga, meditation, and chanting, but found these uncongenial. Gary Snyder, who was a much more serious student of Zen, tried long and hard to teach them meditation, but these sessions usually ended with everyone reading haikus back and forth. Kerouac was unable to bend his knees because of his old football injuries, but "even had he been able to, his head wouldn't have stopped long enough for him to endure it. He was too nervous."

If the Eastern *sadhanas* had one unifying message, it was that the rational mind was the great obstacle. "A psychological impasse is the necessary antecedent of *satori*," the Zen master D. T. Suzuki had written, "and the worst enemy of Zen experience, at least in the beginning, is the intellect, which consists and insists in discriminating subject from object. The discriminating intellect, therefore, must be cut short if Zen consciousness is to unfold itself." From their days with Burroughs they knew that one of the quickest ways to disrupt the rational mind was with drugs. But not all drugs. Marijuana worked fairly well, but an even better disrupter was peyote, and its synthetic cousin, mescaline. LSD didn't enter the Beat scene until the end of the Fifties, but when it did it quickly became the tool of choice for achieving "that ancient heavenly connection."

Ginsberg took some peyote in the fall of 1955, shortly after quitting his market research job to devote himself to poetry. Looking out his window, he had a vision of Moloch, the biblical idol whose worship was distinguished by the burning of children. Moloch was America, Ginsberg flashed, and he began writing a poem about this intuition.

One of Ginsberg's salient character traits was his ability to organize things; before he'd decided to go prelaw at Columbia, he'd considered becoming a union organizer. So one of the first things he did in San Francisco was organize a local poetry reading. It was scheduled for October 13, 1955, in an old gas station turned art gallery called the Six Gallery. "Six poets at the Six Gallery," the promotional postcards said,

> Remarkable collection of angels all gathered at once in the same spot. Wine, music, dancing girls, serious poetry, free satori. Small collection for wine and postcards. Charming event.

On hand for his debut were Kerouac and Cassady, the former distinguishable as the man who was passing around the big jugs of Burgundy wine, while the latter was the source of the punctuating stream of *Wow*s! *Yes*es! and *Go, Go Go*s! that greeted each reader. Ginsberg read next to last. Until this moment his vocation as a poet had been more wishful living than artistic fact. What poems he had written were short epigrammatic lyrics in the style of William Carlos Williams. But tonight he wasn't going to bother with his old work. Instead he was going to read the poem that had come to him through the mediation of dexedrine and peyote, a massive, tumultuous thing called *Howl*, which began

> *I saw the best minds of my generation destroyed*
> *by madness, starving, hysterical, naked,*
> *dragging themselves through the negro streets at*
> *dawn looking for an angry fix.*

By the time Ginsberg reached the middle of *Howl*, where each line began with the cry Moloch!, the crowd was chanting along with him. And by the time he swung into the final stanzas everyone knew something momentous was occurring.

Philip Lamantia, who had also read his poems that evening, likened it to "bringing two ends of an electric wire together." Michael McClure, another of the poets, later considered it the moment when the consciousness that reached full bloom in the Sixties began to flower: "*Howl* was the trigger. Afterwards none of us could step back and say, 'I didn't mean it. It's just too fuckin frightening out there . . . I think Allen standing up there reading—putting himself on the line—was one of the two bravest things I've ever seen. Remember, it was '55. People had crew cuts, and they looked at you like you were misplaced cannon fodder. The country was being run by Luce publications. It was a dangerous, cold, ugly time, and it was scary."

But history is full of extravagant moments that, while momentous to those who witness them, evaporate in the press of time. Given the geography of its premiere—an old garage in San Francisco—it seemed likely that *Howl* and the new consciousness it heralded would remain an isolated, provincial event. Why it didn't is an argument for the personal as opposed to the statistical approach to history. Sitting in the audience that evening, as Ginsberg swayed and chanted, was Lawrence Ferlinghetti, an erudite bohemian (Ph.D. from the Sorbonne) who operated City Lights bookstore in the North Beach, which was arguably the first paperback bookstore in America. Besides the bookstore, Ferlinghetti also ran a small publishing house that printed inexpensive editions of poetry under the logo Pocket Poets. His first venture, published a few months before the Six Gallery reading, had been his own *Pictures of the Gone World.* The morning after the Six Gallery reading Ferlinghetti telegraphed Ginsberg and asked if he could add *Howl* to his list.

Even before *Howl* appeared in the fall of 1956 (with a preface by William Carlos Williams that warned, "Hold back the edges of your gowns, Ladies, we are going through hell.") it was the beneficiary of some priceless publicity in the form of an article in the *New York Times Book Review* in September. Poetry had become a tangible social force in San Francisco, marveled East Coast poet Richard Eberhart: "There are several poetry readings each week. They may be called at the drop of a hat." Chanted or shouted, the poems reminded Eberhart of the role jazz had played in the Twenties, as a catalyst for all the subconscious passions one dared not express.

While recognizing *Howl* as "the most powerful poem" to come out of the San Francisco renaissance, Eberhart was ambivalent about the artistic merit of Ginsberg's "spontaneous bop prosody," as well as disturbed by the poem's air of "destructive violence":

It is a howl against everything in our mechanistic civilization which kills the spirit, assuming that the louder you shout the more likely you are to be heard. It lays bare the nerves of suffering and spiritual struggle. Its positive force and energy comes from a redemptive quality of love, although it destructively catalogues the evils of our time from physical deprivation to madness.

114

Ferlinghetti's first printing sold out almost immediately and another was ordered. It was then that the fledgling Beat literary movement received its most valuable publicity. Because the printer for the Pocket Poets series was located in England, Ferlinghetti's books had to pass the scrutiny of U.S. Customs before being readmitted into the country, and in March 1957 Customs seized the second shipment of *Howl* and declared it obscene. Ferlinghetti protested, and the Customs service relented and let the books pass, whereupon the San Francisco police raided City Lights and charged Ferlinghetti with selling pornography.

The reaction was contrary to what the guardians of public taste must have expected: for years San Francisco had advertised itself as the Paris of the West, and now, having actually managed to produce something comparable to the Montmartre of Hemingway and Picasso, local bluenoses were trying to hound it out of existence. The arrest was condemned by both the local papers. By the time Ferlinghetti was acquitted, sales of *Howl* stood at ten thousand copies, and the Beat writers were the hottest literary copy since the Hemingway-Fitzgerald generation.

If the *New York Times Book Review* had alerted editors to the fact that a curious cultural event was taking place in San Francisco, then the subsequent trial had convinced them of its salacious merit. The spectacle of a bunch of ungroomed, poetry-spouting young men renouncing the American dream of home, job, and family in obscene couplets was irresistible. Articles on the Beat poets appeared in such diverse media as *Mademoiselle, Evergreen Review,* and the *Nation.* The *Village Voice* ran a piece on Kerouac, Ginsberg, and fellow poet Gregory Corso called "Three Witless Madcaps Come Home to Roost," a title indicative of the ambivalence that even the most liberal of liberals felt toward the Beats. Although Ginsberg was still the biggest name (Kenneth Rexroth warned in the *Nation* that he ran "the danger of turning into a popular entertainer—he affects an audience much as Louis Armstrong affects French bobby soxers.") Kerouac was always treated as the undiscovered genius: the man with a suitcase full of Proustian novels that were too radical for the reading public.

On the Road was finally published in the fall of 1957, and again the Beat movement profited from a bit of luck. The regular reviewer for the *New York Times* was on vacation and the chore of reviewing fell to Gilbert Millstein, who had been following the fortunes of Kerouac and Ginsberg ever since he had commissioned Holmes's article in the early Fifties. Millstein didn't pull any punches. *On the Road* was "a historic occasion," he wrote, comparable to *The Sun Also Rises* in the sense that it captured a spirit of rebellion that was gathering strength; in all that followed, Millstein predicted, Jack Kerouac would be "principal avatar." If the rest of the reviews fell far short of Millstein's rave, their tone was sufficiently lively to insure *On the Road*'s place as a literary *cause célèbre*. Despite Herbert Gold's published opinion that it was "proof of illness rather than a creation of art," or the CIA-funded *Encounter*'s sneering dismissal of it as a "series of Neanderthal grunts," *On the Road* spent six weeks on the best-seller lists.

What followed was a cultural tempest. While movies, magazines, and even TV were busy tailoring the Beat movement to appeal to their disparate commercial audiences, another segment of the cultural establishment was aggressively denouncing this manufactured image as a celebration of criminality and bestiality. Reading such jeremiads as Robert Brustein's "The Cult of Unthink" or Norman Podhoretz's "The Know Nothing Bohemians," one soon realizes that the subject is not the real Ginsberg or Kerouac, but the fictional beatnik that *Look* created for its readers in "The Bored, the Bearded and the Beat"; the one Herbert Gold parodied in such odd exercises as "A Frigid Frolic in Frisco." A writer for *Life* described the Beat movement this way: "The bulk of it is comprised of those mobs of 'sick little bums' who emerge in any generation . . . people very like them distributed pamphlets for the Communists in the 1930s, or muttered of anarchism and cadged drinks in the speakeasies of the 1920s, and then as now thirsted cunningly for the off-beat cause which could provide them with some sense of martyrdom and superiority. They are talkers, loafers, passive little con men, lonely eccentrics, mom-haters, cop-haters, exhibitionists with abused smiles and second mortgages on a bongo drum—writers who cannot write, painters who cannot paint, dancers with unfortunate malfunction of the fetlock."

But they were also great copy. Ginsberg was probably the only poet in America whose readings drew the kind of press coverage normally reserved for a prize fight or a society divorce. They were there because they'd heard about the time Ginsberg had challenged a heckler to take off his clothes. It'd happened in Los Angeles, where the director of a local poetry society had invited a few of the San Francisco poets down to share their verse. The crowd had been diverse, some Hollywood arty types, a few students, and a solid phalanx of poetry-loving ladies—and one drunken belligerent whose composure finally had shattered when Ginsberg stood up to read. Over time, as his beard and his belly bushed out, Allen Ginsberg would achieve a kind of rabbinical majesty, but when this happened he was still a rabbity Jewish kid from New Jersey, a bespectacled obscene poet anarchist. To his credit, Ginsberg had tried to ignore the heckler, but finally he gave up and said, "All right, all right. You want to do something big, don't you. Something brave. Well, go on, do something really brave. Take off your clothes." That had startled the drunk, who seemed to be under the illusion that he was going to get into a punchout with this rumpled poet, and he had retreated up the aisle. Pressing his advantage, Ginsberg had followed, tearing off his own shirt and undershirt and flinging them at the heckler. "You're scared, aren't you," he had taunted. "You're afraid." Still moving, he had unbuckled his belt, unzipped his pants and kicked them off. The audience, which had sat in mute anticipation throughout this performance, burst into cheers and noisy argument, as both Ginsberg and the drunk were hustled from the room.

This kind of existential vaudeville was what audiences came to expect from the Beats, and more often than not they went home satisfied.

But beyond the constant retelling of a few choice anecdotes, there was a remarkable sameness to the articles written about the Beats in the late Fifties. They were dirty. "I'm surprised the room didn't smell worse than it did," sniffed Diana Trilling in her account of a Ginsberg poetry reading. They were untalented—"undisciplined and slovenly amateurs who have deluded themselves into believing their lugubrious absurdities are art . . ." They were not deep thinkers—"what they have in common is the conviction that any form of rebellion against American culture (which for them includes everything from suburbia and supermarkets to highbrow literary magazines like *Partisan Review*) is admirable, and they seem to regard homosexuality, jazz, dope-addiction, and vagrancy as outstanding examples of such rebellion." They were sick—one psychiatrist, after studying the beats of San Francisco's North Beach, concluded that 60 percent "were so psychotic or so crippled by tensions, anxieties and neuroses as to be incapable of making their way in the ordinary competitive world of men, and that another 20 percent were hovering just within the boundaries of emotional stability."

Allen Ginsberg's father, who was also a poet, summarized the establishment perspective when he wrote his son that "all your vehement, vaporous, vituperations of rebellion move me not one jot. Your attitude is irresponsible and it stinks."

One of the few intellectuals who did support the Beats was Norman Mailer, although with friends like that who needed enemies like the other Norman, Podhoretz? Mailer published an essay called *The White Negro* in 1957, in which he coined the word *hipster* to describe the social mutation he detected among the young. "One is hip or one is square," Mailer wrote. "One is a rebel or one conforms, one is a frontiersman in the Wild West of American nightlife, or else a square cell, trapped in the totalitarian tissues of American society, doomed willy nilly to conform if one is to succeed."

The hipster, Mailer wrote, was the man who understood the central role Death had come to play within life—in the Fifties death was personified by the concentration camp (cultural death) and the H-Bomb (species death)—and as a result had decided "to divorce" himself from society, "to exist without roots, to set out on that uncharted journey into the rebellious imperatives of the self." But for Mailer these rebellious imperatives did not include looking into the face of God, which was the whole point as far as Ginsberg and Kerouac were concerned. Cultivate the psychopath, was Mailer's message (and one that appalled the Beat braintrust) for the psychopath was the only authentic American. "The psychopath murders," he wrote, "out of the necessity to purge his violence, for if he cannot empty his hatred then he cannot live, his being is frozen with implacable self-hatred for his cowardice."

Mailer's essay, by standing the condemnatory label *psychopath* on its head, was cleverness personified, but most of the Beats thought it silly and beside the point. A better defense would have attacked the legitimacy of the label *psychopath,* which had a distressingly glib currency in the Fifties. It was a kind of therapeutic wastebasket, into which individuals who fell into the gray area between normality and specific syndromes were tossed with impunity. The definition was appropriately vague. According to one psychological dictionary, a psychopath was any egocentric, impulsive, asocial individual—a definition equally applicable to an English eccentric or a Beat poet, and one that hardly warranted the frisson of fear the word evoked.

The key word was probably *asocial.* Psychopaths were a danger to the smooth functioning of the social order. In this sense the Beats consistently and defiantly broke one part of the American social contract: they smoked marijuana. Not even prison terms of thirty years or more could dissuade them from using this dangerous substance, whose consequences were well known. Smoke a marijuana cigarette and you turned into a foaming murderer; you might even rape your sister or murder your parents with an ax.

Marijuana's reputation as a "killer weed" was the result of one of the more successful advertising campaigns of the twentieth century. Appropriately enough, it dated back to the mid-Thirties, just when Madison Avenue was learning how to employ the new sciences of the psyche. The chief copywriter of the marijuana campaign was Harry Ainslinger, the new commissioner of the Bureau of Narcotics. Ainslinger, like most bureaucrats, was looking for an issue that would increase his bureau's budget and prestige, and he chose marijuana, a rather innocuous weed that grew wild in most rural areas. To demonize marijuana, Ainslinger used the same strategy that had been used to criminalize heroin twenty years earlier. First he linked its use to the ethnic minorities that were streaming through Ellis Island—not only were these immigrants weakening the powerful bloodlines of white America, but they were importing dangerous drug habits that would spread like a cancer among the country's young. Then he claimed that marijuana was the source of most of the nation's crime, an honor that previously had belonged to heroin. In New Orleans, for instance, 60 percent of the crimes were attributed to marijuana smokers who "fortified themselves with the narcotic and proceeded to shoot down police, bank clerks and casual bystanders."

Ainslinger kept a file of marijuana atrocity stories—most of them unconfirmed—that he parceled out to complaisant reporters. But the juiciest items he kept for his own books and articles, the most famous being his keynote magazine article, "Marijuana: Assassin of Youth."

Although Ainslinger's figures and assertions were the flimsiest sort of fictions, Congress rushed to pass the Marijuana Tax Act in 1937, and *Cannabis sativa* joined heroin as a narcotic danger (frequently spread by communists and other national enemies) aimed at the nation's heart. The most serious attempt to validate Ainslinger's claims came in 1944 when the mayor of New York City, Fiorello LaGuardia, asked the New York Academy of Medicine to evaluate the pros and cons of the marijuana issue. The Academy's findings, which contradicted Ainslinger at almost every turn, were immediately denounced not only by the law enforcement bureaucracy, but by the medical bureaucracy as well. "Public officials will do well to disregard this unscientific, uncritical study," urged the American Medical Association, "and continue to regard marijuana as a menace wherever it is purveyed."

When it came to certain drugs, even the scientific community was willing to compromise standards of truth if they clashed with those of public morality.

What very few of these critics realized was that the Beats they were denouncing were passé; they belonged to the Forties, to the postwar, postbomb Truman years. It was ironic, but here at the height of their fame the Beats already were mutating toward what a later generation would call hippies. But a few heard a peculiar siren song amid all the bad poetry and smelly feet. Writing in *Playboy,* Herb Gold, who was considered an expert on the Beats largely because he lived in San Francisco, was reminded of some lines that William Yeats (another nineteenth-century man who had thought *Homo sapiens* was in the process of climbing the evolutionary ladder) had written:

> *What rough beast, its hour come round at last,*
> *Slouches towards Bethlehem to be born.*

Could the beatniks, Gold wondered, be Yeats's proto-gods? Naw. "When Yeats looked into the future to find a terrible savior, an evolution up from animality into something strange and wonderful—he did not mean James Dean. Perhaps, as they claim, the tunneling hipster's avoidance of feeling can lead to a new honesty of emotion. Perhaps a ground hog might someday learn to fly, but man O man, that will be one strange bird."

Precisely the point Yeats was making.

In *The Dharma Bums,* Kerouac's second Beat novel, there is a moment when the Gary Snyder character experiences a vision of the future comparable to Yeats's. What he sees is "a great rucksack revolution, thousands or even millions of young Americans wandering around with rucksacks, going up to mountains to pray, making children laugh . . . wild gangs of pure holymen getting together to drink and talk and pray."

That was the Beat fantasy, and it was one that Allen Ginsberg was using all of his market research skills to bring about. Ginsberg became the public relations director of the Beat movement, which irritated some of the more self-reliant poets. He badgered the intellectual journals, particularly hostile ones like *Partisan Review* and *Hudson Review,* to publish the work of his friends; he contacted agents and editors and was rarely without a selection of manuscripts that he was trying to place. If the Beat movement was a modestly glowing goal, he was going to do everything within his power to make sure it burst into flame. Years later Ginsberg described the potential of this moment this way:

> We'd already had, by '48, some sort of alteration of our own private consciousness; by '55 we made some kind of articulation of it; by '58 it had spread sufficiently so that the mass media were coming around for information, and by that time I realized that if our private fancies, our private poetries, were so serious that they absorbed the attention of the big, serious military generals who wrote for *Time* magazine, there must be something strange going on."

What was happening, Ginsberg thought, was an alteration of consciousness that was filtering up through the young into all levels of society. It was as though the country was just catching up to where the New Visionaries had been back in 1944. "That year on the literary scene in New York it was all in fashion to go crazy," remembers Barbara Probst Solomon. "It was the fashion to push things to their ultimate extreme— all kinds of sexual and drug experimentation. Once, at a party, someone put LSD in my drink, and I went home and woke up seeing things. I thought I was going crazy until someone phoned later in the afternoon and asked how I liked my acid trip. . . . It was the beginning of the Sixties, really, and I used to say to Larry Roose, a Freudian friend of mine, that it was all very violent, that I didn't like being part of it."

America, thought Ginsberg, was on the verge of a nervous breakdown.

WILD GEESE

Had you required, in August 1960, a personification of this malaise, you could have found him lazing about a swimming pool in the Mexican resort town of Cuernavaca. He was, by profession, a psychologist, although with his horse-latitudes tan he looked more like a golf pro at the local country club. By inclination he was an atheist, a rational humanist, a borderline alcoholic, and incessant womanizer whose most enduring emotion was boredom. "I had run through and beyond the middle-class professional game board," he wrote in *High Priest,* the first of his several autobiographies. "There were no surprise moves left. I had died even to the lure of ambition, power, sex. It was all a Monopoly game—easy to win but meaningless. I had just been promised tenure at Harvard."

His name was Timothy Francis Leary. He was two months shy of his fortieth birthday. And he was about to take a whimsical first step down a path that would end a few months shy of his fiftieth birthday, when a Federal judge called him the most dangerous man in the world.

Located thirty-seven miles south of Mexico City, on the edge of the central plateau, Cuernavaca had once been a center for soothsayers and magicians, occupying a position in the Aztec world comparable to that of Delphi in ancient Greece. Blessed with a climate that rarely varied from 75 degrees Fahrenheit, it had become, after Cortez, a preserve of the Mexican upper classes, and a favorite spot for American academics "vacationing on research grants." For a few hundred pesos it was possible to live like royalty, with a maid, a cook, even a gardener.

Leary was renting a villa out on the Acapulco road, next to the Cuernavaca golf course. He was sharing it with two other psychologists, Frank Barron and Richard Dettering, plus Dettering's wife, Ruth; another housemate, Richard Alpert, was expected later in the month. It was a comfortable set-up, lounging by the pool watching plumes of snow rise from the twin volcanoes, Popacatapetl and Iztaccihuatl, listening to the whack of golf balls down on the fairway. The air was thick with bougainvillea and the happy shouts of Tim's two kids, Susan and Jack, and there was usually time for a game of touch football, after siesta and before the cocktail hour.

Leary tried to devote at least an hour or two of each day to his writing—he had two books under way, a novel and a long essay that finally explained what he meant when he talked about an existential-transactional psychology. But there always seemed to be distractions, often in the form of pretty girls. One frequent visitor to the villa was Gerhart Braun, an acquaintance of Barron's who taught anthropology at the huge National University in Mexico City. Braun was teaching himself Nahuatl, the language of the Aztecs, and one evening the discussion turned to references he had found concerning *teonanacatl*, the divine mushrooms Gordon Wasson had eaten in Huatla de Jimenez.

It wasn't the first time Leary had spent an evening drinking and discussing *teonanacatl*. Several years earlier, excited by Wasson's article in *Life*, Frank Barron had tracked some down as part of his ongoing research into the psychology of creativity. Tim's reaction at the time had been distaste mixed with worry: experimenting with native drugs had seemed a foolishly dangerous enterprise. But now, after a month of lazy days, his boredom was reasserting itself; he was ready for something different. "Why don't we see if we can find some?" he suggested to Braun.

It had taken Wasson years of patient diplomacy before he had found a *curandera* willing to share her mushrooms, but Braun located a source in less than a week, from a *curandera* named Juana who lived in the village of San Pedro, not far from Cuernavaca.

Saturday, August 9, 1960, was like most days in Mexico's central plateau: hot and clear. Braun arrived at the villa in the afternoon, bringing along his girlfriend and several of her friends, plus a bag of dirty, stringy lumps.

"Are you sure it's not poisonous?" Leary asked, examining one of the fungi . . . *Had the Aztecs really called these things God's flesh?* (Earlier, when Ruth Dettering had decided to pass on the mushrooms, Tim had taught her the Spanish words for "ambulance" and "stomach pump.")

In response Gerhart popped a mushroom into his mouth and swallowed it. Then one of the girls ate one. Then Dettering. Leary placed one of the dirty lumps on his tongue. It tasted worse than it looked. Stuffing it into his mouth, he washed it down with a swallow of beer. Then he picked up another.

Later, when he had time to reflect upon what had happened, he was amazed by the abruptness of the transition. One minute he was registering the fact that someone was vomiting into the bushes and the next he was aware of a subtle sort of pulsing buzz—as if the world was alive, the birds, the bushes, the swimming pool, everything humming with life. As he let that lulling hum take hold, he began to slip back through exotic history, images of Nile palaces and Hindu temples flashing up on some inner screen, passing through the bejeweled vistas of Weir Mitchell, devolving back until he bottomed out in that primordial chemical soup.

In *Flashbacks,* his second crack at an autobiography, Leary playfully imagines that he was conceived on January 17, 1920, the day after Prohibition went into effect, and a few hours after a Saturday night dance at the West Point Officers' Club, where his father, Captain Timothy "Tote" Leary was post dentist, and his mother, the former Abigail Ferris, was "the most beautiful woman on the post: jet-black hair, milky soft skin, curvy Gibson-girl figure." They danced, they drank, they staggered, laughing, back to their quarters where they made love, and eight months and some weeks later, on October 22, 1920, a son was born, emerging into a world that was almost as new as he was. Besides shattering every certainty of the Edwardian Age, the Great War had released a gust of liberating energy that was memorialized by the quintessential adjective of the 1920s, *roaring.* Whether it was business or Broadway, the mood, as Cole Porter understood, was "anything goes." Although Leary was still an adolescent when the good times came to an abrupt end, this didn't diminish the influence that these few years of wild, chic living—the Jazz Age—would have on his later philosophy of life.

This was largely Tote's doing. Tote was a Leary from Springfield, Massachusetts, which might not sound like much now, but back in the Twenties the Springfield Learys were rumored to be the richest Irish Catholics in western Massachusetts. Tote's father, the Old Man, was supposed to have made a fortune out of some shrewd real estate deals. With nine kids in Tote's generation, there was an abundance of aunts and uncles "who dashed in and out" of young Tim's life, "making scenes, scandals, strange disappearances. Aunt Frances ran away to Kansas City with a Protestant, and Tote was dispatched by train to bring her back. Cousin Sissy married a prosperous Episcopalian and then—saints, preserve us!—sailed to Paris for a divorce." Rich, fun-loving, and self-absorbed, the Learys were the antithesis of Tim's maternal relatives, the Ferrises, who lived on a dirt farm east of Springfield. Because of his parents' marital problems, Tim spent a considerable amount of his childhood at the Ferris farm, of which, he would later write, he could remember not "one moment of wild merriment." With both parents dead from the 1918 flu epidemic, the titular head of the Ferrises was Abigail's older sister, Aunt Dudu, "a timid, fantastically religious gnome who futilely tried to direct family affairs with Irish-village piety, sitting on a couch all day clicking her false teeth, mumbling prayers, and reading Catholic tracts." Neither Dudu, nor Abigail's other sister, Mae, had been much impressed by the tall, slim, sophisticated Tote Leary; they had treated Abigail's betrothal and eventual marriage as a tragedy in the making, with Mae crying for three days and begging Abigail not to take a honeymoon.

In the end they had the prim satisfaction of having been right. Abigail and Tote's marriage was not blessed; they did not turn into the respectable solid family of Abigail's fantasies. The last thing Captain Tote Leary wanted was to settle into comfortable domesticity, measuring out his days with dental calipers and baby nappies. He preferred his old life as a fun-loving sport, and more and more, as his pursuit of the past grew dogged, he came home drunk, in debt, angry. What kept Tote afloat was the certainty that one day the Old Man would pass on, and part of the richest Catholic estate in western Massachusetts would be his. In fact, all the kids "believed the wonderful myth that we would all be rich when the Old Man died." Even the stock market crash of '29 and the years of uncollected loans to wayward children like Tote and Aunt Sissy failed to dampen this certainty, which persisted right up until the day the Old Man's will was read in 1934, when everyone learned that there were only a few thousand dollars left in the till.

Tote gave a hundred of his share to his son, a thousand to his wife, and then he disappeared from their lives.

What happens when a father suddenly vanishes? What reserves of anger and sorrow are accumulated to be drawn upon in the years to come? Leary, in his published writings, says little about the pain of his father's abandonment, aside from the parenthetical comment that "my sorrow at his abandonment of me emerged later during a drug session with Jack Kerouac." Rather, in *Flashbacks*, he delivers the following eulogy:

> I have always felt warmth and respect for this distant male-man who special-delivered me. During the thirteen years we lived together he never stunted me with expectations . . . Dad remained for me a model of the loner, a disdainer of the conventional way. Tote dropped out, followed the ancient Hibernian practice of getting in the wind, escaping the priest-run village, heading for the far-off land, like one of the Wild Geese of Irish legend.

Abigail doesn't fare half so well in her son's memoirs. Her pious (she rarely missed daily mass) striving to be respectably middle class, her inbred suspicion of "all things joyous, frivolous or newfangled," bored and irritated Tim, and he reacted by cultivating all the qualities that his mother found obnoxious in her Leary in-laws. How successful he was in this impersonation can be measured by a comment made years later by a Boston *Globe* reporter who, after sifting through the detritus of Leary's high school career at Springfield's Classical High, pronounced him "a figure out of Scott Fitzgerald." He was a smooth social operator, a fixture on various student social committees and the award-winning editor of the school newspaper. His academic record was mixed, with high grades in history and English and less impressive ones in math and science. But his best marks came from the opposite sex, who voted him "cutest boy" in his senior year. "Sigh no more, ladies; sigh no more," sighed his yearbook legend, and on another page, in the Class Will, he left the following bequest: "Tim Leary leaves a 'mashed up' mashie to Bob Calhoun, another assaulter of the little white ball." Only in one respect did the son differ from the father: when it came to women Tim preferred "the wildest, funniest, most high-fashion, big-city girl in town." There would be no Abigails in his life.

But ultimately this was a deceptive exterior, a self-creation, really, of a boy who as an adult would remember not the social whirl, but the awful loneliness that he used to chase away with daydreams of "heroism, history, romance, and exploration." If Tote's genes had combined to produce the smarmy charm that had won him "cutest boy" honors, they had also left Tim a legacy of estrangement, which fed those constant dreams of heroic distinction. Even as a child Leary was conscious of himself as an outsider—the Irish Catholic in a school full of Wasps, the artist in a culture of jocks and businessmen, the nonbeliever in a world of worshipers. Starting in his teens, this sense of otherness brought him continually into conflict with authority, often in willed confrontations that he was instrumental in arranging.

The first of these occurred in his final months at Classical High. For no rational reason, Leary began cutting classes and skipping school, daring the principal—"a wise old New Englander" with a "Supreme Court Justice shock of white hair"—to expel him. He later attributed his survival to the quantity of paperwork involved in expelling a nondelinquent juvenile. But his capricious behavior did cost him a college recommendation. Unlike the "huge swaggering jocks," Tim was turned down by the prestigious Ivy League schools; Abigail had to pull strings with the local monsignor to get him accepted at Holy Cross, a Catholic college run by the Jesuits.

Holy Cross, in the fall of 1938, was ill suited for either social or intellectual adventuring. The curriculum was classical, with an emphasis on Greek, Latin, religion, and football; it was a little like a monastery with an athletic department. Girls were rarely seen on campus. Chapel, at 7 A.M., was compulsory. Tim spent two years in this purgatory, translating Cicero and Horace and running a bookmaking ring with another "restless outsider" named Angelo. At night, after bed check, they would sneak out to the local bars to try their luck with the neighborhood shop girls.

After Holy Cross, in a romantic mistake that he shares with Edgar Allan Poe, among others, Leary used his family's political connections to secure an appointment to West Point, where he lasted slightly more than a year. His fling at being a warrior went awry during a return train trip to the Academy, when several upperclassmen confronted him and accused him of drunkenness—a punishable offence but not a mortal one. Leary always maintained that what followed was a combination of too much alcohol and the sort of existential crossed signals that occur whenever different people try to communicate. The upper classmen, however, interpreted these crossed signals as lying, and the Cadet Honor Court agreed. Cadet Leary had dishonored the Corps; he should resign his commission. But Cadet Leary felt otherwise, and requested an official court martial. This was considered bad form by his fellow cadets, many of whom had been divided on the merits of his case, and they reacted by silencing him. Leary became a nonperson. In *High Priest* he describes sitting in the enormous airplane hangar of a mess hall surrounded by two thousand gray-suited young men, none of whom was allowed to sit next to or talk with him. Any communication he wished to make, like "pass the salt," had to be scribbled onto a piece of paper.

Although the official court martial found him not guilty, this had no effect over the silencing, which dragged on until August 1941, when Leary finally sent the commandant a note. "I am ill adapted to a military career," it began, "I am not satisfied in my present environment and I feel that it would be to the best interest of both myself and the government if I were permitted to resign and pursue another career."

He went south, to the University of Alabama, and it was there that his intellect caught fire. He majored in psychology and minored in English and history, and he discovered Joyce's *Ulysses,* which bowled him over. To one day write a book as intense and artful became his greatest ambition. But if he was cracking the books with a bit more application than before, this didn't mean that he had completely abandoned his old habits. Southern women, for instance. Tim loved them for their flirtatious sexiness, and he was eventually caught spending the night in one of the female dorms and expelled.

His adventures might have continued unabated—an educational picaresque on the order of Tom Jones—but for the war, which he spent as an army psychologist at a Pennsylvania veterans hospital. The war marked a break in Leary's life in roughly the same way as it did with the nation as a whole: Tim came out and went right back to school, eventually earning a doctorate in clinical psychology from Berkeley. He got married, had two kids, settled into a comfortable suburban ranch house in the Berkeley hills, and accepted a prestigious sinecure at Oakland's Kaiser Hospital, as research director of the psychiatric clinic. It was a classic Fifties success story, which made what happened all the more symbolic. If Ginsberg and the Beats represented one end of the emotional spectrum, and the Organization Man the other, then Tim was somewhere in the middle, on the one hand (as he later boasted) "an arrogant disdainer of fear-directed bourgeois conformity," while at the same time an ardent pursuer of all the rewards that fear-directed bourgeois conformity could bring. The tension between these two drives manifested itself in his marriage. When friends were later pressed to characterize the relationship between Tim and Marianne, the analogy that popped up frequently was Edward Albee's play, *Who's Afraid of Virginia Woolf.* Like the older academic couple in Albee's play, Tim and Marianne were masters of the barbed witticism, the ego-toppling put-down. The general impression was that they were trying to drive each other crazy.

But these were also the years when Leary did the work that established his reputation as a promising young psychologist. In the balkanized world of academic psychology, Tim was considered an expert in personality assessment and behavior change, which meant he was a whiz at interpreting diagnostic tests like the TAT and MMPI, while at the same time he was taking a crack at one of psychology's really Big Questions: behavior change. One reason that psychotherapy's success rate was so low was because intellectual understanding did not directly translate into changed behavior. Just because a patient understood what his problem was didn't mean he would do anything about it; too often patients were locked into relationships and routines of behavior that couldn't be broken. But every once in a while something . . . clicked! It was like trying to catch time, that click. "One can make tape-recordings, take motion pictures, count heart beats, measure muscle potentials, note the number of minutes spent together, ask questions (True-False questions, open-ended questions, questions in disguise), get interpretations of inkblots, or do any number of those tricks of the trade with which we are all familiar," wrote Leary's best friend and fellow Berkeley classmate, Frank Barron. But none of these captured that telltale click, that vitalizing transaction, that healing moment.

Frank Barron and Tim Leary were friends for a number of reasons: they were both Irish, both psychologists, both Berkeley grads, and they were both taken with each other's temperament. Tim, with his quicksilver imagination and his natural rebel's skepticism, teemed with wildly implausible theories that Barron artfully brought down to earth. While you could say that Tim, with his passion for Joyce, wanted to embody creativity, Barron preferred to study it, understand it, perfect it, and then use it the way any other tool was used. So they were well gaited for their first collaboration, which played off a situation that Leary was coping with at the Kaiser Clinic. The Kaiser Clinic was being overwhelmed with patients, some of whom had to spend months on a waiting list. Now it was engraved on the heart of every Cinderella scientist that the world would be a better place if everyone was required to undergo therapy. Certainly Leary and Barron accepted this, although perhaps less enthusiastically than some of their colleagues, and when the oversubscription at Kaiser presented itself, they conceived of a tidy little experiment, contrasting those patients who were receiving therapy with those who recognized they had problems but were still waiting for professional help, thus arriving at a nice numerical index of psychotherapy's utility. That was the intention, in any case.

To say they were horrified by what they found is a little strong—amazed, worried, amused, disturbed—you could use any of those. Because what they found was that there was *no* difference: "The therapy patients did not improve significantly more than the waiting list controls," they reported in the *Journal of Consulting Psychology*. In both groups about a third had stayed the same, a third had deteriorated, and a third had gotten better. In that final group something else was occurring, that elusive vitalizing *click* that was "as frail as love or blessedness, as passing as the moment of grace or the beginning of creation," to quote Barron again.

The Kaiser study got Leary noticed, as did his next project, a book-length examination of personality assessment, *The Interpersonal Diagnostic of Personality*, which was lauded by the Annual Review of Psychology as "the most important book on psychotherapy of the year." Leary's professional success seemed assured, and it might have been, had not Marianne chosen to asphyxiate herself in the garage of the Berkeley house on the morning of Tim's thirty-fifth birthday. Whatever the rancors leading up to the suicide, Leary was "destroyed, his hair turned gray in the course of four months, a fantastic reaction," remembers Barron.

But Marianne's death was also liberating, in much the same way that Tote had been released by the Old Man's death. Suddenly all bets were off, all ties binding him to the middle-class domesticity he loathed were broken. He could do anything he wanted, and what he wanted was to get away, go to Europe, live by his wits, and write. A few months after Marianne's death Leary resigned from Kaiser, and, accompanied by his two children and a bundle of research notes, sailed for Spain. The research notes—"thousands of test scores and numerical indices which demonstrated with precision why psychotherapy didn't work"—were supposed to form the backbone of his next book, one that would develop a theory of the vitalizing transaction, and one that just might (if he could only freeze the visions that whirled through his mind) do for the second half of the twentieth century what Freud's *Interpretation of Dreams* had done for the first. But the book refused to jell. Leary drifted, taking gypsy lectureships in Spain and Denmark before holing up in Florence, where Barron found him in the spring of 1958.

Barron brought along a bottle of Jameson's whiskey to celebrate the reunion. As the level in the bottle steadily fell, the two men talked shop. Barron was in Europe on creativity business, having just flown to Ireland to interview the writer Sean O'Faolain. Prior to that he had spent a few days at Harvard attending a seminar on creativity in the sciences, and just before that, before flying out of San Francisco, he had tried some narcotic mushrooms . . . *teonanacatl* . . . *Psilocybe mexicana* . . . perhaps Tim remembered reading about them in *Life?*

That such tiny fungi could stimulate such wild visions in a New York investment banker had been compelling news to Barron; and as soon as a sabbatical had provided the time and money he had made arrangements to retrace Wasson's journey. But on the eve of departure he had learned of two scientists at the National University in Mexico City who had a large supply of mushrooms that they were more than willing to share with a fellow researcher.

Leary was skeptical and a bit put off by Barron's enthusiasm. This was partly because he failed to see what contribution an aboriginal hallucinogen could make toward solving the really pressing problems of psychology, and partly because he was preoccupied with his own equally pressing problems, principally his lack of cash. Which was why he was all ears when Barron mentioned that before leaving Harvard he had visited with his friend David McClelland, the director of Harvard's Personality Clinic, and McClelland had told him he was going to be in Florence at the end of the month. Barron urged Leary to call on McClelland, and Tim did, pedaling up on his daughter's bicycle with a bag of manuscript under his arm, and riding off with a lectureship at Harvard, and the prospect of tenure if things worked out. It was as though, having been cast by misfortune into the role of mendicant medieval scholar, Leary had suddenly been offered a sinecure in Rome, for Harvard was the capital of academic psychology.

"I walked about Harvard Square and the Yard and felt in the presence of the great. The towering elms, the oddly pleasing mix of architectural styles, the to me 'pure' scholars walking the crisscross paths under the trees. This was Athens and I was walking the Agora!"

That was Jerome Bruner describing his arrival to study psychology at Harvard in 1938. Twenty-one years later, when Leary showed up, the Harvard mystique was still as intense, only now the proper analogy was

Rome not Athens. Suave, confident, urbane, Harvard was the cradle of liberal technocracy, the place where the Best and the Brightest were transformed into the kind of managers the American Century was going to require. Harvard was a sexy, powerful place, qualities that were epitomized by its most visible alumnus, the junior senator from Massachusetts, John F. Kennedy, who would run for and win the presidency in 1960. It was also an ironic place for an arrogant disdainer of bourgeois conformity to end up, this Valhalla of Organization Men.

To be fair, Leary loved Harvard's mental voltage: everywhere you turned there were minds capable of striking lightning; the thrust and parry of academic argument was delightful; but he also chafed at the snobbish noblesse oblige of the place, the arrogance, the fatuous certainty that whatever Harvard decided was right, *was* right. Harvard brought out the outsider in Leary, and he delighted in pricking the pomposities of his colleagues. Which was just fine as far as McClelland was concerned. One of the reasons he had hired Tim, aside from the obvious satisfaction of possibly salvaging a brilliant career, was his belief that Leary would stir things up at the Center for Personality Research, which was housed in a little building at 5 Divinity Avenue. The Center had been the godchild of Harry Murray, one of the grand old men of personality assessment. By the time Tim arrived Murray was in semiretirement and the day-to-day chores had passed to McClelland, which was symbolically appropriate in the sense that if Murray represented the generation of psychologists who had created personality tests, then McClelland represented the generation who had learned how to use them. To quote an admiring interviewer in *Psychology Today*, when it came to charting the delicate structures of the subconscious, McClelland had been "the first man to do it well." You created a tool, you figured out what it could do, and then you used it. And that was where Leary became important with all his talk about the existential-transactive matrix . . .

> Existential means you study natural events as they unfold without prejudging them with your own concepts. You surrender your mind to the events.
> Transactional means you see the research situation as a social network, of which the experimenter is one part. The psychologist doesn't stand outside the event but recognizes his part in it, and works collaboratively with the subject toward mutually selected goals.

In retrospect it is clear that transactional psychology was merely one ripple in the upwelling that became humanistic psychology, the so-called Third Force, as distinguished from Behaviorism (the First Force) and psychoanalysis (the Second). Unlike its predecessors, humanistic psychology was not a monolithic philosophy of the psyche; rather, it was a loose confederation of therapies linked by a set of common assumptions: that it was time to ask what made people healthy, not what made them sick; that it was time to recognize that treating the body was almost as important as treating the mind; that such things as vitalizing transactions really happened (Maslow, one of the patriarchs of the Third Force, published his first paper on peak experiences in 1956); that there was room for all kinds of therapy, all kinds of tools—to adhere to a party line was simply a sign of scientific immaturity.

But if existential transactional psychology, as espoused by Leary, was part of this larger backlash, it also had some unique features of its own. The most important was its decision to treat all social roles and behavior as a series of elaborate games, each with its own rules, rituals, strategies and rewards. This was basically a distancing device. For example, Leary was playing the professor game, Ivy League variation. In order to be allowed onto the playing field it was necessary to dress properly, in Leary's case in J. Press and Brooks Brothers, but not as properly as someone playing the banker game. It was possible, for example, to adequately assay the professor game in tennis shoes and red socks, which Tim was partial to. But there were also certain rituals to attend to, the publications, the papers presented at symposiums, the grants, etc., etc.

The kids loved it. Watching Tim lecture, Harry Murray was reminded of the Pied Piper: "When he talked they would look at him with rapt attention." But Tim probably made his biggest impact on some of his younger colleagues, the first-year instructors and the doctoral candidates. They were awed by him, by the fact that he was a front-line veteran, and not just another ivory tower backbencher with no feel for the reality of trench life in the war on mental illness; they were awed by his early professional renown, and the fact that he had walked away from it and could laugh about it. Leary exuded an air of irrepressible confidence; nothing fazed him. And he would say the damndest things, just waltz into your office and launch into a charming story about how he had bounced checks all over Europe.

Maybe it was the voice? Art Kleps used to claim Tim could have recited the alphabet "and those who heard him would have smiled, allowed their own conversation to lapse, and very possibly read all kinds of symbolic meanings into the succession of syllables." He had a "remarkable ability to charm those who came near, to exude a warmth and radiance that made others feel strong in his presence," wrote David McClelland. "When I was near him everything seemed possible," remembered Richard Alpert, who was ten years younger than Leary, but leagues ahead of him in terms of the Harvard game of status and corner offices. Leary didn't even have a proper office: they had him shoehorned into a converted closet at 5 Divinity Avenue like some poor relation. Not that he cared a jot. Others might have better offices, but he had a better time. And that was perhaps the thing that awed his younger colleagues most: Tim was like catnip to women; he was like something out of a Cary Grant movie.

One of the best summations of Tim's effect on his younger colleagues comes from Michael Kahn, a young lecturer who had flown combat missions during the Second World War: "When Timothy arrived, I knew the day he walked in I'd never met anybody like him. During the war what some people developed was a sense, an intuition of who you would want to fly with and who you wouldn't. Everybody knew about it and nobody could quite describe it. There were guys you wanted on your crew, and guys you didn't. If you were in bombers, there were guys you wanted on your flight, and guys you didn't if you were in fighters. Nobody quite knew what that quality was, but everybody knew it was there. It was some sense of strength and competence and trustworthiness and loyalty—some funny combination. 'I'd like to fly with him,' guys would say about other guys. I never quite knew what that meant. But when I met Timothy, the thought that crossed my mind was I'd fly with him."

Leary also impressed them with his contempt for everything middle class, which was nothing exceptional at Harvard, except that Leary's gibes contained an abrasive edge that went far beyond the usual swipes at the sheeplike bourgeois; Tim really did hate those faceless, conforming Organization Men. Charles Slack, a fellow psychology instructor and frequent drinking partner, concluded that one of Leary's most powerful drives was his desire to "escape the middle class . . . his whole career was a flight from middle-class values, relationships, people, scenes, everything." Slack remembers Leary preaching to him about the necessity of creating hybrids. "Make Hybrids," Leary would exclaim, "and you make revolutions. . . . If you could only find a good excuse for bringing certain isolated groups and individuals together and removing their established biases you could cure most of the psychological ills of this lousy, class-bound culture of ours."

Slack's teaching contract expired in the spring of 1960. Shortly before he left he was vouchsafed a glimpse of what Tim meant when he called himself an arrogant disdainer of fear-directed bourgeois conformity. They were sitting in one of their usual watering holes, talking about mainstream psychology's kneejerk habit of labelling "every poor Roxbury street kid who ever stole a hubcap" a psychopath, when Slack proposed that they form a club, the Psychopath Club. Leary gave him an amused look and said, "You know, I really am a psychopath." "I know you are," replied Slack, "but I'm one too." "You aren't in my league at all," Leary said. As proof he offered a simple test: how many times had Slack violated the American Psychological Association's Code of Ethics. Slack couldn't think of a single instance. "Well what about you?" he asked Leary.

"I think I've violated them all except the ones about money."

Thinking his leg was being pulled, Slack mentally reviewed the Association's Code and selected the worst abuse he could remember, the one only a true psychopath would break. "Have you ever had sexual relations with a patient of yours?" he asked.

Leary gave him a sheepish look. "Yes, quite a bit."

Slack left Harvard believing Tim Leary to be one of the most truly radical people he had ever met. In some respects he *was* a psychopath, but he didn't fit the usual profile. He didn't flout the rules because of some desperate and uncontrollable compulsion, but because he had a kind of "social-science curiosity about what would happen if you broke this or that taboo, as opposed to the accepted version of the consequences." During their last meeting Leary talked of his summer plans. He was going to Mexico. And he was finally going to finish that damn book.

Afterward it was all he could talk about. How he had devolved back through millions of years until he had become a single solitary cell. And then returned, passing through the oceanic to the amphibian to the terrestrial, evolving out of the primordial slime and into that smartest of smart monkeys, a Harvard professor.

All the games and strategies that had given his life coherence had melted away. He had viewed his personality, that boozy womanizing totally bored fraud, with the cold objectivity of . . . well, of a god. He might have been looking at an ant through a magnifying glass. "Wow! I learned more in six hours than in the past sixteen years," he enthused to novelist Arthur Koestler. "Visual transformations. Gone the perceptual machinery which clutters up our view of reality. Intuitive transformations. Gone the mental machinery which slices the world up into abstractions and concepts. Emotional transformations. Gone the emotional machinery that causes us to load life with our own ambitions and petty desires."

Gone also, he might have added, was the boredom that had been his constant companion. Taking its place was the overwhelming urge to "rush back and tell everyone":

> Listen! Wake up! You are God! You have the divine plan engraved
> in cellular script within you. Listen! Take this sacrament! You'll see!
> You'll get the revelations! It will change your life! You'll be reborn!

That's the way Leary remembered the feeling in *High Priest,* although by then his context had shifted toward religion and revelation. He hadn't really rushed around talking about God that first morning after; it had been more along the lines of finally experiencing that elusive vitalizing transaction.

Leary couldn't wait to share his discovery with David McClelland, who was vacationing a few miles away in the village of Tepoztlan. McClelland had spent the summer finishing *The Achieving Society,* which was a psychological analysis of why some civilizations prospered and others decayed. He was also making tentative overtures in the direction of motivational training, which was exactly the kind of lucrative marriage between business and psychology that powerhouse schools like Harvard hoped to promote. So Tim's enthusiastic babble about Aztec drugs caught him by surprise. If he was hearing things correctly, Leary seemed to be implying that a mushroom was going to revolutionize psychology. He insisted that McClelland return to Cuernavaca at once and have a vitalizing transaction. And McClelland went, although he was undecided whether he would actually eat any of these things. But when they got there, they discovered that the Mexican maid had destroyed their supply of mushrooms, a reflection perhaps of the years of Catholic propaganda against such pagan practices.

Like William James and peyote, McClelland decided to take Tim's account of his wondrous visions on faith, and he gave a tacit go-ahead for further research.

Leary went rushing back to Harvard, stopping first in Orinda, a suburb of San Francisco, to compare notes with Frank Barron, who had left Cuernavaca a few days before Braun's successful rendevous with the *curandera.* It was like two old campaigners swapping war stories, now that both had been bemushroomed. These things are the key, Tim kept insisting, we should be using them to heal people; it's an axiom of psychology that true insight will lead to true change; why not test that proposition? Why not give the mushrooms to writers and artists, Barron added; imagine the kind of insight into creativity that would produce! By coincidence Barron had a standing invitation from McClelland to spend a year at Harvard, at the Clinic. Why not the coming year?

That's how it started. Indeed the only stumbling block was the problem of finding a steady supply of mushrooms. It would be highly impractical to have to fly to Mexico and scour the hinterlands for compliant *curanderas* every time you ran out. Then someone mentioned that Sandoz was marketing the psychoactive ingredient of *Psilocybe mexicana* under the trade name psilocybin. An order was dispatched, and a few days before Thanksgiving, 1960, a nondescript box arrived at 5 Divinity Avenue. Inside were several brown bottles and inside the bottles were dozens of pink pellets.

Leary and Barron took them back to the house they were renting in Newton, shook a few out, and took off. "For the next six weeks we were on our own," Leary wrote,

> Western literature had almost no guides, no maps, no texts that even recognized the existence of altered states. We had no rituals, traditions or comforting routines to fall back on. In line with our existential-transactional theories we avoided the sterility of the laboratory and the sick man atmosphere of the hospital. We conducted the experiments in faculty homes, in front of comforting fire places, with candles instead of electric lights and evocative music.

Like the wild geese of Irish legend, they were heading for that far-off land.

12

THE HARVARD PSILOCYBIN PROJECT

Inside the small building at 5 Divinity Avenue it was like watching a science fiction novel unfold before your eyes. The plot went something like this: good solid scientists embark upon interesting research program involving native drugs. Come back babbling about love and ecstasy and insisting you haven't understood anything until you've been there, to the Other World, beyond the Door. It was a little like *Invasion of the Body Snatchers,* a cult movie favorite of the Fifties, in the sense that every day the crowd in Leary's shoebox office grew larger, graduate students and junior faculty members, all with these soft intense voices and glowing eyes, talking about the death of the mind, the birth of the uncensored cortex. . . . And it had all started out so innocuously—what research project doesn't?

Summer had always been a time when professors recharged their mental faculties; they always returned full of ambitious plans, full of tasty little experiments that had popped into their heads as they lazed in the hammock, with something other than an undergraduate theme folded against their chest. So Tim's enthusiasm tended to blend in. Everyone knew he was doing something with Mexican mushrooms; they couldn't help but know, owing to the rather grandiose claims (Galileo's telescope was mentioned a lot, and once or twice the invention of fire) that were issuing from the converted closet at 5 Divinity Avenue; but they didn't pay much attention. Something big had bitten Tim, that was clear, but Mexican mushrooms? Sounded more anthropological than psychological. Still it might be fun to watch Leary try to make his case; it might prove whether that big reputation for clinical cleverness was deserved or not. But they couldn't get too excited about it. When Leary offered to run a Psilocybin session for any of the senior faculty members who were interested, everyone refused with the exception of the septuagenarian Harry Murray. And even Murray's tale of being transported back to the Egypt of the pharaohs, of actually standing in front of one of the recently completed pyramids, with a fountain of gold geysering to a great height, failed to move them.

Leary had always talked a great game about the deadening effect of the "adjust or else" brand of psychology that had held sway over the Fifties, but he hadn't realized just how dead in the water most of his colleagues were until he offered them psilocybin, and they refused to try it. My God, these were psychologists yet they lacked the slightest curiosity about their own unconsciouses! And if you made the mistake of rhapsodizing about the marvelous world that was somehow locked up inside their minds, then they treated you with the kind of disdain mature people usually reserve for those who still believe the fairytales of adolescence.

Niels Bohr, the great quantum physicist, made a comment in his autobiography that sheds a little light on Tim's frustrating attempts to get a hearing from the senior psychology faculty. "A new scientific truth does not triumph by convincing its opponents and making them see the light," Bohr wrote. "But rather because its opponents eventually die, and a new generation grows up that is familiar with it."

Leary had better luck with younger colleagues like Michael Kahn, and with the doctoral candidates, either those who had already attached themselves to the personality clinic, or those who were just arriving, and had wandered in to check things out. George Litwin was an example of the first. He and Tim had had a fairly warm relationship prior to Leary's summer vacation; enough so that when Litwin had been experimenting with mescaline the previous spring, Tim was one of the few faculty members he told, and one who had responded with a short lecture about "chemical meddling." So Litwin was a little surprised when he ran into Tim that September and Leary began raving about the mushroom project.

Litwin immediately signed on, trotted down to his cubicle, and trotted back with slim copies of Huxley's *The Doors of Perception* and *Heaven and Hell*. Essential reading, he told Tim.

Then there were the raw recruits, like Gunther Weil. Weil was just back from a stretch in Europe as a Fulbright scholar. He bumped into Leary the first time he stuck his head into 5 Divinity Avenue: "Tim was in a converted closet, which was in keeping with Tim. It didn't bother him. He shot me a big smile, a very warm handshake; very engaging, tremendously engaging, very warm, very funny. He invited me to participate in the project. I said yes."

It was like watching a master salesman at work; before long Tim had smilingly collected an eager platoon of graduate students, which meant a diminution in the amusement of the senior psychology faculty.

It was an unwritten rule that graduate students were community chattel, with everyone receiving a couple to do their research donkeywork, and some receiving more than others owing to their senior stature. By cheerfully urging everyone he met to participate in his psilocybin project, Leary was breaking this unwritten rule. Barron, who was far more experienced in academic protocol, urged Tim to keep things small; he was creating a needless and potentially dangerous jealousy. But Tim couldn't help himself: these drugs were the cutting edge of the future; how could he turn away the very people who were going to create that future?

At its peak, the psilocybin project numbered about two dozen, mostly graduate students and junior faculty, but with a sprinkling of nonacademics, usually creative types like the poet Charles Olson, who had been drawn in by Barron's creativity experiments. Once or twice a week they gathered at the rambling old colonial that Leary and Barron were renting in Newton from an MIT professor who was on sabbatical. Before taking the drug everyone filled out set and setting questionnaires, outlining such variables as specific fears or expectations, plus any other data (such as "Gunther and I had a huge argument yesterday") that seemed pertinent. Then they swallowed the pills and waited for the Door to slide open. During the first several experiences there was always a moment of panic as they passed through to the Other World, but with time the transition became almost routine.

"This is no field for the faint of heart," Leary lectured them. "You are venturing out (like the Portuguese sailors, like the astronauts) on the uncharted margins. But be reassured—it's an old human custom." "There were no freakouts, there were no bad trips in those days," remembers Michael Kahn. "We didn't know what a bad trip was. In hundreds of psilocybin trips, I never saw one. Those were benign, life-changing, growth experiences because Tim's presence was so involving."

In their first experiment—a naturalistic study similar to what Oscar Janiger had done with LSD—they gave psilocybin to 175 different people, to writers, housewives, musicians, psychologists, graduate students. Most were male and young, the average age 29.5 years. Over half claimed they had learned a great deal about themselves, and about the same percentage felt that psilocybin had changed their lives for the better; 90 percent wanted to take it again. Leary interpreted these figures as tentative proof that he was producing a vitalizing transaction about half the time, which was incredible for a preliminary investigation. Every time they ran a session they learned a little more about the delicate calibration between set, setting, and psilocybin.

But if psilocybin promised to make behavior change a practical reality, it didn't diminish for one instant the mysteriousness of what went on in the vitalizing transaction. "I looked in a mirror and was delighted to see that my skin was dissolving in tiny particles and float-ing away," wrote one female graduate student in her postsession ac-count. "I felt as though my outer shell was disintegrating and the 'essence' of me was being liberated to join the 'essence' of everything else about me . . ." And while these essences were commingling, she was "drifting about in a wondrously beautiful heaven of visual imagery and music . . ."

Another graduate student took a massive dose and lost his mind, which did not strike him as a bad thing to have happen. He felt "cosmi-cally alone" and came to the conclusion that "the only reasonable way to live in the same world was to love . . . love and faith in love keeps us from being cosmically alone."

Now when Leary read through anecdotal material like the above, he tended to underscore words like "essence," "liberated," "beautiful heaven," "cosmically," "love." But when others who weren't involved in the psilocybin project read them, they tended to focus on the govern-ing metaphors, in the first case a presumably level-headed young woman disintegrating, and in the second an equally upstanding young man losing his mind! Those were the sorts of analogy one usually associated with breakdowns, not with attaining mental health. Was Tim? . . . no, impossible. But what about those intense voices and glowing eyes, what about the way the members of the psilocybin proj-ect were always hanging out in a group, either crammed into Leary's ridiculous office or monopolizing a corner of the Social Relations cafete-ria? Of course the members of the psilocybin project saw nothing sinis-ter in the fact that they were always together—"taking the drug is such an overwhelming experience that we soon realized that those of us who had done so had something wonderful in common. We wanted to be together constantly, to share time and space," one later explained. But it struck the rest of the faculty as abnormal: whatever else it was doing, Leary's psilocybin research seemed to be promoting a narcissistic self-absorption, with a tendency toward aggrandizement.

One was either fascinated or repelled. A Social Relations doctoral candidate named Ralph Metzner was fascinated. A graduate of Oxford, Metzner had been in his second year when Leary arrived from Italy, and unlike many of his peers he had been unimpressed with Tim's flights of existential-transactive theory; with his "detached quizzical air" and tennis shoes, Leary was just another absentminded professor to Metzner. But there had been nothing detached about the man who had come back from Mexico. Leary had come back obsessed, true, but it wasn't the usual scientific monomania, the jockeying for tenure, the jealous protection of one's turf. He was urging everyone to try the psilocybin and then lend a hand building a model that would explain the effects it produced in the mind. But even more dramatic, as far as Metzner was concerned, was the way the graduate students were changing. Suddenly all they could talk about was love and sharing, the ecstasy of being alive—topics that were "extremely unusual in the austere and cynical atmosphere of the Center for Personality Research."

Metzner *was* fascinated. But he was also scared of drug addiction. So he did the logical scientific thing: he perused the literature and found, much to his surprise, that there was no evidence of physiological damage or addiction associated with any of the hallucinogens. Then he sought Tim out and offered his mind to the psilocybin project. And was almost refused. Leary thought him "too academic, too dainty-British, too ivory tower." But eventually he relented, perhaps because it occurred to him it might be interesting to measure psilocybin's effect on the famous English reserve. Metzner proved a natural, however.

To the world the alchemists were buffoon chemists looking for a way to turn lead into gold, but that was only the cover story. The real lead that concerned the alchemists was ordinary consciousness, and the gold they sought was the golden brilliance of cosmic consciousness. That's the way it has traditionally been with mystery cults—they're Janus-faced, presenting one image to the world and another to their followers. And that's the way it was with the Harvard psilocybin project. When Ralph Metzner joined in the spring of 1961, he discovered that its air of harmonious scientific purpose was an illusion. Beneath the surface it was difficult to tell whether Tim was running a scientific experiment or starting a cultural revolution—a confusion of aims that was symbolized by the "crashing disagreement over the conduct of the sessions" that had sprung up between Leary and Barron.

To fully appreciate the nature of this disagreement, it is necessary to backtrack to those first weeks after Cuernavaca, when the psilocybin project was still an embryonic gleam in Leary's eye. Some serendipitous and ultimately fateful collisions had occurred during those early weeks. The first was probably Leary's reunion with Litwin, when Litwin had jogged off to get his copies of Huxley's psychedelic essays. The sense of recognition, when Tim finally dipped into them, had been profound: here was a man who knew exactly what it was like to travel through the Other World. And then someone at a cocktail party had mentioned that Huxley was spending the semester at MIT, as the Centennial Carnegie Visiting Professor in Humanities, a title almost as big as his fee—nine thousand dollars for nine weeks' work.

Leary sat down and wrote Huxley a letter about being bemushroomed in Mexico, and the project he was setting up to study the therapeutic effects of psilocybin. He was rewarded almost immediately with an excited phone call and an invitation to lunch.

The fall of 1960 was an equivocal time for Aldous Huxley. His lectures on visionary experience were jammed. And not just by students. The public ones at night caused traffic problems more appropriate for the Harvard-Yale game. Huston Smith, who taught religion at MIT, considered it the crowning moment of Huxley's career as a public philosopher. Huxley was less sanguine. For twenty-five years, ever since he had joined Gerald Heard in support of Dick Shepperton's Peace Union, he had been chipping away at his loathing for the public soapbox; in the last twenty years he had addressed everyone from rotarians to nuclear scientists; so by the time he reached MIT he was in top oratorical form. But he found he had little to say. "It's a bit embarrassing," he confided to Huston Smith, "to have been concerned with the human problem all one's life and find at the end that one has no more to offer by way of advice than 'Try to be a little kinder.'"

It was the sort of gentle resignation one might expect from a man who had recently been diagnosed as having cancer of the throat.

Health problems, which he blamed on his stringbean lack of robustness, had always been a complication of Huxley's life; his letters are peppered with self-mocking references to his hypochondria, his blindness, his lack of stamina. But cancer was Maria's disease, there was a finality to it, which may be why Aldous told no one except Humphrey Osmond, whom he swore to secrecy.

With death on his mind, Huxley redoubled his efforts on his recalcitrant utopian novel, which now bore the working title *Island*. Every morning he wrestled with the literary problem of how to portray a psychedelic utopia without boring the reader. "It may be that the job is one which cannot be accomplished with complete success," he confessed to his son. "In point of fact, it hasn't been accomplished in the past. For most Utopian books have been exceedingly didactic and expository. I am trying to lighten up the exposition by putting it into dialogue form, which I make as lively as possible. But meanwhile I am always haunted by the feeling that, if only I had enough talent, I could somehow poeticize and dramatize all this intellectual material."

It was a losing battle. Despite his best efforts, *Island* was becoming a thinly fictionalized anthology of final thoughts on topics that had occupied Huxley for forty years: on education, psychology, metaphysics; on the place of art and creativity in life, and the role of psychedelics in exploring the mind's potential. To dramatize this last theme, he had invented a new mind drug, which he called moksha, "the reality revealer, the truth and beauty pill."

His utopian islanders, the Palanese, used moksha in a carefully modulated system of psychedelic education. Children took the drug once a year, beginning in adolescence and continuing into adulthood. Great stress was laid upon the use one made of these visits to the Other World. "For a while, thanks to the moksha-medicine, you will know what it's like to be what in fact you always have been," Huxley's doppelganger, Dr. Roberts, tells a class of Palanese children who are awaiting their first dose of moksha. "What a timeless bliss!"

> But like everything else . . . it will pass. And when it has passed, what will you do with the experience? What will you do with all the other similar experiences that the moksha-medicine will bring in the years to come? Will you merely enjoy them as you would enjoy an evening at the puppet show, and then go back to business as usual, back behaving like the silly little delinquents you imagine yourselves to be? Or, having glimpsed, will you devote your lives to the business, not at all unusual, of being what you are in fact . . . All that the moksha-medicine can do is to give you a succession of beatific glimpses, an hour or two, every now and then, of enlightening and liberating grace. It remains for you to decide whether you'll cooperate with grace and take those opportunities.

For Huxley, Tim Leary was like a strong breeze in a sail that had started to sag. His enthusiasm, his theoretical orientation, and most of all his connection with Harvard, made him the perfect man to advance Aldous's psychedelic scenario. One night when they were lying in front of the fire at the Newton house, having taken psilocybin, the conversation turned to the proper way to introduce the concept of mind expansion to a culture of organization men. It wasn't something Aldous had to think twice about: turn on the elites, he urged Leary. The artistic elite, the intellectual elite, the economic elite. "That's how everything of culture and beauty and philosophic freedom has been passed on." Use Harvard's prestige to artfully spread the word about these mind-changers. But do it shrewdly and cautiously, always staying within the medical model. "You must expect opposition," Aldous cautioned. "There are people in this society who will do everything within their considerable power to stop our research."

It didn't take much to win Tim over. Like the Palanese, his own encounter with the moksha medicine had made it impossible for him to return to the limited world of academic psychology. He was ripe for something Big, and Huxley's vision, delivered in that wonderfully ironic Oxonian accent, was nothing if not Big: turn on the Best and the Brightest and transform the world! What was, from one angle, a research project into personality and creativity, quickly became, from another perspective, "a pretty good cover for giving drugs to rather famous writers and painters . . . if someone turned up on the doorstep who had written speeches for FDR, he would most likely be invited for a session."

It was an exhilarating feeling to think one might be playing a crucial role in the evolution of the species, a giddy feeling that intensified as the various members of the Huxley circle made their way to

Harvard. "Our project was being contacted and visited by many from this extraordinary network of prominent people, all aware of the potency of Harvard's name," Leary recalled. "The message was clear. Let's keep this knowledge to ourselves. Don't go public or you'll bring down the wrath of the custodians of society."

Gerald Heard stopped by and entertained with a typical Gerald dissertation on the role of drugs in the ancient mystery cults. Following the meandering river of his voice, the graduate students found themselves back in ancient Greece, joining the Athenian elect as they were inducted into the Eleusinian mysteries. And then they were shot forward to the present, which was a new age according to Gerald, a psychological age when *Homo sapiens* would finally figure out what they really were. "They are mines of energy," Heard said. "They are unfinished." Figuring out how to tap those energy fields, how to finish the human masterpiece, that would be the responsibility of the young men of the psilocybin project.

Heard called them intranauts, as opposed to the astronauts of the Mercury space program. And like the investigation of outer space, inner space had its own rigors. "A training is necessary," he stressed. "One has to know the kind of country one is going through, one has to take the kind of supplies, the rations which are necessary, and one has to have the health and the resistances which are necessary to probe through into a world with which we are not wholly familiar."

"We know this is worthwhile doing. This is the future of the human race."

At the other end of the spectrum, but equally compelling, was Al Hubbard. Hubbard came bouncing into Boston with his leather bag and told Leary: "Timothy, you are the key figure; I'm just old deputy dog Al at your service."

Even Humphrey Osmond put in an appearance, arriving in November to attend a psychiatric conference, and joining Aldous and Tim for dinner. After Leary had left, Huxley had pronounced him a capital fellow and predicted that the Harvard connection would do wonders for psychedelics. Osmond, reflecting upon Tim's formal tweeds and short hair, had agreed that the professor was a very nice chap, but didn't Aldous think he was a little bit of a square? "You may be right," Huxley had replied. "Isn't that, after all, what we want?"

Years later Osmond was still telling this anecdote as an illustration of just how wrong these two students of the human temperament could be. It was immediately clear to Alan Watts, when he met Leary a few months later in New York City, that Huxley had completely misread Leary's character. From the "detached and scholarly flavor of Aldous's account of his work," Watts had expected a serious and rather pedantic scientist, "but the man I first met in a New York restaurant was an extremely charming Irishman who wore a hearing aid as stylishly as if it had been a monocle." Watts recognized a kindred spirit.

So it was probably inevitable that Tim, the champion of cultural hybrids, would rebel against the policy of reserving the psychedelic experience for an elite. But it was Osmond, ironically, who precipitated his change of heart. Osmond's main reason for coming to Boston had been to attend a symposium sponsored by GAP—the Group for the Advancement of Psychiatry. GAP symposiums were liberal and topical, having debated in the past such trenchant issues as the Negro crime problem and the immigrant assimilation problem. This year, 1960, they had trained their sights on the beatnik problem, and among those invited to address the psychiatrists was Allen Ginsberg, who was just back from South America, where he had retraced Burroughs's route in search of the visionary vine *ayahuasca*.

Ginsberg had wondered what the psychiatrists would say about his drug-induced poetry, so he treated them to renditions of "Laughing Gas," "Mescaline," and "Lysergic Acid." The reaction was depressing. While a few of the older analysts had been intrigued—reflecting, perhaps, their upbringing in the golden age of Freud and Jung, when it was still possible to explore mental phenomena without a lot of dogmatic baggage—the younger ones had dismissed him as crazy, possibly schizophrenic, certainly psychopathic—the whole "conform or else" litany. Among the intrigued, however, was Osmond, who, perhaps thinking to extend Ginsberg's poetic oeuvre, suggested he might want to contact a Harvard psychologist by the name of Timothy Leary, and try psilocybin.

Allen Ginsberg descended on the Psilocybin Project like a visitation from Leary's personal unconscious. Here was a bonafide arrogant disdainer, "the secretary-general of the world's poets, beatniks, anarchists, socialists, free-sex/love cultists," as Tim affectionately described him. He arrived with his lover, Peter Orlovsky, and with the light bouncing off his black-rimmed glasses, over introductory tea, he began describing his recent cosmic adventures in the Peruvian jungle. He told of spending the month of June in the village of Pucallpa, attending all-night sessions with a *curandero*, "a very mild and simple seeming cat of 38 or so," drinking a mixture of *ayahuasca* and the leaf of a local plant, mescla. The effect was devastating—"the strongest and worst I've ever had," Ginsberg had written to Burroughs. A classic Dark Night of the Soul, with snakes writhing across his body and Death, "that single mysterious Thing which was our fate and was sooner or later going to kill us," making an appearance. And not just some abstract nothingness kind of death, but a powerful, vital Death that covered him like a heavy blanket. And it had been clear that he could die right there, just turn off the body/mind circuit, no more rotting old Ginsberg. But then he had flashed on the grief his friends would feel; that had pulled him back; he had chosen to live.

It was a powerful story, full of the sort of heroic adventuring Leary craved. And full of confirmation. Ever since Mexico, and Braun's Aztec tales of *teonanacatl*, Leary had harbored the suspicion that it was the shamans and mystics of the world who knew how to use these drugs, and not the psychologists. That simple seeming cat had been a maestro of set and setting! We should be setting up seminars with wise old Indian medicine men and mystical Tibetans. Leary felt this in his bones, yet he accepted Huxley's and Barron's argument that staying within the accepted medical model was crucial. But listening to Ginsberg it was borne home to him (yet again) just how culture-bound Western science was. It was all so frustrating, so beside the point . . .

Ginsberg and Orlovsky took the psilocybin the next day. Leary made them comfortable in an upstairs bedroom and then retired to the study to talk with Barron. Both expected a replay of the quiet, contemplative sessions that had become the norm. So they were unprepared when the study door banged open, and two naked poets danced in. "I'm the messiah," Ginsberg announced to the startled professors. "I've come down to preach love to the world. We're going to walk through the streets and teach people to stop hating." Barron went and drew the shades.

Persuaded that this was not the best moment to march naked through the streets of Newton preaching love, Ginsberg decided to telephone Kennedy and Khruschev and "settle all this about the Bomb once and for all." But he was unable to get the two most powerful men in the world on the phone, and had to settle for Jack Kerouac, who was suffering through a boozy retirement in a village on Long Island's north shore. After a lengthy argument that had an anxious Leary mentally totaling his next phone bill, Kerouac had agreed to donate his research services to the psilocybin project. The whole afternoon had been like that, one crazy funny scene after another. Graduate students dropped by to chat and found the house filled with hairy naked people, laughing and kissing. Even the most liberal were scandalized. Tim loved it; he had been in danger of becoming solemn.

By midweek the Social Relations department was buzzing with bowdlerized versions of Tim's beatnik drug orgy. Colleagues who had heretofore been ignorant of his earthly existence looked up from their research protocols and wondered, briefly, whether this psilocybin thing of Leary's was really the sort of research Harvard should be involved in. There was a feeling, not really articulated but certainly there, that Leary had crossed some crucial line.

Which, in a way, he had. As the psilocybin wore off, everyone had gathered in the kitchen, and with Tim bustling around pouring hot milk into cups, Ginsberg had proposed an alternative psychedelic scenario:

> Allen, the quintessential egalitarian, wanted everyone to have the option of taking mind-expanding drugs. It was the fifth freedom— the right to manage your own nervous system. The Grand Plan seemed quite logical. First we would initiate and train influential Americans in consciousness expansion. They would help us generate a wave of public opinion to support massive research programs, licensing procedures, training centers in the intelligent use of drugs.

Sipping his hot milk, Leary realized that Huxley's way was not his. "It was at this moment," he later wrote, "that we rejected Huxley's elitist perspective and adopted the American open-to-the-public approach." Ginsberg had further awakened the rebel within Tim.

Ginsberg's own recollection of the weekend, while considerably less apocalyptic, offers a nice cameo of Leary, who struck the Beat poet as a basically nice but naive scientist. "Like he had no idea that every poet in San Francisco had lived with Indians and taken peyote and mescaline long ago. Or that everybody was smoking pot. He'd never smoked pot . . . Leary had this big beautiful house, and everybody there was wandering around like it was some happy cocktail party, which was a little shocking to me at first because I still thought of myself as a big, serious religious meditator. And they were all so cheerful and optimistic and convinced that their kind of experiment would be welcomed as a polite, scholarly, socially acceptable, perfectly reasonable pursuit and would spread through the university and be automatically taken on as part of the curriculum. Like Leary couldn't conceive of meeting any academic opposition. I kept saying, 'You have no idea what you're going to meet, what you're up against,' but he was already thinking in terms of, 'We'll turn on Schlesinger and then we'll turn on Kennedy'—in terms like that. So I wanted to calm him down a little, and I said, 'Why not begin by turning artists on?' "

But the weekend chez Leary did confirm one of Ginsberg's pet intuitions: everybody was becoming hip. "Something big is happening consciously to consciousness," he told an interviewer a few weeks later. And at the center of this change were the new "wisdom drugs," which were responsible for an emerging spirituality that, as Huxley had predicted, was also a revolution. "People are beginning to see that the Kingdom of Heaven is within them, instead of thinking it's outside, up in the sky and that it can't be here on earth," Ginsberg said. "It's time to seize power in the Universe, that's what I say—that's my political statement. Time to seize power over the entire Universe. Not merely over Russia or America—seize power over the moon—take the sun over."

Ginsberg began promoting Leary's psilocybin project with the same application he had once brought to the unpublished manuscripts of his friends. "I spoke to Willem de Kooning yesterday," he wrote in January 1961, "and he was ready to swing, too, so please drop him an invitation. I figure Kline, de Kooning, and [Dizzy] Gillespie are the most impressive trio imaginable for you to turn on at the moment, so will leave it at that for a while, till they can be taken care of."

Leary began weekending in New York. He gave psilocybin to Jack Kerouac, who came away with the enigmatic, "walking on water wasn't built in a day." Robert Lowell took a small dose and concluded *"amor vincit omnia."* Dizzy Gillespie tried it, then ordered enough for his entire band. A supply was dispatched to Burroughs in Tangier. This was a potentially rich alliance for Leary, since Burroughs had a much more scientific approach to drugs than either Ginsberg or Kerouac, and was working on a theory of neurological geography that divided the cortex into heavenly and diabolical areas. "My work and understanding benefits from Hallucinogens MEASURABLY," he wrote Tim. "Wider use of these drugs would lead to better work conditions on all levels. Might be interesting to gather anthology of mushroom writings. I will be glad to send along my results." (Later he sent a warning about DMT, which a friend of his had synthesized. Like Oscar Janiger and Watts, Burroughs had been overpowered by DMT. It was like "fire through the blood," he warned, plunging one into the diabolical latitudes.)

Leary's entanglement with the Beats ultimately produced mixed results. Ginsberg, after lining up dozens of prospective research subjects, decamped to Paris in the spring of 1961, where he was being considered for the editorship of a "big-time sexual magazine." The salaries would be "vast," he wrote Tim; they would be able "to print anything mad we want." But Orlovsky was lobbying for India, and Allen was torn between pursuing the ancient heavenly connection or the possibility of a real job. His letter concluded with a plea for more mushrooms. "I am looking for French connection, no success yet but have not looked extensively. Can use all you can send." Leary later rendezvoused with Ginsberg in Tangier in the summer of 1961, for a hash-dazed tour of the Casbah. But after that Allen was gone, vanished into the Orient on an inward journey that would climax in *satori* on a train traveling between Kyoto and Tokyo.

As for Jack Kerouac, whatever he was looking for he didn't find it in the Other World, or in this one. Fame had not proved an unguent for his problems. Indeed, it only exacerbated them. The reading public regularly confused Jack with Dean Moriarity, his Cassady-like creation; they expected him to be the high-octane hipster, not this alcoholic manic depressive who was given to interminable boasting. "I'm king of the beatniks!" he had roared at Leary when Tim had arrived with the psilocybin. "I'm François Villon, vagabond poet-rogue of the open highway. Listen while I play you hot-lick spiral improvisations from my tenor typewriter." But the fact was the tenor typewriter was silent, and had been for months. Leary found it depressing. It was his first bad trip. Later, when he asked Kerouac if he could publish a report of the session, Jack refused, although it would still be some time before he began comparing psychedelics with communist brainwashing.

A similar contretemps occurred with Burroughs, whom Leary first met in Tangier with Ginsberg. Burroughs appeared with Leary on an APA panel on psychedelics in the fall of 1961, and then spent a few weeks at the Newton house, never removing his fedora, inhaling gin and tonics and exhaling a mordant commentary that mocked the lovey-dovey softness of the psilocybin project. "He left silently without farewell," Leary wrote in *High Priest.* "And then rumor drifted up like damp smoke from New York that he had published a no-thank-you letter denouncing the Harvard psychedelics."

The letter parodied Leary's claims for psilocybin: "Listen to us. We are serving the garden of delights immortality cosmic consciousness the best ever in drug kicks. And love love love in slop buckets." But what they were really offering, Burroughs wrote, was a "terminal sewer."

In the end it didn't matter. Through Ginsberg Leary was introduced into that curious milieu wherein wealth and avant garde art find each other mutually amusing; a psilocybin weekend at Newton became the in thing to do among the New York jet set. Michael Kahn remembers being "absolutely dazzled" the first time he dropped by the house and found it filled with these larger than life creatures. "I'd never seen women that kind of tough, hard, beautiful, and I'd never seen that kind of casual dyke scene that a lot of those girls were into, sort of exciting to me and very mysterious." For Tim, who preferred the brassiest big city girl on the block, it was heaven. More than once he found himself on the receiving end of declarations of undying love, an aphrodisiacal byproduct of the psilocybin that everyone who used psychedelics was aware of, but one that was seldom mentioned. "I strongly urge you not to let the sexual cat out of the bag," Huxley cautioned. "We've stirred up enough trouble suggesting that drugs can stimulate aesthetic and religious experiences."

But the lush life was tempting. One weekend a woman named Flo Ferguson arrived to try the psilocybin, and when her session was over she drew Tim aside and invited him to spend a weekend at her house. "I could arrange experiments with some interesting subjects," she said. "And show you what life is like in the first class lounge."

Flora Lu "Flo" Ferguson was the wife of big-band leader Maynard Ferguson, and like Mabel Dodge before her she was one of those women whose genius expresses itself in the organization of a salon. Artists, philosophers, scientists, the bohemian rich—Flora Lu Ferguson made it her business to invite the most incandescent minds around to her house in the shady Westchester suburb of Bronxville. And what a house. It was a large, roomy Tudor completely filled with wood panelling, rich carpets, abstract paintings. There was an enormous stone fireplace in the living room and a whole wall full of recording equipment with tens of thousands of records. Upstairs the sheets were silk, the floors fur covered. Walking into that house, Leary later claimed, was his first introduction to "hedonic consciousness . . . pleasure as a way of life." And he loved it.

But it also involved him in a number of balancing acts, not least of which was his prohibition of marijuana. One day Michael Kahn was at Tim's house with a bunch of the beautiful people when someone pulled out a bag of marijuana and began to roll joints. An obviously agitated Leary ordered that the bag be put away. "Dave McClelland has been a loyal and good friend to me," he said. "And I'm not going to get busted out here with a lot of people smoking grass and violate my contract with him. Psilocybin is legal in this house. Everybody knows I've got it. I get it from Sandoz. I'm doing a research project. Grass is against the law. I'm not going to get busted and do that to him." Everyone was astonished at this outburst; Gunther Weil thought it was the first time he had ever seen Tim lose his cool.

But could you truthfully call it a research project? With so many people dropping by to take the drug—vital people in terms of the Grand Plan—science tended to get lost in the glamorous shuffle. For a while Leary drove himself crazy trying to make sure that everyone filled out a set and setting questionnaire and took a Personality test or two, but then he gave up. Most weekends everyone in the house was beyond the Door, both researchers and subjects. Which wasn't a unique situation as far as the psychedelic research community went, although it certainly would have raised eyebrows back at 5 Divinity Avenue. Early on, researchers had discovered that communication improved if both people were at least partway into the Other World; Osmond's group in Canada had gotten so they could function perfectly fine on 100 milligrams of LSD. But no one, anywhere, had a research program quite like Leary's; with all the dazzle and excitement of those exotic weekends, it was understandable that some of the finer points of scientific method got overlooked.

But science was still one of Leary's main motivations. He really did want to know what was happening beyond the Door, in the Other World. He had a theory, of course, one that owed equal debts to Huxley, transactional analysis, and the fact that the Harvard psychology department had just purchased its first computer—its first artificial mind. From Huxley he borrowed the "reducing valve" analogy that had the brain screening out the millions of messages that arrived every second. But from there he modified Huxley to fit his own theoretical vocabulary:

> Let's assume that the cortex, the seat of consciousness is a millionfold network of neurons. A fantastic computing machine. Cultural learning has imposed a few pitifully small programs on the cortex. These programs may activate perhaps one-hundredth of the potential neural connections. All the learned games of life can be seen as programs which select, censor, alert and thus drastically limit the available cortical response. The consciousness-expanding drugs unplug these narrow programs. They unplug the ego, the game machinery, and the mind (that cluster of game concepts). And with the ego and mind unplugged, what is left? . . . What is left is something Western culture knows little about. The open brain. The uncensored cortex, alert and open to a broad sweep of internal and external stimuli hitherto screened out.

So if that was theory, then ask yourself what would happen if you began to disconnect the game structure of Western culture? What would happen if you began to systematically unplug the egos of America? These were the questions Leary was asking himself, and the answer he arrived at was that whatever happened, it would be for the best. It was time to unplug the old mind of *Homo sapiens,* so a new one could take shape. This was the psilocybin project's hidden agenda, and the odd thing about it was that it seemed to come from a higher level of consciousness, a higher power. "We began to see ourselves as unwitting agents of a social process that was far too powerful for us to control or more than dimly understand," was the way Leary described the sensation. "A historical movement that would inevitably change man at the very center of his nature, his consciousness."

They had glimpsed the future, and it was themselves.

The role of unwitting social agent, however, didn't appeal to Frank Barron, who was alarmed by the way his friend was consuming psilocybin. By March of 1961, Leary had taken the drug fifty-two times, which factored out to a little less than once every three days. And the more he took the drug the less concerned he was in dotting the scientific *i*'s and crossing the experimental *t*'s. Which was a tactical mistake as far as Barron was concerned; he agreed with Huxley that one shouldn't needlessly create trouble by scorning the accepted scientific models. He also, if pressed, favored Huxley's elitist perspective over the democratic visions of Ginsberg and Tim. Their differences became obvious whenever they argued about nuclear disarmament, a political cause that Barron was particularly passionate about. It was his position that the Bomb had been made by an elite and it would take an elite to unmake it, albeit one with a fundamentally altered consciousness, which was where psychedelics came in. But Tim disagreed. America's nuclear madness was a symptom of the elite's quest for power: to truly remake a society you would have to begin from the bottom up. Which meant everyone should have the right to take psychedelics. But what about the casualties, Barron always protested. "A weakened ego, forced to drop all its defenses suddenly, would shatter." To which Tim usually replied that everyone had the right to go out of their mind, to have a psychosis, if that was their future.

It was, Barron later decided, a species of military thinking. Leary was arguing that it was foolish to quibble over a few lost souls when the stakes were the literal salvation of the world. But Barron was unwilling to take that kind of responsibility, and he began to distance himself from the psilocybin project.

His place as senior advisor to the project was filled by an up and coming member of the psychology department named Richard Alpert. Alpert took his first psilocybin in early March 1961, on the night of the winter's worst blizzard. At five the next morning he trudged the several miles through the snow to his parents' house. Grabbing a shovel, he began clearing a path to their door, which woke them up. Rushing to the window, they peered down at their son, the Harvard professor, laughing and flinging shovelfuls of snow into the air.

"Come to bed, you idiot! Nobody shovels snow at five in the morning."

It was his mother. Raising the shovel above his head, he danced a little jig and then went back to shoveling. It's okay to shovel snow, he thought, and it's okay to be happy.

Those transforming pink pills had claimed another.

When Richard Alpert was a teenager he wore double Z pants with balloon seats. He was an extremely fat kid and at Williston, the Massachusetts private school he attended, the seniors used to tease him mercilessly. He was bookish, bad at sports, Jewish. Once he was caught wrestling with another boy and word went around that he was queer. Ostracized by most of his classmates, it had seemed for a time that he might leap from the roof of one of Williston's dormitories. Instead he became a grind, one of those compulsive fourteen-year-old intellectuals who has read all of Dostoevsky and who plans to become a brain surgeon.

"Until you know a Jewish middle-class, upwardly mobile, anxiety-ridden neurotic," Alpert wrote years later, "you haven't met a real achiever."

He got that from his father, who started life as the son of an immigrant junk dealer in Boston's West End. George Alpert's passport was education—first Boston University, then law school. By the time Richard, the third of his sons, was born in 1928, George Alpert had become wealthy by speculating in railroads and real estate. Weekends and vacations were spent on a 190-acre New Hampshire farm, a portion of which had been converted into a three-hole golf course. A temple trustee and a founder of Brandeis University, George Alpert was also influential in Boston's Jewish community, although his Judaism tended to be social rather than spiritual. If he believed in anything, it was the sanctity of a professional career, and he encouraged his sons to become doctors and lawyers. He showered them with reinforcements, giving Richard a biography of the Mayo Brothers for his Bar Mitzvah.

Like a lot of youngest sons, Alpert was particularly close to his mother, who wanted more than anything else for her son to go to Harvard. But Harvard rejected Alpert and he was forced to enroll at Tufts, in nearby Medford, where he embarked on a rigorous program of self-improvement. He dieted and exercised until the fat preppy became boyishly handsome. He made a rigorous study of wine and antiques, and he began spending vacations in Hemingwayesque pursuits, motorcycling in New England, scuba diving in the Caribbean. As his self-esteem increased, so did his sex life: Alpert was furtively bisexual.

The only sour note during this period were his grades. Deciding he had no chance of being accepted at any of the top medical schools, he decided to pursue graduate work, a decision that was strenuously opposed by his father, who refused to pay for anything but medical school. No doubt this wasn't the first clash of wills between Alpert and his father, but it was probably the first time that young Richard emerged the victor. On his own he had applied for and received a research assistantship in psychology at Wesleyan University. And the man responsible for this assistantship, the chairman of Wesleyan's psychology department, was Dr. David McClelland.

Over the years McClelland would spend considerable time pondering the personality of this "charming, intelligent, witty" young man who had become first his protégé, then his very good friend. Early on in their relationship Alpert struck McClelland as being "unusually sensitive to the opinion of others, he generally tried to please people and make them happy." And he was a natural nuturer—what Alpert always referred to as his Jewish-mother condition. When McClelland's twin sons were born, he asked Alpert to be their godfather, and Alpert turned out to be a wonderful one: "It gave him great pleasure to provide them with new and wonderful experiences, to take them up to his family farm where they could tear around the lake in his speedboat or play the slot machines all night long; or he would give them a ride in his airplane and land on the fairway of the Alpert private golf course."

Alpert went to Stanford for his doctorate. He spent long hours in the library carrels, mastering Freudian theory and motivation, which was one of his specialties. For his thesis he chose academic anxiety and devised a test capable of predicting whether a student was the sort of personality that thrived on exams regardless of preparation, or whether he belonged to the camp that broke out in a cold sweat and could barely remember his own name. If you guessed that Alpert belonged to the latter category, you'd be right. Despite his academic success, he felt like a fraud, particularly when he began working as a therapist at the Stanford Health Service (where his very first patient, a kid named Vic Lovell, turned him on to marijuana). But he liked the image, and he became a fixture at the wilder Stanford parties, siouched in the corner, listening to the inevitable jazz, feeling a little superior, "the shrink."

George Alpert had become president of the New Haven Railroad while Richard was still at Stanford. When the railroad encountered financial difficulties, he turned to his youngest son for advice. Alpert began flying to New York to attend corporate meetings. It was his first taste of real power—"in Palo Alto I had a job buying coffee cups for the student lounge, in New York I was advising my father on deals worth millions"—and it was sufficiently alluring for him to consider abandoning psychology for business. What changed his mind was an invitation from David McClelland to join him at his new post, which was director of Harvard's Center for Research in Personality. It was a dream come true, at least for Alpert's mother.

Harvard was a paradise after the cramped graduate cubicles of Stanford. Alpert had a corner office with windows overlooking Divinity Avenue, plus two secretaries to handle his correspondence. He surprised himself by becoming a popular lecturer, and before too long there was a small platoon of graduate students eager to handle the tedious aspects of his research projects. He got on well with his colleagues, particularly McClelland, and within three years held appointments in four Harvard departments. He wasn't even thirty.

Most of Alpert's colleagues attributed his swift rise less to an ability to do original work, than to an almost uncanny skill in the academic bureaucracy game; he was exactly the sort of smart professor-politician who ended up department chairman, or even dean. And he knew it. "I wasn't a genuine scholar but I had gone through the whole academic trip," he later wrote. "I had gotten my Ph.D; I was writing books. I had research contracts . . . I was living the way a successful bachelor professor is supposed to live in the America of 'he who makes it.'" He drove around Cambridge in a Mercedes sedan when he wasn't out for a spin on his Triumph motorcycle or cruising the Eastern seaboard in his

Cessna. He had an antique-filled apartment where he "gave very charming dinner parties."

And underneath he was disintegrating.

Whenever he lectured he got diarrhea. He was drinking heavily and his sex life, when he had a sex life, was a sham. His sporadic attempts at heterosexuality only confirmed what he had suspected since his classmates at Williston had called him a queer: he preferred men. Although he concealed his growing despair behind a convivial facade, a curious double bind was developing: craving affection and approval, Alpert felt angry whenever these were given. You like me, went his logic, but you like a me that isn't me. On top of this he was becoming increasingly skeptical about the profession of psychology: "All the stuff I was teaching was just like little molecular bits of stuff but they didn't add up to a feeling of anything like wisdom. I was just getting more knowledgeable. And I was getting very good at bouncing three knowledge balls at once. I could sit in a doctoral exam, ask very sophisticated questions and look terribly wise. It was a hustle."

Part of the problem was analysis. Alpert had been in psychotherapy since Williston. His analyst, during his five years at Stanford, had collected close to twenty-six thousand dollars in fees, and when he learned Alpert was bound for Harvard, he urged him to find a new therapist as soon as possible. "You're too sick to leave analysis," he had said.

If a dozen years of analysis had not helped him, how could he possibly hope to help others?

This was Alpert's mood when he returned to Harvard in the fall of 1959. Entering 5 Divinity Avenue for the first time, he noticed that one of the closets had been converted into an office. The place was ridiculous—barely big enough for a desk and bookshelves—and it was occupied by this trim, tanned guy with a bright grin who was studying a map of Europe. "I'm just back from Europe," Tim Leary had said to him, "where I spent a lot of time bouncing checks."

"He was capable of taking wild risks in his thinking," was the way Alpert later explained the powerful attraction he had felt for Tim; hanging around with him restored Alpert's enthusiasm for psychology. Leary, for his part, considered Alpert an "ambitious, academic-politician—engaging, witty, a big tail-wagging puppy dog." But he also intuited that, like himself, Alpert was an outsider. His homosexuality, combined with his Jewishness, gave him "that precious alien perspective." They became frequent drinking companions and co-taught a course in existential psychology, and when it came time for summer vacation, Leary suggested they fly Alpert's Cessna to Mexico and points south. But Alpert had to lecture at Stanford during the early part of the summer, so the plan was revised to have him rendezvous with Tim in Cuernavaca, and go adventuring from there.

But the aerial tour had been scrapped. Alpert had landed a few days after Tim had been bemushroomed, and all his risky-thinking friend could talk about was getting back to Harvard and getting to work. Since Alpert had contracted to spend the fall semester at Stanford, there was nothing for him to do but listen to Tim rhapsodize about devolving back to the primordial soup. The whole thing reminded him of the few times he had smoked marijuana.

How wrong he had been, he discovered that first night at Newton. The crucial moment of Alpert's session happened when he was sitting all alone on a couch and suddenly a curtain in his mind whisked open to reveal a vaudeville comedy act. Alpert the professor came out in cap and gown, mouthing profundities, followed by Alpert the social cosmopolite, Alpert the airplane pilot, Alpert the lover, and Alpert the little boy who had wanted to please his parents by becoming a brain surgeon. One by one they appeared, then vanished. It was like riffling through a deck of cards at high speed and at first Alpert had been amused. "I worked hard to get that status but I don't really need it," he'd thought as the professor swished off. But then he started to panic. If all his roles disappeared, what would be left?

The answer, when the last shreds of his ego had vanished, was his body. At least I've got my body, Alpert thought. I can always get a new identity. But then his body vanished. Alpert knew this because there was a mirror on the far wall and whenever he snuck a look at it the couch was empty! *What if his body never returned?* A simple enough question when you read it on a page like this, but when it flashed through Alpert's mind it triggered the most intense adrenalin rush he had ever experienced. He opened his mouth to scream, but just as the howl was about to burst from his lungs, this soft, pleasant voice inside his head asked, "who's minding the store?" And like magic the scream died, the adrenalin rush bursting like a soap bubble. *If his self had disappeared, and even his body, then where was that voice coming from?*

> When I could finally focus on the question, I realized that although everything by which I knew myself, even my body and this life itself, was gone, still I was fully aware! Instantly with this recognition I felt a new kind of calmness—one of a profundity never experienced before. I had just found that "I", that scanning device—that point—that essence—that place beyond.

Laughing happily, he dashed outside into the snowstorm.

"We made a straight out deal," Leary had said of Alpert's role in the psilocybin project. "He said, 'Listen, I'm better at handling the outside world, let me do that and I'll protect you.' That was a very explicit contract we made. And he was incredible at it. I can remember staff conferences where we'd be kind of sitting around and he would walk in and have a list in his pocket of the agenda or of the students he thought we should work with. He was like our majority whip."

Alpert worked hard. On weekends they climbed into his Cessna and sailed off as far as North Carolina, where they ran some sessions for J. B. Rhine's parapsychology institute at Duke. But their usual destination was New York, where they participated in a series of cock-tail parties designed to explain the possibilities of mind expansion to selected intellectuals, artists, and socialites. Of all the socially promi-nent people that they met during these months, the most important, in terms of our story, was Peggy Hitchcock, the artistically inclined twenty-eight-year-old jet-setting heir of the Mellon millions. Peggy, as Leary later wrote, "was easily bored, intellectually ambitious, and look-ing for a project capable of absorbing her whirlwind energy." Mind expansion fit the bill and she joined Flo Ferguson as the unofficial patronesses of the psilocybin project.

Ironically, in the midst of this social whirl, Leary dreamed up an experiment that actually had the potential of proving his contention that psilocybin was a powerful behavior-change tool. One day, purely by chance, he noticed a flyer from the Massachusetts Department of Corrections soliciting psychology interns to work in the prisons—a request that routinely provoked little response, prison psychology being comparable, in terms of prestige, to working in a leper colony. Leary contacted the Massachusetts Department of Corrections and invited the appropriate officials to lunch at the Harvard Faculty Club. There he made his proposal: clear up the red tape involved in giving convicts drugs and he would supply more graduate students than they could handle. A week later he was on his way to Concord State Prison.

The beauty of the prison project was this: where else could you find an environment of such experimental cleanliness, with limited varia-bles, rigidly defined roles and, the coup de grâce, a statistical measure of just how dismal the current rehabilitative techniques really were: the recidivism rate in the Massachusetts prison system was running close to 70 percent. Using psilocybin, Leary told the prison officials, he could cut that rate. Privately, to his grad students, he joked, "Let's see if we can turn the criminals into Buddhas."

Taking psilocybin at Newton had been one thing, but ingesting it with a bunch of hardened criminals in a locked room in the prison infirmary was quite another. The prison psychiatrist had cheerfully provided Leary with a cross-section of criminal types: two murderers, two armed robbers, an embezzler, and a heroin addict. They reminded Metzner of "big cats in a zoo," the way they glided nervously around the room. The psilocybin was in a bowl on the table. Leary took six of the pink pellets and passed the bowl to one of the cons. The man hesitated and then downed six of his own. The arrangement was that Leary would guide a session for three of the men in the morning, to be followed by Metzner, Gunther Weil, and three others in the afternoon.

As the drug took hold ("the loosening of thought, the humming pressure in my head, the sharp, brilliant, and then brutal intensification of the senses") Leary began to feel dreadful. "Why is that, doc?" asked one of the prisoners. "Because I'm afraid of you," Leary finally admitted. The man started laughing. "Well that's funny, doc," he said, "because I'm afraid of you." "Why are you afraid of me," Leary asked. "Because you're a fucking mad scientist," came the answer, which started everyone laughing, and broke the ice.

As the prison gates clanged shut behind them that evening, it was hard not to whoop and yell. "We had put our faith in human nature and the drug experience on the line," Leary later said. "A bit of pagan magic had occurred. . . . It was a heroic moment in our lives."

After that they were back at Concord several times a week, sometimes just to talk, other times bringing personality tests whose rationale had to be patiently explained to the suspicious inmates. And every few weeks they ran another session. The changes, whether measured by the tests or simply by their own perceptions, were dramatic. Within a month these hardened convicts were talking about love and ecstasy and sharing, concepts that were as rare at Concord prison as they once had been at the Center for Personality Research.

Word began to spread that there was a weird shrink thing going on in the infirmary that could get you off work duty. One day two of Concord's biggest and meanest cons cornered Leary and announced they were joining the project. The others were dismayed. These guys were fearsome presences in the prison power hierarchy, they warned Tim; ignoring them could be dangerous, but including them would ruin the project's increasingly spiritual tone. Tim listened to their concerns, and then pointed out that before these guys could join the group, they were going to have to take psilocybin. As the implications of this sank in, the other inmates began to smile, then laugh.

Imagine the Humphrey Bogart of *Angels with Dirty Faces* suddenly transported into *Alice in Wonderland* and you will have some idea of what transpired. One of the newcomers became paranoid and decided the whole thing was a fiendish police trick to get him to confess to all the crimes he had never been caught for. He stared murderously at Gunther Weil, which worried Weil quite a bit, although he would have been more unnerved if he had known that the man was feverishly working out all the steps he would have to take to arrange an accident for this smart-aleck Harvard punk who had outwitted him. But then—smart manipulation of set and setting—his paranoia vanished, he forgot about revenge, forgot about his standing in one of Boston's Irish Mafia families; he started thinking about love, about how everyone was really the same, no difference between him and this Harvard boy, really.

The early results of the prison study were so promising that Leary flew to Washington to discuss the possibility of introducing psilocybin therapy throughout the penal system.

But the prison study also highlighted one of psilocybin's main sticking points. The prisoners were changing, true enough, but they were changing in a way that made science uncomfortable: they were getting religion. And if psilocybin could do that to hard-core cons, imagine what it was doing to the members of the psilocybin project. Barron, knowing they were going to find themselves in places that would sorely test their agnostic principles, had brought from California a small library of mystic texts. "I think you should start with the William James," he'd advised. And after James, Swedenborg, George Fox, William Blake, the French surrealist Rene Daumal, the Taoists, the Buddhists, the Sufis, the Tantric psychologists of the *Bardo Thodol.*

It never would have occurred to them to read books like this before psilocybin. But now, as they slipped deeper into the rich literature that comprised what Huxley called the perennial philosophy, it seemed that these mystic texts were better explanations for what they were experiencing than any of the scientific monographs.

What they were on to, Leary decided, was a kind of applied mysticism. This, anyway, was the gist of a paper he read in August 1961, at the Congress for Applied Psychology in Copenhagen, Denmark. "The most efficient way to cut through the game structure of Western life is the use of drugs," he said. "Drug-induced *satori.* In three hours under the right circumstances the cortex can be cleared."

13

WHAT HAPPENED AT
HARVARD

Sitting in the Copenhagen audi-
ence was a colleague of Leary and Alpert's named Herb Kelman, who
was the Clinic's resident social psychologist and who, for the past year,
had been on sabbatical in Norway. Having known Alpert for several
years and Leary for a few months and having thought them both charming and competent, Kelman was astonished at the direction the panel
on New Directions was taking. Up on the stage Leary was thanking
Barron for turning him on to the sacred mushroom, and Alpert was
thanking Leary, and the whole thing was sounding more like a convention of evangelists than a scientific symposium. One amazed listener
later told Kelman that Leary acted as though he were brain damaged.

Sitting there, Kelman suddenly understood what his friends had
meant in their letters when they had alluded to strange doings at 5
Divinity Avenue. But even so he was unprepared for what he found
when he returned to Cambridge: instead of being roundly criticized for
sloppy science, Alpert and Leary had become powerful influences. Leary
acted as though he had discovered the master reconceptualization of
late-twentieth-century psychology. It would have been laughable but
for the fact that everyone involved with the psilocybin project seemed
so confident. This included not only some of the sharper graduate students, but also faculty members like Alpert and Kahn. On top of this,
Leary and Alpert were team-teaching the seminar in introductory clinical, which was arguably the most important course a psychology doctoral candidate would take at Harvard, and they were using that forum
to imply that the old methods of doing psychology were obsolete: the
future belonged to the new behavior-change drugs like psilocybin.

There was always the possibility, of course, that Leary might actually be on to something. Who could forget that Freud had been hissed

by his peers, and now he was legend and they mere foolish footnotes. But the corollary didn't necessarily follow. Not all men with novel ideas were Freud. Most were quacks and charlatans, and the more Kelman learned of the psilocybin project, the more certain he became that Tim belonged in this category, however brilliant and personally attractive he might be. In fact, the more Kelman studied the psilocybin project, the more convinced he became that it was just a clever excuse for a drug party.

This was not a new criticism, per se. Since day one Leary had had a difficult time persuading his colleagues that candles, mattresses on the floor, and Hindu *ragas* on the stereo were the stuff of Great Science. He'd usually responded with a short lecture on set and setting, and that had been enough at least to earn him the benefit of the doubt. But by the fall of 1961 it was no longer possible to conceal the dual purpose of the project. "I began to realize," David McClelland later told a magazine reporter, "that there were only a few subjects and many researchers, which meant that the researchers were taking more of the drug than anybody else."

McClelland's initial attitude of cautious optimism—he'd brought Tim here to shake things up, after all—was turning to anxiety. Instead of producing oneness and love, psilocybin was causing dissension and fear. It was dividing 5 Divinity Ave. into two camps: those who had had *the experience* and those who hadn't, with the former displaying a "blandness, or superiority, or feeling of being above and beyond the normal world" that bordered on the pathological. But even more troubling were the persistent rumors that, contrary to Tim's hearty assurances, some subjects were ending up in the hospital. Although McClelland was never able to prove any of these rumors true, one of Tim's graduate students did confess that "she knew she was becoming psychotic, but she'd never been so happy in her life."

McClelland aired his reservations at a faculty meeting in October, passing around a memo entitled "Some Social Reactions to the Psilocybin Research Project": "The history of the project has been marred by repeated casual ingestion of the drug, group decisions made which are not carried out etc. One can hardly fail to infer that one effect of the drug is to decrease responsibility or increase impulsivity." He also took a poke at Tim's recent infatuation with the mystic East:

> It is probably no accident that the society which most consistently encouraged the use of these substances, India, produced one of the sickest social orders ever created by mankind, in which thinking men spent their time lost in the Buddha position under the influence of drugs exploring consciousness, while poverty, disease, social discrimination, and superstition reached their highest and most organized form in all history.

Give me proof, McClelland was saying, and not just some narcissistic comparison with the Mercury astronauts.

Realizing that the heart of McClelland's critique—the lack of controls, the scarcity of hard data—was unimpeachable, Michael Kahn said to Alpert, "Timothy is like a great director who has lost touch with the realities of the theater. He needs a production manager who will remember to get the props to the theater on time." Together Kahn and Alpert began tidying up Tim's professional life, copy editing his grant proposals, making sure that data was collected, collated, and written up. In February 1962 they distributed a thirteen-page memo that apologized for "the inadequate communication on our part" that had led "to a number of rumors and speculations concerning the purposes of this research." They were patiently gathering evidence, the memo continued, which would prove their assertion that "psilocybin has the potential to facilitate major insight of an intellectual-emotional nature, which, if guided properly, could lead to genuine behavior change." So far, ninety-one out of ninety-eight subjects reported "pleasurable experiences," with sixty-one experiencing "insights that resulted in positive changes in their lives." Of the thirty-four prisoners who were now taking the drug at Concord, most showed marked increases on the MMPI in the categories of responsibility, socialization, tolerance, and achievement.

The memo also touched upon their growing interest in the religious implications of the psychedelic state, what McClelland had scornfully dismissed as "undergraduate navel-gazing." In December, they reported, they had begun a series of informal seminars with local theologians like Huston Smith, Huxley's friend who taught religion at MIT, and Walter Houston Clark, a sexagenarian psychologist who was teaching at Andover-Newton seminary. Nine of these religious experts had taken psilocybin, with the result that four underwent a classic mystical epiphany. "I think religion will neglect the consequences of this powerful instrument, with its implications, at its peril," one was quoted as saying in the memo. "The experience recalls Otto's *mysterium tremendum.* It was awesome."

But whatever qualms the memo soothed were quickly resurrected on February 20, when the Harvard *Crimson* printed a story about the psilocybin project that contained this worrisome paragraph: "The directors of the Center envision the use of psilocybin in a 'mushroom seminar' for graduate students in theology, behavioral science and philosophy; the course would be based on taking the drug once a month and spending the intervening sessions applying the insights gained to problems in their respective fields."

Apparently, despite the warnings of everyone around him, Leary still found it impossible to believe that any university could turn its back on a teaching tool like psilocybin. During the fall semester he had urged all his introductory clinical students to avail themselves of a trip or two. Only one had refused.

But this one exception was an advisee of Herb Kelman. Brooding that his refusal to take psilocybin might weigh against him (certainly it marked him as a retrograde psychologist in Tim's eyes), he finally went to Kelman and confessed his fears. Kelman was outraged. Leary and Alpert were blurring the lines between what was optional and what was required; they were becoming advocates, not educators. Kelman interviewed other introductory clinical students. Some admitted feeling pressured, others told scary anecdotes about what had happened in the Other World. Armed with these stories, Kelman went to McClelland and demanded a department meeting in which the psilocybin project could be freely debated. McClelland consulted Leary, who agreed it was a good idea. Notices were posted, the rumor mill began to hum, and on March 16, 5 Divinity Avenue's "psychodrama room" was standing room only.

David McClelland moderated the debate, which went on for about ninety minutes, and he strove to maintain a posture of skeptical support. The most vigorous opponent was Kelman, who demanded that the psilocybin project either be radically restructured or terminated. "I wish I could treat this as a scholarly disagreement," he said. "But this work violates the values of the academic community . . . the program has an anti-intellectual atmosphere. Its emphasis is on pure experience, not on verbalizing findings. It is an attempt to reject most of what the psychologist tries to do."

Kelman's critique was echoed by others in the room. "Have you bothered to read the literature in your field?" demanded Brendan Maher, whose debating style reminded Leary of a prosecuting attorney.

"Yes, I've read those papers."

"Then how can you continue administering these drugs outside a mental hospital?"

Although he had expected criticism, the vehemence of the attack surprised Leary, and he had to work at remaining outwardly unruffled. The same couldn't be said for Alpert, whose reaction was described as cold anger. Leary later claimed that before the meeting Dick had been drawn aside and told that "nothing could be done to save Tim, but if he kept quiet his career could probably be salvaged." Whether this was true or not, Alpert did remain silent for about half the meeting before jumping to his feet and attacking Kelman and Maher. In the end, the conflict was resolved, in true academic fashion, with the recommendation that a committee be appointed to thoroughly investigate the differences. "The meeting ended on a note of civilized calm," Leary wrote in *Flashbacks*.

The calm lasted less than twenty-four hours. Next morning the biggest thing on the front page of the Harvard *Crimson* was "Psychologists Disagree on Psilocybin Research." From the *Crimson* the story jumped to the Boston dailies and thence to the wire services, the combination of Harvard's prestige and experimental mind drugs proving irresistible. But that was only the preliminary hoopla. Suddenly agents of the Bureau of Narcotics were calling at 5 Divinity Avenue and the local office of the Food and Drug Administration was making investigatory noises.

Harvard reacted with suave demurrals. The problem had been taken care of, they told reporters. The psilocybin project was now under the supervision of a faculty committee, and the project's supply of psilocybin had been turned over to Dr. Dana Farnsworth at the University Health Service, to be released only with the committee's approval. In addition, Leary and Alpert had been asked to turn over all personal supplies of the drug, a request that raised interesting questions about academic freedom, but one to which Leary had cheerfully acquiesced. Indeed, by the end of spring term, 1961, it seemed that the problem of the psilocybin project had been artfully contained, if not solved. All that remained was to wait until Leary's teaching contract expired the next spring, and then they would be rid of him and his band of applied mystics forever.

Unfortunately, Harvard was not in full possession of the facts. For all Leary cared, Dr. Farnsworth could lock up the psilocybin and throw away the key. Psilocybin was passé, it had been for months, ever since Leary had scooped a teaspoonful of LSD paste out of Michael Hollingshead's mayonnaise jar and soared off the map. Later he wrote: "From the date of this session it was inevitable that we would leave Harvard, that we would leave American society."

He was English, of course, a tall, balding man in his midthirties with peculiar scars on his forehead and a plummy upper-class accent. An accomplished mimic, he told hilarious stories about public school and psychoanalysis with Anna Freud. Leary called him a "divine rascal" and was endlessly entertained by his "witty, multi-reality tales." Others considered him a sociopath. "Getting involved with Hollingshead was one of the worst mistakes Tim ever made," said one.

In his first telephone conversation with Tim, Michael Hollingshead introduced himself as a protégé of the British philosopher G. E. Moore. He was in Boston, he said, because Aldous Huxley had mentioned Tim as a man who understood psychedelics. Leary invited him to lunch at the Harvard Faculty Club, where he spent most of the time outlining the plot of a novel he planned to write. He also boasted of having ingested more LSD than anyone else in the world. Tim politely listened, wished him luck, paid for the meal and returned to his office. The phone rang. It was Hollingshead: he needed help, he was suicidal, he had no place to stay. Leary brought him back to the Newton house and called a New York connection for information on his new lodger: stay away from Hollingshead was the message, he's a con man. But he was a con man with a mayonnaise jar full of LSD.

How Hollingshead came to possess that mayonnaise jar illustrates how quickly the psychedelic ripples were spreading out from the epicenter of our story. Hollingshead came to New York in 1953, and for most of the decade was associated with an organization known as the British-American Institute for Cultural Exchange, which was supposed to promote amity between the English-speaking cousins and the continent. Huntington Hartford was on the board, so was the poet W. H. Auden. One of Hollingshead's acquaintances, another British expatriate, was a young doctor named Michael Beresford. And Beresford, an admirer of *The Doors of Perception,* was part of a small psychedelic cadre whose community center was an obscure store in Greenwich Village that sold all kinds of native roots and potions, peyote, harmaline, ibogaine, some mescaline, all legal. Hollingshead joined Beresford in a number of experiments that finally culminated in their joint purchase of several grams of LSD. Hollingshead came out of the deal with one gram (at a cost of $285), which factored out to about five thousand doses. Back at his Greenwich Village apartment he proceeded to dilute the chemical with distilled water and then poured in a box of confectioner's sugar. When this mess was thoroughly mixed, he transferred it to an old mayonnaise jar, and then unthinkingly he licked the spoon. Now 250 millionths of a gram, which is a healthy dose of LSD, is little more than a speck, so you can imagine what happened to Hollingshead after his impulsive lick. He went roaring off to the Other World, where he experienced a rare but not unknown problem: he couldn't come back completely. It was as though he were lost midway between this world and the other one, a little like a spirit who ends up in limbo because of improper burial. Hollingshead eventually wrote a letter to Huxley (who was interested in the problem of reentry) and Aldous responded with Leary's name and address. "A splendid fellow," he wrote.

Despite the warnings from New York, Leary invited Hollingshead to stay at the Newton house as a kind of unofficial babysitter for Susan and Jack. Metzner thought he performed his duties rather well, "considering what he was pouring into his system all the time." A typical day started with a spoonful of LSD icing, a drink, and a few hours of TV. Hollingshead called LSD his daily consciousness vitamin.

Leary wouldn't touch the stuff at first. He was too busy shepherding the psilocybin project, worrying about the mounting criticism within the Social Relations department. Despite Hollingshead's insistence that it was like comparing a house cat to a lion, Tim stuck to his belief that there was no difference between psilocybin and LSD. And it was only after Maynard and Flo Ferguson arrived for a weekend and agreed to try some of Hollingshead's LSD, that he relented. "You gotta try this," Flo had whispered, and he had.

It was the most shattering experience of his life.

Metzner ran into him the next day and was appalled. He barely recognized Tim. He had the "blank look of someone who is seeing too much" and he kept babbling about the "plastic doll world" and the "total death of the self." And he was following Hollingshead around like one of Konrad Lorenz's imprinted goslings. "We've lost Timothy," Alpert warned, don't touch LSD. But eventually Leary snapped back to normal. "Wow," he said.

If psilocybin had been about love, LSD was all death and rebirth, and it quickly changed the tone of the psilocybin project. Everyone began taking massive dosages and going off on solitary treks that no one else could share. The sense of community crumbled. "We got snotty, we got put-downy, we got 'in' and 'out,' " Kahn remembers. "We got looking at the people who hadn't had 'the experience' as though they were inferior to us. We would go to parties and there would be 'drug people' and 'non-drug people,' and we would be in little groups and we would tell 'in' jokes, and we would be groupy, and we'd put down people who tried to get in with us."

Alpert, in particular, was dismayed by LSD's arrival. Psilocybin was a comfortable experience; after a year of work they were close to creating a manageable model of what happened; the trip through the Door had become almost routine. But LSD . . . LSD threw you back into the chaos. It was too much! There was no way they could wrestle this explosion into the available psychological categories. The whole thing made him nervous. Of course it was possible—this being a story about psychologists—that subconsciously Alpert recognized that if he followed the lure of LSD then it might be goodbye Harvard, goodbye Nobel Prize, possibly even goodbye Dick Alpert.

But Tim urged them on. New circuits, he exulted, a better broom to sweep the cortex clean!

Actually, if anyone symbolized the changes brought about by LSD, it was the bringer, Michael Hollingshead. In a matter of weeks Hollingshead acquired a status coeval with Alpert. Metzner felt he was a disruptive presence who loved to mock the spirituality of their little family. To share a session with Hollingshead was a dangerous thing, for he loved to manipulate the suggestibility of the state. Watching Hollingshead, Metzner realized for the first time that psychedelics didn't necessarily make you holy or wise. But whenever he confronted Hollingshead, the latter would blink and proceed to deny it in "such a guileless, humorous, friendly manner, that it was impossible not to like the man." Plus he had the wholehearted support of Leary, who, as a consequence of that shattering first trip, believed him to be an agent for some higher intelligence who had been sent to earth to . . . well, possibly to guide Tim Leary onto the chosen path.

One of the difficult questions to answer in Tim Leary's biography is the question of when he first began to think of himself as a prophet. At what point did the guru game begin? Where did the transformation that culminated in *High Priest* start? Leary, of course, always denied that it ever did. Outwardly he always ridiculed the suggestion that he was divinely elected. Tim would "laugh and laugh," remembers Kahn, "he never for a moment got thinking of himself as a guru." But Metzner believed differently: "I know that inwardly, starting at an early stage of our work together, he saw himself as a prophet. And the growing attacks on him and his actions by the authorities and the media only confirmed this, because he believed that a prophet is always misunderstood and hounded by his contemporaries."

And this prophetic mission was assuming an increasingly spiritual tone. If psilocybin had progressively weakened the foundations of what Leary liked to call "the Tim Leary game," LSD had swept it away in an "ontological confrontation" from which "I have never recovered." Although it would still be several years before he could pronounce the word *God* without wincing—such was Aunt Dudu's legacy—for the first time in his life Leary understood why competent people like Ginsberg and Watts had chosen the spiritual game.

By the spring of 1962 Leary was deep into Tantric Buddhism. During this period a young psychologist named Stan Krippner arrived to take the psilocybin. Although Tim was supposedly in the middle of negotiations with Harvard, the FDA, and the State Bureau of Narcotics concerning the future of the psilocybin project, and although he had reportedly turned over his entire supply to Dana Farnsworth, he scared up some of the drug for Krippner, telling him, "You're exactly the sort of person we want to have this experience." Later, when Krippner had time to reflect upon his whirlwind visit to Harvard (the high point of his session was a clairvoyant foreseeing Kennedy's assassination) one of the things he remembered most clearly was the thematic tension of Leary's desk. Half had been littered with protocols bearing those peculiar concentric circle graphs Leary had popularized in *The Interdiagnostic of Personality*. But when Krippner had complimented him on the success of that book, Leary had waved his hand dismissively and said, "That's antediluvian stuff." The drugs, he implied, were taking him in wholly revolutionary directions, and although he didn't specify what these were, it had been impossible not to notice that the other half of the desk was piled high with books on Buddhism and Hinduism.

But books were no substitute for direct experience. In early 1962 a former Air Force major turned Hindu monk named Fred Swain arrived at the Newton house. Swain was associated with Boston's Vedanta ashram, although he was not adverse to seeking higher awareness through drugs, and had once spent a bemushroomed night with Gordon Wasson's *curandera* in the hills outside Oaxaca. Swain took LSD at Newton and reciprocated by inviting Tim to the ashram. Leary the atheist was amazed. "The ashram itself was a turn-on," he later wrote. "A serene, rhythmic life of work and meditation all aimed at getting high." He eagerly conducted an LSD session for the ashram members and they responded in much the same way that he had with Hollings-head: "The monks and nuns treated me as a guru. To them it was obvious. I was not a Harvard psychologist with a staff of research assistants. Come off it, please. I was, like it or not, playing out the ancient role."

Despite Kahn's observation that whenever the ancient role came up, Tim would laugh uproariously, his religious pose became more pronounced with time. Was it a sham? A clever public relations ploy? Or was Tim serious? Had he tapped into that ancient heavenly connection and received the usual message: go forth and spread light! Something Alan Watts once wrote about himself should be kept in mind when considering these questions:

> On the one hand I am a shameless egotist. I like to talk, entertain, and hold the center of the stage, and can congratulate myself that I have done this to a considerable extent—by writing widely read books, by appearing before enormous audiences. On the other hand I realize quite clearly that the ego named Alan Watts is an illusion, a social institution, a fabrication of words and symbols without the slightest substantive reality; that it will be utterly forgotten within five hundred years, and that my physical organism will shortly pass off into dust and ashes.

As Watts realized, few professions are as ambiguous as the philosopher of egolessness who achieves fame. The *I* who writes the books and gives the lectures is merely a player in the theater of the self, and, from that perspective, life becomes a tragi-comedy whose merit is enhanced by the amount of wit and grace one brings to the playing.

Actually, when it came to pointers on how to play the "ancient role" in modern dress, there was no better teacher than Alan Watts. He was a generation younger than Huxley, yet he had the same English fluidity of mind, the same noble dedication to a life of ideas. But unlike

Huxley he was a bohemian, although here he personified a rather more elegant conception of bohemian style than Ginsberg or the beatniks. One of Watts's quibbles with the Beats, besides their near-beer brand of Zen, was their dowdy attitudes; they "lacked *gaiete d'esprit,"* he felt. When he wasn't globetrotting around as a freelance philosopher, Watts lived on a houseboat in Sausalito Bay. He was a wonderful entertainer. His days with the London Buddhists, plus his years as an Anglican clergyman, had left him with a talent for ritual and mystery. One Easter Sunday he stage-managed an entire psychedelic ceremony at Leary's Newton house, offering a liturgy composed of readings from the New Testament interspersed with parables and Zen jokes. The sacrament— LSD—was served in goblets along with French bread. Then he led them outside to chase snowflakes. Everything about Alan was balanced yet refreshingly different. Watching him, Leary was envious; he too wanted to be a freelance philosopher, living off his intellectual wits.

Watts was a frequent presence at Harvard. He was always turning up at the Divinity School, although he was equally at home at the psychology department. With the exception of Harry Murray, he considered the psilocybin project people to be the liveliest on campus, although Tim's recklessness worried him: "It seemed to [Tim] more and more that, in practice, the procedures of scientific objectivity and rigor were simply an academic ritual designed to convince the university establishment that your work was dull and trivial enough to be considered 'sound.' " Although he sympathized with the dilemma, Watts repeated Huxley's counsel: don't abandon scientific principles, transcend them.

Tim did manage to come up with an experiment that approached Watts's ideal. The stimulus came from a medical doctor turned theologian named Walter Pahnke, who for his doctoral thesis wanted to give twenty theology students psilocybin and then measure their reactions against a nine-category model of mystical experience that he had derived from the work of Princeton philosopher W. T. Stace. At first Leary balked, but he was soon won over by the combination of Pahnke's "fresh-faced, gee whiz" enthusiasm and his careful experimental design. What Pahnke proposed to do was divide the twenty students into five groups, with two members of the psilocybin project assigned to each group. No one, neither the students, nor Pahnke, nor the grad students, would know who had received psilocybin and who the placebo. Afterward, the students would fill out a 147-item questionnaire, with another to follow in six months. To evaluate their answers, Pahnke had lined up some housewives who were all ex-schoolteachers. A double blind study. It was the most scientific thing the psilocybin project had ever attempted. Unfortunately, Harvard refused to release the drugs.

The ad hoc committee, less than a month old, felt it needed more time to evaluate the request. This angered Leary, although he was certainly aware that the committee's main brief was the containment and elimination of the psilocybin project. Yet they had said again and again that legitimate research would be allowed to continue. And if Pahnke's experiment didn't meet that condition, then nothing would. Irritated and feeling obligated to Pahnke, Leary scrounged around and came up with enough psilocybin, and on Good Friday, in Boston University's Marsh Chapel, with twenty divinity students from Andover-Newton (supplied by Walter Houston Clark) on hand, the experiment commenced. Half the young theologians were given psilocybin, the other ten nicotinic acid, a substance that caused one's face to flush, but nothing else. No one knew who had what at first, but within an hour the division was clear. While half sat attentively listening to the Easter service that was being piped in from the main chapel, the others were all over the place, lying on benches moaning, or wandering around fixating on the various religious icons. One sat at an organ, playing "weird, exciting chords." Of the ten receiving the nicotinic acid, only one reported experiencing anything that fell within Pahnke's nine categories; of those who took the psilocybin, nine reported four or more categories of mystic experience.

For Harvard, the "miracle of Marsh Chapel," as it became known, was final proof that Leary had no intention of abiding by the rules. It was rumored that the Divinity School was going to reject Pahnke's thesis, and there were demands for the immediate firing of Walter Houston Clark at Andover-Newton. For Leary, it was further confirmation of what might be called the finger syndrome. A man points at the moon, do you stare at his finger or do you look at the moon? Harvard was a finger watcher; it didn't care about the moon. My God how could you give those kids that dangerous drug, was all it could say. The fact that everyone had had a perfectly fine time, on top of which nine of those kids had seen God, or a reasonable facsimile thereof, was entirely beside the point.

To hell with Harvard and psychology, Leary wanted to shout, to hell with boring old bourgeois science. To hell with boring old bourgeois religion. Mind-expanding drugs were going to be the religion of the twenty-first century ("Pursuing the religious life today without using psychedelic drugs is like studying astronomy with the naked eye," Leary remarked), and he was going to be chief avatar. "He began to turn into a mystic and a poet," remembers Walter Houston Clark. Tim became Prometheus, "with a prophetic sense of mission to change others as he had been changed through profound religious experience." Harvard was too small to contain him; science was too small. According to Michael Kahn, Tim "wanted out of science. I said to him, as I have always said to him and I guess always will, 'wherever you're going, I want to go there too. Go ahead and I'll move right along.' "

It was a feeling shared by many of the other members of the psilocybin project. The adventures of the past fifteen months had made it impossible for them to return to traditional psychology, despite the warnings that their professional prospects were nil if they didn't renounce Leary. Most finished their doctorates quickly and readied themselves to follow Tim, in this case to Mexico. What Leary had in mind was a summer retreat, far from the pressures and hyperintellectuality of Harvard. He wanted to find an isolated research station, maybe a deserted hotel, somewhere warm and lazy where there would be no interruptions and they would have the leisure to venture as deeply into the Other World as possible. Aldous Huxley's novel, *Island*, had just been published, with its dreamy evocation of a psychedelic utopia isolated from (and ultimately destroyed by) the world of the Organization Mad. Tim was looking for something comparable and he found it in the faded Mexican resort town of Zihuatanejo, which was a couple of hours up the coast from Acapulco. It was a twenty-room, slightly seedy hotel called the Catalina, run by a Swiss emigré. And it was free for the summer.

Leary didn't fly immediately to Zihuatanejo when the semester ended. First he went to California and made the rounds of the research community. In Los Angeles he attended a number of parties that were similar to the ones he and Alpert had organized in New York, full of literate, intelligent seekers quietly discussing their trips to the Other World. One night after one of these affairs, a sloshed Marilyn Monroe slipped into Tim's bedroom and asked him to turn her on. There were moments when Leary had to agree with Allen Ginsberg: everyone was becoming hip.

This was an illusion, of course. Maybe 10 percent were becoming hip, the rest were getting nervous. And one of the focal points of their anxiety was LSD.

14

THE POLITICS OF CONSCIOUSNESS

"The whole goddamn climate changed. Suddenly you were conspirators out to destroy people. I felt like Galileo. I closed my practice and went to Europe. I felt violated."

That was the way Oscar Janiger remembered the change in mood that began in the summer of 1962. Suddenly LSD was no longer innocuous. It was a dagger pointed at the heart of psychiatry, the next thalidomide, a time bomb that was cheerfully being constructed by deluded members of the profession.

"If you want to know, it was Leary and the others who were ruining what we had worked so hard to build."

That was Janiger retrospectively laying blame. At the time no one knew where to point the finger. With the exception of some of the Lab Madness boys, who had been a tad bitter when their work was dismissed as passé, things had been proceeding with benign optimism, new recruits swelling the research ranks every week.

In a major city like Los Angeles, it was as easy to go on an LSD trip as it was to visit Disneyland. Interested parties could either contact the growing number of therapists who were using LSD in practice, or they could offer themselves as guinea pigs to any of the dozens of research projects that were under way at places like UCLA. Representative of the first approach was Thelma Moss, a former character actress turned "slick fiction" writer. Moss had heard Aldous Huxley talking about the Other World on a local television show, and before learning of Arthur Chandler and Mortimer Hartman, she had been prepared to search out some of Gordon Wasson's magic mushrooms in Mexico. Moss made an appointment with Chandler and Hartman, and after deciding on a psychological problem that would focus the sessions (she chose frigidity), she took the first of twenty-three LSD trips.

Moss was not a novice when it came to psychoanalysis. She had been in therapy for years. But she had never really, in her heart of hearts, believed that there was such a thing as the unconscious. LSD convinced her. During one session she suddenly became a legless beggar caught in a desert sandstorm, a scene right out of *King Solomon's Mines,* except that deep inside herself she heard a voice whispering, *I died here.* Another time she watched her insides explode into flames with such force that she was flung against the wall. It reminded her a little of how emotions sometimes multiplied until every pore was engulfed, only this was "a vastly more ruthless force" (students of *kundalini* take note). "What is it," she kept crying to her therapist, who finally gave her a tranquilizer.

Moss never knew where she would land after she passed through the Door. "Truth and lies and absurdity and grandeur were all mixed together in the psychedelic experience," she wrote. "In an effort to separate them, I would return for the next session, and the next, hoping each time that with this next session the truth would be revealed." It never was. But what did happen was so incredible, so contrary to the slick fiction that was her bread and butter, that she began keeping notes.

The other way to the Other World, the research project route, was exemplified by George Goodman, who is probably better known as the economist and writer Adam Smith. Goodman signed up for a UCLA project and was told by the director, "You are the astronauts of inner space. You are going deeper into the mind than anyone has gone so far, and you will come back to tell us what you found."

One of the things Goodman found was that he could see all "the basic molecules of the universe . . . all the component parts, little building blocks of DNA." He conscientiously drew a picture of what he thought was DNA, but it turned out to be a plastic monomer marketed by Dupont called Delrin. That didn't dampen Goodman's amazement, however, because up until taking the LSD he had had a banker's knowledge of molecules and chemical notation, which is to say he knew absolutely nothing about them.

There was something in the American psyche that craved spiritual adventure, something which writer Peter Mathiessen described as a "deep restlessness." Mathiessen had been a leader of the postwar Parisian expatriate scene, one of the founders of *Paris Review.* But he'd also become involved with the Gurdjieff work and that stirred a yearning that he described this way: "One turns in all directions and sees nothing. Yet one senses that there is a source for this deep restlessness; and the path that leads there is not a path to a strange place, but the path home." In Peru Mathiessen experimented with *yage.* Then he hooked up with a "renegade psychiatrist" in New York and started using LSD. "Most were magic shows," he later wrote. "After each—even the bad ones—I seemed to go more lightly on my way, leaving behind old residues of rage and pain."

Mathiessen was fortunate. Whenever his girlfriend took LSD it precipitated a terrifying confrontation with her own death. Since this was a fairly common occurrence for anyone who spent much time in the Other World, it is worth quoting Mathiessen's description of a bad trip:

> She started to laugh, and her mouth opened wide and she could not close it; her armor had cracked, and all the night winds of the world went howling through. Turning to me, she saw my flesh dissolve, my head become a skull—the whole night went like that. Yet she later saw that she might free herself by living out the fear of death, the demoniac rage at one's own helplessness that the drug hallucinations seem to represent, and in that way let go of a life-killing accumulation of defenses. And she accepted the one danger of the mystical search: there was no way back without doing oneself harm. Many paths appear, but once the way is taken, it must be followed to the end.

If people like Mathiessen had a code, it was "there are no casual experiments."

One of the reasons LSD therapy was booming was because qualms about the drug's safety had been laid to rest in mid-1960, when Sidney Cohen published his findings on adverse reactions. Cohen surveyed a sample of five thousand individuals who had taken LSD twenty-five thousand times. He found an average of 1.8 psychotic episodes per thousand ingestions, 1.2 attempted suicides, and 0.4 completed suicides. "Considering the enormous scope of the psychic responses it induces," he concluded, "LSD is an astonishingly safe drug." With the question of safety out of the way, interest then focused on the best way to use mind-expanding drugs. There were two schools of thought: those who saw LSD as a "facilitator" of traditional therapy, be it Freudian or otherwise, and those who followed the Hubbard-Osmond practice of giving huge dosages and trying, through the subtle use of cues, to produce a psychedelic or integrative experience. This became known as *psychedelic* therapy, as opposed to the more mainstream *psycholytic* therapy. It got so astute students of the literature could guess the theoretical orientation of an LSD monograph simply by its title: psycholytic papers had headings like "LSD as a Facilitating Agent in Psychotherapy" or "Resolution and Subsequent Remobilization of Resistance by LSD in Psychotherapy"; whereas psychedelic ones favored things like "LSD; Alcoholism and Transcendence" or "LSD and the New Beginning."

There were certain constants, of course, set and setting being the most notable. But from there the different techniques diverged rather dramatically. Psycholyticists like Chandler and Hartman took a lot of time, using small dosages, establishing a path to the unconscious—sort of a maintenance road—before any real exploration began. What they tried to do was create a state of conscious dreaming, and the way they did it was by masking the various senses. With the eyes blocked, the mind would begin projecting inner movies, sort of like "a 3-D film tape . . . being run off in the visual field," as one therapist described it. Some of these film loops were of actual incidents, forgotten since childhood, but most were composed of that symbolic patois that Freud felt was the true language of the unconscious, of psychic reality rather than objective reality.

The patients, asked to maintain a running commentary on what they were seeing, would report things like: *I'm in a black tunnel . . . there is a grayish light at the end of it . . . I'm moving toward it. . . .* There was a moment in one of Thelma Moss's sessions when she came to an abyss. Explore it, the doctor suggested:

> As I plummeted down, I felt myself growing smaller and smaller . . . I was becoming a child . . . a very small child . . . a baby . . . I was a baby. I was not remembering being a baby. I was literally a baby. (The conscious part of me realized I was experiencing the phenomena of "age regression," familiar in hypnosis. But in this case, although I had become a baby, I remained at the same time a grown woman lying on a couch. This was a double state of being.) The leg of the baby that I was (my own adult leg) suddenly jerked into the air and I whimpered in the voice of a little child: "They stuck me with a needle!" Before I could find out who had stuck me with a needle, I was playing with round violet-colored marbles . . . which changed into squares . . . then rectangles . . . which grew long and high and became the four sides of a playpen. I was inside the playpen. My brother was outside it, playing. I whined like a baby: "They let him play outside but I have to stay in here . . ."

Then the playpen vanished and Moss found herself gazing into a big purple jewel, which became an amethyst pendant hanging from her mother's neck, which became her mother's face, purple with rage, and she was shaking someone that turned into a rag doll that turned into Moss.

That was what was at the bottom of that abyss.

No doubt because they were Freudians, Chandler and Hartman elicited a lot of childhood sexual trauma, Oedipus complexes, penis envy, but they also observed elements of the Jungian unconscious, the wise old man archetype, the symbol of evil archetype. Sometimes mythological creatures appeared, dragons and Japanese devil gods. And just as Huxley had written, there was a hellish dimension to the Other World, a Dark Wood that everyone stumbled into eventually. A few passed through to something else and returned convinced that they had looked into the heart of creation. *Had they?* After some thought, Chandler and Hartman decided this mystical *gnosis* was one of LSD's potential drawbacks, since the patient was generally uninterested in further therapy.

But it was precisely this mystic *gnosis* that interested the psychedelic therapists. Using one large dose and a grab bag of nonverbal cues, after hours of interviewing, testing, analyzing, and prepping, the psychedelic therapist tried to lead the patient to that self-shattering point where he merged with the world—the point known to the Buddhists as *satori*, to the Hindus as *samadhi*, and to the psychological community as "a temporary loss of differentiation of the self and the outer world." It was a realm of pure potential, and if the psychedelic therapist was skilled, the effects could be dramatic. Osmond and Hoffer's success rate with chronic alcoholics was hovering between 50 and 70 percent, while Al Hubbard's clinic at Hollywood Hospital reported a figure in the low eighties.

An update on Mr. Hubbard. Despite the misgivings of Humphrey Osmond, who felt it would create more problems than it would solve, Hubbard had gotten his Ph.D in psychology from a Tennessee diploma mill. He was now Dr. Hubbard, at least on his stationery. It may be that in some sense Al felt he needed proof of intellectual parity, poor barefoot boy that he was, surrounded by the likes of Huxley and Heard. Perhaps he coveted their Oxbridge erudition. If so, it was an ironic situation, he longing to discourse intelligently about Jung and the Other World, while they envied him his simple American ability to get things done, whether it was a business deal or a guided tour of the Other World. But whatever Hubbard did, there was always a lot of shrewd practicality to it, and getting his doctorate was no different. Hubbard had decided—I lapse momentarily here into Leary's transactional terminology—that the one game he wanted to play was the psychedelic research game, with his own clinic, patients, colleagues, and before he could do that he needed credentials.

To be blunt, Hubbard had burned his bridges to pursue LSD; he had let his business interests wither from inattention, which can be stressful for a man with a Rolls Royce-island-estate lifestyle. Despite his genuine human hunger to find out what was happening in the mind's depths, Hubbard had not been unaware of the possibility that an LSD clinic might prove profitable. What he had needed was a doctor to provide the necessary medical expertise, and he had found him in the person of Ross McLean, the administrator of Hollywood Hospital, in New Westminster, British Columbia. McLean had given Hubbard a suite of rooms and in 1958 the first private Canadian clinic to use LSD therapy opened for business.

Hubbard's clinic became the testing ground for psychedelic therapy. In 1959 it attracted the attention of Ben Metcalfe, a local reporter. Hubbard invited Metcalfe to stop by for a two-day session, and Metcalfe did. He took the drug in Al's specially designed session room—Dali's Last Supper over the couch, Gauguin's Buddha on the far wall, another Dali, a crucifix, a small altar, a stereo system, burning candles, a statue of the Virgin. Metcalfe landed in a part of the Other World that was comparable to MGM's film library, particularly the section where historical epics were stored. There were Flashes of Carthage and ancient Rome seguing into landscapes out of Titian; great battles fleetingly glimpsed; figures that were unmistakably Shakespearian. It would have been immensely entertaining had it not ended in a fit of weeping. Not sniffly little whimpers, but great heaving sobs. "This is all repressed material coming out," Doctor Hubbard said. "This is what we bury to become men."

It went on like that, with Metcalfe emoting and crying and mumbling to himself, while Al sat meditatively alongside, rarely interrupting. One of the most difficult things that a psychedelic therapist had to learn was how to do nothing, how to become transparent, yet remain attentive enough to respond at the crucial moment, like when Metcalfe began shouting, "I must be insane! I must be." A good therapist had to know which cue would untie this particular knot. Which picture, which whispered observation. "We're all insane when it comes to confronting ourselves," Al murmured. And there was a big click in Metcalfe's mind and he went shooting up toward this bright central sun, and as he flew, it seemed to him that his earthly ties, his kids, his wife, his job, all floated away from him like "flashes of multi-colored snow vanishing in the darkness while I sped upwards."

It felt like death.

"Did I die?" Metcalfe asked.

"No one really dies," said Captain Al.

Hubbard's one published work, "The Use of LSD-25 in the Treatment of Alcoholism and Other Psychiatric Problems" (*Quart. J. Stud. Alcohol*, 1961), was frequently cited in the literature, but his biggest contribution was the Hubbard room, the stereo playing Bach, the vaguely spiritual pictures. Although few researchers knew its provenance, duplicates appeared wherever psychedelic therapy gained a foothold.

Though there were some classic psychedelic therapists—Hoffer and Osmond in Saskatchewan come to mind, the Kurland group in Catonsville, Maryland—who used LSD in an almost old-fashioned way, a lot of the psychedelic therapists were new to the profession, either recent graduates or converts like Hubbard and his former protégé, Myron Stolaroff, and this was going to cause problems. In their enthusiasm they returned from the Other World with a childlike energy that was often obnoxious to their middle-aged peers. They cut corners and bruised feelings and this more than anything contributed to the jealousy that lay behind the aura of "bad science" that began to surround LSD therapy.

Myron Stolaroff was a good example. Stolaroff had been in charge of long-range planning at Ampex, one of the first of the big electronics firms to settle south of the Bay Area, when he had been bitten by the psychedelic bug. Together with Hubbard he had tried to interest Ampex's management in a program that would use LSD to solve all kinds of corporate problems, interpersonal problems, design problems, long-range planning problems. But the plan had foundered on Al's penchant for Christian mysticism. Stolaroff didn't let go, though: he started holding weekly LSD sessions for some of Ampex's more adventurous engineers; Hubbard came down from Canada one weekend and took them all to a remote cabin in the Sierras where he guided them through the kind of ontological earthquake only Al could manufacture. The senior management of Ampex had been horrified. Having gotten to know Hubbard through rather extraordinary circumstances, it didn't seem at all irrational for them to be worrying, "What if this nutball drives our best men crazy?" So there had been sighs of relief when Stolaroff decided to leave Ampex and set up his own nonprofit psychedelic research center in Menlo Park, California—the International Foundation for Advanced Study.

The Foundation, which opened in March 1961, wasn't the only organization working with LSD in the San Francisco area. The Palo Alto Mental Research Institute had been studying the drug since 1958, and had been instrumental in introducing dozens of local psychiatrists and psychologists, as well as interested laymen like Allen Ginsberg, to the perplexities of the Other World. But the Institute's composure had been shaken by several terrifying incidents—colossal bad trips in which the subject returned from the Other World in questionable shape—and interest in LSD's therapeutic potential had diminished. LSD programs were also under way at the Palo Alto Veterans Hospital, the San Mateo County Hospital, and Napa State Hospital, but no one was offering psychedelic therapy, and what little research was being done was unexciting: Leo Hollister (who will soon reappear in association with a hopeful young writer named Ken Kesey), at the Veterans Hospital, was still doing model psychoses work.

The point was that most LSD researchers were fairly conservative. So when a couple of engineers set up shop (Stolaroff's vice president, Willis Harman, had been an engineering professor at Stanford) and began poaching bread and butter patients—unlike Osmond and Hoffer, Stolaroff wasn't just concentrating on chronic alcoholics, he was soliciting the man off the street, who in this case was the neurotic professional in the high tech-high education hub that surrounded Stanford—there were more than raised eyebrows. Charging five hundred dollars for one session with a highly questionable drug? The whole thing smacked of chicanery, despite the fact that Stolaroff had a licensed psychiatrist running the actual therapy sessions. But what was worse, it was chicanery with good word of mouth. The San Mateo *Call Bulletin,* scenting a medical scandal, had interviewed a number of Stolaroff's patients and found them laudatory to the point of hyperbole. At the Foundation's first and last open house, Stolaroff had been cornered by a disgruntled therapist who growled, "One of my ex-patients thinks you're a saint," making it clear that he thought Stolaroff was a charlatan. What was one to make, after all, of the *Call Bulletin*'s statement that the Foundation's aims were "partly medical, partly scientific, partly philosophical, partly mystical"? The first two, okay, but philosophy was for philosophers, and mysticism? mysticism was for cranks!

It was a situation that was a little analogous to Leary's at Harvard, in the sense that the local therapeutic community was so totally absorbed with the pointing finger (questionable professionals using questionable drugs to produce questionable cures) that it was almost as if it didn't want to look at the moon. The Foundation was not reticent about the data it was seeing. Seventy-eight percent of its patients claimed an increased ability to love; 69 percent felt they could handle hostility better, with an equal percentage believing that their ability to communicate with and understand others had improved; 71 percent claimed an increase in self-esteem, and 83 percent returned from the Other World with the conviction that they had brushed against "a higher power, or ultimate reality."

Robert Mogar, the Foundation's expert in such diagnostic tools as the Minnesota Multiphasic Personality Inventory, had never seen anything that could produce the kind of dramatic changes that LSD routinely produced. Part of the usefulness of the MMPI was the fact that some of its scales were remarkably stable, which provided a background against which other personality changes could be measured. But under LSD these stable scales, which generally pertained to beliefs and values, fluctuated wildly. To augment the MMPI, Stolaroff began using a variant of Oscar Janiger's elaborate card distribution system. This consisted of a hundred statements that the patient arranged in nine piles, ranging from those he agreed with least (pile one) to those he wholeheartedly endorsed (pile nine). Three times the cards were sorted into piles, once at the beginning of the program, two days after the LSD session, and then again in two months' time. The changes were consonant with what other researchers were beginning to report. Cards with statements like, "Although I try not to show it, I really worry quite a bit about whether I will prove adequate in meeting the challenge of life," tended to move down the scale. While those bearing statements like, "I believe that I exist not only in the familiar world of space and time, but also in a realm having a timeless, eternal quality," jumped to the top.

Of course there were some negative reactions. One patient felt he had been harmed mentally and roughly a quarter of the others complained that they now tended to lapse into daydreams with greater frequency. More troubling, but entirely understandable if the data about changes in worldview were correct, was an increase in marital problems—27 percent of the experimental subjects and 16 percent of the paying patients reported increased friction with their spouses.

The Foundation's theoretical manifesto—*The Psychedelic Experience: A New Concept in Psychotherapy*—was submitted for publication in late 1961. In it, the psychedelic experience was broken into three broad stages: (1) evasive maneuvers, (2) symbolic perception, and (3) immediate perception.

The evasive stage, according to the authors, was what earlier therapists had confused with schizophrenia, leading to LSD's misclassification as a psychotomimetic. What happened was this: the drug, by its very nature, released such a flood of new thoughts and perceptions that the patient's normal conceptual framework was overwhelmed, producing a panic condition with overtones of paranoia. But with skillful manipulation of set and setting, the therapist could guide the patient smoothly through the evasive stage to the point where the overly famous hallucinations began. These shifting geometrical patterns were a last gasp of an ego which, "having lost the battle to divert attention through unpleasantness, seeks to charm and distract the conscious mind by throwing up a smokescreen of hallucinations to hide the inner knowledge which it fears."

Actually, the hallucinatory level was a preparation for the realm of symbolic perception, which was where the psycholyticists spent most of their time, deciphering the curious symbolic patois: "The subject constantly works off repressed material and unreality structures, false concepts, ideas, and attitudes, which have been accumulated through his life experiences. Thus a form of psychological cleansing seems to accompany the subjective imagery. This results in considerable ventilation and release almost independent of intellectual clarification. Gradually the subject comes to see and accept himself, not as an individual with 'good' and 'bad' characteristics, but as one who simply is."

But there was also a higher level still. Past the symbolic stage was a land of no boundaries:

> The central perception, apparently of all who penetrate deeply in
> their explorations, is that behind the apparent multiplicity of things
> in the world of science and common sense there is a single reality,
> in speaking of which it seems appropriate to use such words as
> *infinite* and *eternal.*

As Abram Hoffer had told the last Macy Conference, if you could lead
a patient to this point, then nine times out of ten a cure would miracu-
lously occur. Why this happened was not easily explained in psychological terms (as Leary had realized when he decided to opt for the rhetoric
of applied mysticism). But it seemed to be something like this: overwhelmed by the realization that one was an "imperishable self rather
than a destructible ego," the patient underwent a kind of psychic expansion, in which "the many conflicts which are rooted in lack of self
acceptance are cut off at the source, and the associated neurotic behavior
patterns begin to die away." As the self expanded, it burst the webbing
of unhappy relationships that had tethered it to the ground.

Another analogy: Imagine the self as an oxbow lake, which is
formed when a meander is cut off from the main body of a shallow,
slow-moving river. Over time, unless fresh sources of water are found,
the oxbow begins to stagnate, becoming first a marsh, then a swamp,
as vegetation (thickets of received ideas, neuroses, etc.) starts to compete for oxygen. Psycholytic therapy, you might say, contented itself
with removing the vegetation; psychedelic therapy, on the other hand,
operated by dynamiting the obstruction and restoring the oxbow to
what, in fact, it had always been: a lazy curve in a broad, flowing river.
Both methods achieved the desired result, which was health, but in the
second case something totally new (from the perspective of the oxbow
world) was created. The psycholytic therapist used LSD to heighten the
traditional psychotherapeutic values of recall, abreaction, and emotional release. But the psychedelic therapist was doing something entirely new, and whether he followed Tim Leary and called it applied
mysticism, or the psychedelic experience, the integrative experience, or
peak experience, it had an unmistakable and unwelcome odor. To discover, in the recesses of the mind, something that felt a lot like God, was
not a situation that either organized science or organized religion wished
to contemplate. Yet this was the implication of psychedelic research
everywhere, not just at Harvard.

What sprang up was more a climate of criticism than any one
specific charge. The profession began to worry. It worried about
whether LSD, with its plunge into the deep unconscious, was an appropriate direction for a mental health movement whose raison d'être was

the molding of healthy, adjusted egos. Could it promote the right sort of behavior change? It worried about the cure rates—Hubbard's 80 percent with chronic alcoholics was unbelievable—which was the start of the bad science criticism, one variant of which went like this: "LSD is a hallucinogen, researchers are taking it as well as giving it, therefore they must be hallucinating their data." That was the charitable bad science interpretation. The uncharitable interpretation maintained that LSD therapists, besides hallucinating their data, were actually making their patients sicker. And they didn't even realize this because the drugs were giving them delusions of grandeur (comparing themselves with the Mercury astronauts or Galileo, what rot!). Psychedelics were revealing a nasty (or a rival) strain of evangelism within the Cinderella science: everywhere you looked therapists were turning into lower-case gurus, with adherents rather than clients.

Roy Grinker put it as bluntly as possible in the Archives of General Psychiatry: "Latent psychotics are disintegrating under the influence of even single doses; long-continued LSD experiences are subtly creating a psychopathology. Psychic addiction is being developed."

Grinker cited no data to back up these rather serious charges. He cited no data for the simple reason that there were none—Sidney Cohen's 1960 study on adverse reactions was still unchallenged in the literature. What Grinker was doing was projecting his own professional biases. Believing that your average citizen was a barely functioning tissue of neuroses and incipient psychoses, Grinker found it inconceivable that the opening of the Pandora's box of the unconscious could be anything but disastrous. Whether they knew it or not, people who used LSD had to be disintegrating; Grinker's whole model of consciousness depended upon it. To a traditional psychiatrist like Grinker, consciousness expansion meant unconsciousness expansion, and that was unconscionable.

Actually, a lot of the criticism over LSD can be reduced to a politics of perspective. A psychotomimeticist, for example, watching the ego dissolve under the press of LSD, would jot down "depersonalization," while a Myron Stolaroff or a Tim Leary, faced with the same phenomenon, might record an instance of "mystical union" or "integrative experience." Observing the flights of internal imagery caused by the drugs, the former would choose "hallucination" while the latter might select "visionary or symbolic interaction." As for the emotional highs that followed, the enthusiasm, one could either choose the psychopathological term, "euphoria," or go with the new psychedelic candidate, "ecstasy." When Abraham Maslow, a psychologist far removed from the LSD debate, published his first work on the curative effects of peak experiences (PE), psychedelic therapists like Hoffer quickly appropriated his vocabulary and the debate jumped to a new rhetorical level.

What was happening was basically a turf war over who would control traffic to the Other World. Were mere psychologists, to say nothing of artists, theologians, or an engineer like Myron Stolaroff, competent and responsible enough to investigate the extremes of consciousness, even if it was their own consciousness? Who owned the scientific prospecting rights to the Other World? The medical community claimed it did. According to one *Journal of the American Medical Association* editorial, anything which altered a person's "mental and emotional equilibrium" was a medical procedure and "should therefore be under medical control." In other words, LSD and its chemical brethren were part of psychiatry's weaponry, but not psychology's. Implicit in all this was the understanding that whoever received the mineral rights to the Other World would also be allowed to define its borders.

Thus it was the theme of "irresponsibility" that rose to the fore in the summer of 1962. LSD "was a useful adjunct to psychotherapy" went the refrain, but unfortunately it attracted "unstable therapists" who derived an "intoxicating sense of power" from bestowing such a fabulous experience on others. And these unstable therapists were the main reason why LSD was escaping, so to speak, from the lab. In July 1962, Sidney Cohen and Keith Ditman, writing in the *Journal of the American Medical Association,* drew attention to the phenomenon of the "LSD party"—a phenomenon that the California Narcotics Bureau, when queried by the LA *Times,* knew nothing about. Of course LSD parties had been part of the Los Angeles psychedelic scene since the mid-Fifties, but what was changing was the quality of the participant. A lot of kids were taking LSD, and not just college kids, but the beatnik kids, the maladjusted rebels. To Cohen's way of thinking, the Beats were exactly the sort of borderline personality types who should be kept away from LSD at all cost. If not, then Grinker's editorial would become a self-fulfilling prophecy.

Besides alerting the medical community to the growing misuse of LSD, Cohen also solicited more examples of adverse reactions. He published his findings in the spring of 1963. Nine incidents were explored, ranging from a psychologist who took LSD three times and then spent the next few weeks contemplating bizarre plots, one of which entailed the seizure of Sandoz's entire LSD supply, to a secretary for a therapist with a large LSD practice who had taken the drug somewhat more than two hundred times and less than three hundred—she was unsure of the exact figure. What she was sure of was that whenever she looked in a mirror, she saw a skull.

Although adverse reactions were still rare, Cohen predicted that this would change as more therapists added LSD to their practice. The "inexpert" use of LSD could become a major health hazard, he wrote, and he recommended that use be "restricted to investigators in institutions and hospitals where the patients' protection is greater and appropriate countermeasures are available in case of adverse reaction." Projects like Leary's were precisely what Cohen wanted to see ended.

The debate over who was a responsible therapist and who an irresponsible charlatan became moot when Congress passed a law in the summer of 1962 that gave the FDA control over all new investigational drugs. Scheduled to take effect in June of 1963, the law was principally aimed at the misuse of amphetamines. But the result was that all researchers using experimental drugs would now have to clear their research projects with Washington. No longer would it be possible to mail a form to Sandoz and receive in return LSD or psilocybin.

It was unclear what effect the new regulations would have on LSD research, but a partial answer appeared at Oscar Janiger's door in the autumn of 1962, in the form of a regional FDA official. Well dressed, polite, he asked to review Janiger's LSD work. Then he told Janiger to turn over his remaining supply of the drug. Janiger was stunned, then angry. He made some phone calls and learned that others had received similar visits.

Someone was turning off the research machine.

But it was too late to turn off the publicity machine. The psychedelic bookshelf—once limited to Huxley and possibly the Wassons' massive *Russia, Mushrooms and History*—was expanding in rapid fashion, as Adelle Davis's *Exploring Inner Space,* Thelma Moss's *Myself and I,* and Alan Watts's *The Joyous Cosmology* arrived in the bookshops. All three were anecdotal accounts of the Other World, but the similarity ended there. Adelle Davis, who'd taken LSD as part of Janiger's creativity study, had been transported to a phantasmagoric land suffused with the aurora borealis of God. "The most lasting value of the drug experience," she wrote, "appears to be a number of convictions, most of them religious in nature, which are so strong that it makes not one iota of difference whether anyone agrees with them or not." LSD had led her to "a new faith in God, a faith so satisfying and rewarding that my lasting gratitude goes to the Sandoz Pharmaceutical Laboratories." Thelma Moss, on the other hand, had spent her sessions harrowing the Freudian Id. The flap copy on her book said it all: "I traveled deep into the buried regions of the Mind. I discovered that in addition to being, consciously, a loving mother and respectable citizen, I was, unconsciously, a murderess, a pervert, a cannibal, a sadist and a masochist." And then there was Watts's smooth essay, which Leary and Alpert in the introduction lauded as "the best statement on the subject of space-age mysticism" available. "Watts follows Mr. Huxley's lead and pushes beyond."

Watts had a nice poetic feel for what it felt like to travel in the Other World, which is worth quoting:

> Back through the tunnels, through the devious status-and-survival strategy of adult life, through the interminable passes which we remember in dreams . . . all the streets, the winding pathways between the legs of tables and chairs where one crawled as a child, the tight and bloody exit from the womb, the fountainous surge through the channel of the penis, the timeless wandering through ducts and spongy caverns. Down and back through ever narrowing tubes to the point where the passage itself is the traveler . . . relentlessly back and back through endless and whirling dances to the astronomically proportioned spaces which surround the original nuclei of the world, the centers of centers, as remotely distant on the inside as the nebulae beyond our galaxy on the outside.

The Joyous Cosmology was widely read by Watts's many fans, but it was not the most popular psychedelic guidebook to appear in the summer of 1962. That honor went to *Island,* Huxley's utopian blueprint for what a psychedelically enlightened society might be like. Already *Island* had attracted one enthusiastic social engineer, who was putting its precepts into practice in the appropriately exotic locale of Zihuatanejo, Mexico.

15

THE FIFTH FREEDOM

If the psychedelic movement can be said to possess a nostalgic highpoint, it would probably be those weeks at Zihuatanejo in the summer of 1962, when thirty-five experimenters (and nine children) arrived at the Hotel Catalina for a collective assault on the Other World. Leary had gathered together a fascinating mix of psychologists, artists, jet-setters like Peggy and Tommy Hitchcock, and his Harvard graduate students, their wives and friends; an agglutination of talents and temperaments poised for an Everest expedition of the mind. They had come together to push the envelope of consciousness as far as it would go, although this didn't mean that they intended to ignore the Mexican *dolce vita:* Tim had left plenty of time for baking on the beach, ordering drinks from the Catalina's bar, which would come rumbling down the little funicular railway a few minutes later.

The Catalina, two miles outside of Zihuatanejo, at the end of a long dirt track, was built into a steep hillside, with cabanas at various levels. Except for the lazy curve of the Pacific to the west, with its miles upon miles of virgin beach, the hotel was completely surrounded by jungle. "We were swimming in a sea of tropical energy," remembers Gunther Weil, who attended with his wife and baby daughter. "Cut down a banana plant and 24 hours later it would be an inch out of the ground."

On any given day approximately a third of the group were off to the Other World, with another third acting as guides, and a remaining third recuperating and writing reports about what they had seen during their voyages of the previous day. The sessions were under the nominal control of Metzner and Alpert, while Leary acted as a kind of psyche-delic *pater familias*—his first crack at the ancient role. Actually, Tim was curious to see whether he could create the kind of community that Huxley had only imagined in *Island,* a transpersonative community

185

(*transpersonative* was the newest buzzword among the Harvard group), which meant a group of people who had evolved past the ego, who were living beyond "the persona, the role, or mask, which we normally are compelled to exhibit socially."

Could he take three dozen high-powered egos and meld them into a true spiritual brotherhood?

A month was certainly not sufficient time to prove anything, but it was a start, and with a few notable exceptions—Myron Stolaroff being one—it promised to be a good one. Stolaroff had met Leary in the spring of 1962, had been charmed and impressed by him, and had quickly assented when Tim invited him to join the Zihuatanejo project. But now he was regretting it. He felt completely at sea in Tim's transpersonative community: the women were moody, the men aloof. Some of Stolaroff's negativity derived from the fact that he was forever having to defend his Foundation against the charge that it was selling enlightenment the way you would a dinette set—*five hundred bucks a pop! Disgraceful!* Whenever he tried to explain the difficulties involved in financing research the health bureaucracy chose not to support, he was met with an indifference that verged on the hostile. There was an us-against-them quality to Zihuatanejo that perplexed Stolaroff, particularly since the us faction, the Learyites, never tired of talking about the love and openness LSD supposedly inspired. And he was equally disconcerted by all the "in phrases, in concepts, in ways of describing experiences. I couldn't understand a lot of it and I thought I had a pretty good handle on the psychedelic experience." Having struggled long and hard to build a model of the psychedelic experience that would be acceptable to mainstream psychology, Stolaroff was unprepared for Leary's infatuation with religious terminology. Everything was *bardo* this, *bardo* that, soon we'll be Buddhas.

The word *bardo* came from one of Huxley's favorite books, the *Bardo Thodol* or *Tibetan Book of the Dead.* It described the stages the soul presumably passes through after leaving the dead body. One day, while guiding a session for Metzner, Leary had opened up the *Tibetan Book of the Dead* and read a few pages, and Metzner, after initially fighting the strange Tibetan concepts, had felt his mind go lifting up through the layers of consciousness just as the Tibetan lamas had written. Everyone had been stunned. Had they unwittingly stumbled across an ancient psychedelic guidebook? As Alpert later put it, the *Tibetan Book of the Dead* contained "the most vivid descriptions of what we were experiencing with psychedelics but hadn't been able to describe. We were saying it was ineffable, and there it was, described in this book that was 2500 years old."

It quickly became one of Leary's main props (rather in the way Hubbard used Christian iconography and texts), albeit one that was freely translated to fit the moment. "O nobly born, you have departed from your own self," the guide would chant. "Even though you cling to your mind you have lost the power to keep it. You will gain nothing more in this plastic doll world . . . Remember, when your body and mind were separating, you must have experienced a glimpse of the pure truth. Be not daunted thereby, nor terrified, nor awed. That is the radiance of your true nature. Recognize it."

However odd it sounded to Stolaroff, it seemed to work, and in the back of his mind Tim was considering modernizing it and publishing it as the first psychedelic Baedaker to the Other World.

But Myron wasn't the only source of negativity that Leary had to contend with. There was also Alpert, who was filled with an unspecified dread, a feeling of impending calamity, whether for himself or the whole group, he couldn't say. One night he swallowed a massive dose of LSD and walked into the surf and remained there until morning, teetering on the brink, wondering whether he would live or die, and not caring which way the decision went.

The last few months had been both hard and ironic for Alpert: ironic because his meteoric career had stalled at the very moment when he was at last doing some original work ("This was the most exciting thing we'd ever been involved in," he later told a reporter. "And here were all these people putting obstacles in our way."); and hard because the people putting obstacles in their way were friends whose good opinion he coveted. Although Alpert rationalized the criticism of the Kelmans of the world as simple colleague jealousy, he couldn't use that excuse with McClelland. From the moment he'd leaped to Tim's defense, it had been clear to everyone that he'd chosen a new mentor. And to his old one he'd said, "I'll help him with pleasure because he's that great a being. And I'd help raise money and run the kitchen and clean the house and raise the children."

But would he leave Harvard for Tim? Having concluded that the tensions within the Social Relations department were what anyone with the temerity to introduce a "powerful, non-verbal, meta-intellectual agent into a community which is fervently dedicated to words and intellectuality" should have expected, Leary was planning to leave Harvard when his teaching contract expired in June 1963; the future of psychedelic research lay outside the ivory tower. Thus Alpert was faced with a dilemma: abandon academia and continue as first lieutenant to a man he considered one of the wisest in the world, or remain safely in his comfortable professorial niche.

It was all LSD's fault, Alpert decided. The drug was more powerful than they guessed. "I think we're pushing the edge of this system," he told Leary, after Metzner and another man found him standing in the surf the next morning and led him back to the hotel. "I think we better cool it, because otherwise we're going to blow it somehow or other."

Unperturbed, Leary suggested a long shower and some hot tea.

"Cool it" was the opposite of what he was planning to do. For months he had been kicking around the concept of internal freedom. In a speech to the Harvard Humanists he had proposed that one's right to do what one wished with one's own consciousness was in effect a "fifth freedom," and one that ought to be amended to the Constitution. *Congress shall make no law abridging the individual's right to seek an expanded consciousness.* This fifth freedom was necessary, Leary told the Humanists, to prevent America from becoming "an anthill civilization," in which all of us were "mere puppets playing out roles in complex games." We were all becoming Organization Men, but this wasn't the only choice. Through a judicious use of psychedelics, Americans could recover a spiritual dimension that would free them to do great things—to explore the stars, conquer disease, eliminate poverty—in short to attain the goals of Kennedy's New Frontier while eliminating the greed and self-serving motives of the old frontier.

When he closed his eyes and fell into dreamy reverie on the Zihuatanejo sand, Leary saw a world modeled after Huxley's *Island,* in which the educational potential of psychedelics was obvious. But Huxley's fantasy had offered no guidance on the important problem of how the moksha medicine could be introduced to a complex society like the United States. Tim had already rejected the notion of turning on just the Best and the Brightest. And he was already bored with the Bohemian and the Beautiful. What was needed were more people like Ralph Metzner or Gunther Weil, a corps of well-trained guides capable of training others in the techniques of psychedelic guidance. The key to the psychedelic revolution, Leary realized, was the guide:

> A medical degree doesn't equip one to pilot a jet plane, or to understand the incredible complexities of consciousness. The LSD experience is so novel and powerful that the more you think you know about the mind, the more astounded and frightened you'll be when your consciousness starts to flip you out of your mind. A new profession of psychedelic guides will inevitably develop to supervise these experiences. The training for this new profession will aim at producing the patience of a first-grade teacher, the humility and wisdom of a Hindu guru, the loving dedication of a minister-priest, the sensitivity of a poet, and the imagination of a science fiction writer.

Later, in *The Politics of Ecstasy,* he compared the psychedelic guide to

> . . . control tower in La Guardia Tower. Always there to receive messages and queries from high-flying aircraft. Always ready to

help them navigate their course, to help them reach their destination . . . the pilots have their own flight plan, their own goals, and ground control is there, ever waiting to be of service.

"We're through playing the science game," Leary told McClelland when he returned to Harvard that fall. Instead they were going to play the social movement game, and their chief counter was going to be an organization with a serious-sounding name: The International Foundation for Internal Freedom, IFIF for short. In theory, IFIF would be a cluster of autonomous cells, each built around the nucleus of an IFIF-trained guide. These cells, as they grew, would divide, forming other cells, until the world was speckled with mini-Islands. IFIF central, in Boston, would train the guides, supply them with LSD, and act as a clearinghouse for the various research reports that each cell would be required to send in. This was crucial. Due to the recent law requiring FDA approval for all experimental drugs, IFIF was going to have to cultivate the appearance of a legitimate research project in order to receive LSD or psilocybin.

Addressing the Harvard Humanists a few weeks after his return from Mexico, Leary described his decision this way: "very tricky social and cultural dilemmas emerge if your consciousness extends beyond the language you know and the culture in which you exist. The question has been: do you attempt to harness the ongoing cultural games to the possibilities of expanded consciousness or do you attempt to set up new social forms?"

In Mexico they had opted for the new form, that small transpersonative band of evolutionary pioneers, the psychedelic cell.

"It tears my heart out to see what's happened to them," was McClelland's reaction to IFIF. "They started out as good scientists. They've become cultists." Andrew Weil, who was following the psilocybin project story for the *Crimson*, felt that Leary and Alpert had become glorified salesmen, therefore sacrificing any claims they might have to traditional academic freedom. And when John Monro, one of Harvard's deans, asked the *Crimson* to keep him informed of their findings, Weil acquiesced without too much professional soul searching. For Dean Monro, and by extension the Harvard administration, IFIF was further proof that Leary wouldn't abide by his promise not to involve Harvard students with psychedelic drugs.

Although what remained of the psilocybin project was safely off campus, flyers promoting IFIF were a common sight on university bulletin boards. To drum up readers for IFIF's house journal, *The Psychedelic Review*, one enthusiast had scattered mimeos proclaiming "MESCA-

LINE! EXPERIENCE OF MYSTICISM! ECSTASY! LSD-25! EXPAN-
SION OF CONSCIOUSNESS! PHANTASTIKA! HASHISH! VISION-
ARY BOTANY! OLILUQUI! PHYSIOLOGY OF RELIGION!
INTERNAL FREEDOM! MORNING GLORY! POLITICS OF THE
NERVOUS SYSTEM!" throughout the dormitories. Indeed the debate
over mind drugs threatened to overtake the Harvard-Yale game as a
topic of undergraduate small talk. The street price of a sugar cube laced
with LSD was said to be five dollars, and if you believed the rumors,
every third person in Harvard Square had them for sale.

This was the situation Dean Monro and Harvard's chief health
officer, Dr. Dana Farnsworth, hoped to defuse when they published a
letter in the *Crimson* warning that LSD and psilocybin "may result in
serious hazard to the mental health and stability even of apparently
normal persons." Although no fingers were pointed, the Dean later told
the *Medical Tribune* that the letter had grown out of the need to respond
to a "fairly persistent campaign to interest students in such drugs." A
few days later the *Crimson* carried a response from Leary and Alpert,
which brushed aside the question of health hazards to focus on the Fifth
Freedom. "A major civil liberties issue of the next decade will be the
control and expansion of consciousness," they warned. "Who controls
your cortex? Who decides on the range and limit of your awareness? If
you want to research your own nervous system, expand your consciousness, who is to decide that you can't and why?"

The argument jumped from the pages of the *Crimson* to those of the
New York Times. (HARVARD MEN TOLD OF MIND-DRUG PERIL, read one headline;
USE OF MIND-DISTORTING DRUGS RISING AT HARVARD, another.) Dean Monro
told the *Times* that Harvard's problem could be traced back to "the
interest shown by Aldous Huxley and others" in these drugs, which was
surprisingly astute, but also a little unfair. Because the Huxley circle was
even more alarmed by IFIF than Harvard.

Osmond visited Boston soon after the first public statements regarding IFIF, and reported back that no amount of argument could shake
Tim's conviction that everyone could safely take psychedelics. This
confirmed what Huxley had felt during his last trip to Harvard, when
Tim had "talked such nonsense . . . that I became quite concerned. Not
about his sanity—because he is perfectly sane—but about his prospects
in the world; for this nonsense-talking is just another device for annoy-
ing people in authority, flouting convention, cocking snooks at the
academic world."

But however outrageous Tim became—and with IFIF he was endangering Aldous's whole vision of legitimizing psychedelics—Huxley
couldn't bring himself to dislike this "mischievous Irish boy." Instead
he tried guile. When the Maharajah of Kashmir sent him an admiring
letter about *Island* and expressed a personal interest in trying psychedel-

ics, Aldous recommended that he contact Tim Leary at Harvard; should his Highness put a house at Leary's disposal, he wrote, it was likely Tim would jump at "an opportunity of working with the psychedelics in relation to subjects brought up within another culture than his own." Owing to Tim's recent passion for the mystical East, it was a shrewd gambit, but it came to nought.

Myron Stolaroff took a much more direct approach, firing off a letter that described IFIF as "insane." It will "wreak havoc on all of us doing LSD work all over the nation," Stolaroff predicted. "The medical profession in this country has had these materials available for years. Yet outside of the Canadian groups, and a very few individuals in this country, no one has really learned how to use these materials and get the benefits from them in spite of years of trying.

> Tim, I am convinced you are heading for very serious trouble if your plan goes ahead as you have described it to me, and it would not only make a great deal of trouble for you, but for all of us, and may do irreparable harm to the psychedelic field in general.

But, as Stolaroff admitted in his closing paragraph, "I suppose there is little hope that with the bit so firmly in your mouth you can be deterred."

In early January 1963, IFIF filed incorporation papers with the state of Massachusetts. Leary was designated president, Alpert, director, with Gunther Weil, Ralph Metzner, George Litwin, Walter Houston Clark, Huston Smith, and Alan Watts listed as members of the Board of Directors. In February it began the difficult job of wooing followers and generating revenue. Thousands of information packets were mailed out, each including a résumé of the psilocybin project—"91% of our subjects enjoyed pleasant experiences; about 66% reported insights and positive life change"—and a membership blank charging ten dollars per year in dues. Money, if it didn't exactly pour in, didn't trickle in either. Although some of the beautiful people made nice donations, the bulk came in ten- and twenty-dollar increments—dues from the hundreds of people who responded to IFIF's first membership drive.

Alan Harrington, who was profiling IFIF for *Playboy*, attended a New York fundraiser, along with a few dozen "rich people, aficionados of psychoanalysis, editors and writers, and a few others who just wanted to be saved." Leary and Alpert worked the crowd like "two fatigued basketball players, passing off the ball to one another." Watching them, Harrington was particularly impressed with Tim, who struck him as a man who "would never be without disciples." Leary had that "abstracted look of a person who can see with absolute clarity what no one else will believe is there"; he was playing the ancient game, and he was doing it with style. After the sales pitch a dazzling young girl, part of the IFIF entourage, entwined herself around Leary and gazed soulfully into his eyes. As for Alpert, Harrington dismissed him as a "quick and kindly young man," a useful appendage to the main prophet.

Harrington, who later went up to Boston and visited the Other World under the guidance of Ralph Metzner, was right on target when it came to IFIF's unpublicized agenda. "In my opinion," he wrote in his *Playboy* article, "the IFIF people are social revolutionaries with a religious base using these extraordinary new drugs as both sacramental material and power medicine. I think they hope to establish a Good Society in the United States. . . . It may seem ridiculous to take a fledgling group so seriously, but Christ and Hitler started small; all revolutionaries meet initially in ridiculous barns and barrooms. So what is especially minor league about a hotel on the Mexican Coast that sleeps forty?"

With a twenty-two-month lease on the property, Leary intended to convert the Hotel Catalina into a year-round psychedelic research center and academy. For two hundred dollars, interested researchers and apprentice guides could spend a month at Freedom Center (the hotel's new name) learning how to guide high-flying internal aircraft. In travel brochure prose, Zihuatanejo was described as "unspoiled by commercial civilization . . . the inhabitants are friendly, honest and happy . . . life is open, and is close to the sea, palms and sun." Prospective seminarians were instructed to pack a dozen or so of their favorite paperbacks for the library.

Because Freedom House would occupy most of his energies for the next several years, Leary announced that he was severing his connection with Harvard when his contract expired in June. And he was also saying goodbye (temporarily, everyone hoped) to Alpert, who had decided to stay on at Harvard for at least another year, having finagled an extension of one of his four teaching contracts. Whether Dick would eventually follow Tim down the path of freelance philosopher was unclear, but for now he was content to stay in academia.

Later, writing in *High Priest,* Leary was retrospectively blunt about what he hoped to accomplish with IFIF: "In 1961 we estimated that 25,000 Americans had turned-on to the strong psychedelics . . . at that rate of cellular growth we expected by 1967 a million Americans would be using LSD. We calculated that the critical figure for blowing the mind of the American society would be four million LSD users and this would happen by 1969."

That was IFIF's hidden agenda. It was time for the old mind to die, so that a new one, with expanded sensitivities, could be born.

Now one might think that this was a pretty aberrant notion in a culture whose generalized symbol of the *Übermensch,* the Overman, was still James Bond, and in that sense it certainly was, but the important thing to remember is that it made perfect sense to the kids! News of IFIF crackled through the hipper filaments of the student subculture. Out at Stanford a young writer named Kesey was writing to another young writer named Ken Babbs, who had been temporarily displaced to the Republic of South Vietnam, about this wild thing that has descended on the land: IFIF.

Reporters began beating a path to Cambridge; radio stations called for interviews; TV producers asked to be put on the IFIF mailing list. As Michael Hollingshead (who was back in New York and busy with a multitude of schemes, one of which involved the inclusion of a mind-expansion pavilion at the 1964 World's Fair) put it, Internal Freedom was this year's Zen. And that meant trouble. "Even in the hands of Tim, the external juggler, things began crashing about their heads as 'news' about IFIF circulated in the media and through casual gossip, which may or may not have been true but was certainly extravagant, contradictory, scandalous, libelous, comic and inspirational."

The best tidbits were usually about what went on at the two old colonials—"colonies for transcendental living"—that IFIF had rented in Newton. In the IFIF literature, these ménages were described as having been

> influenced by the ideas elaborated in Aldous Huxley's recent novel, *Island.* A serious attempt is made in these communities to develop an atmosphere of transcendental and genuinely self-giving relationships. Raising children in such an atmosphere has proven to have many advantages, and has been enthusiastically accepted.

That was the theory. The reality was what was later referred to as the standard hippie commune. Sometimes a dozen stereos were going at the same time, Hindu *ragas* flowing out of one room to merge, in the hall, with Tibetan bells and Thelonious Monk. The cumulative din drove the neighbors crazy, as did the sight of bare-chested young men practicing yoga in the yard. "They all wear a beatnik uniform—tight pants and jerseys, no shoes or stockings," complained one neighbor, who compared the Leary-Alpert house to a weekend motel. "One young man in his twenties is letting his blond hair grow down to his shoulders; every time I look at him I want to vomit." Then you had the decor. There was something about the psychedelic experience which stimulated the urge to decorate, particularly if there were any white or monochromatic walls in sight. The kitchen was filled with Rohrschach's inkblots and the rest sported collages that daily grew more bizarre. The one in the living room consisted of nudes clipped from magazines, with a single solitary bra pinned to it—a visual non sequitur that strengthened the impression that underneath the rhetoric about consciousness expansion and mystic enlightenment, a lot of uninhibited sex was taking place. About the only room at all congruent with the contemplative tone of *Island* was the meditation room, a quiet little nook of wall to wall mats, smelling of incense, with the dim mysteriousness of "a gypsy tea-leaf reader's tent."

As might be expected when a dozen individuals live in close proximity, there were times when people failed to live up to the transpersonative ideal. Indeed, not all the inhibitions released by LSD were life affirming; some were downright antisocial. The most dramatic example of this developed after Alpert fell in love with one of his housemates, a married student with a history of mental illness and a wife and child who also lived in the house. In many ways it was a replay of the Lucien Carr-David Kammerer affair, and it threatened to have the same tragic consequences. According to Metzner, "on certain days the tension lay in the air like dynamite with a crackling fuse. Foster threatened to burn the house down. We had a tribal meeting to try to talk him out of it, but he claimed not to know why he wanted to do it."

Ultimately the situation fizzled out, to be replaced by other minor tempests. It was exhausting, it was exhilarating. As with any group who lived together and took LSD regularly, the outlines of a group-mind began to form, with all the strange nonverifiable phenomena (precognition, telepathy, ESP) that that implies. One byproduct of this phenomenon was a quantum increase in the us-versus-them mentality. When Barron returned for a visit in late 1962, he was alarmed at how much they resembled a cult—and one that excluded him. Suddenly he was an outsider. The implication was that they had gone so far into the Other World that it was useless trying to explain to a relative *naif* like himself. Barron was unimpressed: "They were all standing around saying 'wow' and this expletive never sufficed for me."

Unable to tolerate further degradation of the neighborhood—Leary's dog was rumored to have bitten seven people—the citizens of Newton Center circulated a petition urging the town to enforce the zoning laws, which stipulated one family per dwelling. A hearing was scheduled. IFIF hired Alpert's father, who was a member of the Massachusetts bar, to be their defense attorney, and he carried the day by pointing out that the law didn't specify that the families had to be consanguinous—related by blood.

When Leary left Boston in April, bound for Zihuatanejo, he left behind an increasingly tense situation. Not only was IFIF under investigation from the Massachusetts Office of Public Health, but it was also out on the street, having been evicted from the suite of offices it had rented in Boston's newest medical building. The other occupants had protested to the landlord after reading about their new tenant in a Boston *Globe* story entitled "Banned Drug Research Crosses Charles," and the landlord had tossed them out so fast their furniture hadn't even arrived. Eventually IFIF found an apartment a few blocks from Harvard Square and hung out its shingle, but it was a far cry from the headquarters Tim had had in mind.

But these were minor quibbles compared to the situation at Harvard itself. For months *Crimson* reporters like Andrew Weil had been hanging around the Newton houses, picking up whatever tidbits happened to drop from the unguarded lips of the transcendental colonists. Now they were ready to turn over their findings to Dean Monro. According to the *Crimson*'s evidence, which was all hearsay, Leary and Alpert had broken their agreement with the advisory committee at least twelve times. Dean Monro called the various individuals involved in these infractions into his office and asked them to implicate Leary and Alpert. With one exception, all showed "absolute allegiance to the two psychologists." That one exception was a young friend of Alpert's, whom Dick had given psilocybin to, long after he was supposed to have turned over his personal supply.

It was an ironic turnaround, in the sense that Alpert, by wrangling an appointment with the Education Department, had in effect chosen Harvard over IFIF and Tim. Frank Barron, who ran into him at a National Education Association meeting in Washington, remembers him turning ashen whenever the subject of the Dean's investigation came up: "He was being brave about it and going to see it through, but I could tell that that was not what he wanted to have happen." There was an inevitable bitter confrontation with McClelland and then the dead days while he awaited Harvard's decision. In particularly despairing moments, Alpert was convinced he was going to be censured by the American Psychological Association. "Not because we're dirty boys doing dirty things," he told a magazine reporter, "but on the grounds that we have failed to concern ourselves with behavioral toxicity and emotional side-effects of the drugs. This is not true. We are watching these things very closely. We don't deny that personality changes are occurring. But we think they are changes for the better." To the same reporter he complained that he had been so good. "I turned down over two hundred guys," he said. "But my friend had a buddy who got very irate and went to the authorities. Some day it will be quite humorous that a professor was fired for supplying a student with 'the most profound educational experience in my life.' That's what he told the Dean it was."

Alpert was fired on May 27. At the same time, Leary was relieved of his teaching duties for "failure to keep classroom appointments," and his pay was docked as of April 30. As Leary had no classroom appointments, and had already publicly severed his ties with Harvard, this was more face saving than punitive. The *Crimson* devoted most of its front page to a recapitulation of the psilocybin project and the investigation that had brought it to a crashing end. It was the first in a small anthology of articles devoted to IFIF and Harvard, and in many ways it was the best. Unlike most of the big-league journalists, the *Crimson* writers at least understood what Leary was planning:

> The shoddiness of their work as scientists is the result less of incompetence than of a conscious rejection of scientific ways of looking at things. Leary and Alpert fancy themselves prophets of a psychic revolution designed to free Western man from the limitations of consciousness as we know it. They are contemptuous of all organized systems of action—of what they call the "roles" and "games" of society. They prefer mystical ecstasy to the fulfillment available through work, politics, religion and creative art.

Leary and Alpert left a response of sorts, written before their dismissals, in the summer issue of the *Harvard Review*. "The game is about to be changed, ladies and gentlemen," they wrote in a cheery nose-thumbing at the Harvard Corporation. "Man is about to make use of that fabulous electrical network he carries around in his skull. Present social establishments had better be prepared for the change. Our favorite concepts are standing in the way of a floodtide, two billion years building up."

A lot of Tim's friends thought he was making a bad mistake by not returning to Boston to contest, or at least correct, Harvard's version of his firing. But Leary couldn't be bothered. Harvard was part of his past; Zihuatanejo and IFIF were the future. And they were, for at least two more weeks, which was when the Mexican government closed Freedom House and deported everyone involved with IFIF.

16

HORSE LATITUDES

If this story were occurring twenty years in the future, the popular press would probably describe Leary's Freedom House as a "Club Med of the Mind." And this wouldn't be too far off the mark, as long as somewhere in the lead paragraph they also compared it to an "Outward Bound of the Mind." Within thirty-six hours the first group of prospective guides—the usual mixed bag, three dozen psychologists and social science types, with a sprinkling of artists and idle rich, a stockbroker, a TV actress, a French author, a yogi—were reduced to their bathing suits, and were slurping Zihuatanejo Zombies, which the Catalina bartender had created in honor of the returning gringos. But good fun and deep tans were clearly a secondary consideration: these people were here to learn how to guide an LSD trip, plus go on one themselves.

The prevailing mood was one of serious cosmic fun. Upon arrival every prospective guide was handed the Freedom House philosophy:

> The aim of the transpersonative community is to liberate members from their webs so that they can soar, at will, through the infinite space/time of the energy fields surrounding them. IFIF has come 4000 miles to get away from YOU! You may be frustrated to find people here who are uninterested in playing the game of YOU! Don't feel hurt. Climb out of your web and float after them.

And most did, enthusiastically throwing themselves into little rituals like "the tower," which was a wooden lifeguard platform down on the beach. The idea was that the tower would be occupied at all times by somebody who was pushing the envelope of consciousness, kind of a living symbol of their higher purpose. Once a hurricane blew up the coast and the guy who was up in the tower refused to come down. He sat up there in the howling wind like Ahab at the prow of the *Pequod,* and when it was over all he would say was "fantastic."

That word described a lot of things that happened, particularly the group mind. The group mind was one of those nebulous, subjective things that seemed to happen under LSD, which always evaporated when you applied objective standards of truth. "All I can say is our consciousness linked up, formed a new entity that was not human, and wasn't inhuman either," is the way one psychologist who was at Freedom House that summer remembers it. "I was one element in a larger entity. It was neither pleasant nor unpleasant and I felt no fear or alarm." What they felt was curiosity. Could you do anything with these group minds besides sit around and feel linked up? Was there any way to prove this was happening? One time a scorpion crawled into Metzner's bed and stung him; he had a violent allergic reaction to the antidote and broke out in a rash from head to toe. What a wonderful opportunity to see if they could telepathically heal the rash. They took LSD and gathered around Metzner and started bathing him with—I hate to say healing vibes but that was what it was—and Metzner felt this "tremendous heat; it started in the feet, moved slowly up the legs and body, the rash disappearing as it moved, and finally, it dispersed through the top of my head and I was clear!"

What a moment! If only somebody had remembered to bring a movie camera. Without documentation it was just another paranormal fish story.

A lot of the sessions took place down on the beach, in the surf, which had a remarkably soothing effect, particularly on those who got trapped in the Dark Wood and began freaking out. Which wasn't a rare occurrence: the first lesson a good guide had to learn was how to get their charges past what Stolaroff had called the evasive stage, which were all those maneuvers the terrified ego went in for in a futile effort to escape from the clutches of the Other World. There was always a moment when the inevitability of madness had a terrible clarity, and it helped to have somebody there to whisper, "Feel the waves and the sand. This was what it was like when we crawled out of the water eons ago."

It was a pleasant time (group minds and Zihuatanejo Zombies) and the only thing that made it less than carefree, at least for Metzner, was the steady stream of indigent young Americans who kept trying to gate crash. These kids weren't beatniks exactly, and they were still a few transformations away from being hippies; what they were was a relentless nuisance that got on the nerves of the locals, which started some familiar grumbling. Transpersonative Community? *Casa Libre? Que pasa?* Just as Leary's dog was supposed to have chewed up half of Newton

Center, the gringos at the Catalina began to be blamed for all sorts of mishaps, some of which (like the murder of a local man) had happened months before Leary's arrival.

Actually the parallels with Harvard went even deeper. You'll remember that the psilocybin project's most vigorous opponent was Herb Kelman, whose antagonism had been aroused by a speech Leary and Alpert had given to a convention of peers. This repeated itself in Mexico. The previous summer, after those first halycon weeks at the Hotel Catalina, Leary and Alpert had been invited to address the Mexican Psychoanalytic Association and had obliged with an account of their psilocybin work. Sitting in the audience was a Dr. Dionisio Nieto, who was director of the Medico-Biological Institute at the University of Mexico. Like Kelman before him, Nieto had been appalled by what he was hearing. "I felt Leary had done no original work," he later told a magazine writer. "His paper was absurd, confused, valueless. Attempting to release creative mental activity with hallucinogens is nonsense, since it is well established that no community ever achieved social or cultural progress thereby. Look at India with its hashish eaters. Look at our own Mazatec Indians with their sacred mushrooms. Nobody should encourage people to take LSD. I was tempted to protest to Harvard."

But when Nieto learned that Leary intended to establish a permanent research center at Zihuatanejo, he protested to the Mexican government instead, and they sent two *federales* posing as newspaper reporters to investigate. Thinking they were genuine journalists, and wishing to ingratiate IFIF with the native media, Metzner gave them the royal treatment. One even took an LSD trip. But the charade ended on June 13, when the men revealed their true identities and announced that IFIF had five days to pack up and leave the country. The reason? Operating a business on a tourist visa.

The deportation highlighted two serious and rather immediate problems. The first was their dwindling supply of LSD. The previous January, realizing that unless they could finesse their way around the new FDA ruling IFIF would be dead before it began, Leary had ordered a huge amount of LSD and psilocybin from Sandoz, enclosing a ten-thousand-dollar check that he half-hoped would divert their attention from the fact that he lacked the necessary FDA import license. But it hadn't. They had been turned down. The possibility of a drugless IFIF had loomed, before being averted by the timely arrival of Al Hubbard, who had reached into his leather bag and swapped five hundred hits of LSD for the remainder of Leary's psilocybin. But that was only a stopgap, and Leary had spent most of his time in Mexico beating the bushes for a chemical company willing to synthesize IFIF's LSD. Deportation had ended those negotiations, and the supply problem was back to square one, or worse, because their last little bit of LSD, the final few ampules, the ones they'd hidden in a hair tonic bottle, had shattered during deportation, leaking all over a suit jacket—which was admired and chewed on for months.

How could you expand the mind of America without mind expanders?

The temporary answer was: morning glory seeds. A few months earlier the botanical world had been startled by Albert Hofmann's announcement that he'd found an LSD-like compound in *Ipomea violacea*, the common morning glory. Or rather the botanical world was startled by the sudden demand for *Ipomea violacea*. People who didn't know a bulb from a sack of bone meal suddenly appeared at the counter asking for hundreds of pounds of morning glory seeds—seeds which bore such wonderfully suggestive names: Pearly Gates, Heavenly Blues. IFIF had prudently bought several hundred pounds (the growers, alerted to the nongardening use of their product, soon began treating the seeds with a noxious chemical), although no one had bothered to confirm Hofmann's data with a personal experiment until Metzner ground some up and mixed them with Coca Cola. It was one of the most nauseating things he'd ever swallowed, and barely psychedelic.

But it was going to have to do, because pressing problem number two was even more serious: money, of course. Unless IFIF found another site for Freedom House fairly soon, it was going to have to refund the deposits of the several hundred people who had signed up for Zihuatanejo—deposits that had already been spent. This was why Gunther Weil found himself winging toward Dominica, a sleepy little black volcanic rock in the Caribbean that was one of the last outposts of the British Empire. It was a drowsy languid *manana* land, run by an alcoholic civil service, and hotter than blazes: at midday the only things moving were the ceiling fans and the chickens.

IFIF had been invited to relocate on Dominica by the leader of a local free-love cult, who was also an enthusiastic fan of *Island*. He had read about IFIF's troubles in *Time* and had immediately fired off a letter to Tim singing the praises of Dominica. Weil had been sent to check things out, although by the time he learned the full story, it was already too late: Leary was on his way accompanied by a dozen or so IFIFers. The full story went something like this: a few months earlier, the free-love cultist had dashed into a burning building and pulled a couple of people to safety. This act of bravery had made him a national hero, which had brought him to the attention of what passed for the Dominican Liberation Front, a handful of excitable revolutionaries who were hoping to replicate on Dominica what Fidel had accomplished in Cuba. Pressed to become the figurehead of the revolution, the man had agreed. Weil had known nothing of this until the day he had been taken to a ramshackle hut in the jungle and there, under the glare of a bare bulb, the plot had been explained to him: Dominica would become a psychedelic paradise, but only after the revolution.

Of course the English, veterans of a century of native unrest, were privy to this rebellion. And in their context Leary became a chemical warfare expert who was being imported to do something nefarious, like dumping LSD in the water supply at the start of the revolution. From the day it landed, the IFIF contingent was blatantly shadowed by the police, and after a few days they were summoned to the office of the colonial governor and ordered to leave the island immediately. During their brief interview with the governor, he kept referring to several documents on the top of his desk, which, to everyone's astonishment, turned out to be Hofmann's original articles on LSD.

Deported from Dominica, they tried Antigua, bivouacking in a deserted Navy canteen called the Bucket of Blood. Although they worked hard at retrieving the pleasant mood of Zihuatanejo, almost without exception the sessions were terrible. And for the first time one of the graduate students went psychotic. He stood for hours in a standing Buddha posture, with kids scampering between his legs, and then he vanished. What was alarming about his disappearance was the fact that before vanishing he seemed to fixate on the notion that a sacrifice was needed to free IFIF from its bad luck, and that he was the anointed victim. Everyone fanned out and searched the island, but there wasn't a trace of him anywhere. Finally they notified the Antiguan authorities to be on the lookout for a tall American who might be acting a little strange, and settled down nervously to wait. Days passed, and then word came that he was being held in a special mental asylum in the middle of the jungle.

One of the first things Tim had done after arriving on Antigua was visit the half dozen local doctors to familiarize them with IFIF's research aims. One of these doctors was a Hungarian psychiatrist, a seedy character who made a good living traveling around the Caribbean doing lobotomies and receiving medals from the local *jefes;* the grad students were convinced he was really an ex-Nazi; and it was in this man's private asylum that their friend was being held. Dreading that he might already be lobotomized, Gunther Weil was sent to retrieve him. Weil found him, intact, way out in the jungle in a wooden stockade, sitting in a tiny cell surrounded by dozens of other tiny cells, each containing a living corpse. He was quite sane and blessedly free of all thoughts of sacrificing himself for the psychedelic cause. They put him on a plane and sent him home. A few days later the colonial governor of Antigua called Tim into his office and did the same for IFIF.

In less than three months they had been thrown out of three countries and one world-class University. Their plans were in disarray; they were deeply in debt; it was not an auspicious beginning for the ancient game. All they wanted was a hole they could crawl down and sleep for a few weeks. And it was then that Peggy Hitchcock mentioned an estate her twin brothers, Tommy and Billy, owned in Millbrook, New York, a village ninety miles north of New York City.

Estate was the *mot juste.* The acreage measured five miles by five miles and was dotted with ponds, streams, and seven or eight houses, one of which was a sixty-four-room Bavarian *château* that the brothers were thinking of tearing down rather than pay the taxes on it. Alpert was dispatched with Peggy Hitchcock to look the place over, and he reported back that it was exactly the sort of grandly isolated environment they were seeking. To enter the grounds you had to pass through a gatehouse with portcullis, and then wind up a twisty mile-long, maple-lined drive until you reached the decaying mansion, which was known locally as Alte Haus, or the Big House, built around the turn of the century by William Dietrich, a German immigrant who'd made a fortune wiring American cities with electric lights.

Leary interpreted this precedent of illumination as a good omen, and in mid-September, having packed the detritus of their Boston years into several rental trucks, a small band set out to colonize the huge musty relic. It was dusk when they arrived. The house, boarded and vacant, "loomed Transylvanian under its two high turrets and steep gables." Since the electricity was still off, they built a fire in the massive fireplace and waited for morning, tossing the I Ching for amusement. Up came hexagram #1, the double creative.

Before going to ground at Millbrook, Leary had stopped by the annual APA convention in Philadelphia, where he addressed a group of Lutheran psychologists. "You are witnessing a good, old-fashioned, traditional religious controversy," he'd said. "On the one side the psychedelic visionaries, somewhat uncertain about the validity of their revelations, embarrassedly speaking in new tongues . . . and on the other side the establishment (the administrators, the police, the fund-granting foundations, the job givers) pronouncing their familiar lines in the drama: 'Danger! Madness! Unsound! Intellectual corruption of youth! Irreparable damage! Cultism!' The issue of chemical expansion of consciousness is hard upon us. You can hardly escape it. You are going to be pressed for a position. Internal freedom is becoming a major religious and civil rights controversy."

He was right about the controversy. But wrong about the larger picture. "Harvard Profs Fired in Drug Scandal" was good copy and that's the way the media treated it. By the fall of 1963 negative pieces chronicling IFIF had appeared in *Esquire,* the *Saturday Evening Post,* and *Look,* the latter written by none other than Andrew Weil. The dominant theme was that LSD was a potentially useful substance that had become dangerous in the hands of irresponsible scientists like Leary and Alpert, whom *Esquire* described as "rivals for the title of world's worst bores." Any mention of the Other World or expanded consciousness was usually dismissed with a reference to "parlor-game mystics," "armchair pilgrims," and "illusory utopias." The most intellectually edifying discussion of the subject could be found in the summer issue of the *Harvard Review*, edited by the ubiquitous Andrew Weil, who to his credit had solicited the complete spectrum of psychedelic perspective. Leary and Alpert were represented with a by now characteristic defense of the Fifth Freedom, IFIF style. "Licensing will be necessary," they wrote. "You must be trained to operate. You must demonstrate your proficiency to handle consciousness-expanding drugs without danger to yourself or the public. The Fifth Freedom—the freedom to expand your own consciousness—cannot be denied without due cause." There were articles that argued that due cause existed for refusing to let everyone willy-nilly expand their consciousness. What if they screwed up, asked contributors like David Ricks. Does a person have the right to do something that "might be harmful when he is in no position to pick up the pieces?"

There was even, in early September, an editorial from Leary's old Harvard nemesis, Dr. Dana Farnsworth. Writing in *JAMA*, Farnsworth warned that "the siren song of expanded consciousness" was ringing in the ears of the American student.

> Our young people are being told that there is little hazard in the use of hallucinogens—"less harmful than aspirin or alcohol, less dangerous than riding in a motorcar"—and that the spiritual and intellectual rewards are vivid, wonderful, inexpressible. The case is made that men's minds are now "imprisoned" in verbal habits and formalities, and that the drugs offer an escape to a word free paradise. The claim is advanced that the drugs "free" the mind for creative activity that would otherwise be beyond the reach, and that subsequent psychological functioning, after the effects of the drugs have worn off, will be better than before.

This was a fair assessment of the IFIF philosophy, and Farnsworth was quite right when he pointed out that despite the "rhapsodic talk and writing" there was, as yet, no proof that any of these claims were true. There was so far only individual anecdote, which was inadmissible as scientific evidence. Of course Farnsworth's own assertion that psychedelics exerted "powerful and often damaging effects on the human system," was equally anecdotal. He repeated Grinker's unverified assertion that latent psychotics were disintegrating after one experience with LSD and he mentioned an article published the previous June in the *Saturday Review* with the sensational title: "They Split My Personality."

It's worth pausing to take a closer look at this last exhibit, because it is a good example of a genre of psychedelic story that, in a less polished, articulate, and often anonymous form, became extremely popular. Harry Asher, the article's author, was a lecturer in physiology at the University of Birmingham in England. His specialty was visual functions, which was why he was curious about LSD in the first place. He wanted to hallucinate and "the day came when I sat in a chair in a laboratory, and a man in a white overall handed me a beaker containing thirty millionths of a gram of lysergic acid."

Asher was in the hands of a fairly common type of LSD researcher: interested in physiological data, they paid little attention to things like set and setting; if they subscribed to any of the larger theories of what LSD did in the mind, it was usually that of the psychotomimeticist. They took Asher's EEG, they asked him to look at a flashing light and dictate into a tape any hallucinations he might have. "A lady psychiatrist sat by the side of the couch with a notebook in her hand. She could control the frequency of the flashes by turning a knob." After six hours of this he was escorted to the cafeteria for afternoon tea, and it was on the way back that he realized he had split into two distinct people.

Panicked, Asher asked to be taken home and the psychiatrists obliged. At home he began compulsively walking around the block—"Keep the children away from me, will you please?" he told his wife, who had been briefed by the psychiatrist—in an attempt to integrate his several selves. The next morning Asher couldn't get out of bed. He lay there weeping. When a contingent of worried researchers arrived from the hospital, their faces appeared green. He wanted to jump out the window, which was why he was usually heavily sedated. This went on for several months before the symptoms faded away.

Stories like this drove Leary up a wall. Through a thorough disregard of set and setting, Harry Asher's doctors had driven him crazy. Yet this kind of psychedelic malpractice was considered responsible, while his own work was dismissed as bad science.

Perhaps the only halfway positive article about IFIF that appeared in the fall of 1963 was Allen Harrington's account of his LSD session with Metzner, which *Playboy* published in November. Besides being one of the few journalists who actually took LSD with one of Leary's guides, Harrington was also rare in his feeling that you ridiculed Tim Leary at your own peril. Fired from Harvard, exiled from Mexico, reviled by his more conservative colleagues—instead of falling on his face in disgrace, the man had ended up in a mansion in upstate New York enjoying the patronage of one of America's wealthiest families.

But that November *Playboy* was special for reasons other than Harrington's article. It was special because it contained a short piece entitled "Hallucinogens: A Philosopher's Visionary Prediction," which was the last thing Aldous Huxley would ever write about his psychedelic dream.

The crab, in remission since 1960, had come creeping back, and by autumn it was touch and go. Huxley checked into a Los Angeles hospital and tried to ignore the disease that was ravaging his throat. He was unable to write because of the pain, but he did have a dictaphone and in lucid moments he worked on an essay on Shakespeare. Although his condition was obviously grave, he refused to acknowledge the possibility of death. Did he know he was dying? It was a question his wife, Laura, couldn't answer:

> We read the entire manual of Dr. Leary based on the *Tibetan Book of the Dead.* He could have, even jokingly, said: "Don't forget to remind me when the time comes." His comment instead was directed only to the problem of "reentry" after a psychedelic session. It is true he sometimes said things like, "If I get out of this," in connection with his new ideas of writing, and wondered when and if he would have the strength to work. He was mentally very active and it seemed that some new levels of his mind were stirring.

But on the morning of November twenty-second, a Friday, it became clear the gap between living and dying was closing. Realizing that Aldous might not survive the day, Laura sent a telegram to his son, Matthew, urging him to come at once. At ten in the morning, an almost inaudible Aldous asked for paper and scribbled "If I go," and then some directions about his will. It was his first admission that he might die. Soon after he murmured, "Who is eating out of my bowl?" When Laura asked what he meant he dismissed it as a private joke. "At this point there is so little to share," he told her, a statement that she interpreted as meaning no questions. Around noon he asked for the pad of paper and scribbled

LSD—try it
intermuscular
100mm

In a letter circulated among Aldous's friends, Laura Huxley described what followed: "You know very well the uneasiness in the medical mind about this drug. But no 'authority,' not even an army of authorities, could have stopped me then. I went into Aldous's room with the vial of LSD and prepared a syringe. The doctor asked me if I wanted him to give the shot—maybe because he saw that my hands were trembling. His asking me that made me conscious of my hands, and I said, 'No, I must do this.' "

An hour later she gave Huxley a second 100mm. Then she began to talk, bending close to his ear, whispering, "light and free you let go, darling; forward and up. You are going forward and up; you are going toward the light. Willingly and consciously you are going, willing and consciously, and you are doing this beautifully; you are doing this so beautifully—you are going toward the light—you are going toward the light—you are going toward a greater love. . . . You are going toward Maria's love with my love. You are going toward a greater love than you have ever known. You are going toward the best, the greatest love, and it is easy, it is so easy, and you are doing it so beautifully."

All struggle ceased. The breathing became slower and slower and slower, until, "like a piece of music just finishing so gently in *sempre piu piano, dolcamente,*" at twenty past five in the afternoon, Aldous Huxley died.

And it was only then that Laura Huxley really had the time to fathom the other great tragedy of the day, the assassination of the President in Dallas.

Reading the official obituaries, it was hard not to feel that Huxley had wasted the last third of his life after a brilliant couple of furlongs. But he had a second audience, as yet without a voice aside from the *Psychedelic Review,* and it was here that he received his due. He was that "rarest of alloys," wrote Gerald Heard, "taste combined with temerity, daring speculation delivered in a perfect rendition of lucid and elegant restraint." Alan Watts predicted that in twenty years "It will be clear to all of us that Aldous Huxley had a genius for raising the right questions." He was a "calypso guru" remembered Tim. "Under what heading do we file the smiling prophet? The nuclear age bodhisattva?"

Psychedelics had made Huxley, in some quarters, an object of ridicule, what with his cheerful espousal of mysticism and drugs, and his rather schoolmarmish pep talks about human potentials. *Island,* while enthralling members of the psychedelic movement, had received lukewarm or negative reviews elsewhere. As Sybil Bedford, Huxley's biographer, observed: "To a number of his readers [*Island*] with its happiness and kindliness and good sense was immensely moving. . . . To a great many others, and this must be faced, the book was a boring tale of preaching goody-goodies." Having fun with fungi, was the way one reviewer dismissed the book. And in *Playboy,* Huxley responded: "Which is better," he asked, "to have Fun with Fungi or to have Idiocy with Ideology, to have Wars because of Words, to have Tomorrow's Misdeeds out of Yesterday's Miscreeds?"

In a world of "explosive population increase, of headlong technological advance and of militant nationalism," *Homo sapiens* had to discover, and very soon, "new energy sources for overcoming our society's psychological inertia." Mankind could no longer afford the luxury of a Bronze Age psyche in a world of hydrogen bombs. What was needed, Huxley wrote, was a specialized course of education:

> On the verbal level an education in the nature and limitations, the uses and abuses of language; on the wordless level an education in mental silence and pure receptivity; and finally, through the use of harmless psychedelics, a course of chemically triggered experiences or ecstasies—these, I believe, will provide all the sources of mental energy, all the solvents of conceptual sludge, that an individual requires . . . if the number of such individuals is sufficiently great, if their quality is sufficiently high, they may be able to pass from undiscriminating acceptance of their culture to discriminating change and reform. Is this a hopefully utopian dream? Experiment can give us the answer, for the dream is pragmatic; the utopian hypotheses can be tested empirically. And in these oppressive times a little hope is surely no unwelcome visitant.

But while Huxley was content to speculate, he had always backed away from the larger implications of his vision. "The last thing I want is to create an image of myself as 'Mr. LSD,' " he once wrote Osmond. "Nor have I the least desire (being without any talent for this kind of thing) to get involved in the politics of psychedelics." Unfortunately, this left the game entirely in the hands of people whom Aldous referred to as the "white hot enthusiasts." But this was changing. If only he had lived a year or two longer, Humphrey Osmond always felt, then his example of "elegant restraint" might have prevented that rash chap, Tim Leary, from cocking the snooks he was destined to cock.

17

PUSHING THE ENVELOPE

Memoirs of Millbrook are rarely coherent. What is offered is a series of snapshots: Tim astride a horse painted blue on one side, pink on the other; Tim popping into the kitchen exclaiming, "Jesus Christ, do I have to fuck every girl who comes into this place"; Metzner tinkering in his electronics laboratory, producing eight-hour tapes that Leary and Alpert would listen to in the meditation room, waiting for the whispered instructions to lift their imprints; R. D. Laing performing a *sufi* ballet in the kitchen; Alan Watts interpreting the *I Ching*, fire crackling in the huge central fireplace, shadows dancing like Tibetan temple gods across the ceiling; or Maynard Ferguson standing on the rooftop sending long trumpet rills snaking out over the gardens, in which another jazz legend, Charlie Mingus, could sometimes be found pruning the rosebushes. "A golden year," was Alpert's memory of those first months at Millbrook. Leary, characteristically, was more dramatic: "On this space colony we were attempting to create a new paganism and a new dedication to life as art."

In some accounts Millbrook resembles an ashram or monastery, a refuge for seekers on the higher paths of consciousness; in others it emerges as a unique research institute, a place where psychologists frustrated with the accepted models of mind could pursue their research in peace. Both descriptions are correct, as far as they go. But Millbrook was also a school, a commune, and a house party of unparalleled dimensions. Mel Brooks would have had no problem casting a movie there, recalled one habitué. Others, echoing the movie analogy, felt Fellini a more appropriate director.

At the center of all these memoirs is the astonishing Victorian labyrinth that was Alte Haus, the Big House, dark and mysterious, the halls carpeted with a frayed red fabric, the walls covered with psychedelic frescoes. Marya Mannes, who spent a memorable night there in 1966, described Dietrich's dream house as "unparalleled ugliness—the nadir in turrets, porches and fretted woodwork"; while the assistant district attorney for Dutchess County, making an unannounced call late one night, was appalled to find almost no furniture, aside from the carcass of a seemingly dead (actually he was only stoned) dog. Millbrook was a "strange mutation of Thoreau's Walden and a Tantric Buddhist temple," wrote an anonymous reporter for *Time*. "In the drafty hall of the main house, part of a grand piano sits on its side, its strings waiting to be plucked. The rooms are furnished with legless tables, bedless mattresses and mandalas on which the eye of the true believer is supposed to 'lock' during drugless exercises."

That is a future snapshot. With less than a dozen occupants, the rhythm of that first autumn is peaceful, almost scholarly, the days spent browsing through the library (which already contains an impressive collection of esoteric and scientific texts) or writing: the second issue of *The Psychedelic Review* is in the works, and the updated version of the *Bardo Thodol* is almost ready for the printer. As autumn deepens into winter, the long meditative walks in the woods give way to afternoon skating parties on frozen ponds. At night, after dinner, there is talk and games, sometimes poetic little psychodramas of Tim's devising, and sometimes actual poetry, like the Japanese *renga*, with everyone contributing a line.

From the towers, on a clear night, across acres of pine, the village of Millbrook twinkles, while up above, the galaxies of the Milky Way wheel through limitless space. It is as though, after the upheavals and uproar of the past few months, they have stumbled across a fairytale castle, entering a timeless dimension where the gap between psychedelic time and real time doesn't exist. They were "anthropologists from the twenty-first century," wrote Leary, "inhabiting a time module set somewhere in the dark ages of the 1960s."

One of the first things they do is convert one of the tower rooms into an experimental laboratory. They paint the ceiling gold and install unobtrusive speakers so that music and whispered instruction can be piped in from below, the ultimate in unobtrusive guiding. (They favor Indian or classical music, for nothing is more jarring to psychedelic balance than a three-minute rock song about hormonal lust.) Next to the bed are statues of Shiva and the Buddha.

Once a week each member of the household ascends the tower and embarks upon a carefully programmed "ontological adventure." The objective is the complete mapping of the Other World. Leary dreams of the day when it will be possible to program any trip—early childhood? the Dark Wood? an afternoon of archetypes?—just tell the guide where you wanted to go, what mental spaces you wished to explore and then lie back and watch the Door open. But before this can happen, the Other World has to be charted, guidebooks assembled and published. This is the rationale behind *The Psychedelic Experience,* which is what they've renamed the *Tibetan Book of the Dead,* and which is now merely volume one in an extended guide to psychedelia; there are plans to work similar transformations on Dante's *Divine Comedy,* the *Egyptian Book of the Dead,* Bunyan's *Pilgrim's Progress,* and the Tao *Te Ching.*

"It became apparent that in order to run exploratory sessions, manuals and programs were necessary to guide subjects through the transcendental experience with a minimum of fear and confusion," Leary writes in *The Psychedelic Review.* "Rather than start *de novo* using our own minds and limited experiences to map out the voyage, we turned to the only available psychological texts which dealt with consciousness and its alterations."

Momentarily free from the political and professional disputes that have drained so much of his energy during the past eighteen months, Leary returns to his old love, behavior change, and to his old problem: how to explain, in scientific terms, the mechanism that allows psychedelics to change behavior. Convinced psychology offers few fruitful avenues, he begins exploring the latest discoveries in genetics, quantum physics, and biology, and eventually zeroes in on ethologist Konrad Lorenz's theory of imprinting. Lorenz happened to be present one day when some goose eggs hatched in an incubator. Consequently he was the first large thing the goslings saw after pecking their way out of the eggshells. To his utter astonishment they reacted by treating him as their mother. The attachment was irreversible: Lorenz's goslings would have nothing to do with other geese. It was as though, in those first moments of consciousness, the mind had taken a snapshot of reality— "a sudden, shutterlike fixing of the nervous system" was the way Leary described it—that was inalterable:

> Once taken, the picture then determines the scope and type of subsequent "lawful learning." Imprinting, a biochemical event, sets up the chessboard upon which slow, step by step conditioning takes place.

Aldous Huxley had theorized that psychedelics temporarily disrupted the mind's reducing valves, thereby allowing information that was usually screened out to flow freely into consciousness; Leary was now proposing that these same drugs momentarily neutralized those primary biochemical imprints, those deep behavior patterns, those metagames. But as every psychedelic therapist knew, the open cortex lasted only so long before the patient started to slide back into old behavior patterns, before the imprints reasserted themselves.

But was this inevitable?

Leary doesn't think so. Why can't they amuse themselves trying to find a way to lift their own imprints and reinsert new ones? They do this by creating, after much trial and error, eight- and ten-hour tapes. For a time, it is routine to find Tim and Dick lying with their heads touching in the meditation room, gazing up at the golden ceiling, while from all sides come whispered instructions and pulses of music, the work of Metzner who spends long days making guide tapes in his little laboratory.

But it soon becomes apparent that tapes are not enough to weaken all their behavior patterns. They need to develop additional techniques that will undermine their normal conditioning when they are not in the drug state. This becomes known as "breaking set," and in the early months a number of experiments are devised to jar them out of their usual habits. The first involves communal child rearing, which sounds ideal in theory and which Huxley has heartily recommended in *Island*. Besides easing the parental burden, it is thought that everyone will profit from proximity with that state of spontaneous innocent curiosity that children are so famous for. In practice, however, Alpert and Metzner end up as full-time nannies, which they endure for a few weeks before rebelling, thus ending the communal child-rearing experiment.

Thereafter the kids are left to shift for themselves, an increasingly out of place element in the adult funhouse that Millbrook is becoming.

The next experiment might be called the desert island strategy. In this one, two names are drawn at random and the couple is obliged to spend the next five days alone together in the little coach house that contains a bowling alley, sometimes tripping, sometimes straight, but always seeking new levels of friendship. Although this experiment is soon abandoned as too artificial, it paves the way for what becomes known as "the third floor experiment." This one focuses on sexual possessiveness and includes anyone who wants to move onto the third floor where beds were communal property, available to anyone who wanted to climb between the sheets. Except for a "bisexually promiscuous lesbian," most of the participants find the experiment more daunting than they expected: "We did a lot of sitting in bed and talking about how it felt," writes Metzner. "It was unsettling not to know where you could go to sleep, or who you would be sleeping with, when you were tired. So this experiment also was discontinued after a week or two."

* * *

In November they announce the death of IFIF. "In the evolutionary sense," Tim writes in the final IFIF newsletter, it was "too soon, too-weak, and too-rigid to deal with the external pressures. Rather than limp along as a bypassed species, we believe it better that the form be scrapped." But while he is happy to forego the bureaucratic headaches involved in an international organization, Tim is reluctant to relinquish his dream of a tropical island. A committee, he assures the IFIF membership, is already vetting possible locations. If all goes well, an island institute will be operational by the summer of 1964. Meanwhile IFIF has mutated into a new organization: Castalia.

The name comes from an obscure novel, *The Glass Bead Game,* written by an obscure Nobel prize winner named Herman Hesse. Although Hesse's work attracted admirers like T. S. Eliot and Thomas Mann, he is unread in the United States, an obscurity that the *New York Times,* in its obituary, attributed to his "profound spiritual themes" and the "melancholy mandarin quality" of his heroes—precisely the qualities that attracted first Metzner (who was part German), then Leary. Reading novels like *Steppenwolf, The Glass Bead Game,* and *A Journey to the East,* they became convinced that Hesse was a psychedelic adept from an earlier age. And one who had succeeded where Huxley had failed, in the sense that while his books were about the internal drama of the psyche, they were also compulsively readable stories. *Narcissus and Goldmann,* read on one level, was the story of two medieval friends, one a monk, the other a man of the world. Taken on another level, it was a parable about the personality and the soul.

A Journey to the East began: "It was my destiny to join in a great experience. Our goal was not only the East, or rather the East was not only a country and something geographical, but it was the home and youth of the soul, it was everywhere and nowhere, it was the union of all times."

At first only the mailman disrupts their solitude. He brings huge cartons of mail, the fruits of a clipping service that Leary has engaged to keep them abreast of developments concerning psychedelics. The volume is extraordinary—by summer the service will be billing them for so much work it will have to be discontinued—and although the tone is largely negative, the sheer magnitude of product indicates that psychedelics have touched a nerve, has awakened something powerful in the American psyche. As word of Leary's whereabouts spreads, cartons of letters begin arriving, soliciting information, offering advice, asking for drugs.

Quietly, almost secretly, they begin training guides. Some are the result of the short-lived IFIF, but others simply write requesting information and are invited for a visit. Art Kleps, a school psychologist in upstate New York, was leafing through the *New York Times* one day when he came across an article about Castalia. Having previously experimented with mescaline, Kleps was astonished to discover that "a group of perfectly respectable intellectuals were taking LSD and psilocybin and apparently functioning with great practical efficiency at the same time, having a ball, setting out on great adventures and taking over mansions in Dutchess County."

Kleps drops Tim a note expressing his interest in psychedelics and is rewarded with a postcard invitation. He arrives a few days after Christmas, 1963, joining several other psychologists and an artist who is about to undergo his first ontological adventure in the tower.

Although there is some grumbling over accommodations—"Making your own bed and helping with the dishes?" groused one of the psychologists. "I have always been very happy to pay for that kind of service."—it is more than compensated for by the air of harmonious pleasure that fills the Big House. It seems to Kleps that the quality of life at Millbrook is "better, more lively, more meaningful, funnier, happier . . . Timothy Leary, I thought, was a magician who seemed to change life as it was lived."

Kleps is in the kitchen drinking coffee when the artist appears after his first session in the tower. He drifts in "like a ghost, his big brown eyes shining and dilated," murmuring "beautiful, beautiful . . . but I seem to have switched sides. My left side is now my right side and my right side is my left side. As a matter of fact I think I left part of myself up in the tower. I have to go back and get it."

Watching him drift off, it occurs to Kleps that there is a deeply serious side to all the talk about behavior change. The idea of taking LSD is beginning to "scare the living piss" out of him.

A common enough reaction. It is Castalia policy that a beginner needs at least fifteen carefully guided trips before even the most modest level of proficiency is attained.

As the months pass, occupancy of the Big House becomes increasingly fluid. Maynard and Flo Ferguson arrive with their five kids to occupy a suite of rooms on the second floor. A few doors down is a young friend of Alpert's who is reportedly having adjustment problems, and a young woman who was one of their research assistants at Harvard. Michael Hollingshead makes a reappearance, as do a number of old friends from the Harvard and IFIF years—Frank Barron, Walter Houston Clark, Alan Watts.

The weekend parties are famous. For a time a weekend at Millbrook with the cosmic Castalians is *de rigeur* if you are a member of the wealthy New York young adult set and know any of the Hitchcock kids. The Hitchcocks don't stay at the Big House; they all have their own places on the grounds. The most spectacular, in the sense of driving home how the rich really are different, is Billy's little copper-roofed bungalow, with servants' quarters, swimming pool, tennis courts, billiard room, formal library.

Billy Hitchcock is new to the psychedelic movement. He has been working in London for Lazard Frères during the IFIF years. Tall and blonde, with an uncomplicated and rather nice attitude toward the world, Billy reminds Art Kleps of a "Frank Merriwhether type who had somehow fallen into a pool of gold and came up smelling of marijuana." Before guiding an LSD session, Tim usually asks the person what they hope to accomplish in the Other World. Most reply that they are seeking ego loss or cosmic unity. But not Billy. "How can I make more money on the stockmarket," was his answer.

Had Aldous Huxley lived to attend a Millbrook weekend, he probably would have been reminded of those epic houseparties during the First World War at Garsington. Of course in those days the elixir had been conversation, witty and heretical and always elegantly phrased. At Millbrook the weekends are powered by an expanding shelf of party favors—hashish, DMT, psilocybin, LSD, mescaline, peyote, mushrooms, marijuana (Tim has gotten over his paranoia), and alcohol. Although the media will shortly dub him the high priest of psychedelia, Leary still likes his Jameson's.

Some weekends Metzner counts over a hundred new faces: "jazz musicians, avant garde painters, underground filmmakers, high level procurers, mysterious Orientals, night creatures with huge eyes and chromatic chiffon dresses floated softly through the house, carrying large chunks of hashish . . . sometimes Millbrook felt like a kind of orbiting astral space station, where beings on different levels of consciousness converged to exchange communications."

Once a novice who is undergoing his inaugural session in the tower blunders into the middle of one of these frolics. He stands there transfixed, and then blurts out, "Christ, it's crazy enough up there. But down here it's completely insane."

How to describe the feeling that steals over them that winter? It is like a melody whose vibration is felt rather than heard, a tune that grows stronger as the weeks pass, until it blots out all the theories about imprinting and breaking set.

The Buddha, after six years of meditation and fasting, sits down under a Bo tree and after forty-nine days of mental struggle pierces the final veil, attaining enlightenment. That's what the melody says to them: it's time to sit under the Bo tree and push the envelope to its final limit; it's time to storm heaven.

Imagine a climbing expedition that is trying to scale Everest. Hundreds of people are involved: Sherpa guides and technicians and porters, who drop away as the goal nears, until it is just the one or two climbers who try for the top.

Tim is the first climber. On March 21, the Vernal Equinox, they escort him to the meditation hut with a torchlight parade. Alan Watts consecrates the moment with a candlelight reading of the *I Ching*, then everyone files out, leaving Tim alone for a week of solitary voyaging. Swallowing his first LSD, he wraps himself in a heavy winter coat and walks outside into the late-winter chill. There is a full moon. He howls at it. The Big House is dark, remote. He lies down on one of the hills and stares at the stars, listening to the wind in the pines, an antenna tuned into a million channels of information.

The days pass. The envelope holds.

Leary is granted a vision, though, an intuition, which seems to tell him that mankind must link up with womankind; only when these two specialized consciousnesses are psychedelically entwined can the next stage of evolution occur.

The attempt on the envelope also pushes him deeper into the ancient role, which is perhaps to say it burns out a lot more of his old imprints. Talking with Tim becomes an exercise in indirection:

"Tim, is anything more important than anything else?"
"Look at the way the snow shines in the moonlight. Beautiful isn't it?"

One day he is in the orchard with an enthusiastic market gardener who wants to cut down the twisted old apple trees and replace them with some hybrids. "You realize this is a very reckless conversation you're involved in," Leary says. The gardener, unsure if he is being spoofed, says "Yeah, the trees can hear, right?" "You notice that I've said nothing except friendly and protective things about these trees," Tim says. "There's no testimony from me."

Is he serious? It's impossible to fathom his almost perpetual smile. Here is a man who has been fired from Harvard and ridiculed by most of the major media; he should be despondent, depressed, repentent, yet he is smiling broadly and surrounded, as often as not, by beautiful women.

But are any of them suitable dyad material?

With the warm weather they purchase a lawn mower and mow the enormous lawn. They restore the formal flowerbeds, one shaped like a moon, the other like the sun. They prune the maple trees and whitewash the stones along the drive, an act which prompts Alpert to remark that the place is starting to look like a Jewish country club. They plant a vegetable garden. The Millbrook *Round Table* runs a picture of Tim pushing a power mower with the caption: "Woodchucks in his Fields."

Their industriousness is not lost on the villagers of Millbrook, many of whom are related to the craftsmen that Dietrich imported to build the Big House. Art Kleps observes that "in town Tim [is] greeeted warmly by storekeepers and townspeople and he seem[s] genuinely happy playing the role of one of the boys, fellow villager and good neighbor with a few easy bantering words for one and all."

Luckily the locals haven't seen the interior improvements that have been taking place at the Big House. Most of the furniture has been thrown out, or the legs cut off so that you can live right down on the floor. Ceilings are in the process of being painted gold, walls are filling up with mandalas, and corners are becoming impromptu shrines, mingling Hindu and Tantric symbols with whatever esoteric practice is ascendent this week. Georges Gurdjieff is a new discovery, and several times a week a group drives into New York to attend a lecture on "the work," which is what the Gurdjieffians call their assorted exercises.

Alpert is off to Canada in his Cessna, ostensibly to rendezvous with a shipment of Czechoslovakian LSD, most of which is going to Millbrook, but a small portion will be distributed to researchers whose work has been curtailed by the FDA. But Alpert is also scheduled to meet with a wealthy dowager who has become interested in using LSD as a possible preparation for death—Eric Kast, at the University of Chicago, was doing the best work in this area. Castalia was happy to oblige the old lady's curiosity. Wealthy old dowagers frequently leave nice bequests in their will, and right about now Castalia could use a nice bequest.

Lack of money, that eternal foe of utopian dreams, has once again shown its craven face.

One obvious solution is to charge an admission fee to visit Castalia, a popular proposal since the weekend crush has become so intense that a few of the regulars have taken to camping out in the woods, appearing only for meals. They could resurrect the old Freedom House plan and turn the Big House into a summer academy that would give seminars in nondrug ways of expanding consciousness and breaking set. A reporter from *Newsweek* is lured up to publicize the academy, and while the tone of the eventual piece is mocking ("Now, after fighting their way to a commanding height hard by the Catskills, the two tanned and sinewy proponents of better living survey an empty plain."), it serves its purpose. It also reveals a growing canniness on Leary's part concerning the media. The previous autumn, when *Time* ran a dismissive piece on IFIF, they illustrated the story with a picture of Alan Watts and Tim bending over an extremely glamorous research subject. Although the text was negative, the context implied that beautiful women and psychedelic drugs went hand in hand. A similar bit of message mixing was prepared for the *Newsweek* writer, who couldn't help but remark how "girls in bikinis . . . prowl loose-limbed" throughout the Big House.

The summer sessions pose a number of interesting problems: to wit, how in thirty-six hours can you accomplish your stated aim of altering the consciousness of these refugees from the normal world? How can you awaken them to the rich mental experiences that are normally ruled out of bounds by the rational, nine-to-five mind?

Thinking it better to ease them slowly into the looking-glass world of the Big House, they decide to hold a get-to-know-one-another cocktail party for the first group. Bad mistake. "The straights immediately plunged into the cocktail party game of which they were experts," remembers Hollingshead. " 'Hi, I'm Jack Smith from Denver, who are you?' 'Jack Smith, eh?' And so on. As we were novices in the cocktail party game we were completely flattened."

To compensate they decide to "break set" as soon as the weekenders arrive. Social roles, titles, and habits will be checked at the door. No talking the first night. Everyone will wear identical white robes. Art Kleps is there when one of these Friday-night transformations takes place: "I had seen perhaps twenty of them, mostly conservatively dressed and middle-aged, come in the front door, smiling grimly but with fear in their eyes, to follow a silent but beaming Dick Alpert up the stairs. When they came down a couple of hours later, however . . . I could hardly believe my eyes. They were all wearing white robes made out of bed sheets. The robes were intended to obliterate social distinctions. It was like a gathering of the Klan."

Hollingshead is a genius at ingenious ways to break set. His most famous suggestion was the food-dye-in-the-breakfast-food suggestion. "We are very much affected by the imprints we have, particularly those of color associations," Metzner says as the guests contemplate their green eggs and black milk. "When someone says *sky,* we think of blue, when someone says *meadow* we think of green, when someone says *scrambled eggs* we think of yellow. But this is a mental hangup. It doesn't really make any difference whether scrambled eggs are green, as they are today, or whether they are yellow."

Although great pains are taken with explaining the theory here, appetites tend to vanish along with the imprints. Which prompt certain wits to point out that regardless how useful the dyes are in "breaking set," they are a financial godsend, since food consumption always drops considerably.

Visitors arrive daily. A writer named Robert Anton Wilson arrives to do a piece on Castalia for the *Realist*, a satirical magazine edited by Paul Krassner. He finds everyone out on the lawn playing baseball, although Maynard Ferguson is standing on the roof playing jazz on his trumpet. Wilson is probably the only journalist who has ever read Tim's first book, and Leary responds to his obvious passion.

"LSD takes you out of the normal space-time ego," he says. "I always go through a process in which the space game comes to an end, the time game comes to an end, and then the Timothy Leary game comes to an end. This is the peak, and at this point a new neurological imprint can be made, because all the old imprints are suspended for a while then."

Warming to the topic, Tim outlines one of his current fantasies: a national chain of imprinting clinics. Prospective patients would meet with a behavior change expert who would explain the pros and cons of psychedelic imprinting. Loaded with literature, the patient would take a week to think it over, then meet a second time with the behavior-change expert and work out exactly what program they want to pursue. "The most important rule," Leary keeps stressing, "is that the tripper decides what behavior change is desired. Nobody else has the right to decide for him."

Another time two FDA officials drop by. "We are shocked by what you people are doing," Leary remembers them saying. "For centuries drug taking has been considered a vice. Now you are not only defending it, you're suggesting it's moral, educational, even religious. Maybe Kennedy went along with this kind of thinking, but Johnson is different."

"The people in law enforcement—and believe me, they have the power—can't wait for these drugs to be illegal so they can bust your ass."

An acquaintance of Myron Stolaroff arrives for a visit and sends letters to the West Coast describing daily life in the Big House: "Our days pass like any other Charles Addams family—with some people on a macrobiotic diet, the family around the fireplace smoking pot after dinner (dinner being served from 10:30 to midnight), palm reading, the reading of Jung, Gurdjieff and Ouspensky, Tantric chants, bells continually ringing, wrestling matches, children, popcorn, motorbikes, raccoon coats.

"Emotionally the place is satisfying. There is a middle-aged Baronessa from Sweden and she is teaching me to cook and we spend time together—she's Mother. Tim is Father, and when I ask him what I am supposed to do he says 'Be happy, for once in your life.' There are numerous brothers and sisters and, as I say, emotional needs are fulfilled. They don't know it, but Millbrook is really a transcendent therapeutic community."

The middle-aged Baroness is actually Tim's future mother-in-law. Her daughter, Nena, is locally famous as the striking blonde who comes sailing up the Hudson in a Viking warship in the Eric the Red cigar commercials. She is, according to *Harpers Bazaar*, "an avid concert and ballet goer . . . born in Mexico and raised in Peking, she became a seasoned traveler at a youthful age, so today it's only natural that she spends much of her time jetting from her New York base to various and sundry European and Asian destinations."

Tim met her at Millbrook's huge Fourth of July party and instantly knew she was the long-lost other half of his personal dyad. Their lovemaking in the afternoon is so vigorous that Alpert, who occupies the room below Tim's, can't meditate. But it is obvious that it's less the lovemaking than the love that bothers Dick. "In many ways I was like Dick's father," Leary later writes. "In our household, Dick, who was extremely close to his mother, took on what he has often described as the maternal wifely role. He was definitely closer to Susan and Jack than I."

For a time it seems Alpert might boycott the planned nuptials, which are set for December 12, 1964. But then he agrees to act as best man and begins "treating the ceremony as high camp." Leary plans to honeymoon in India, which means that Dick will be in complete charge of Castalia.

Ralph Metzner is already in India, having left early in autumn with members of the same Boston Vedanta ashram that Tim had given LSD. His letters paint an idyllic portrait: "This morning I sat in the woods with a far-out German book on Tibetan medicine, written by a Benedictine monk, which Lama Govinda loaned me. The landlady's dog was chasing monkeys up the tree. . . ."

Tim couldn't wait to go. Writing to Metzner, he confesses that he is eager to surrender his responsibility and settle into connubial bliss in the Himalayan foothills, pursuing "the incredible complexities that develop when two people begin to explore their potentialities together." His one fear is that there won't be enough senior staff at the Big House to keep Castalia on track, but "Richard has mutated. He has taken over 'Tim's role' whatever that means and is genial, hospitable, radiating plans and welcomes. He is filling the house with creative and beautiful women."

In the same letter he describes two recent lectures he has given in Palo Alto and San Francisco. Overflow crowds, he writes. And in cynical

New York he packs the one thousand, three hundred-seat auditorium at Cooper Union, forcing hundreds to stand in the back. "It was like whispering things in your lover's ear . . . the political-educational battle over psychedelics has been won. From now on it's just a matter of time."

That's the official Millbrook slideshow, ending with Tim and Nena's wedding, a completely surreal affair that saw the happy couple showered with drugs, instead of china and silver patterns. This was not going to be a Blondie/Dagwood dyad.

But there are other snapshots of those first few months that have been left in the drawer, because no one knew their significance at the time. The most interesting of these was taken in August. It was a hot, calm day. People were sunning themselves on the lawn. Leary was upstairs in the middle of a three-day trip when this fever on wheels came tearing up the drive, its progress punctuated by the green smoke bombs its occupants kept tossing from the windows. It was a school bus, true, but the sort of school bus Hieronymous Bosch might have produced had he been a tormented maintenance man at a local high school. The thing seethed with color. Sliding to a stop, it broke open and disgorged some equally loud and obnoxious hatchlings.

The sun bathers scurried for safety.

Ken Kesey and his Merry Pranksters had arrived.

18

THE BOY MOST LIKELY TO
SUCCEED

Richard Todd, writing in the Harvard *Alumni Bulletin,* once observed that "the reason Timothy Leary has puzzled and interested people, and appalled them, is that once he was someone else. One day he was an energetic and respected psychologist, and the next—the magic mushrooms—he was on his way to becoming a drifting head." Change a noun or two and that observation could apply with equal acuity to Ken Elton Kesey: one day he was a superb athlete, an upstanding civic example, voted "most likely to succeed" by his high school classmates; a promising novelist, author of two highly praised books before his thirtieth birthday, a committed family man, married to his high school sweetheart, sober, abstemious, but then—LSD—he became . . . like Leary, it depended upon your perspective. To his companions, the Merry Pranksters, Kesey was "the Chief," having penetrated deeper into the wilderness of the Other World than any of them. To a young girl who met him at a Unitarian conference he was "the Prophet Kesey." To the authorities he was a dangerous crank who abused his God-given talent for leadership.

But if Leary and Kesey had arrived, via psychedelics, at equivalent stations of respect and approbation, the roads they had taken to get there were markedly different. While Leary's Irish forebears were dreaming of displacing the Wasp brahmins from their drafty, expansive castles, Kesey's antecedents—"hard shell Baptists," "root-hungry folksingers"—were slowly moving through Tennessee and Arkansas, to Texas and New Mexico, and thence to LaJunta, Colorado, where Ken Kesey was born on September 17, 1935, the first child of Fred and Geneva Kesey.

When Kesey was in the third grade, Fred Kesey moved the family to Springfield, Oregon, a town in the Willamette Valley where he became foreman, and later manager, of a milk cooperative called Dari-Gold. Although the Keseys were comfortably middle class, with a suburban ranch house on Debra Lane, they always felt slightly apart, as though they hadn't yet shaken the pioneer dust from their boots. Kesey remembers his dad as a "kind of big, rebellious cowboy who never did fit in." Fred Kesey brought his boys up to be self-sufficient and tough. He taught them how to hunt, fish, swim, fight, wrestle—how to compete! Even manhood was a contest. When Kesey came of age, his father arranged a delicate ritual in which the son was allowed to defeat the father. "A boy has to know he can best his father, and his father has to present him the opportunity," Kesey once told an interviewer. "It's got to be the right way and at the right time—when the boy really needs to make his pitch. He's got to know he can outrun, outwrestle, outlove, outanything his old man. My father's a wise man and he gave me the chance. Perhaps this is a father's most significant duty."

Kesey was a model Fifties teenager, blonde, blue eyed, athletic, intelligent. He played guard on his high school football team and wrestled during the winters. Summers he worked at Dari-Gold, making ice cream. He was theatrically inclined, and an interest in magic and ventriloquism led to a modest career as a stage magician, performing at parties and club meetings. He also told stories, weird, loopy tales that suggested an imagination at odds with his image as a smart jock. In his senior year his classmates voted him "most likely to succeed." And succeed he did. At the University of Oregon, in nearby Eugene, Kesey became a collegiate wrestling champ, undefeated in his last season and second in the AAU tournament. He pledged Beta Theta Pi fraternity, where his verbal talents were instrumental in making the Theta Pis a contender in the various song and skit competitions that enlivened collegiate life. At the end of his junior year he married his high school sweetheart, Faye Haxby, a woman whom Tom Wolfe later described as "one of the prettiest, most beatific-looking women I ever saw." On the night before their wedding, Kesey got drunk for the first time in his life, "and even then not too drunk—just a token toot for my brother's benefit."

But this is only half the iceberg. Years later, reflecting on the urges that had lifted him out of the comfortable, circumscribed world of Springfield, Kesey remarked that, "in every high school there is always the weird kid interested in stuff nobody else is interested in—doing tricks, studying the stars, reading science fiction, boiling strange things. He usually has a bad complexion, and the girls aren't big on him because he's so weird." Except for the pimples and the implied social awkwardness, this was an accurate reading of Kesey's inner geography. He was a weird kid with large dreams and a rich fantasy life nourished mainly by comic books and pulp adventures. Kesey devoured the entire oeuvres of Zane Gray and Edgar Rice Burroughs; he kept monthly tabs on the surreal exploits of Plasticman and Captain Marvel. Later, at Stanford, he would confound his better-read peers with witty and trenchant defenses of the comic book as a legitimate source of national myth, maintaining that "a single Batman comic book is more honest than a whole volume of *Time* magazines." But the allure of these modern illuminated manuscripts went deeper than simply being a pretext for an amusing bit of pedagogy. What most considered cheap proletarian entertainment, Kesey interpreted as Nietzschean parable. At a gut level he identified with the concept of the superhero. In a sense this was the same teleological yearning for a transformed man that Huxley indulged in; only the symbols were different. Whereas Huxley might close his eyes and imagine the Buddha, Kesey interposed Billy Batson, orphan newsboy, who, deep in the bowels of an urban subway system, had met an ancient Egyptian wizard and—shazam!—became Captain Marvel.

Ken Kesey was exactly the sort of maverick in all-American-boy clothes that the corporate personality testers were paid to spot and eliminate.

It was a schizophrenic situation, being part jock and part aesthete (the jocks wondered what he was doing associating with a bunch of wimpy artists, while the wimpy artists wondered what he was doing wasting time with a bunch of ignorant "thumpheads") but Kesey managed it with the finesse one might expect from someone voted most likely to succeed. Still, it was a dichotomy that would aggravate and stimulate him for years to come. The tension within Kesey between the natural man and the trained intellectual was always intense. It cropped up in undergraduate stories like the one entitled "The Gentle Jock," and, more significantly, it would become the theme of his second novel, *Sometimes a Great Notion,* in which the two Stamper brothers, one a logger, the other a neurotic intellectual, were personifications of Kesey's split personality. "I want to find out which side of me really is," Kesey told an interviewer at the time, "the woodsy logger side—complete with homespun homilies and crackerbarrel corniness, a valid side of me that I like—or its opposition." Although in conversation he tended to slight the "opposition," he found it difficult to shed the analytical tools he had so painstakingly acquired.

Kesey's plans, when he graduated from the University of Oregon in 1957, were very much up in the air. Moving back to Springfield, he worked days at the Creamery and nights on a novel about college football. In the spring of 1958 he received two important notices: the first announced that due to a wrestling injury he was receiving a military classification of 4F; the second congratulated him on winning a Woodrow Wilson Fellowship, to be used to further his education in any way he saw fit. Kesey decided to spend the money learning how to write fiction, and in the fall of 1958, age twenty-four, he arrived in Palo Alto, California, to attend the Stanford Writing Program.

Entering the Stanford Writing Program was like trying out for a Triple-A ball club. Everyone there was competing for a spot in the majors, for a chance to prove that their best stuff was equal to that of Norman Mailer or Algren or the young Updike. The tendency to rank each other according to who was good, better, and best was strong, and within this crop of aspiring Hemingways (including Larry McMurtry, Robert Stone, Ed McClanahan, Wendell Berry) Kesey was quickly tagged as a contender. As Tom Wolfe put it,

> He had Jack London Martin Eden Searching Hick, the hick with intellectual yearnings, written all over him. He was from Oregon— who the hell was ever from Oregon—and he had an Oregon country drawl and too many muscles and callouses on his hands and his brow furrowed when he was thinking hard, and it was perfect.

A spot was found for him on Perry Lane, next to the golf course, which was the closest Palo Alto came to a bohemian community. Because of its modest size—scarcely a dozen weather-beaten cottages that could be had for sixty dollars a month—the Lane was like a private club: many applied, few were admitted. Kesey arrived under the sponsorship of Robin White, author of an award-winning novel called *Elephant Hill,* and the Lane's reigning literary prince. Like San Francisco's North Beach, which its inhabitants emulated in their adherence to "that old Zorba the Greek romanticism of sandals and simplicity and back to first principles," Perry Lane was a hotbed of cultural rather than political rebellion. Kesey grew a beard and began plunking out folksongs on a guitar. He got drunk for the second and third times in his life and he ate his first marijuana brownie. But his cornball enthusiasm remained undiminished, as did his love for the sport of wrestling. In the spring of 1960 Kesey participated in an AAU tournament for seniors at the San Francisco Olympic Club, in a close but fruitless bid for a spot on the Olympic team.

Despite his obvious literary promise, Kesey's maturation as a writer was slow. His football novel, which had gained him admittance to Stanford, was abandoned: it lacked the gravity of theme that he felt a first novel should have. For a time he toyed with writing a novel about Perry Lane, a kind of *Tortilla Flat* of the bohemian literary world, but then he discovered San Francisco's North Beach, which was just entering its twilight phase as a beatnik haven. This was Kerouac country, full of nihilistic jazz musicians and junkies—Zen junkies, heroin junkies, even car junkies, locked into a Neal Cassady world of speed and movement. Kesey had an ambivalent reaction to the Beat writers. He considered Kerouac more a reporter than a novelist. ("A thousand years from now when they want to know what was going on in our day, they'll have to read Kerouac.") The rest were flawed by what was probably a necessary but nonetheless crippling experimentalism. "Have you read Trocchi's work for Evergreen, *Cain's Book?*" Kesey wrote to a friend. "Some of the best prose going. Almost as good as *Naked Lunch.* Both have power and honesty, but lack something I plan to add—control."

Zoo, for that was the working title, was a characteristic Kesey composition. The plot involved the son of a rodeo rider turned chicken farmer, who arrives in the North Beach full of the kind of self-sufficient, depend-on-no-one-but-yourself values that Fred Kesey had instilled in his own son. Narrative tension was generated by the conflict between this heritage and the sort of primitive communalism that was emerging in the North Beach. Although *Zoo* won the two thousand-dollar Saxton Prize in 1959, it was turned down by the New York publishers. The rejection didn't tarnish Kesey's growing reputation—like Kerouac, and like Hemingway a generation earlier, his success was thought to be inevitable—but it did intensify his bursting urge to accomplish great feats. Perry Lane, which had seemed so exotic just two years earlier, was losing its capacity to surprise. "I've snuggled me out a comfortable niche here that has pretty near everything I want, and I'm loathe to move outta something so nice," Kesey wrote to a friend. "But I've come to a point of diminishing returns as far as learning new things goes."

Kesey's best friend in the writing program, Ken Babbs, was going directly from the classroom to the Marines, a fate that might have befallen Kesey but for his old wrestling injury. "I'm afraid this military is doing things to me," Babbs wrote. "Unpleasant things, like getting used to shaving every day. Like sirring assholes I'd normally kick in the crotch. Like going to work on time." To which Kesey replied: "You get out and my word we'll move to Mexico and sell jumping beans. Next week! Tomorrow! Don't deal with the lunatics of the world."

Kesey needed a new challenge, perhaps a change of scene, and as if on cue his wish was granted.

With his wild black hair, his lean intensity, and his Freudian take on life and love, Vic Lovell was a Perry Lane fixture, having moved there in 1957 after becoming a psychology graduate student at Stanford. Lovell, Tom Wolfe once wrote, came on "like a young Viennese analyst, or at least a California graduate-school version of one." He had a probing, restless mind, and a sympathy for the bohemian lifestyle. Lovell had been the student who had introduced Dick Alpert to marijuana when the latter was getting his Ph.D at Stanford. He was keenly interested in what was happening on the frontiers of psychology, so when he learned that the Menlo Park Veterans Hospital was advertising for volunteers to test a range of psychotomimetic drugs, he suggested to Kesey that they both volunteer. The pay was twenty dollars a session.

The Menlo Park experiment was under the auspices of one Dr. Leo Hollister, who was sort of an updated version of the Lab Madness boys. Hollister had great contempt for most of the psychedelic and psycholytic work that was under way, and was probably the sharpest local critic of Myron Stolaroff's Foundation. He was also one of the researchers the CIA had turned to when it decided to farm out its MK-ULTRA program.

The first drug Hollister gave Kesey was psilocybin. Nothing much happened until a squirrel dropped an acorn outside the hospital window and Kesey didn't just hear the soft thump: he felt it, as if his heart had given a vigorous pump. It was as though someone had taken his senses and turned up the volume as far as it would go: it was weird, certainly, but a benign weirdness, and it would have been quite pleasant if only this researcher hadn't kept popping in with his clipboard with all sorts of odd little requests: Could you add up this column of numbers? How's your sense of time? Could you tell me when you think a minute has elapsed? Answering was difficult because whenever Kesey looked at the guy, he felt he was looking right into him, right into the pinball game of his central nervous system, see the synapses fire, watch the messages rocket up and down the nerves. A hallucination? Maybe. But it made concentration damned difficult.

In the ensuing weeks, Kesey was dosed with LSD, the superamphetamine IT-290, and Ditran, which was a synthetic relative of belladonna. Kesey always knew it was Ditran because the fibers on his blanket would turn into a field of thorns and then he'd throw up. Ditran was real "bad scene stuff," he later told Gordon Lish, "intended to demonstrate to the whining neurotic how much worse off he can be."

But the others, particularly LSD and psilocybin, were wonderful. "Suddenly I was shifted over to where I had been looking full front at a world; and by shifting over, I was seeing it from another position. It became dimensional." It was the sort of multiple perception that a fledgling novelist might find extremely useful.

By midsummer Kesey was working at the Veterans Hospital as a psychiatric aide. He worked the graveyard shift, midnight to eight, hours when the hospital was deserted and the medicine cabinet where the psychotomimetic drugs were stored was wide open for anyone who wanted to borrow an experimental chemical or two. One time he swallowed an enormous dose of mescaline and "managed the night by mopping fervently whenever the nurse arrived so she couldn't see my twelve-gauge pupils, and the rest of the time argued so heatedly with the big knotty pine door across the office from me that I finally chalked a broad yellow line across the floor between us and told the door, 'You stay on your side, you goggle-eyed son of a bitch, and I'll stay on mine.' "

It was a pleasant routine—swab the floor, chat with the nurses, chat with the crazy insomniacs, gobble an experimental chemical, and do a little typing. The hospital authorities had let him bring a typewriter onto the ward, the idea being that he would use the solitude to whip *Zoo* into publishable shape, but before long Kesey was tapping out sketches of hospital life, long skeins of prose that "came more easily to my hand than anything else before or since." Gradually a story began to shape itself.

After two years of intense literary training, Kesey was not unaware that a mental hospital had wonderful possibilities as an extended metaphor for the America of the 1950s. Here the game was simpler: one conformed or was made to conform via drugs and electroshock therapy. There was no room for either personal assertiveness or mild eccentricity. Anything that fouled the smooth workings of the system was crushed. Even if one wished to rebel, this was impossible because the Combine, which was Kesey's word for the politics of adjustment that permeated everything, was invisible and impersonal, operating through a variety of willing but nevertheless unwitting agents, in this case, Big Nurse.

To liven things up, Kesey introduced a swaggering proletarian named Randle P. McMurphy, who had opted for the mental hospital in lieu of a stretch in prison. An itinerant logger and roustabout, McMurphy was the sort of fast-talking carny con man that Kesey had been so good at in improvisation classes back at the University of Oregon. He was a classic outside agitator, his vitality momentarily jarring the inmates from their tranquilized stupor. In the end, of course, the Combine would crush McMurphy, lobotomizing him, but in true gospel fashion his defeat would liberate some of his followers, specifically Chief Broom, the giant schizophrenic Choctaw Indian who narrates the story, and who, in the last pages, breaks free of the hospital and runs like crazy for open ground. Kesey planned to call the book *One Flew Over the Cuckoos Nest.*

While Randle P. McMurphy was a familiar character in Kesey's imaginary pantheon, Chief Broom was unique. For Kesey, the discovery of the Chief was the missing link, as it allowed him to assimilate both objective storytelling with the weird flights of fantasy that he was tapping out during those wild experimental nights on the ward. Chief Broom was a gift from the Muse; he'd come to Kesey in the midst of a peyote haze.

* * *

The drugs divided Perry Lane. In general the older crowd, the Robin White crowd, were dead set against them, while those a few years younger were eager to experiment. In a sense what was happening on Perry Lane was a repeat of what had happened to Oscar Janiger when he'd been swamped by the Los Angeles painting set. The word was that Kesey had stumbled across some creativity pills, and that was why he was working like a madman on his new book.

This was, of course, a limited perspective. "When you start fooling around with dope," Kesey once said, "what you're doing is asking to see your books. The first few highs are gratis. There's a grace given you, but then it's like they say, 'You want to see your books, huh?' This hand grabs you by the back of the neck and turns you and for eight hours you're forced to look at your own history of transgression against your fellow creatures. Not only that, but you're forced to look at the fact that you will, one day, be worms. That your physical body will turn into this. Your soul will continue on. It's how your soul is doing in its path to eternity, not how your body is doing in its path through this life, that's important."

Those lacking the nerve to go through the Door and take a good look at their books were left behind with their wine bottles and Zen. It was a syndrome that all fledgling psychedelic communities seemed to go through, the separation of the world into the aware and the rest, and Perry Lane was no different.

People began gathering at Kesey's for mutual exploration, wolfing down bowls of venison chile liberally seasoned with LSD, listening to Ken extemporize in his soft country purr about what it all meant. That voice was all that was left of the Jack London Searching Hick who had come to Stanford to learn how to string sentences together in a marketable manner. Kesey had changed in the last few months, he seemed bigger, bursting with vitality, and primal, as if he was tuned in to Something Big. During the winter of 1961 he conducted his own literary salon out at Perry Lane. Watching him, Malcolm Cowley, who was lecturing at the writing program that semester, was reminded of the glow that had surrounded the young Hemingway in the Paris of the Twenties. Kesey had become "the man whom the other young rebels tried to imitate."

By June 1961, ten months after he'd begun, *One Flew Over the Cuckoos Nest* was ready for the publishers. Viking bought it immediately, paying Kesey one thousand five hundred dollars, their top advance for an unpublished writer. The book was published in February 1962, to wonderful acclaim. The *Saturday Review* called Kesey a "large robust talent" who had written "a large robust book." Kesey was twenty-six, he was famous, and if the twenty thousand dollars he had just received from the sale of his movie rights was any indication, he was going to be rich.

228

* * *

A first novel, particularly a successful one, always presupposes a second novel, if only to show that the first was no fluke. Even before the fanfare from *Cuckoos Nest* had faded, Kesey was at work on a second novel, a tale about loggers and union politics in the Pacific Northwest. As an aesthetic exercise, *Sometimes a Great Notion* was largely an attempt to see how many perspectives a contemporary narrative could hold before it burst. The ostensible hero of the book was Hank Stamper, an independent logger who, in his desire to just keep working, ends up at odds with the campaign to unionize the lumber industry. But of equal importance was the Oregon weather, mostly rain, and the brooding physical presence of the Oregon mountains. Despite positive reactions from his agent and editor, Kesey was nervous about the new book and there were times when he felt like he was on a shooting course where people kept congratulating him on his shooting, but no one ever mentioned how close he was coming to the bullseye.

Kesey finished the book in the spring of 1963, and having never been to NewYork, decided to deliver the manuscript in person. During the return trip, he began to think seriously about collecting together his friends and putting down roots, somewhere warm, with plenty of privacy, somewhere in the woods, perhaps. Kesey had been procrastinating over leaving Perry Lane, but now he had no choice. A developer had bought the property and was planning to raze the cabins to make room for a modern development. On the last Saturday before the bulldozers rolled in, about a hundred Perry Laners gathered for a farewell party fueled by pot after pot of psychedelic venison chile. At the height of the festivities they hauled an ancient upright piano from the depths of Kesey's cabin and began flailing away at it with axes. "It is the oldest living thing on Perry Lane, its annihilation is symbolic," Kesey told the startled reporters who had gathered to record the final moments of what the San Francisco *Chronicle* called "Menlo Park's distinguished patch of rustic bohemia."

Perry Lane received a more fitting memorial six years later when Vic Lovell published a series of autobiographical sketches in the local underground newspaper. By now a radical organizer and therapist, Lovell traced his personal transformation back to those carefree years in the Lane: "It was there that I first felt love, sensuality, creativity, spontaneity, and the sense of human community, and it was also there and thereafter that I first felt the possibility that total disaster could overtake mankind if something were not done, by each in his own way, if only to drop out. When I get disoriented, I try to remember how it felt."

Although they didn't know it, that night as they flailed away at the piano, they were already on the path.

* * *

Kesey found what he was looking for in La Honda, a town fifteen miles east of Palo Alto. It was a modern log cabin, six large rooms, paneled, with a massive fireplace and a pair of elegant French doors that opened onto six acres of redwood forest. To reach the house you had to cross a wooden bridge spanning a little stream. The nearest neighbor was a mile away, the nearest outpost of civilization a few miles beyond that, at Baw's General Store.

The original plan was that the Perry Laners would move out to La Honda and live in tents up in the woods, immersing themselves in Kesey's fantasy of a community of psychedelic adventurers pushing deeper into the Other World—it was Millbrook, but with an artistic slant. But Kesey's increasing autocracy ("Just when you're starting to lie back and groove on your thing, he comes in—Hup!—Hup!—Everybody up! and organizes a tramp through the woods.") grated on a number of his old friends and they elected to stay in Palo Alto, within easy visiting distance but nevertheless apart from whatever plans their old friend had up his sleeve.

Kesey didn't know what he had up his sleeve, really, but he kept getting intimations whenever he was in the Other World, that he was on the track of something, and he was going to need help before it was over. He needed a band of adventurers willing to undertake this quest, and he began to find them. Some were friends or friends of friends, but often virtual strangers arrived, as though summoned. One day in the summer of 1962 Kesey turned into his Perry Lane driveway and there coming toward him, bobbing and weaving and talking a mile a minute, was that icon of the New Vision, Neal Cassady.

Fortune had been less kind to Neal Cassady than it had to either Kerouac or Ginsberg. In April 1958, a year after *On the Road* had made him famous as the quintessential angel-headed hipster, Cassady had been arrested in San Francisco and charged with operating a marijuana-smuggling ring. The evidence (two joints that Neal had give to a plain-clothes cop in exchange for a ride to work) was ludicrous, but it was enough to earn him two concurrent sentences of five years to life in San Quentin. One might expect, given his compulsive energy, that prison would've been unbearable for Cassady, but in an odd way he thrived on what he referred to as his period of enforced meditation. "Worldly failure was always Cassady's most creative element," William Plummer wrote in *The Holy Goof,* his biography of Cassady:

> Gavin Arthur, grandson of the twenty-first president and comparative religion professor at San Quentin, would later say that Neal was at his most sublime in prison. It was the one place where he could use his magnificent mind, said Arthur, adding that it was the

only place where Neal was not a slave to the "desire body." The very first day of class Arthur picked Neal out of a group of sixty inmates: Neal was shining with unearthly fire.

He was paroled in 1960 and went back to his old life of railroad work and monologuing. Then he happened to pick up a copy of *One Flew Over the Cuckoos Nest*. He was Randle P. McMurphy. This man Kesey had stared into his soul. He felt summoned, and there he was when Kesey arrived back from an Oregon vacation, bobbing and weaving, waiting to finally meet the man that he would henceforth call "Chief."

The Perry Laners regarded Cassady as an amusing sort of museum piece, as though the soul of Rousseau's natural man had transmigrated into the body of a 1950s hotrodder. He was quaint but a little tiresome, what with his habit of constantly flipping a small sledgehammer into the air, catching it by its handle, then reflipping it, without missing a syllable of whatever manic rant he was in the middle of. But Kesey kept saying, listen to Cassady, *he's there*. Cassady, on his own, had achieved a state remarkably similar to what the Zen Buddhists referred to as *Zazen:* total nonattached mindfulness. Cassady had always had this ability, even as far back as his first meeting with Kerouac and Ginsberg, but over the years it had grown in power, until now he was able to carry on three or four conversations at once. Gordon Lish (at the time editor of a small art journal called *Genesis West*) met Neal at one of Kesey's parties and was stunned when Cassady "started to recapitulate the talk going on around us and to comment on it, even while he was keeping up his end of our conversation. It was breathtaking." Lish, who had been puzzled by Kesey's admiration for Neal, came to regard Neal as "one of the greatest minds I've ever known—certainly the quickest intelligence."

Cassady's unique abilities were most apparent when he was in his favorite meditative position, behind the wheel of one of Detroit's finest. To ride with Neal, Jerry Garcia later admitted, "was to be as afraid as you could be, to be in fear for your life. You'd be driving along in some old Pontiac or Buick, one of those cars Neal was always borrowing— with no brakes. You'd be racing through San Francisco at fifty or sixty miles per hour, up and down those streets with blind corners everywhere and he'd cut around them in the wrong lane and make insane moves in the most intense traffic situations and you'd just be amazed that people weren't getting killed. He could see around corners. And while he was doing this he'd be talking to everybody in the car at once and dialing in the radio and fumbling with a roach." Kesey called it Neal's "careening, corner-squealing commentary on the cosmos," and he began to believe that it represented an archetype of what post-psychedelic man would be like.

What happens when you pass back through the Door? How do you keep these new states of awareness alive so that you can enjoy what Huxley used to call "the best of both possible worlds"?

These were questions that confronted anyone who pondered the social utility of psychedelics. How do you keep the growth growing? At Millbrook they were working on ways to "break set"; they were sending out survey crews, hoping that one of them would find a way through the envelope, they were drawing maps and talking about brain circuits and bardos; the best job description for them was scientist-explorer/ religious novitiate; they were monkish scientists or scientific monks, and they were about as different from the Kesey crowd as could be imagined. The Merry Pranksters (a collective name that was shortly to crystallize) never verbalized about the Other World. It was the unspoken thing! the weird shit! the zone! And when they did talk about it, it was with comic-book hyperbole. The ideal became a place called Edge City, which was that part of the spectrum of being that lay between the ego, with its layers of conditioning, and the annihilating energy bath of the Void. To live in Edge City meant to live totally in the here and now. "We got so we could do it and be right there, in the present, for long periods of time," Kesey told an interviewer. It was like being in a boat, at sea, drifting, except that "powers are available to you that you couldn't find in the past or in the future."

About the only acknowledgment they made to this palpable sense of personal mutation was their habit of rechristening every recruit with a Prankster name: Gretchin Fetchin, Mal-Function, Cool Breeze, Hassler, the Cadaverous Cowboy, Mountain Girl; Kesey became the Chief, Cassady was Speed Limit, and Babbs, newly returned from Vietnam, became the Intrepid Traveller. If you had to write a job description for the few good men (and women) Kesey was looking for, it would be, "superheroes wanted for real life movie work."

A lot of the impetus for what became the essential Prankster style came from Babbs, who'd returned, "like a great hearty grizzly bear roaring a cosmic laugh" from Vietnam in the fall of 1963. It was Babbs who came up with the concept of the Prank, those great cosmic put-ons that seemed to come bubbling out of some ribald sector of the Other World. And this in turn led to the Bus.

The Bus was actually the culmination of several contingencies, primarily Kesey's tentative plan to drive to New York in the summer of 1964, arriving in time for the publication party of *Sometimes a Great Notion* and the opening of the World's Fair (which, incidentally, had turned down Michael Hollingshead's plan for a mind-expansion pavilion). There was also talk of using some of the movie equipment that Kesey had been buying with the royalties from *Cuckoos Nest* to make a film of their trip, sort of an *On the Road* fifteen years later. Then someone spotted a newspaper ad offering for sale a pre-war International Harvester bus that had been outfitted with all the amenities (a refrigerator, bunkbeds) of a gigantic camper. Kesey bought the bus, wired in a sound system that allowed them to converse with the outside world, and then expanded the cross-country fantasy to epic-film proportions: they would make a genuine high quality road epic and then sell it to Hollywood: Intrepid Traveller and His Merry Pranksters Search for a Cool Place.

They would embark upon a voyage of discovery (not theirs so much as America's), a sublime mission that would require a sublime vehicle. When the knights of medieval Europe rode off to the crusades, they didn't just jump on any old nag and canter off to the ships; they pushed off in style, on horses that were as gaudy as a Macy's Thanksgiving Day parade float. And so it was with the Pranksters. "It was as though somebody had given Hieronymous Bosch fifty buckets of Day-Glo paint and a 1939 Harvester and told him to go to it," wrote the Pranksters' chronicler, Tom Wolfe. By the time their decorating frenzy had cooled, they had created a vehicle that seemed to pulse and vibrate, like some mad inventor's spaceship. On the front, where the destination sign was supposed to be, they wrote the word FUURTHER. On the back: CAUTION: WEIRD LOAD.

They left in July 1964, planning to swing through the South and then up the Eastern seaboard. They filmed everything, constantly. The world was their movie, or rather the world was a rivalry of movies. People were always trying to trap you in their movie (Leary would have said game) and the only way to prevent this was to create alternative movies. For example: whenever they attracted the notice of the local constabulary, which happened quite frequently, they would hop out with their cameras and microphones and disrupt the cop movie with their own script:

> New Orleans [Tom Wolfe writes] was a relief because they got out and walked around the French Quarter in their red and white striped shirts and Day-Glo stuff and the people freaked over them. And the cops came while they were down by the docks, which was just comic relief, because by now the cops were a piece of cake. The city cops were no more able to keep their Cop Movie going than the country cops. Hassler talked to them like the college valedictorian and Kesey talked sweet and down-home and Hagen filmed it all like it was some crazed adventure in cinema verite and the cops skedaddled in a herd of new Ford cruisers with revolving turret lights.

Coming down the Blue Ridge mountains, Cassady switched the ignition off and downshifted all the way, without once touching the brake. Kesey was riding outside, on top, and as the bus began to slither through the hairpins it suddenly flashed through his mind that if he felt fear it would instantly be communicated to everyone within the bus, with possibly disastrous consequences. For Kesey it was a first flash of the group mind: we are all one brain connected to . . . what? Some universal power source? An Overmind? What the Mahayana Buddhists referred to as Mind-only and the Zen sects as the One Mind? The Pranksters didn't want to put a borrowed name to it; "they were all deep into some weird shit now," Wolfe wrote, "as they would just as soon call it by way of taking the curse . . . off the Unspoken thing."

They reached New York in mid-July, in time for the publication of *Sometimes a Great Notion*. The reviews were mixed. The critic for the *Herald Tribune* praised it as "a towering redwood" in the scraggly wilderness of contemporary fiction, while Orville Prescott of the *Times* pilloried it as a "Tiresome Literary Disaster," calling it "the most insufferably pretentious and the most totally tiresome novel I have had to read in many years." Some of Prescott's venom may be attributable to his odd belief that Kesey was actually the prototype for Dean Moriarity in Kerouac's *On the Road*, a "beatnik type," in other words, who had no business bringing his passion and bad manners to the comfortable literary barbecue that had prevailed through the Fifties. Prescott's mistake was ironic, since a few days before the review appeared Kerouac and Kesey had met, with less than amicable results.

Kerouac was living with his mother in alcoholic semiseclusion in Northport, Long Island. He was forty and tired, with a potbelly and a streak of bitterness that seemed to widen whenever he confronted the new enthusiasms of Ginsberg and Cassady. He was growing increasingly conservative, increasingly Catholic, denouncing old friends like Ginsberg as atheist communists. His opinion of psychedelic drugs was equally low. Nevertheless he let himself be persuaded by Cassady to attend a party with Kesey—a typical Prankster affair full of weird costumes, movie cameras, squawking tape recorders, LSD punch. Kerouac stood it for a few minutes and then left, but not before making a symbolic gesture of contempt: spotting an American flag carelessly draped across one of the couches, he removed and carefully folded it up. He wanted no part of the Prankster movie . . . the days of his own superhero ambitions, when it was only the mad who stirred him, the ones who burned burned burned and never said a dull word . . . you might as well have been talking about another person.

Kesey felt bad about his botched meeting with Kerouac. An opportunity had been missed largely through an inexcusable lack of sensitivity. To the Pranksters, Kerouac was like a symbolic big brother, who'd given them confidence and direction when they'd most needed it, but had been unable to follow his own example. He had been King of the Beats, but he'd renounced his crown.

Hoping to regain their momentum, the Pranksters packed the bus and headed north along the Hudson. Somewhere in the valleys and pockets of the Taconic hills was another symbolic brother, Tim Leary. If anyone understood the Unspoken Thing, it would be him. As they neared the Big House, they broke out their smoke bombs, intending to make a friendly, yet festive arrival.

Kesey probably expected an Eastern version of La Honda and the Pranksters. What he found was a bunch of Ivy League eggheads walking around in robes and talking like comparative religion professors. Millbrook was a bore, and hostile to boot. The Castalians regarded the Pranksters, in their Day-Glo costumes, as the sort of thing that might happen if you put LSD in the punch at a Greek mixer—a bad fraternity prank. They were the Romans and the Pranksters were the Goths and the Vandals, and when these primitives asked for some LSD to enliven their return voyage, they responded by offering them some of the sacks of morning glory seeds that had been lying around since the IFIF days.

The Pranksters, recognizing a snub when they received one, politely declined, piled back in the bus, and vanished through the stone gates, heading west.

19
TURN AND FACE THE STRANGE

Millbrook's nonwelcome strengthened the Pranksters' sense of their own psychedelic identity, which was both more macho and less intellectual than Leary's. Except for the *I-Ching,* the Pranksters avoided the religious psychologies of the Orient, scorning the Tibetan mumbo jumbo that the Castalians found so profound. They rejected the reliance on guides and careful programming, believing limits of any kind were inimical to the experience. Go with the flow, became their maxim; freak freely, their slogan. For the Pranksters, the true test of psychedelic selfhood was one's ability to plunge into the whitewater of this new experience and, using only one's wits, reach the calm mystic pools downstream.

Here were the seeds of disaster: what if the Leary doctrine that everyone could profit from LSD, provided the trips were rigorously controlled, got confused with the Prankster doctrine that no controls were necessary? What if the whole country began to freak freely?

In a sense, Kesey stood in relation to Leary as Leary did to Huxley: each represented a radicalization of the other's position.

Returning to La Honda, they became infatuated with the feeling that they were acquiring new powers. Most of the Eastern commentaries on the Other World mention these powers in passing and counsel the apprentice adept to observe them and then pass quickly by lest these intriguing sideshows seduce them from the toilsome path that leads to complete awakening. But for the Pranksters, with their fondness for comic-book metaphysics, these powers became an index of their success, and they formed the basis for all that follows.

In Cassady these powers manifested themselves in his ability to

236

devote his full attention to several things at once. One time Cassady was driving up one of the long, climbing curves that led into La Honda with Norman Hartweg, and Cassady was talking a mile a minute in his trademark hallucinatory way, not looking at the road, but at Hartweg, who was watching an enormous truck hurtle right at them. Seconds before impact, Cassady shut up, swerved the wheel, fishtailed onto the opposite apron, squealed around the truck on the wrong side, fishtailed back, and picked up where he had stopped a couple of seconds before. "Cassady doesn't have to think anymore," was Kesey's explanation when he encountered the badly shaken Hartweg wandering around La Honda; Cassady was a permanent Edge City resident. Hartweg was digesting this when it suddenly occurred to him that he hadn't told anyone about his close call with Cassady. How had Kesey known? Well, that was Kesey's power. If Cassady could do a couple of things at once, Kesey had a disturbing habit of popping up and answering your questions before they had even formed in your mind.

Although there was something of a power hierarchy, with Kesey, Cassady, and Babbs occupying the top rungs, everyone had their moments, which was why the atmosphere at La Honda was heavy with portents and intersubjectivity: think about closing a window and someone across the room would get up and close it. Kesey had no interest in designing experiments to test this phenomenon; he was beyond the point of questioning the validity of these powers. What he wanted to do was find a way to fuse all these little individual powers into one large whole. As one participant described it: "There was the tantalizing idea that if we could find the missing link, that the abilities of this gestalt— this group entity—would be multiplied and we would be able to do really fascinating things." The phrase that they used for this hypothetical state was "leaving the planet."

One of the consequences of all this was Kesey's decision to abandon writing. Although a few of his old Stanford classmates tried to dissuade him, his mind was made up. LSD had revealed the limitations of language, and by extension, of literature. Whenever he thought about writing, he told a friend, all he saw were the holes that the medium left unfilled. Yet he was still an artist at heart. He confessed in his notebook,

> After two successful novels and ten times two successful fantasies I find myself wondering "What to prove next? I've shown the buggers I can write, then shown them I can repeat & better the first showing, now what do I prove?"
>
> The answer seems to be "prove nothing."
>
> "A clever challenge, Chaps, and one, I confess, that stirs the fight in me. Now anyone can crank out a nice compact commercial, slide it between covers and vend it as literature, but how many are

there capable of advancing absolute proof of nothing [under-
lined]?"

"Not many, no, not so very many."

"Then, by jingo," slapping his thigh vigorously, "let's do it."

Then Resounding How?

Do something by doing nothing—the challenge of every Taoist—
just let it develop organically.

But before he could concentrate on any of these paradoxes, Kesey
had to resolve one of his more opulent fantasies: *Intrepid Traveller and His
Merry Pranksters Search for a Cool Place.* Kesey meant to finish and distribute
Intrepid Traveller, if only because the cost of color processing thirty hours
of raw film had left him seventy thousand dollars poorer. But he had
also never lost the conviction, nurtured by a couple of adolescent summers spent in Hollywood, that his true creative metier was film. When
Kirk Douglas had bought the screen and stage rights to *Cuckoos Nest,*
Kesey had offered his services as both screenwriter and director, assur-
ing Douglas that he had seen far more movies than he had ever read
books. The romance of moviemaking faded quickly, however, killed by
the postproduction tedium of whittling thirty hours of badly lit, badly
focused action into a reasonably commercial package. Deciding that he
needed a professional editor, Kesey approached Los Angeles playwright
Norman Hartweg, who was also a columnist for that city's first alternative newspaper, the *Free Press,* and invited him to move to La Honda,
where he had set up an editing room.

The La Honda that Hartweg arrived at resembled a marathon encounter session that already had been running for months. Or it was like
wandering into a movie set where only a few people had read the script,
or claimed they had read it, since they wouldn't talk about it, not about
the Unspoken Thing. Some arrivals had no trouble synchronizing
(synching up) with the higher ideals of Pranksterhood, while others,
like Hartweg, were completely baffled. Hartweg was astonished, for
example, to find himself criticized for smoking and reading, on the
grounds that these were selfish pleasures which added nothing to the
group gestalt.

"There were no official rules," wrote Tom Wolfe about the Prankster method of induction. "There was no official period of probation,
and no vote on is he or isn't he one of us, no blackballing, no tap on
the shoulders. And yet there was a period of proving yourself, and
everyone knew it was going on and no one ever said a word about it
. . . the Pranksters probed everybody, to make them bring their hangups
out front, live in the moment, spontaneously."

Newcomers at Millbrook were usually given some of Leary's
writing or one of Hesse's novels as an inkling of what to expect. These
kinds of guidebooks existed at La Honda as well, but most were sci-

ence fiction novels. The Pranksters were particularly drawn to Robert Heinlein's *Stranger in a Strange Land*, which told the story of Valentine Smith, an American who had been raised on Mars, where he had learned certain mystic and occult arts. Returning to earth, Smith begins gathering a "nest" of followers, whom he instructs in the arcane technique of "water sharing." Heinlein is never specific as to the mechanics of water sharing, but the result was a blending of the various personalities in the "nest" into one entity; water sharing allows them to grok with each other, grokking being a kind of all-encompassing telepathy. As the story progresses, these internal changes get translated into a communal lifestyle that eventually spreads out until earth is faced with a religious revolt, as more and more kids begin grokking that the culture they live in is seriously flawed. Heinlein had published *Stranger* in 1961, and the Pranksters chose to interpret the timing as a precognitive myth which they were in the process of embodying. Running across *Stranger* was an experience comparable with what Cassady must have felt when he opened *Cuckoos Nest* and discovered that, as Randle P. McMurphy, he was living in the recesses of another's imagination.

Another book they treated as a precognitive myth was *Childhood's End*, by Arthur Clarke, the English scientist who later wrote *2001, A Space Odyssey*. Clarke's fantasy revolved around the appearance of a generation of superkids—super in the sense that they were more highly evolved and were able to tap into mental powers that their parents had heretofore dismissed as fairytales. With the birth of this generation, the evolutionary line *Homo sapiens* comes to an end. At the end of the book the children are ushered into the spaceship of the Overlords (read gods) and they leave the planet.

Finally there was an obscure novel by Theodore Sturgeon called *More Than Human*, which told the story of a group of social outcasts who discover that they can telepathically merge to form a powerful compound personality: *Homo gestalt*.

These were the fantasies that gave form to the Pranksters' intentions. Using LSD, they were able to grok with each other, to tap into mental regions that promised unlimited energy, unlimited power. Like the kids in *Childhood's End*, they believed that a special destiny awaited them. And like the outcasts in Sturgeon's book, they sensed they were on the verge of evolving into *Homo gestalt*. Every Friday they held a briefing—*briefing* being a term Babbs had brought back from Vietnam—and Kesey would lead off with either a theme or an anecdote or some whimsical perception. Then the others would join in, embroidering and reworking the evening's topic, piling on poetic pirouettes, metaphysical can openers off the high board, until the group mind synchronized and the tethers started to loosen, drifting, drifting, until they were . . . leaving the planet.

Kesey's neighbors would have been grimly amused to learn what went on at these Friday briefings, since they already considered the Kesey place another planet. The Pranksters had repainted the redwood forest in Day-Glo colors, so the whole side of the hill glowed in the dark like some postholocaust mutant forest. People driving past shouted "dirty beatnik," a term Kesey found offensive in the extreme, and bullets were fired into the mailbox and the windshield of one of the trucks. There were also rumors that the police had the place under surveillance, and once when the Pranksters climbed up a nearby hill they found a mound of cigarette butts on top.

The Pranksters reacted to the growing animosity with their usual *esprit*. When word came that William Wong, a well known narcotics officer, was planning to raid the ranch, they hung a huge sign on the side of the main cabin reading WE'RE CLEAN WILLIE. But the sign failed to convince officer Wong and on the morning of April 23 he led a cavalry charge across the bridge and into the heart of Kesey's domain. He found the author in the bathroom in the process of either painting flowers on the toilet bowl (Kesey's story) or hurriedly disposing of an illegal narcotic, namely marijuana (Wong's story).

At the time, the arrest seemed a minor blip on the screen of their well-being. Having worked the kinks out of their group mind act, the Pranksters were becoming interested in seeing what they could do with this new sense of power. Could they draw people into their movie? Teach them how to go with the flow? A few weeks after the bust Kesey was invited to participate in a Unitarian encampment, the theme of which was social change in the Sixties. On the surface this was a week of songs, symposiums, and hikes along the Pacific coast, but the conference also had a hidden agenda, which was the bridging of the gap that was growing between the older liberal Unitarians and their increasingly radical children. Someone had thought that Kesey and his friends might provide a possible bridge.

And the Pranksters were a bridge, but not one that led back to the comfortable liberal world. From the moment they piled off the bus in their superhero costumes, the Pranksters had the place in an uproar. Midway through his first public talk, Kesey pulled the American flag off the stage and stomped on it to illustrate his point that the symbol of one's emotion was not the same as the emotion. Outraged gasps came from the Unitarians, but before they could calcify into righteous anger, the flag had been picked up and everyone was singing "America the Beautiful."

The conference began moving at a dizzying, and to many of the older Unitarians, an unhappy pace. Half the time the kids were down on the beach, clustered around that obscene bus, playing the Power game. The point of the Power game was to allow the chosen leader approximately a half hour of unlimited power over the rest of the players. At La Honda it had led to moments like the time Babbs auctioned off everyone else's personal possessions; here it resulted in such strange tableaux as everyone sitting in the surf, washing each other's feet.

Don't talk about it, do it was Kesey's message. To illustrate his point, he spent one whole day with his mouth taped shut—a gesture that further enhanced his stature as a teacher.

To gauge the impression the Pranksters made upon the young Unitarians, it is useful to quote Tom Wolfe's reaction to them some months later. Wolfe, the dapper, cynical, New York sophisticate with a Yale Ph.D, was overcome by what he described as a kind of mysto steam. "This steam, I can actually hear it inside my head, a great ssssss, like what you hear if you take too much quinine. I don't know if this happens to anybody else or not. But if there is something startling enough, fear, awesome, strange, or just weird enough, something I sense I can't cope with, it is as if I go on Red Alert and the fogging steam starts . . ."

By the last day of the Conference that mystic sssssss was ringing in dozens of ears.

On a scale of one to ten, bringing the Unitarians into the Prankster movie had a difficulty rating of five; adequate but hardly impressive. By August 1965, the Pranksters had a much more worthy target, one that would really test the group mind's ability to control events: the Hells Angels.

The midwife for this experiment was a freelance writer named Hunter Thompson, who was in the process of writing an informal history of the Hells Angels, arguably America's most prominent non-Mafia thugs. The Angels' public reputation dated back to the previous Labor Day, when they had terrorized the California coastal town of Monterey, buzzing through the streets like a swarm of unwashed hornets; an emanation from the dark side of the American psyche—big, gross, drug-using, alcohol-abusing psychopathic nonconformists. As in any true brotherhood, one didn't become an Angel without first undergoing a ritual initiation, part of which involved the extended wearing of a pair of jeans soaked in the urine of your brother Angels.

About the only derogatory label that couldn't be pinned upon the Angels was pinko. Long before the hardhats won national favor by attacking antiwar protestors, the Angels indulged in commie bashing. For a time there was even a rumor that the army was recruiting a crack

combat team (a la Dirty Dozen) of Hells Angels to mop things up in
Vietnam. But these instincts were slow to surface and prior to becoming
the protector of the flag the Angels enjoyed a brief run, in certain hip
intellectual circles, as the embodiment of Alienated Existential Man.
According to Thompson, by the summer of 1965 hostesses were clamoring for an Angel or two to station by the wet bar, where they would
discourse on what it was like to geeze crystal and then bang down the
coast highway at 100 mph. Thompson, besides being the informal historian of this criminal subculture, suddenly found himself in the odd role
of social director: "There was a feeling in the air that I could produce
them whenever I felt like it. This was never true, though I did what I
could to put the outlaws onto as much free booze and action as seemed
advisable. At the same time I was loath to be responsible for their
behavior. Their preeminence on so many guest lists made it inevitable
that a certain amount of looting, assault and rapine would occur if they
took the social whirl at full gallop."

Thompson met Kesey in early August 1965 at WQEVD, San Francisco's educational television station. After repairing to a nearby bar for
some drinks, he invited Ken to tag along to a nearby bike shop and meet
a few of his research subjects. Kesey was an instant hit, and "after
several hours of eating, drinking and the symbolic sharing of herbs," he
suggested that the San Francisco chapter of the Angels come down to
La Honda for a weekend-long party.

On the day of the party a huge sign, fifteen feet by three feet, was
displayed near the gate: THE MERRY PRANKSTERS WELCOME THE
HELLS ANGELS. The sign had, as Thompson, who attended, observed,
"a bad effect on the neighbors." Stopping at Baw's General Store, he
overheard the following conversation:

> "That goddamn dope addict," said a middle-aged farmer. "First
> its marywanna, now it's Hell's Angels. Christ alive, he's just pushin
> our faces in the dirt."
> "Beatniks!" said somebody else. "Not worth a pound of piss."
> There was talk of divvying up the ax handles in the store and
> "going up there to clean the place out." But somebody said the cops
> were already on the job: "Gonna put em in jail for good this time,
> every damn one of em . . ." So the ax handles stayed in the rack.

The San Mateo police had four cars on the scene, their lights revolving in the dusk. Each new arrival was stopped and questioned,
while his license and registration was checked for outstanding traffic
violations. At least one was handcuffed and driven off to jail. But
otherwise the police were powerless to interfere in the weird scene that
was developing across the stream. It was a scene, Thompson wrote,
"that must have tortured the very roots of their understanding. Here

were all these people running wild, bellowing and dancing half naked to rock 'n' roll sounds piped out through the trees from massive amplifiers, reeling and stumbling in a maze of psychedelic lights. . . . WILD, by god, and with no law to stop them." Girls in scarlet tights and long soft hair danced with a "steady stream of college professors, vagrants, lawyers, students, psychologists and high style hippies." Kesey was dressed like a druid priest in a hooded white robe. Cassady was in a corner rapping. Allen Ginsberg was sitting on the living room floor, tapping his finger cymbals and chanting.

The Angels never had a chance. From the moment they roared en masse across the bridge, their Harleys momentarily competing with the thundering rock 'n' roll, they were firmly within the Prankster movie. Far from being fawned upon, the Pranksters treated them with the same calculated rudeness that all new arrivals received. No sooner had they killed their bikes than one of the Pranksters began serenading them over the sound system with a kind of talking blues about Angel life, punctuating each stanza with

> Oh, but it's great to be an Angel
> And be dirty all the time!

Beer was pressed upon them—the Pranksters had laid in a prodigious supply—and LSD, which most of the Angels swallowed under the impression that it was a kind of superamphetamine. It wasn't, of course, and within the hour strange explosions were occurring within their frames of reference. An Angel named Freewheeling Frank, for example, suddenly discovered that he could read the thoughts of all his brother Angels. Watching Ginsberg tap his finger cymbals, he felt like he was "in the land of Oz." Someone said, "Allen Ginsberg is a fruit," but Freewheeling's once potent homophobia had vanished. Like Albert Hofmann, twenty years before him, Freewheeling Frank was feeling like he had been reborn.

"The real Hell's Angels are the ones who've taken LSD and had the carpet jerked out from under them," he later said. "I never really became a Hell's Angels until I took LSD. Not to speak of becoming a man and finding myself . . . LSD is a medicine not a drug. I only hope it gets in the right hands, and is used for Love rather than Fortune and Fame."

According to Hunter Thompson: "Contrary to all expectations most of the Angels became oddly peaceful on acid. With a few exceptions, it made them much easier to get along with. The acid dissolved many of their conditioned reflexes. There was little of the sullen craftiness or the readiness to fight that usually pervades their attitude toward strangers. The aggressiveness went out of them; they lost the bristling, suspicious quality of wild animals sensing a snare. It was a strange thing, and I still don't quite understand it."

But eventually the Angels peaked on LSD and began to slide back down the anti-cline into their former selves. In October they won the hearts of conservative editorial writers everywhere when they beat up some antiwar protestors in Berkeley. And they threatened to do it again should any more marches take place. Kesey, accompanied by Allen Ginsberg, spent a day with the Angel leadership, trying to persuade them that their logical role lay in aiding the antiwar activists, not the establishment. But the Angels saw the protestors as communist traitors, a perception that no amount of LSD could dispel. The meeting had ended with Ginsberg leading everyone in a Buddhist chant. "That goddamn Ginsberg is gonna fuck us all up," one of the Angels later told Thompson. "For a guy that ain't straight at all, he's about the straightest sonofabitch I've ever seen. Man you shoulda been there when he told Sonny he loved him."

In a matter of weeks the Hells Angels went from being darlings of the left to darlings of the right, and their sense of self-importance rose dramatically. They called press conferences, they issued policy statements, and their national president, Sonny Barger, sent the following telegram to President Lyndon Johnson:

> On behalf of myself and my associates I volunteer a group of loyal Americans for behind the lines duty in Vietnam. We feel that a crack group of trained gorillas would demoralize the Viet Cong and advance the cause of freedom. We are available for training and duty immediately.

Why no farsighted public official took them up on this offer is one of history's little mysteries.

Although the Hells Angels were the star attraction at Kesey's that weekend, two other partygoers deserve mention. The first was Allen Ginsberg. In the five years since he had sat drinking hot milk with Tim Leary in Newton, Ginsberg had logged thousands of miles on a spiritual pilgrimage that had taken him across India to Japan. The point of it all, at first, had been to become a saint, a bodhisattva. But this had been replaced by a deep depression by the time he reached India. His life had become a "vague haphazard slow motion death," Ginsberg confided to his notebook. The depression continued into Japan, where Ginsberg visited Gary Snyder, who was studying in a Kyoto Zendo. And then it happened. Returning to Tokyo by train, he suddenly burst into tears and felt a great weight—specifically the weight of his desire to disappear into cosmic consciousness—lift free of his body. It was *satori,* of a kind. "No more mental universe arguments," Ginsberg had written to Kerouac. No more wandering. He was returning to America to put his queer shoulder to the wheel.

Ginsberg's first intimation that he had returned to a different world, one where the syndrome of shutdown was beginning to fragment, came in Czechoslovakia, where for a few weeks in mid-February 1965 he was a familiar sight, strolling the snowy streets of Prague in a used overcoat and white tennis shoes. The official journal of the Czech Writers Union playfully described him as "a large blackbird standing on one leg and listening until the music of life reveals itself to him." But then the young students of Prague elected him King of their May Day parade; Ginsberg was borne down the boulevards in a rose-covered chariot. This was too much for the communist bosses, apparently, because a few days later Ginsberg was arrested for disturbing the peace, and a few days after that he was expelled; fame had not dulled his talent for irritating official power.

The particulars of Ginsberg's expulsion involved the loss and recovery (by a loyal comrade) of one of his personal notebooks. Inside, interspersed between such comments as "it seems that everyone in Czechoslovakia is drunk," were descriptions of his amours with various handsome Czech youths. This was no jolly blackbird, railed one of the party journals, but a pernicious influence who espoused "those things which must be condemned: bisexuality, homosexuality, narcomania, alcoholism, posing, and a social extremism verging on orgies." A copy of this editorial was duly translated and inserted in Ginsberg's file at the Federal Bureau of Narcotics.

Six weeks later Ginsberg was in London for a poetry reading at the Albert Hall. Seven thousand students turned out to cheer his poems, and those of Gregory Corso, Lawrence Ferlinghetti, and the Russian poet Andrei Voznesensky. Almost overnight Ginsberg found himself an authentic culture hero, an elevation that was paying unexpected dividends: with almost a hundred thousand copies of *Howl* in circulation, Ginsberg was starting to make money, which was a troublesome prospect. Unwilling to give up the lifestyle he had created during his penurious youth, Ginsberg hired Bob Dylan's manager to organize his bookings and look after his earnings, and he formed himself into a nonprofit corporation and began giving grants to friends.

Although the media still treated him as the notorious beatnik of old—would he take his clothes off!—Ginsberg had changed during his Eastern *hegira;* his public persona was much more contemplative and oracular. Privately, with his famous address book and boundless enthusiasm, he was becoming what Jane Kramer, the *New Yorker* writer who profiled him during the height of the psychedelic movement, called "the central casting office of the underground." He knew everyone, lawyers, gurus, poets, mystics, businessmen, professors, even senators. Unlike most of his younger admirers, he was not scornful of the straight world, preferring an ethic of gentle persuasion to one of raucous rejection. But bridging the spreading gap between the children of the Sixties and their parents was not his major concern: more than anyone else Ginsberg would try to heal the rift that was developing between the hippies, who were his natural constituency, and the political activists, whom he saw as a resource (they knew how to organize) that the counterculture could not afford to squander.

Stimulated by this diplomatic role, Ginsberg tried to tutor the activists in what might be called right logistics. The old popular-front style of marching through the street shouting slogans only served to reinforce the Establishment stereotypes, he counseled in a long article in the Berkeley *Barb*. Slyer tactics were called for, particularly if one ran the risk of being attacked by riot police and marauding Hells Angels. "Marchers should bring CROSSES," he wrote, "to be held up in front in case of violence; like in the movies dealing with Dracula." They should try chanting the Lord's Prayer or "Mary Had a Little Lamb." And if that didn't work, sound systems should begin playing the Beatles' big hit, "I Wanna Hold Your Hand," and everyone should start dancing.

Ginsberg's stance on LSD, circa 1965, was that it wiped out conditioned reflexes, a possibility that had first been raised in the late Fifties by a Czechoslovakian researcher named Jiri Rubichek. LSD allowed you an objective look at your own conditioning, at all the categories you had been taught to filter experience into, first as an infant and later as a functioning member of a complex, highly organized society. This was more or less in line with Leary's belief that psychedelics revealed the games one had unconsciously adopted, but it put matters in a starker, more appealing light: take LSD and wipe the slate clean of all that Madison Avenue-Big Business-Behaviorist crap.

But what happened after that? No one knew. Having just won a Guggenheim grant which brought him another six thousand dollars, Ginsberg had decided to purchase a VW van and, with Peter Orlovsky in tow, spend the winter of 1966 touring the college campuses of the Midwest, hoping to learn firsthand how deep the ferment went. But until then he attached himself to the Prankster entourage, renewing his friendship with Cassady and writing at least one poem that captured the La Honda milieu:

> in the huge
> wooden house, a yellow chandelier
> at 3 AM the blast of loudspeakers
> hi fi Rolling Stones Ray Charles Beatles
> Jumping Joe Jackson and twenty youths
> dancing to the vibration thru the floor

a little weed in the bathroom, girls in scarlet
tights, one muscular, smooth skinned man
sweating dancing for hours, beer cans
bent littering the yard, a hanged man
sculpture dangling from a high creek branch,
children sleeping softly in bedroom bunks,
And 4 police cars parked outside the painted
gate, red lights revolving in the leaves.

The other notable partygoer that sultry August night was Richard Alpert, who for reasons that will be explained had left Millbrook and was now living in the Bay Area, working as a consulting psychologist on the Stanford project that was developing the new math. He was also trying to establish himself as a lecturer on the psychedelic circuit and having pretty good response. The Los Angeles *Free Press,* after attending one of his early efforts, gushed that his "sunny disposition and genuine sweetness, joined onto his first-rate science-trained mind, make him almost archetypical of the psychedelic hero." Alpert usually eschewed the label of scientist, however, and presented himself as a fellow explorer who was bringing his colleagues the latest, most up to date information about the Other World. "I am merely the East Coast representative checking in," he told the LA audience. "A progress report."

As LA was an early crucible for the psychedelic movement, it is worthwhile quoting at some length from the *Free Press* article, which was obviously written by someone who was no stranger to the Other World. First off, the reporter noted, the five hundred or so attendees were not members of the lunatic fringe:

> These were peaceful, beautiful-looking people of all ages and colors. Their aura was that of law-respecting and life-positive citizens, who want, more than anything, to live and enjoy life. And yet all of them asked the sort of questions and followed the kind of answers that clearly showed they were not merely curious, but directly, intensely, involved with psychedelics. What they knew of LSD did not come from books. Obviously, upwards of 90% of the audience were, in varying degrees, using the psychedelics in their own lives.
>
> These people were obviously more than theoreticians which means that all of them have been knowingly breaking the law and given the nature of the psychedelic experience, I suspect it grieves most of them to do so. Yet do so they must. Yet on the plus side, it is a unique kind of black market, the psychedelic supply system, for the profit motive is not yet paramount in it. Harassment, at the moment, is minimal, for psychedelic people want to and in the main manage to stay out of trouble; but a . . . cloudless sky is unrealistic

to expect. There will be trouble, no doubt, and perhaps it should
even be structured trouble.

The trouble arrived sooner than anyone expected and at its center
were the Merry Pranksters. As Alpert, who perhaps caught an intimation of the future that evening in La Honda, described it: "We thought
we had a few more years of sneaking under the wire with legitimacy
before the whistle got blown. But Ken made them blow the whistle. I
mean, the day after the San Jose 'acid test' the big headline in the paper
was about a 'drug orgy.' Then the legislators had to act. Their hand had
been forced."

The Acid Test was Kesey's experiment on the nature of group mind
and a possible new art form. It was total experience, Kesey explained
to Wolfe, "with all the senses opened wide, words, music, lights,
sounds, touch—lightning."

The first Acid Test was a dry run held at Babbs's place in Soquel,
a town outside of Santa Cruz. Except for an enigmatic poster—Can You
Pass The Acid Test?—that appeared in a local bookstore, no effort was
made to publicize the event and aside from a contingent of San Francisco bohemians who came with Allen Ginsberg, attendance was limited
to the Pranksters and their friends. The second Test, in San Jose on the
night of a Rolling Stones concert, was closer to the Grand Design.
Although the Pranksters failed in their quest to find a public hall, they
managed to procure a rambling old house out in the suburbs that was
owned by an aging and somewhat gullible bohemian named Big Nig.
When the Rolling Stones concert ended and the doors opened to emit
the flood of satisfied rockers, there were the Pranksters, dressed in their
Day-Glo finery, pressing handbills bearing that enigmatic . . . Can You
Pass . . . plus Big Nig's address . . . into eager hands.

Kesey had hired a band for this Acid Test, a group of Palo Alto
rockers who called themselves the Warlocks, although they shortly
would change their name to the Grateful Dead. Consequently Big Nig's
living room was filled with electronic equipment—amplifiers and assorted Prankster playthings, microphones and tape recorders that were
hooked into each other, feeding Cassady's voice or Babbs's voice—
"Have you lost your mind yet?"—out over the suburban turf and into
the suddenly wide-awake consciousness of the neighbors. Who
promptly called the police. Who found hundreds of people milling
around Big Nig's yard, a few freaking out, but most totally absorbed
into whatever meaning the Pranksters plus the LSD had been able to
create.

"They had film and endless kind of weird tape recorder hook ups
and mystery speaker trips and all," recalls Jerry Garcia, the Warlock's

lead guitarist. "It always seemed as though the equipment was able to respond in its own way. I mean it . . . there were always magical things happening. Voices coming out of things that weren't plugged in . . . it was just totally mind boggling to wander around that maze of wires and stuff like that. Sometimes they were like writhing and squirming. Truly amazing."

In a sense, the electronic whisperings, the bop raps of Cassady, Babbs's metanoic chants—these were comparable to the huge eight-hour tapes that Metzner had devised at Millbrook. Both were designed to manipulate the suggestibility of the psychedelic condition, to move the tripper in novel directions, except that the Acid Test piled on roaring guitars and flashing lights and hundreds of ecstatic fellow voyagers going wherever the flow led them. The ideal was to get everyone participating, adding their own creative juice to the gestalt. To get hundreds, maybe even thousands, synched up . . . to leave the planet!

Primed by the San Jose success, the Pranksters decided to turn the Acid Test into a traveling magic show. Their next appearance was in Palo Alto, where they rented a plush little nightclub called the Big Beat that was owned by two sweet middle-aged ladies. It was a more polished replay of San Jose, except for the fact that the Pranksters sported quasi-official uniforms: Day-Glo harlequin jerseys of alternating green, orange, and white stripes. A few of Kesey's old Palo Alto friends came to check out his latest incarnation. Most tended to agree with what a lot of the other psychedelic pioneers were saying: the Acid Test was too high powered for the uninitiated. "You can freak out in there," they were warning. But according to the Pranksters, freaking out was good for the soul. And judging from the legion of postadolescents who frequented the Tests, a lot of kids agreed.

Who showed up at the Tests? "Thousands of people," remembers Garcia, "all helplessly stoned, all finding themselves in a roomful of other thousands of people, none of whom any of them were afraid of. It was magic, far out, beautiful magic." One participant was a Berkeley undergraduate named Jann Wenner, who wrote a column for the student newspaper, the *Daily Cal.* Using the pen name Mr. Jones, Wenner pub-crawled through the hip underside of the Bay Area, a job that inevitably brought him into contact with the Pranksters. What attracted Wenner to the Acid Test wasn't the drugs or the higher purpose, but the music and the dancing: "Once the music stops it becomes very dull," he wrote.

As 1965 drew to a close the leading edge of the Baby Boom was turning twenty; at San Jose, at Palo Alto, you could feel their restlessness coming to a boil.

As one of the most obvious catalysts of this ferment, Kesey and the

Pranksters began to attract organizers and entrepreneurs who saw in the Acid Test a format that could be profitably expanded, until it rivaled such acts as the Beatles or, a better analogy perhaps, the religious crusades of Billy Graham. Among these newcomers was a young man named Stewart Brand, who was the creator of a multimedia presentation called the "American Needs Indians Sensorium." A Midwesterner by birth, educated at an elite New England prep school, Brand was characteristic of the sort of young person who was beginning to flock to California, and to San Francisco in particular. He had first fallen in love with the state through the novels of John Steinbeck, an infatuation that had resulted in his subsequent enrollment at Stanford University, where he "wasted four years" studying biology. Stanford, Brand quickly learned, was not Steinbeck country. For that he had to discover the North Beach, where the Beat culture, although waning, was still exotic enough to captivate a young romantic.

Of the older Beats, only Gary Snyder had recognized that the Native Americans, particularly in their relationship with the earth, had as much to offer the children of the Fifties as the *roshis* and gurus of the East. Snyder's sympathy had grown out of his training as an anthropologist; with Brand it was that recent extension of biology known as ecology. In the course of his research Brand lived with two different Indian tribes, the Oregon Silcots and the Navajos of the southwestern desert. Of the latter he has said, "Anything I know about organization, I learned at a Navajo peyote meeting one night."

It is these organizational talents that concern our story. Having fallen in with the Pranksters around the time of the Palo Alto Acid Test (his slide show blended into the Acid Test without a blemish), it wasn't long before Brand was organizing a mammoth spectacle, which became known as the Trips Festival. Whereas previous Acid Tests had relied on posters and word-of-mouth, Brand hired his own publicist, adman Jerry Mander, and managed to rent the huge Longshoreman's Hall, one of San Francisco's favorite convention venues. Publicity stunts were arranged for the media. For one, three weather balloons were released in Union Square to coincide with the lunch hour crowd. As the balloons lofted over the city, bearing a banner containing the single word NOW, Brand exclaimed over the PA: "Look at it go right into the sun. It's trying to get a little bit closer to the sun before it burns its wings off. Pray for that balloon." "Let's get out of here before we lose our wallets," a name-plated conventioneer was heard to mutter.

The Trips Festival was scheduled for the third weekend in January 1966. Besides the Pranksters and his own Indian Sensorium, Brand invited local theater groups to participate, as well as local businesses. Scattered throughout the hall were booths selling Trips Festival sweatshirts, booths offering incense and psychedelic literature, booths promoting political causes, even booths selling books on insects. Five separate movie screens, each filled with its own surreal montage, were attached to the walls. Strobes washed over the crowd.

Despite all this, Friday, which was devoted to local theatricals and the Sensorium, was dull. "A bust, a bore, a fake, a fraud, a bum trip," lamented the *Chronicle*'s Ralph Gleason in his "On The Town" column. Gleason, who had come expecting the "unspeakable delights" promised by Jerry Mander's publicity, described how "one of the frustrated customers got on stage halfway through the dull evening and said, unselfconsciously, 'this is a bore even on acid.' A little while later, the guy behind me said to his partner, 'let's go out in the car and listen to the radio.' It seemed like a bright idea." But Saturday, which belonged to the Pranksters, redeemed Gleason's opinion of the Trips Festival. It reminded him of a book called *The Circus of Dr. Lao.* "The place was jammed with a congeries of exotics Dr. Lao would have been proud to exhibit," he marveled. "There was a man bandaged all over, with only his eyes peeking out through dark glasses, carrying a crutch and wearing a sign: 'You're in the Pepsi Generation and I'm a pimply freak.' "

An estimated ten thousand people paid admission to the Trips Festival. They came, they gawked, and some of them grokked in the true sense of the word. As one participant described the feeling: "It was like we were all born at the same time in some ways. Like all brilliant children. And we liked to be around our fellow brilliants."

It was Kesey's biggest moment. A few days after the Trips Festival ended, Jerry Mander told columnist Herb Caen that a New York promoter wanted to book the Acid Test (which had grossed sixteen thousand) into Madison Square Garden. "We'll let him, if he'll call it Madison Hip Garden," Mander quipped.

It seemed like a glorious first act, but in reality the show was about to close. Three days before the Trips Festival began Kesey had been rearrested for possession of marijuana. And what was worse, this new arrest came less than forty-eight hours after he had been sentenced for the Willie Wong raid back in April at La Honda. And what was even more ironic: once again he was an innocent bystander. It had happened like this: on Tuesday, January 18, Kesey had stood for sentencing in a San Mateo courtroom. The judge, while not exactly throwing the book at him—the sentence was six months in the county jail with three years' probation and a fifteen hundred-dollar fine—had treated Kesey to what the newspapers described as a "tongue lashing," the gist of which was that he had abused his gift of leadership in a way that society could not tolerate; he had become a negative influence on the young. "If it weren't that your record until now is clean," the judge had warned, "you'd be going to State Prison." As it was, the terms of probation required Kesey to sever all contacts with the Pranksters and the Acid Test.

Two nights later Kesey was at Stewart Brand's apartment on Telegraph Hill, ironing out some last-minute details concerning the Trips

Festival. After the festival, as per the judge's orders, he planned to bid the Pranksters adieu and repair most probably to Oregon, while his legal appeal ran its course. Someone mentioned that one of the Pranksters, Mountain Girl, was on the roof and Kesey went up to join her. Earlier a whole crowd of people, Pranksters and Hells Angels, had been up there smoking marijuana and tossing pebbles at the passersby below, one of whom had notified the police. But now there was only Kesey and Mountain Girl, lying on a rubber mattress, peering over the edge at the street below. They watched as a police car drew up to the building and two officers got out. It never entered their heads that the intended goal was the very roof they were sitting on until the officers appeared in the doorway. And even then, there was no evident problem until one of the policemen spotted the half-hidden Baggie containing about three joints' worth of green vegetal matter. Realizing that history was about to repeat itself, Kesey wrenched the bag from the officer's grasp and flung it over the edge of the building.

He was arrested on charges of possession of marijuana, assaulting a police officer, resisting arrest, and trespassing.

With jail now a certainty, Kesey chose to vanish, missing his bail hearing on February 2. Four days later the bus was found parked near the ocean, outside the northern California town of Eureka. On the front seat was a suicide note, plus a belated endorsement for Barry Goldwater's 1964 presidential campaign. "Last words," it began. "A vote for Barry is a vote for fun." Then:

> Ah, the Fort Bragg sign and that means the ocean and that means time to drop the acid (not that I really need it, mind you; I've courage enough without chemical assistance, it's just that I'm scared. . .)
>
> Driving along, checking the abyss at my left like I'm shopping for real estate prospects. Ocean, ocean, ocean. I'll beat you in the end. I'll go through with my heels at your hungry ribs.
>
> I've lost the ocean again. Beautiful, I drive hundreds of miles looking for my particular cliff, get tripped behind acid. I can't find the ocean, end up slamming into a redwood just like I could have slammed into at home. Beautiful.
>
> So I Ken Kesey being of (ahem) sound mind and body do hereby leave the whole scene to Faye, corporation, cash, the works. And Babbs to run it. (And it occurs to me here that nobody is going to buy this prank and now it occurs to me that I like that even better.)

And nobody did buy it. The police didn't for a minute believe that Kesey had killed himself. APBs were put out throughout the Northwest, although the strongest rumor maintained that Kesey had actually fled south, across the border to Mexico.

20

IN THE ZONE

On Saturday, April 16, 1966, a tall young man, blind in one eye and wearing the flowing brown robes and the traditional tonsure of a Buddhist monk, arrived at Millbrook and requested an audience with Dr. Leary. He identified himself as a former Harvard student who was living at a Tibetan lamasery in New Jersey, from whence he had come that morning, bearing an urgent personal message. The gist of this communique was that Leary should reject the mantle of LSD leadership and do nothing further to anger the authorities.

"When two dogs fight over a bone," he said, "and one of them drops the bone, the other will drop it too and walk away." He left shortly after delivering this cryptic warning, claiming that the atmosphere surrounding the Big House was full of negativity and danger.

Although it was not every day that a one-eyed, Harvard-educated monk showed up on Leary's doorstep counseling Buddhist nonattachment, Millbrook had become a sufficiently strange place that the monk's warning was duly noted, then forgotten. It was mid-April; there were dozens of details to attend to before Millbrook would be ready for the influx of summer guests; armed with power saws and axes, Leary had spent the day with a group of the men thinning a stand of trees known as the "sacred grove."

The monk's image of two dogs fighting over a bone was appropriate. In the past month Leary had participated in a number of media debates, frequently in tandem with his new nemesis, Dr. Donald Louria, Chairman of the Subcommittee on Narcotics of the New York County Medical Society. The previous night, in fact, they had met on a New York radio show to rehash the same argument that Leary had been having with representatives of the medical community for four years—the one about who was going to draw the line between public safety and personal prerogative.

While there was no clear answer to this dilemma, at least from Leary's perspective, Louria was adamant in his belief that only doctors had the breadth of knowledge and the training to handle psychedelic substances, and then only in the most rigorous of experimental situations. And while Leary disagreed, he was usually forced to admit that some form of preparation and training was necessary before embarking upon an LSD trip. However strongly he argued that the government did not have the authority to abridge an individual's right to explore his or her own consciousness, he did recognize that some sort of learner's permit was necessary. But they jumped on him whenever he admitted this: so, Dr. Leary, even you believe controls are necessary! The answer was, yes, certainly, but not by you people. The more Leary debated the representatives of his own professional generation, the more he became convinced that his decision to concentrate on the young was correct: "Fifty-year-olds have lost their curiosity, have lost their ability to make love, have dulled their openness to new sensations, and would use any form of new energy for power, control and warfare," he told one interviewer.

Twenty-six people were staying at Millbrook on the Saturday of the monk's visit. Most were regulars, although there was the usual complement of visitors—a young secretary from Washington, a research psychiatrist, a documentary filmmaker, a drygoods manufacturer, a fashion editor, plus one journalist, Marya Mannes, who was profiling eighteen-year-old Susan Leary for a woman's magazine. Mannes's first impression of Millbrook: "I saw mattresses on the floor, on one of which lay a young man, on another a huge Great Dane. To the left was another bare living room, without mattresses, but with a Victorian sofa on which were two large paper kites and a pith helmet with yellow ostrich feathers on it. Stuck on the newel post of the massive staircase was a stuffed tiger head with a large pink flower in its mouth."

Mannes found the rooms dusty, the sinks piled with dishes, the floors spattered with mud, the closets crammed with junk, the dogs . . . the dogs were everywhere. She was initially assigned a bedroom that had a huge slit-eyed deity painted on the wall, but was moved to the library after complaining that the thought of "sleeping or waking in its presence was not palatable."

One of the few things she did find palatable was the food. Dinner was a splendidly seasoned fish. But afterward the oddness returned, as everyone retired to the sacred grove for singing and meditation. Later they moved back inside for a preview of the audiovisual extravaganza Leary planned to take on the road that summer. Employing numerous synchronized projectors and speakers, the experience was supposed to simulate a psychedelic trip. One of the film loops involved an extended meditation on the movement of water beetles.

Around midnight everyone retired. Leary was up on the third floor with his new girlfriend, Rosemary Woodruff, when the trouble began.

Imagine the kind of sound made by several dozen state troopers pounding up one of those sweeping Victorian staircases and you will have some idea of the noise Leary heard ascending toward him. Leading this phalanx was a wiry pitbull of an assistant district attorney with the no-nonsense name of G. Gordon Liddy.

For the second time in four months Leary was under arrest for possession of marijuana that wasn't even his. For a long moment, hand-cuffed in the back of the police cruiser, he must have wished he could turn back the clock, transport himself back to the safety of that hut in the Himalayan foothills; return to those months in the fall of 1964 when his trajectory had seemed so true, when the future had seemed clear and inevitable.

India had been a succession of magical tableaux. Arriving with Nena in Calcutta, Leary followed Ginsberg's advice and visited the Ganges to watch the corpses being burned. The dead were placed in makeshift craft that were then set aflame and pushed out into the sacred waters of the Ganges. Watching the burning vessels dance in the current, Leary noticed that the sky was full of black buzzards and the air reeked of marijuana smoke. He breathed deeply, feeling extraordinarily alive, and the thought popped into his head: "What's death but the end of breath?"

In Benares, while Nena slept, he bribed a boatman to paddle him across the Ganges to a section of shore that was supposedly haunted by devils. Wading ashore, uncertain what to do now that he was actually here, he was startled by an old man in a ragged *dhoti* who materialized out of the gloom, babbling in a fast, mysterious tongue, with eyes that blazed like lanterns. Fear made him retreat into the water.

> Suddenly I understood: he was some special ancient teacher who had been waiting for me all my life. I wanted to run forward and throw myself at his feet. But I was paralyzed with fright, thinking at the same time that he could be a crazed fanatic. He might attack me, a profaner of holy ground.

Leary waded back to the boat, hoping the boatman could interpret this strange vision. But the boatman was equally terrified, was leaving that instant in fact, and Leary, unthinkingly, scrambled back aboard. Half-way across, the immensity of what he'd done struck him, and he burst into tears: he had met the Buddha and run away.

In Delhi they rendezvoused with Ralph Metzner, who took them to the Taj Mahal for a moonlit LSD trip. Then it was on to Almora in the Himalayan foothills, where Metzner was studying with Lama Govinda, an Austrian who was one of the foremost interpreters of Tibetan Buddhism. Leary and Metzner had discovered his writings during their initial plunge into Eastern cosmology at Harvard; in gratitude they had sent him a copy of *The Psychedelic Experience,* and he'd replied with an invitation to visit Almora should they ever be in India.

Although he had always refused to become a guru, Lama Govinda agreed to spend one hour each day instructing Tim and Nena in Buddhist mysticism. During one of these tutorials, conducted with European elegance over tea and pastries, Lama Govinda suggested to Tim that he was merely a cog in a grand design:

> In recent years, said the Lama, many of the guardians of the old philosophic traditions had realized that the evolution of the human race depended upon a restoration of unity between the outer science advanced by the West and the inner yoga advanced by the East. It had become necessary to break centuries of public silence, to bypass the master-disciple tradition, and actively seek to enlighten the West. This infiltration of Oriental philosophy into Europe and America would be carried out by publishing books and sending forth charismatic teachers . . . Translations of the *Tibetan Book of the Dead* by Evans-Wentz was part of the plan. When word came to the philosophic community of India that a group of Harvard psychologists were using the ancient Buddhist text as a manual for drug-induced *satoris,* there was great interest.

"You," the Lama told Tim, "are the predictable result of a strategy that has been unfolding for over fifty years . . . you have been the unwitting tool of the great transformation of our age."

This was, of course, the subtext of many of Tim's conversations with Huxley and Heard, even with Watts, but to hear the scenario described over tea, in a cabin in the snowcapped Himalayas, with such calm certainty, was unnerving. It made one wonder whether all the legends about the Masters weren't true, after all.

Lama Govinda wasn't the only Western expatriate living in the Almora foothills. A few valleys away was Sri Krishna Prem, who as Ronald Nixon had been a slightly younger contemporary of Huxley. Having read philosophy at Cambridge, Nixon originally had come out to India to teach, had been seduced by the mystical (like so many of that generation) and had become a devotee of Krishna. He was sixty-seven when Leary met him, a tall, vigorous man with a thick wedge of white hair, and underneath his saffron robe still the English gentleman. He too had heard of the Harvard psilocybin project and he broke his rule of no visitors to offer Leary and Metzner lunch. Metzner later considered it to be the "one day that made the whole Indian journey worthwhile."

Over sherry, Sri Krishna Prem had talked about the proper way to approach the Eastern concept of guru. The true guru, he told them, was the inner voice of one's highest self. But very few people were attentive enough to hear that murmurous whisper. They needed an outer guru, a teacher, who would act as "a sort of amplifier for the inner guru." But in accepting an external teacher, one should never lose sight of the fact that one day it would be necessary to pass beyond the outer teacher, and return to the inner path.

It was Metzner's impression that Sri Krishna Prem "was probably as close as Tim has ever come to accepting a teacher." If this was the case, then his teaching, brief as it was, contained an explicit warning. At one of their last meetings, Sri Krishna Prem grew serious and said to Leary, "It is time that I tell you some things that you should know. Over the centuries our Hindu philosophers have seen everything come and go. Empires, religions, famines, good times, invasions, reforms, liberations, repressions. And drugs. Drugs are among the most influential and dangerous powers available to humans. They open up glorious and pleasurable chambers in the mind. They give great power. Thus they can seduce the searcher away from the Path."

Then he proceeded to tell a long allegorical anecdote about a yogi who had been falsely accused of rape. The man was vilified and spat upon and ostracized by the same people who yesterday had thought him a wise man. But the yogi took no notice of his fallen stature and continued to pursue the inner path. The years slipped by and eventually the girl who had accused him confessed and named the true rapist. Now the villagers tumbled all over themselves proclaiming the yogi to be a wise and good man. But the yogi took no notice of them and continued to follow the inner way.

Months later the prescience of this allegory would be borne home to Leary, but at the time it was just another spice in the heady, mystical broth that he found in Almora, a variant of those conversations with Lama Govinda in which the latter would tell stories of how, in the higher realms of consciousness, systematic telepathy and out-of-the-body travel were commonplace.

Upon arriving in Almora, Tim and Nena had moved into a cottage that was rented by the local Methodist missionary. A Moslem cook was hired to handle the meals. Once a week Leary sent him down to the village market and he returned with some of the best hashish Leary had ever smoked. The hash provided the proper mood for his sole utilitarian project while in India, which was the translation of the *Tao te Ching* into the "lingua franca of psychedelia." Leary had brought along seven or eight translations of Lao Tze's gnostic verses. After absorbing each version, filtering it through his own store of psychedelic images, he would produce a new version, stripped of all fat, just the psychedelic kernel of the *Tao.*

Almora should have been the ideal honeymoon for Tim and Nena. But it wasn't. Unaccountably the strain between them grew with each passing week, prompting Metzner, who had been staying in one of the cottage's extra rooms, to hasten his departure for Millbrook. What was particularly sad about the disintegration of Tim's third marriage was the fact that in Lama Govinda and his wife, Li Gotama, Tim had found the perfect illustration of the loving, evolving couple whose consciousness, linked in tandem, was "the key to personal evolution." Try as he might, he was unable to achieve a similar rapport with Nena. LSD, which was normally a powerful aphrodisiac for Leary, pushed them further apart.

The marriage was over before the honeymoon was over. They "limped back to Millbrook with no flags flying," Leary wrote in *Flashbacks.*

They found a shambles. Castalia, under Alpert's management, had self-destructed. Gone was the atmosphere of adventurous yet serious monasticism; the Big House had become "a playground for rowdy omnisexuals." Charles Slack, unaware that his old friend was honeymooning in India, had dropped by one Saturday and had found the place full of Greenwich Village hustlers "lying naked and freaked out all around the mansion."

"I went into the kitchen to try to find Jackie and Susan but instead, standing by the sink, which was piled shoulder high with a heap of dirt-encrusted dishes, I found a nice looking blonde haired lady who could have been from *I Remember Mama* or a TV Swedish maid. She was Birgit Baroness von Schlegrugge, Nena's mother."

Metzner, who returned about a month before Tim, thought he had stumbled into an occult version of hell. The walls had turned into bizarre frescos, covered with glittery shards of mirror and grotesque faces. Metzner found the place divided into two warring camps. On one side were Nena's relatives and a handful of others who wanted to keep the mansion clean and orderly. Allied against them were the trip-all-the-time party, which included Michael Hollingshead ("reincarnated in Scottish kilts and scarlet capes, zanily lecturing on the relativity of the brain") and a charismatic artist named Arnie. Arnie, oddly enough, had usurped Tim's role as philosopher-king, and was promoting a creed of psychedelic extremism that called for constant tripping. The trip-all-the-time party kept a mayonnaise jar full of LSD in one of the bed-rooms. Two or three times a day they would stick a finger in and lick it clean, receiving twenty to thirty times the normal dosage. Metzner thought it a "ridiculous waste of LSD."

The antagonism was such that actual blows had been struck, and it was clear to Metzner that although Dick pretended to be impartial, he favored the constantly high crowd.

His was a complicated mood. On one hand, Alpert felt exploited. It seemed to him that the harder he had worked at creating an atmo-sphere of calm orderliness, the more outrageous Tim had become. Old, uptight Dick, had been Tim's standard attitude, particularly when the subject was money, for which Leary professed an airy disregard. It had been Alpert who paid the bills and collected the rent and cajoled the creditors into waiting a few more weeks for money that always seemed to materialize in sufficient quantity at the very last moment—an oner-ous task for a nice Jewish boy who had been brought up believing in the sanctity of one's credit rating. And what about Leary's kids, Susan and Jack? Alpert had been both mother and father to them, making sure they were fed and attempting, as best he could, to empathize with the enormity of being a teenager in the bizarre adult funhouse that Mill-brook had become.

One day Alpert took some LSD and went for a spin in his Cessna, an astonishingly stupid act. It was a replay of the night he had walked into the surf at Zihuatanejo. There were days when he ached for his old life as a hip professor, tooling around Cambridge in his Mercedes, entertaining clever young men in his antique-filled apartment; days when he pined for the familiar routine of lectures and staff meetings, the easy conversations with Dave McClelland. Although there were times when he saw the purpose and potential of Millbrook Castalia clearly, there were others when he felt lost, completely at sea with what Tim and Ralph were doing. He saw no purpose, for instance, in adul-terating the *Tibetan Book of the Dead* into a modern guide book. Sure the parallels were striking, sure it might make a little money. But it was a side issue, surely. What they should be concentrating on was how to stay permanently high!

After hundreds of trips to the Other World and back, a subtle kind of depression was settling in. Alpert found himself playing the "Do You Know" game, meaning were you enlightened:

> People were constantly looking into my eyes, like, "Do you know."
> Just that subtle little look, and I was constantly looking into their
> eyes—Do You Know? And there we were, "Do You?" "Do You?"

"Maybe He?" "Do You. . . ." And there was always that feeling that everybody was very close and we all knew we knew, but nobody quite knew.

Much more than Leary, Alpert wanted to push the envelope, to pierce that final veil that stood between himself and enlightenment. One time he shut himself up in the bowling alley with a few of the other trip-all-the-timers. For several weeks they stayed aloft, upping the dosage as tolerance built up, until they were ingesting thousands of micrograms.

But the envelope held. They came back down. Nothing had changed except Alpert's neurotic need to keep things under control. Two weeks of constant LSD had cured him of cash-flow nightmares, which was just as well since their debt was mounting at a dizzy pace. Metzner estimated Castalia was spending five or six times what it was bringing in. To raise money he and Alpert began giving public lectures, which culminated in a communal effort on April 5, 1965, at the Vanguard Theater in Greenwich Village. The communal effort was what Hollingshead dubbed transart—transcendental art—a combination of film projectors, music, and theater, which strove to overload the senses, creating a kind of psychedelic frisson. The Pranksters would have felt right at home.

The audience was evenly divided between an older Upper East Side set and younger college-age kids, who displayed (thought a reporter from the *Times*) a rather sophisticated knowledge of arcana like cosmic consciousness, reentry, and set and setting. The significance of those flashing images of Mount Rushmore and the Buddha, interspersed with what seemed to be a high school biology film, was not lost on them. They wolfed down the jelly beans distributed at intermission (a few people worried that the jellybeans might be treated . . . you never knew with these drug fiends) and gaily waved the balloons.

After the psychedelic light show ended, a single spot clicked on and Alpert appeared carrying a stool, which he plunked down in the middle of the stage. He made himself comfortable and then he launched into a series of hilarious anecdotes about Harvard, his eccentric father, Tim, his search for enlightenment in a world that considered Vince Lombardi a great American philosopher. The crowd rolled in the aisles.

"You are a natural-born comedian," the owner of the Vanguard told Alpert after his final bow. "Would you like to try a week here as a comedian, doing what you did tonight?"

Alpert agreed and a few days later returned for another engagement, this time in front of a normal audience. He bombed. His routines hung there like a bad smell. The problem, as Hollingshead quickly perceived, was you had to be high to think Dick was funny. Straight people, who had come to the Vanguard to escape their own quiet desperation, found nothing comical about a man who "could jeopardize an enviable family security and a top academic job to live as Dick was doing then."

Tim, had he been in the audience, might have agreed with them. It was amazing how quickly life could pivot one hundred and eighty degrees. On the eve of his wedding, everything had seemed glorious to Leary. Thrown out of Harvard, booted around the Caribbean, he had managed to land on his feet, and in Castalia he had a facsimile of what Huxley had dreamed of in *Island:* a stable, mentally enriching environment detached from the stresses of the modern industrial state. And in Nena he had found, after almost a decade of industrious womanizing, a woman to whom he could commit himself, something he had long desired in theory, if not practice. Now, four months later, none of that existed.

At Alpert's urging, Leary agreed to participate in a three-way LSD session with Dick and Nena, a decision he later came to regret as "the height of folly—we were three willful wary souls, already alienated from each other." As the drug took hold, Alpert suddenly accused Leary of being a prude, of constantly making subtle condemnations of his homosexuality, which was hardly a sign of enlightenment. Leary was taken aback: "How I reacted to this first move would be crucial. Response A: I laugh and genially point out that the love and humor among us three will conquer all. Outcome: fusion. We unite as a merry trio of divinities . . . But I could do no better than Response B: guilty silence. Outcome: fission . . . If Dick or I had been more secure, either one of us could have strobed the other out of low spirits with a blast of loving humor. But no. This acid session was about severing connections. The lines went down, and we never got the current going again. It was the last time we took acid together."

Alpert flew off for a long vacation in the south of France. When he returned, he was told there was no place for him at Millbrook.

The other problems were less soluble. Instead of easing the financial crunch, the transart performances only exacerbated matters by attracting more weekend pilgrims to Millbrook. To stave off bankruptcy, Leary decided to resurrect the nondrug "experiential weekends" of the previous summer.

Every Friday at 7:30 in the evening the guests arrived at the Big House, usually between fifteen to twenty, although the size and complexion of the group varied from week to week. Most were urban professionals who had read about Millbrook in the newspapers or had chanced upon an issue of the *Psychedelic Review* in a progressive bookstore and had impulsively mailed off the experiential weekend coupon. The cost was little enough—sixty dollars—when weighed against the brochure's tantalizing prose:

> The first step is the realization that there is more: that man's brain, his thirteen billion celled computer, is capable of limitless new dimensions of awareness and knowledge. In short that man does not use his head.
>
> The second step is the realization that you have to go out of your mind to use your head; that you have to pass beyond everything you have learned in order to become acquainted with the new areas of consciousness. Ignorance of this fact is the veil which shuts man within the narrow confines of his acquired, artifactual concepts of 'reality,' and prevents him from coming to know his own true nature.
>
> The third step (once the first two realizations have taken place) is the practical theoretical. How can consciousness be expanded. What is the range of possibilities outside of our current verbal-cognitive models of experience? . . . How can the new levels of awareness be maintained?

With those phrases echoing in their heads, the guests ascended the winding drive, past the whitewashed stone and the gardens, coming at last to the Big House, which was strangely and disturbingly silent, like a church. A girl in a sari greeted them at the front door and handed them a printed sheet:

> Welcome to an experiential weekend. Your weekend in Millbrook has been planned to provide a series of consciousness-expanding experiences. The first step in the process of going beyond your routine and familiar patterns is a period of absolute silence.

No hellos. No small talk. About the time they were unpacking their suitcases, and worriedly contemplating the strangely painted walls, two more messages were borne in by another saried girl:

> Please do not engage in conversation of any kind until the breaking of silence is publicly announced. For now, look. Listen to the non-verbal energy around you. Experience directly.

The final slip of paper contained a rather lengthy essay on how to "play" the experiential weekend game and it was at this point that a certain amount of attrition usually occurred. Every weekend two or three of the guests quietly but quickly stole away, not saying a word to anyone. "They think they've fallen into the hands of a mad scientist," laughed Tim. "And that's when we hear them creeping down the back stairs and screeching out of the driveway."

The silence continued into dinner. The menu varied: sometimes spaghetti, sometimes fish, sometimes exotic mixtures of brown rice, vegetables, and chewy homemade bread. The table was only a foot off the floor, with cushions instead of chairs. Unable to swap statuses, everyone listened to the collective chewing, wondering who the others were, where they worked, how much they made. Their glances were amused or puzzled. Midway through the meal a soft voice floated out of a hidden speaker: "Contemplate on the wonders of the body . . . where this food goes . . . how it is digested . . . how it is transformed into energy . . . into you . . . think carefully as you chew the next mouthful."

Afterward they were led to the session room—a richly panelled sitting room that made Hollingshead feel like he was inside a cigar box—and arranged on the mattresses that covered the floor. At the back of the room were a half dozen film and slide projectors, calibrated to operate in tandem, which threw alternating images of the Buddha, etc., upon the walls, while a voice would jump from speaker to speaker intoning:

> That which is called ego-death is coming to you
> Remember:
> This is the hour of death and rebirth;
> Take advantage of this temporary death to obtain the
> perfect
> State—
> Enlightenment.

And so on.

The next morning, for early risers, there was a sunrise yoga session with Metzner. Then a series of lectures on topics like neurological politics, tantra, breaking set. Then back to the session room. At noon Sunday the guests left, and Millbrook reverted to its delightfully odd self. Some nights a hundred people sat down to an elegant meal prepared by a German in a chef's toque; a few days later there wouldn't be a scrap of food in the house. Usually, though, the kitchen hummed with continuous activity. Someone was always making a salad or frying bacon or brewing coffee, at three in the morning. It was like wandering into an all-night diner somewhere in the Twilight Zone: the girl in the black sarong, for instance, might pull a pack of tarot cards out, and give you a reading whose accuracy made your hair stand on end.

Just as the medieval Christian monastics spent their hours pursuing grace and practicing penance, someone at Millbrook was always dreaming up new ways to break set and lift imprints. For a time they employed Gurdjieff's technique of randomly ringing a bell and having everyone stop to assess whether they were centered in the here and now or lost either in fantasy or memory. Had they had the money, they might have dispensed with the bells and trained a flock of parrots to bark attention! attention!, just like in *Island*. Although the desire to escape one's mental ruts had its serious side, it frequently tended to shade off into the form of humor known as the "put on." Millbrook was not impervious to that facet of the psychedelic experience that compelled one to dress in an English Commodore's uniform or Arabian desert robe. "I'd wake up to see Tim dressed as a cowboy driving a covered wagon pulled by two horses, one sprayed pink Day-Glo and the other bright green," remembers a guest. "I just sighed to myself, O, well, here we go again." Once some psychologists from Yale were visiting and Leary told everyone to act as professional as possible. He in particular addressed this request to one of the semipermanent artists (for whom the Big House was a huge canvas; by 1968 every available space had been filled with psychedelic daubings), a fellow partial to bizarre harlequin outfits. They had been in the middle of a polite lunch when the artist had arrived in a three-piece suit, carrying the *New York Times*. Nodding to them, he opened the paper and began to read. Everything seemed normal until the green vegetable dye began dribbling from his mouth. No one said a word but everyone was riveted on the green slime that was gushing down his chin and all over his suit. Then he calmly folded his *Times* and left. It was the first happening Hollingshead had ever seen: "Tim said nothing at all about it. Neither did we. It seemed the wisest course to smother the scene in silence."

Working hard to retrieve the shattered air of normality, Leary suggested that they visit the house pet, which was a Tibetan monkey. Usually the monkey had free rein, but he was caged during mealtimes as he had a bad habit of perching atop the kitchen cabinets and throwing eggs at the diners. Leary led psychologists to the second floor, threw open the door, and there in the monkey cage was the artist, reading the *Times* and eating a banana.

This kind of zaniness was beginning to wear on Metzner. He believed that the mapping of consciousness should be their primary goal and was therefore disturbed that sidelines like the experiential weekend and the psychedelic theater shows were consuming more and more energy. One night, returning from an evening of transart, they ran into Maynard Ferguson (who was now living in the gatehouse) and his band at a roadside café. After the surprise and pleasure at this unexpected meeting abated, Metzner was struck by the realization that like Ferguson, he too was an entertainer. And he was reminded of a dream that had come to him during those first weeks at Millbrook: "In the dream the three of us, Tim, Dick and myself, were vaudeville artists, doing a song and dance routine, with exciting music and chorus girls, to try to present something that was deeply serious and even sacred." It was not the future Metzner had imagined for himself.

But Millbrook was never going to revert to the quiet research center it had been in the beginning. Tim was moving away from research toward politics. They had mapped the Other World, was his position, had mapped it to the point where others could follow. They had trained guides and published guidebooks. Now the issue was how to preserve what they had accomplished, and to do that they were going to have to combat the attempts by the medical and political bureaucracies to paint psychedelics as worse than heroin.

"There are three thousand Americans who die every year from barbiturates," Leary complained. "And it never hits the papers. Thousands more die in car crashes and from lung cancer induced by smoking. That isn't news, either. But one LSD kid rushes out and takes off his clothes in the street and it's headlines in the New York *Daily News.*"

Leary's current favorite proposal called for the establishment of a Commission of Psychochemical Education, which he saw as "a blue ribbon panel of neurologists, pharmacologists, psychologists, educators and religious leaders," who would survey the field of psychochemicals and propose guidelines for further research, both governmental and personal. Although Leary asked for no part in this Commission, he did favor the adoption of two psychedelic commandments:

1. Thou shalt not alter the consciousness of thy fellows by psychochemical means.

2. Thou shalt not prevent thy fellows from changing their consciousness by chemical means. If there is clear evidence that someone's change of consciousness harms society, then, and only then, can you take preventative measures. But in every such case, the burden of proof must be on society to demonstrate that harm is being done.

In private, though, Tim admitted that his chances of forestalling prohibition were slim. When Frank Barron visited Millbrook that summer, one of the things Tim stressed was his intuition that if he played his hand to the end and continued to proselytize for psychedelics, he would end up in prison. "I'm going to jail," he told Barron, and Barron didn't disagree. Leary came from a race who valued the brave lads who defied the authorities; they were honored if and when they got out of jail. It was a damned hard thing to stop an Irish rebel from going to jail if he wanted to, Barron thought to himself.

Curiously, Leary's Irish heritage manifested itself in another context that summer. During one of his frequent LSD explorations, Tim stumbled upon a neurological eddy that seemed to contain ancestral memories, past lives and such. "I've charted my own family tree back to Ireland and France, swimming in the gene pool," he told an interviewer. "I freak out and open my eyes and stop it. In many of these sessions, back about three hundred years, I often run across a particular French-looking man with a black moustache and a rather dangerous-looking guy. And in Ireland or England, moments of propagation . . . scenes of rough ancestral sexuality in Irish barrooms, in haystacks, in canopied beds, in converted wagons, on beaches, on the moist jungle floor." Of course these might be nothing more than "luridly melodramatic Saturday serials conjured up by my forebrain. But whatever they are—memory or imagination—it's the most exciting adventure I've ever been involved in."

Running this adventure a close second, however, was Rosemary Woodruff, a stunningly beautiful thirty-year-old who had turned up at Millbrook one weekend looking like a vision out of Leary's subconscious. The first time Tim met her she was wearing tennis shoes (his favorite form of saddlery) and carrying both a bottle of wine and a copy of Wittgenstein. His attraction was so intense that for a moment he "wondered idly if she was an intelligence agent assigned to my case. If so, the psych-tech boys sure had my number."

To commemorate their first night together, Leary painted two eight-foot-tall interlocking triangles on the chimney. The message, for those who knew the Oriental symbol for sexual union, was that finally Tim had found his perfect complement.

Rosemary's influence was immediate and multifarious. She found the concept of becoming a holy man "too amusing for words" and whenever Tim began to display an overabundance of Hinduism, she turned on the humor. More importantly, she introduced him to science fiction. Like the Merry Pranksters, Leary found the genre a rich source of psychedelic models and over the years it would replace Eastern mysticism as a source of images and vocabulary. But Rosemary's greatest impact was in the area of domesticity. For years Susan and Jack had been shunted to the sidelines while their father pursued the ancient path, to be raised by Alpert, Metzner, and whoever else happened to be around the Big House. Rosemary changed that equation, arousing in Tim pleasurable fantasies of living in a single-family house, with one woman, his kids, his books, his work. Pick a successor and retire to emeritus status. New American Library had offered him a ten thousand-dollar advance for his autobiography. If that book was a success, then Rosemary wanted him to try his hand at science fiction. If it wasn't . . . well, he could always obtain a professorship at some small college. In either case, they would "find a house with a white picket fence, and have babies."

Leary's domestic fantasies were symptomatic of the fatigue that had settled over Millbrook by the fall of 1965. There were too many distractions and not enough money to maintain the dream of a scientific community devoted to pushing the envelope. It was time for a break. Metzner was planning to move to New York, where he would continue to edit the *Psychedelic Review* and finish his own book on consciousness. Hollingshead was off to London to spread the psychedelic vision across the Old World. He took along hundreds of copies of the *Psychedelic Review* and *The Psychedelic Experience,* and these became the basis of the World Psychedelic Center, which he opened in a Belgravia flat. Initial fantasies had Tim flying over in a few months to conduct an enormous session in the Albert Hall.

As for Leary, a few days before Christmas he set out for Mexico, where once again he planned to write a book, this time his autobiography. With Tim and Rosemary in the front seat of the station wagon, Jack and Susan in the back, they resembled a typical suburban family, except for the marijuana joints that passed back and forth between the seats.

Although it was only two years since Leary had been deported from Mexico, he was under the impression that he had obtained special permission to enter as a tourist. But when he reached the border at Laredo, Texas, he was refused entry, and the man who refused him was the same official who had handled his deportation. The official, after examining Leary's papers, suggested he try again the next day. With the feeling that this might be a set-up growing, Leary prudently made sure the car was free of marijuana before driving back through US Customs. But for some reason Susan decided to conceal a small vial in her underwear, where it was discovered during a strip search. And in the confusion that followed Leary spoke the words "that were to change my legal status for the rest of my life: 'I'll take responsibility for the marijuana.' "

With bail set at ten thousand dollars Leary spent Christmas Eve in the Laredo jail. And it was there, during his first meeting with his lawyer, that the gravity of his situation became clear: in Texas, possession of marijuana was punishable by a possible sentence of life in prison. His lawyer suggested that he throw himself upon the mercy of the court.

Now the theoretical mercy of a Texas jury was not likely to console a Yankee intellectual like Leary; in any case, it was Tim's nature to fight. Ignoring the qualms of his lawyer, Leary mapped out a novel legal strategy based on two mutually conflicting arguments. On one hand he argued that it was his right, as a scientist whose specialty was consciousness, to use marijuana as a research tool; while on the other he claimed that during his honeymoon in India he had become a Hindu, and since marijuana was a religious sacrament of certain Hindu sects, the Texas law was an abridgment of his religious freedom.

The result was a parade of scientists and Hindus who entertained the jury but did not sway them from the salient facts. To wit: marijuana had been found on Susan Leary's person and Tim had accepted responsibility for it. Thus, on March 11, 1966, the court sentenced Tim Leary to thirty years in prison and fined him thirty thousand dollars. Susan was remanded to a Federal Reformatory.

Leary appealed, of course. Billy Hitchcock, who had provided the original bail money, established the Tim Leary Defense Fund, with offices at UN Plaza. Full-page solicitations appeared in the *New York Times,* along with a petition signed by numerous New York intelligentsia, among them the two Normans, Mailer and Podhoretz. Dick Alpert generously came forward with an open letter. "Timothy is the most systematically creative person I have ever known," he wrote. "His ability to break set and see beyond the cultural veil has continued to awe and amaze me." Contributors, Alpert suggested, should regard their donations as a "head tax" that would be used to educate the public on the realities of marijuana and psychedelics.

Leary lunched with Marshall McLuhan during this period, and the master of technological paradox advised him to fight the psychedelic battle in the real court of power, the media. "Lysergic acid hits the spot," he sang to a charmed Leary. "Forty billion neurons, that's a lot." Absorbing McLuhan's advice, Leary began wooing the press, granting as many interviews as possible. Four days after the Texas verdict, he held a press conference at New York's Overseas Press Club, arriving in his old professorial tweeds and cheerfully telling the assembled scribes that they could identify his occupation as "visionary prophet."

But while Tim was certainly news, he was generally shunted off to the "local color" pages, his speeches reported alongside stories of clairvoyant housewives and Appalachian hill feuds. When he was taken seriously by the liberal press, the response was usually negative. The *New York Times,* for example, was so outraged by the nature of his Texas defense that it ran an editorial condemning it: "The First Amendment casts a wide net, but it does not protect antisocial or self-destructive practices under the guise of religion. It does not and, in our view, it should not protect the use of marijuana and other drugs. . . . Whether Dr. Leary deserves the severe sentence that he has received is for the courts to decide. But the speciousness and quackery of his specific defense on 'religious' grounds are as worthless as marijuana itself."

Ultimately it was a trade-off. Some of the interviews, like the one to *Playboy,* paid extremely well. And with mounting legal expenses, money was of the essence. But the price extracted was Tim's sense of self. Tim was floundering, thought Metzner. Although "outwardly he still maintained the front of cheerfulness and everything is moving according to plan," it sounded "more and more hollow."

Martin Garbus, one of the lawyers who was handling Tim's appeal, put it even more bluntly: "[Tim's] creative energies were being subverted into publicity stunts; the prospect that he would be arrested at the slightest provocation was intimidating. He might win one case and later another, but ultimately he would lose, face jail, and be destroyed."

Destroyed the way Socrates was destroyed, for asking uncomfortable questions and corrupting the young. That, as Leary liked to quip, was the traditional fate of visionary prophets.

Even before the Texas court sealed his fate, his Millbrook neighbors were clamoring for his removal. At Bennett College, students were shown a slide show of Leary and the other Castalians and warned that fraternizing with any of them was grounds for expulsion, while the county sheriff, John Quinlan, was quoted as saying, "I'll do anything we can to drive Leary out of town." The Hitchcock estate was placed under constant surveillance, some of it by air, and a Grand Jury was convened to investigate whether there were grounds for any kind of indictment. Much of the questioning centered on Tim's role as a father. Did he encourage his children to take drugs? Who looked after them? Did Leary have many girlfriends? Did he sleep with them openly?

To exacerbate matters, Leary chose this moment to reopen the Millbrook Summer School. He issued a slick eight-page brochure that was a paragon of New Age persuasion, advertising grounds "studded with natural and man-made shrines," and rooms that were "ecstatic settings tied to specific psychedelic themes." Participants would spend two weeks learning how to produce a psychedelic experience, how to guide it ("Unless the voyager is trained to prepare a detailed voyage plan, to recognize landmarks, use internal compasses, arrange setting, psychedelic states can be confusing. A complex series of navigational aids has been worked out and will be taught."), and how to talk about it. The cost was four hundred dollars for each trainee, with a hundred dollars knocked off for each married couple, a bargain that testified to Leary's newfound belief in psychedelic monogamy.

The brochure undoubtedly raised a few eyebrows around town. What was one to make of a line like, "The aim is to make Millbrook for these brief, warm, green sunny days a beautiful and advanced spot on this planet." Over at the Dutchess County Prosecutor's office a line like that meant only one thing: a summer-long sex and drug orgy. Up at Millbrook, it was rumored, "The panties are dropping faster than the LSD."

Over at the Dutchess County Prosecutor's office, there was one man in particular who felt Leary had to be stopped. This was an assistant DA, a gun-toting ex-FBI agent named George Gordon Battle Liddy. Leary, sequestered behind the stone portals of the Hitchcock Estate, reminded Liddy of Dr. Frankenstein, and in one of his fantasies he imagined himself leading a mob of enraged citizens up the steps of Alte Haus—an appropriate mise-en-scène since both Dr. Frankenstein and Dr. Leary were convinced they were creating a New Man.

But when the time came, Liddy had to settle for two dozen sheriff's deputies. On the night of April 16, as Marya Mannes and the other guests chanted in the sacred grove, Liddy and his men were hunkered down in the woods, waiting for everyone to retire. Millbrook's fluctuating population—surveillance indicated an average of thirty to fifty occupants—raised certain legal difficulties. In order to make the charges stick (drug possession, crossing state lines for immoral purposes, etc.) it was necessary to treat the mansion like a hotel and surprise the guests in their rooms. Liddy intended to perform a classic "no knock" entry, which meant that after the lights went out they would kick in the front door.

But the lights didn't go out. After the sacred grove, Leary led his charges inside for a preview of his latest multimedia show. Given the mindset of the sheriff's department, the projector's blue flickering light meant only one thing: pornographic movies. And there was considerable competition as to who would sneak forward and reconnoiter.

The lucky fellow was back in a few minutes, snorting in disgust.

"It ain't no dirty movie. You'll never guess what them hippies are watching. A waterfall."

"A what?"

"A waterfall for crissake! It's just a movie of a goddamn waterfall. It goes on and on and nothing ever happens but the water. I kept watching, you know? I figured there'd be, you know, broads jumping in and out of the water or something."

When the last of the lights finally went out, Liddy led the troopers up to the door, kicked it open, and went racing up the sweeping staircase. Deputies charge down the halls, to stand guard at every room. Leary appeared in a shirt but no pants. Guests, ignoring the orders to remain inside, tumbled into the halls. Marya Mannes pulled out her notebook and began writing down everything that was happening. Someone else grabbed a guitar and improvised a folksong:

Oh they're busting Doctor Leary
Cause the evening, it was dreary

And the fuzz had nothing better else to do.
We got the sheriffs out the ass
Cause they're looking for our grass.
And they hope to find a ton of acid too!

Before he was hauled off in handcuffs, Leary had the following exchange with Liddy.

"This raid," he said, "is the product of ignorance and fear."

"This raid," Liddy replied, "is the product of a search warrant issued by the state of New York."

"The time will come," Leary said, "when there will be a statue of me erected in Millbrook."

"I'm afraid the closest you'll come is a burning effigy in the village square." Liddy smiled.

21

PSYCHOTIC REACTION

Had you suggested, at the 1962 White House Conference on Narcotics, that in just four short years America would resemble what *Time* magazine described as a "psychedelic smorgasbord," you would have been laughed from the podium. Marijuana and heroin were the chief concerns back then; LSD barely rated a footnote. The general consensus was that, "in spite of lurid statements by some popular writers," psychedelics were a fringe phenomenon, limited to "long hair and beatnik cults." That people other than kooks might seriously believe a drug could expand consciousness, or propel one up the evolutionary ladder, had seemed too ludicrous for words.

But no longer. Nineteen sixty-six was the year America awoke to the gravity of the psychedelic movement and reacted with all the cultural power it could muster. Before the year was half over, the governors of California and Nevada were publicly competing for the prestige of being the first to sign anti-LSD legislation, an eagerness that was more than matched by their peers in Washington, where three different Congressional subcommittees convened hearings to study the LSD problem—the Juvenile Delinquency Subcommittee of the Senate Judiciary Committee; the Subcommittee on Intergovernmental Relations of the House Government Operations Committee; and the Subcommittee on Executive Reorganization of the Senate Subcommittee on Government Operations. This last had originally been scheduled to hear testimony on the problems of the handicapped, but at Robert Kennedy's urging the subject was switched to LSD.

By July open-ended research would be a thing of the past, as the FDA and the NIMH sharply curtailed existing projects; by August the first agents of the newly formed Bureau of Drug Abuse Control

(BDAC) would be rooting out underground sources of supply; by October possession of LSD would be illegal in every state of the Union.

Although the backlash against LSD had been gathering strength since the early Sixties, it wasn't until 1965 that concrete evidence of its danger appeared. That was when William Frosch, a psychiatrist working at New York's Bellevue Psychiatric Hospital, began noticing an increase in LSD-related admissions. From a handful a year the figures jumped to two or three a month, then to five or six. Most were young men—median age twenty-two—and all were middle class, which was a significant departure from the usual narcotic patient. Several were the children of physicians; one was a judge's son. Besides being well educated and well-to-do, they shared two other variables: all had taken LSD in the hope that it would improve personal insight, and all had a history of previous psychiatric disorder.

What the critics of Leary's enthusiasm had feared was coming to pass: unstable personalities, exposed to LSD in uncontrolled settings, were disintegrating.

Between March and December 1965, Frosch treated sixty-five patients whose etiology fell into three broad categories. By far the largest group were those admitted in an anxious or panicked state, what the Pranksters would have called "freaked." These were given thorazine and released after a few hours. They were lucky: approximately a third of Frosch's patients were admitted in a fully psychotic state, for which there was nothing to do but hope that eventually one or another of the treatments would work. Without question these were the most serious of Frosch's patients, but the gravity of their condition was matched by the scientific curiosity of the final category, which contained people who had taken LSD, often with no complications, except that months later, while sitting in a restaurant or strolling down the street, the drug state had suddenly reasserted itself. This reoccurrence became known as a flashback, and while its existence and implication was hotly debated—some researchers never encountered a flashback; others saw them all the time; still others dismissed them as no big deal: moments of depersonalization and hallucination happened frequently to people who had never touched an illicit drug—it quickly became a journalistic staple.

For six years the media had blown hot and cold on the subject of psychedelics, but in early 1966, as Frosch's data began to be replicated in other cities, particularly those with student populations, the breeze turned decidedly chill. *Time* magazine in March 1966 announced that America was in the midst of an LSD epidemic:

The disease is striking in beachside beatnik pads and in the dormitories of expensive prep schools; it has grown into an alarming problem at UCLA and on the UC campus at Berkeley. And everywhere the diagnosis is the same: psychotic illness resulting from the unauthorized, nonmedical use of the drug LSD-25.

According to *Time,* LSD psychotics were literally flocking to the nearest emergency rooms.

Time was exaggerating, of course. No hard data existed as to how many people were suffering from LSD-related problems. Within the research community the most frequently quoted figure was 2 percent—2 percent of those who took LSD in unsupervised settings were experiencing the sort of complications that Frosch was seeing at Bellevue. And of that 2 percent, about a third were becoming psychotic. That meant that for every thousand people who took LSD, seven would suffer a breakdown. That was seven too many, but it was hardly epidemic material. Which was perhaps why the qualifying figures had a way of disappearing, until instead of a third of 2 percent it became a third of 100 percent.

When William Frosch presented his Bellevue data before one of the three Senate subcommittees who had convened hearings on the "LSD problem," he was careful to stress that his findings were limited to the 2 percent of the psychedelic community who had problems with the drug. That's what went into the Congressional maw. What came out was the perception that

> One of the most common recurrent reactions to LSD use is a psychotic breakdown of an extended but unknown duration. What this means, of course, is that many LSD abusers become insane in a few short hours under the influence of the drug.

Even Frosch's statement that it tended to be those with a history of psychiatric disorder who experienced complications underwent a subtle transformation, until it was thought that what he had really said was that anyone who took the drug was "already psychologically deranged, or can be, or at least the predominance that are using it in that way."

But if the LSD psychotic was of questionable statistical reality, in an aesthetic sense it seized the public imagination and didn't let go for the rest of the decade. Scarcely a week went by that this curious creature wasn't in the news columns, either raping or murdering or committing suicide in stories that were usually anonymous, uncheckable, and bizarre. It is difficult to pinpoint the precise moment when the LSD psychotic first entered the public consciousness, but a good starting point would be April 1966, when the FDA invited reporters in to examine its LSD dossier. Among the stories contained therein was the one about the psychiatrist, a three-time user of LSD, whose breakdown had distinct megalomaniacal shadings; for a month he hatched grandiose scheme after grandiose scheme, the most grandiose being his plan to invade Sandoz and capture the world supply of LSD. Subsequent retellings of this story improved upon it until a few actually had him breaking into the lab. Another file told of a fifteen-year-old girl who became involved with a college professor who hosted weekend LSD orgies. The girl came home acting a bit strange after attending one of these parties and was promptly hospitalized by her family. She escaped, however, and tried to stab her mother.

Following the FDA's lead, police departments around the country opened their own files to reporters eager to get a local angle on a breaking national story. The result was an almost geometric intensification of LSD's negative image. "Cases of attempted rape, assault, murder, suicide and self-mutilation," began one Los Angeles police-file story, before going on to tell about the seventeen-year-old who had attempted to tear out his eyeballs and the twenty-year-old who, postingestion, cruised the suburbs looking for a girl to rape. Spotting a fifteen-year-old outlined against the windowshade of her living room, he tore off his clothes and stumbled inside, only to be thwarted by the girl's quick-witted younger brother, who telephoned the police. Then there was the heavy user who, believing LSD had transmuted him into an orange, refused all human contact for fear of being turned into orange juice.

Given the cavalier way the press treated research statistics, it is prudent to ask how credible most of these stories were. Aside from their uniform tone of vague anonymity, certain discrepancies exist that support a moderate amount of skepticism. It is interesting to contrast, for example, the Congressional testimony of Commander Alfred Tremblay, head of the LAPD Narcotic Division, with newspaper stories published within a few weeks of his appearance suggesting that his files were full of LSD-inspired rape, murder, and mutilation. As a committed opponent of drugs and drug-users, one would have expected Tremblay to choose his most heinous cases to present to Congress. But there was little of that in Tremblay's testimony, which verged on the weird rather than the horrible, offering anecdotes like the time the LAPD found two guys sitting on a suburban lawn eating the grass and nibbling on tree bark. Or the time they received a complaint that a young man was standing beside the Coast Highway making obscene gestures at the traffic. When the police arrived, the guy dashed into the ocean, fell to his knees and began to pray, all the while yelling "I love you! I love you!" Then there was the time someone reported screams in a downtown apartment building and the police found a boy and girl having sex in the hall and shouting "GOD" and "LIFE" at the top of their lungs.

In fact the only example of violence that Tremblay had to offer occurred the day before he flew east to testify, and involved a naked man who rampaged through a local housing development, smashing windows with a two-by-four.

Again, reading the Los Angeles newspapers, one would have thought that scarcely a day passed that LSD didn't contribute to some calamity, usually involving teenagers. Yet police files show that in the first four months of 1966, out of 543 juveniles arrested for narcotics, only four involved LSD.

So where did all the horror stories come from? Part of the problem may have been the media's ignorance of psychosis. No matter how often researchers like Sidney Cohen stressed that rage was a rare occurrence—unless it was self-rage, leading to suicide—rage was the emotion the journalistic community most often associated with LSD; kids eating grass and bark just didn't fit the stereotype of the crazed psychotic.

But there was another possibility besides ignorance, one that had to do partly with journalistic style and partly with the way the dominant powers of a culture influence the value system of that culture. Addressing the problem of truth versus fancy during one of the Congressional hearings, Senator Abraham Ribicoff remarked that, "Only when you sensationalize a subject matter do you get a reform. Without sensationalizing it, you don't. That is one of the great problems. You scientists may know something, a senator may know something, but only when the press and television come in and give it a real play because it hits home as something that affects all the country, do you get action."

Halting the spread of LSD had become part of the national agenda; thus it was necessary for the press to sensationalize the subject. And the press was an old hand at sensationalizing dangerous drugs. The prevailing style was the one perfected by Harry Ainslinger back in the Thirties, during his "reefer madness" campaigns against marijuana. Ainslinger had maintained a voluminous file of anonymous marijuana horror stories, which he periodically fed to a credulous press. One began:

> The sprawled body of a young girl lay crushed on the sidewalk the other day after a plunge from a fifth story of a Chicago apartment house. Everyone called it suicide, but actually it was murder. The killer was a narcotic known to America as marijuana.

Or another:

> It was an unprovoked crime some years ago which brought the first realization that the age-old drug had gained a foothold in America. An entire family was murdered by a youthful addict in Florida

... the boy said he had been in the habit of smoking something which youthful friends called "muggles," a childish name for marijuana.

It was a curious thing, but if you changed a few nouns in any of the antimarijuana stories of the Thirties, you ended up with a reasonable facsimile of the standard "LSD madness" story as it began appearing in the spring of 1966.

Not that there weren't legitimate examples of LSD-inspired violence. The most famous, occurring in late April, involved a New Yorker named Stephen Kessler who stabbed his mother-in-law dozens of times with a kitchen knife. When the police came to arrest him, Kessler reportedly said, "Man, I've been flying for three days on LSD. Did I kill my wife? Did I rape anybody? What have I done?"

A Harvard graduate (class of '57) and a medical school dropout, Stephen Kessler had a history of psychiatric problems; a few weeks before the murder he had checked himself into Bellevue for treatment, and while he was there his wife had moved back with her parents in Brooklyn. Apparently it was this separation, exacerbated by the LSD, that precipitated the murder. Although the press characterized the Kessler case as an "LSD KILLING," most of the experts were less assured. Two things bothered them. One was the infrequency of rage as an LSD reaction; *Time* quoted Sidney Cohen to the effect that suicide was much more likely than murder. But more troublesome was Kessler's claim that he had been "flying" for three days and could remember nothing of what had happened. Unless one kept taking LSD, constantly upping the dosage to offset body tolerance, the effects wore off after twelve hours. And the whole uniqueness of the experience was the fact that one remained relatively clearheaded throughout; it was not an alcoholic fog or stupor. So the Kessler case was a toss-up. In terms of his psychiatric profile, Stephen Kessler was a perfect candidate for a psychotic episode had he taken LSD. But given his educational background, he was also astute enough to realize that LSD, in the spring of 1966, was the perfect alibi for what might have been nothing more than a common act of rage and revenge.

To be fair, after the years of positive sensationalizing that Leary had indulged in, a certain amount of negative sensationalizing was inevitable. Confronted with a pro-LSD password like "instant nirvana," the opponents countered with "chemical Russian roulette." Expanded consciousness? Distorted consciousness! Or, as James Goddard, the new commissioner of the FDA put it, "pure bunk."

Goddard, because of his position within the health bureaucracy, was the point man in the campaign against LSD. In April he sent more than two thousand letters to college administrators warning that

> Both students and members of the faculty are being secretly approached to engage in hallucinogenic "experiences." There is direct evidence of widespread availability of a number of drugs which have profound effects on the mental processes. I wish to alert all educational administrators to the gravity of the situation and to enlist their assistance in combating an insidious and dangerous activity.

He was a fixture at the Congressional hearings, appearing in all three venues. Asked to judge the magnitude of America's LSD problem, he estimated a user population of around 3.6 million, a figure far in excess of Leary's personal guess of one hundred thousand. Goddard arrived at this number using a curious differential: for every reported incident of illegal drug use, the FDA assumed that ten thousand went unreported. And LSD had come to the Agency's attention 360 times.

Who were these 3.6 million? Not the evolutionary vanguard of Leary's rhetoric, but "middle-aged underachievers, stale artists, and postteenagers." "They are life's losers," said Sidney Cohen. "Dissatisfied, restless people, afflicted with problems they can't handle. A lot of them wallow in self-pity and denigrate those who have made it in the 'square' world." Maladjusted failures. Nonconformists. At one point during his Congressional testimony, Captain Tremblay of the LAPD pulled out a photograph taken at one of Kesey's Acid Tests and passed it to the congressmen, saying, "I'm sure you'll agree that this young lad is certainly a nonconformist. He is presently under the influence of LSD when this photograph, this colored photograph was taken. He has painted his face and his jacket, the nonconformist signs on the back of his jacket together with his face would certainly indicate the young lad was a nonconformist with our society as we know it today."

In the end it wasn't the horror stories or the juggled figures on psychotic breakdowns that worried the congressmen. That, as Senator Ribicoff understood, was just the necessary PR froth: good for headlines, but largely beside the point. The real reason LSD needed to be eliminated wasn't because it was making a tiny percentage of its users crazy, but because of what it was doing to the vast majority. Contrary to what Captain Tremblay believed, LSD wasn't attracting nonconformists so much as it was creating them.

Back in 1963 Grinker had warned that LSD was "subtly creating a psychopathology"; by 1966 the contours of that pathology were clearly visible:

Those who use (LSD) frequently or chronically almost inevitably withdraw from society and enter into a solipsistic, negativistic existence, in which LSD is not merely an experience in the totality of living, but becomes synonymous with life itself. These individuals, colorfully described by their confreres as acidheads, engage perpetually in drug-induced orgies of introspection and are no longer constructive active members of society . . . they withdraw not only from society but also from meaningful family ties. Were the numbers of such individuals to increase markedly, such a group could constitute a real threat to the functioning of our society.

This was the real message the opponents of the psychedelic movement brought to the Congressional hearings. LSD was eroding the work ethic, it was seducing the young into religious fantasies, it was destroying their values. "We have seen something which in a way is most alarming, more alarming than death in a way," testified Sidney Cohen. "And that is the loss of all cultural values, the loss of feeling of right and wrong, of good and bad. These people lead a valueless life, without motivation, without any ambition . . . they are deculturated, lost to society, lost to themselves."

If psychedelics continued to spread, then America ran the risk of becoming a society of spaced-out mystics; a communist society no doubt, since the drugs would have sapped the will to confront Soviet aggression.

It was an odd debate, with the opponents arguing that LSD had the potential to destroy America, while the proponents claimed the exact opposite. For them, LSD was therapeutic; it corrected the neurotic excesses brought on by a consumer culture; it jarred one free of mental ruts, allowing old problems to be seen from new angles; it accessed higher levels of information, some of which were spiritual in nature. If America was to remain a world power, it could not afford to turn its back on such a useful tool.

Curiously, the one thing both sides agreed on was that LSD was capable of altering personality in a fundamental way. But was this really true? Bill McGlothlin, a psychologist who had participated in several of Oscar Janiger's early studies, published a study in the summer of 1966 that offered some interesting answers to this question. To study the problem, McGlothlin recruited seventy-two graduate students through a blind newspaper ad. After screening out those with doubtful profiles, he divided the group into thirds and gave them a complete battery of personality tests, measuring things like creativity, anxiety, personal values, etc. The first group then received a full dose of LSD, the second a tiny one, while the third received amphetamine. Then the personality tests were repeated, once immediately after the drug trip, and again at an interval of six months. McGlothlin found that statistically the changes in personality were minimal, despite the subjective impression that enormous changes had taken place. Only in one area did significant change occur, the Ways-to-Live scale. After three doses of LSD, McGlothlin's subjects were suddenly having second thoughts about settling into a nice corporate job, they were now leaning toward something a bit more contemplative.

But even this change wasn't permanent; it faded with time and the absence of LSD. After six months the changes in the Ways-to-Live scale had diminished, only to be replaced by significant changes in the "Self-Perception" and "Self-Approval" categories.

McGlothlin's paper was part of a healthy crop of LSD-related research that found its way into the technical journals in 1966; a varied and frequently confusing bounty that may explain why the popular press generally avoided the scientific aspect of the LSD story. It was too complex, too partial in the way that most basic science is.

A researcher at UCLA's Neuropsychiatric Institute, for instance, announced that LSD seemed to help severely autistic children, but was counterproductive in those with milder autism. An NIMH study of forty-three alcoholics undergoing LSD therapy reported that twenty-three had not resumed drinking, seven were drinking occasionally but were able to hold jobs, and two had fallen back off the wagon. Another researcher, studying the good trip/bad trip problem, suggested that extroverts were constitutionally equipped to enjoy the Other World, whereas introverts often had hellish experiences. Intriguing stuff, all in all, but hardly in the same league as an LSD murderer or a mad scientist scheming to seize control of a powerful multinational drug company.

Even within the therapeutic community itself, which had enthusiastically embraced other classes of mind drugs, the tranquilizers, the antipsychotics, LSD research was given short shrift. The old problem of replication remained, and with it the charge (never proven) that much of the research was counterfeit. The alcohol studies drew the most heat in this regard. Some, like the one mentioned above, achieved marvelous results; others were unable to cure even a single alcoholic. The former tended to attribute their success to the sensitive way in which they wielded this powerful new tool, while the latter muttered about bad science and charlatans. But even among those researchers who were pro-LSD there were deep divisions as to the worth, and the ethics, of certain kinds of work, particularly the personality-change therapy that was going on at places like Myron Stolaroff's Foundation. "How should one evaluate the outcome if an individual were, for example, to divorce his wife and take a job which paid him less but which he stated he enjoyed more than the one which he had previously held?" asked one critic. "If a person were to become more relaxed and happy-go-lucky, more sensitive to poetry or music, but less concerned with success or competition, is this good?" Change and be happy was a direct challenge to the adjust-or-else ethic that had reigned supreme during the Fifties, and in this sense the in-house skirmish over the direction LSD therapy was taking reflected a much larger battle that was being waged over therapy's appropriate social role.

But most members of the therapeutic community had little time or patience for the nuances of the LSD argument. *Unpredictable* was probably the word most of them associated with LSD—an unpredictability that manifested itself in the personages of Tim Leary and Dick Alpert, who were seen as cautionary tales on how not to conduct promising careers. But the fact was that there were casualties wherever LSD therapy had gained a foothold, either therapists who had gone crazy or developed cult followings or ones who, post-LSD, had abandoned the traditional methods as too conservative and had begun exploring the kind of esoterica practiced at places like Esalen, the spa turned New Age academy midway up the California coast at Big Sur. Group therapy. Nude therapy. Water therapy. It was no accident that the group leaders at Esalen's first public seminar were all veterans of the psychedelic movement.

This then, in broad outline, was the mindset of the therapeutic community on the eve of *Time*'s announcement that LSD psychotics were flocking to the local emergency room. The result, not surprisingly, was panic. The *New England Journal of Medicine,* declaring that "There is no published evidence that further experimentation is likely to yield invaluable data," called for an end to all LSD research, which must have come as a surprise to the NIMH, who were funding thirty-eight different LSD projects at a cost of $1.7 million. Apparently the editors of the *NEJM* were convinced they had another thalidomide scandal on their hands, a fear that might also account for Sandoz's decision, in early April 1966, to sever all corporate ties to its problem children, LSD and psilocybin. On April 7, Sandoz telephoned the FDA and announced that they were terminating all research contracts and would be willing to turn over their entire supply of the two drugs to the federal government. LSD had become a public relations disaster: Sandoz received dozens of phone calls from journalists and doctors every time it made the news, each requesting a copy of its LSD bibliography, which was now nearly ten inches thick.

Researchers were ordered to return all supplies of LSD and psilocybin to Sandoz, and then resubmit their research proposals to the NIMH for reapproval. Confusion reigned. *Letters to Science* lamented the "state of hysteria" that had driven Sandoz to the unprecedented move of disowning its own discovery. "For Sandoz to be so timorous suggests the Cowardly Lion of Oz," wrote one scientist. "Who is our Dorothy? The FDA? The NIMH? The National Research Council? Who will assume the responsibility for the necessary investigative work with LSD?"

But the scientific bureaucracies lacked the pluck of Frank Baum's Kansas heroine. Researchers attempting to resuscitate projects halted by Sandoz's decision encountered obfuscation and foot-dragging. A typical experience was that of John Pollard, a researcher at the University of Michigan, who had been in the early stages of an experiment measuring LSD's effect on behavior and performance when the "send-it-all-back-to-Sandoz letter" had arrived in his mailbox. Told he must reclear his research proposal with NIMH, Pollard had immediately set out to do so. Since the NIMH had already given him one grant for LSD research, he anticipated little difficulty. But things had changed. After a "summer of one-way correspondence and long-distance phone calls" he was told that while he had the approval of NIMH he must now secure the FDA's okay. "I had spoken to only four different individuals at NIMH," he wrote to *Science.* "But after speaking to five at the Food and Drug Administration, I despaired and hoped that my correspondence would eventually filter through to the appropriate person. The summer passed, the research assistant worked on his thesis, and I ran up a phone bill."

In this midst of this confusion, in mid-June a conference on LSD opened in San Francisco. Chaired by Frank Barron, it was the last time that all the factions in the psychedelic debate were together under one roof. Within weeks politics and public opinion would render scientific debate on the danger/usefulness of LSD moot. In fact, the opprobrium was already so strong that friends of Barron urged him to dissociate himself from the conference, warning that to go ahead would be professional suicide. And Berkeley, at the very last minute, refused to let the conference take place on its campus, so it was hastily moved to an off-campus building associated with the UC extension service.

Barron opened the proceedings by observing that there was still no scientific proof that LSD expanded consciousness. What was needed, he said, was more research. Not just to answer the basic questions, but also to address the reason why so many of the brightest students were turning to LSD "in the hope that it will tell them something about themselves." Barron was followed at the podium by Sidney Cohen, who warned that "just as hypnosis was lost to use for fifty years—while it was used on the vaudeville stage and in the parlor—the same is going to be true of LSD." "We are losing control," he said, and while he clearly felt that the majority of the blame belonged to irresponsible enthusiasts like Leary and Kesey, Cohen also urged that the medical model be modified to allow certain professionals—he suggested theologians, philosophers, and anthropologists—access to the psychedelic experience.

A bit of excitement occurred when one of those irresponsible enthusiasts, Allen Ginsberg, arrived at the auditorium and was greeted with a standing ovation. This actually was an act of displeasure directed toward Barron's superiors, who had crossed Ginsberg's name off the list of speakers on the pretext that he was not a scientist. But aside from that, the Conference was a model of professional decorum. Abram Hoffer, Humphrey Osmond's former colleague, reported that his cure rate with alcoholics was running close to two-thirds. And Eric Kast, a researcher at the University of Chicago's Medical School, sent along a paper describing LSD's therapeutic potential with the terminally ill. Of eighty patients who had taken the drug with Kast, seventy-two wanted to repeat the experience.

Given the newsworthiness of LSD, one might have expected significant media coverage. But that wasn't the case. The newspapers seemed to be perplexed by the multiplicity of opinions—"everything you hear about LSD is nonsense, including what I'm telling you," quipped one pharmacologist at the beginning of his talk—and what little coverage there was tended to focus on the eminently quotable duo of Dick Alpert and Tim Leary, both of whom addressed the conference. Alpert, whom *Newsweek* dubbed an LSD "High Priest," in contrast to Leary's "LSD Messiah," suggested that the government solve the problem of illicit use by establishing an Internal Flights Agency, which would license prospective LSD users, and provide them with up-to-date maps of the Other World. Leary, "radiating light in white chinos and tieless white shirt," with a "dazzling blonde traveling companion" on his arm, spent most of his time soliciting funds for his legal appeal. But he also delivered what Myron Stolaroff thought was "the most carefully prepared address I have ever seen him give."

Unfortunately, wrote Stolaroff to Humphrey Osmond, Tim quickly reverted to "his usual inconsistent, confusing self. After having recently appeared on TV requesting a one-year moratorium on all psychedelics, he ended this address by exhorting the audience to do their own private research and not let anyone stop them."

It had been a difficult few months for Leary, what with the Liddy raid following so closely on the heels of the Texas marijuana conviction. Although he had often joked about the usual fate of prophets, the reality left him subdued and dejected; his number-one priority changed from raising consciousness to raising money, as his lawyers scrambled to keep him out of jail.

It was at this low ebb that Leary agreed to testify before one of the Congressional subcommittees, joining Allen Ginsberg and Art Kleps, among others, on the advocate side of the aisle. Kleps, you will recall, was one of the Millbrook-trained guides. Since then he had gone on to form an LSD-based religion called the Neo-American Church, of which he was Chief Boo Hoo. ("Are you really called a boo hoo?" one of the senators asked him. "I'm afraid so," said Kleps.) Although Leary was not active in the Church, he was, Kleps informed the senators, a holy figure, the equivalent of Jesus Christ or Mohammed. "On the day the prison doors close behind Tim Leary," warned the bearded Chief Boo Hoo, "this country will face religious civil war. Any restraint we have shown heretofore in the dissemination of psychedelics will be ended."

After such a dramatic build-up, the senators must have been a bit nonplussed when Leary sat down before them in his old professorial tweeds. He began by stating his *bona fides:* 311 personal LSD trips; three thousand guided trips. LSD was a form of energy, he said, consequently some sort of control was necessary: "I believe that the criteria for marijuana, which is about the mildest of the psychedelic drugs, should be about those which we now use to license people to drive automobiles, whereas the criteria for the licensing of LSD, a much more powerful act, should be much more strict, perhaps the criteria now used for airplane pilots would be appropriate."

Training centers, modeled after Castalia, should be established around the country, with LSD lab courses a part of every college curriculum. This was too much for Senator Ted Kennedy. "And what is going to happen to the boy who doesn't get to college?" he asked sarcastically.

"There would be special training institutes for him," replied Leary, refusing to be drawn.

"Are we going to have high school courses as well?"

"I would let research, scientific research answer the question as to at what age the nervous system is ready to use these new instruments."

All in all, it was a temperate performance—too temperate for zealots like Art Kleps, who concluded that Tim's legal problems had destroyed his nerve. An assessment that received further confirmation a few days later when Leary publicly proposed a year-long moratorium on LSD use. "I do not say we should stop studying consciousness expansion," he told a crowd of eight hundred gathered at New York's Town Hall. "But we must learn to have psychedelic experiences without the use of drugs."

But by June he had regained some of his old flair. After delivering his paper at Barron's conference, Leary called a press conference and announced that 2 million doses of bootleg LSD were about to descend upon California. Not surprisingly, all thoughts of alcohol cure rates vanished from every reporter's thoughts, as they raced to take down what Tim was saying, which was: "Our social duty now is to publish manuals, give training sessions, and prepare the young to use this powerful, consciousness-expanding drug."

Whether he realized it or not, by calling that press conference he had managed to sabotage the whole point of the Conference.

Myron Stolaroff had driven up to San Francisco principally to hear Abram Hoffer's paper. In truth, he was no longer part of the LSD research scene, his Foundation having lost its license to investigate new drugs—a forfeiture for which it was difficult not to blame Mr. Leary. Eighteen months earlier, while Tim was in India immersing himself in the ancient wisdom, Stolaroff had been on the verge of a major coup. During a trip to Washington, Bill Harman, the Foundation's associate director, had completed the groundwork for a project that would bring selected federal officials to Palo Alto for a thorough initiation into the potentials of psychedelic drugs. "I don't know what more we could want," Stolaroff wrote to Osmond:

> I can't think of anything that would help the overall cause more at this time than to have selected persons well placed in the government receive first hand exposure to our work. Al [Hubbard] has assured us that he will be on hand to insure that their exposure is complete, and that they will not get away without having had a profound look at the situation.

But then, while the project was still in the planning stage, the political climate surrounding psychedelics had changed. Black market LSD, once a trickle, had become a sizable flow; and the impressionable young, stimulated by the claims of Kesey and Leary, had begun taking it wherever and whenever they could, with the upshot being the kind of fallout Frosch was seeing at Bellevue. Instead of being invited to give LSD to selected members of the government, Stolaroff now found himself pressed for funds, as grants that he had counted on were suddenly withdrawn.

When it became apparent in early 1965 that psychedelic therapy was no longer economically feasible, Stolaroff and Harman redirected the Foundation's energies toward the private sector: if the government no longer wanted to fund individual therapy, perhaps industry could be persuaded of LSD's problem-solving potential. In one sense this was a return to Stolaroff's first impulse, when he and Hubbard had dreamed of using LSD to transform Ampex into an enlightened supercorporation. But with a difference. In the interim Stolaroff had become a bit more sophisticated where presentation was concerned: you didn't just waltz into the president's office and invite him to sample a strange drug. You needed documentation, graphs, hard data. You needed a pilot study, which is what the Foundation set about doing, rounding up thirty different professionals—physicists, furniture designers, architects, mathematicians, engineers—who were alike insofar as each had a problem that was eluding solution.

The architect, for example, was wrestling with the design of an arts and crafts shopping center. He came into Stolaroff's office, took the LSD, and later wrote this account of what happened:

> I looked at the paper I was to draw on. I was completely blank. I knew that I would work with a property 300′ square. I drew the property lines and I looked at the outline. I was blank.
>
> Suddenly I saw the finished project. I did some quick calculations . . . it would fit on the property and not only that . . . it would meet the cost and income requirements.
>
> I began to draw . . . my senses could not keep up with my images . . . my hand was not fast enough . . . I was impatient to record the picture (it has not faded one particle). I worked at a pace I would not have thought I was capable of.
>
> I completed four sheets of fairly comprehensive sketches. I was not tired but I was satisfied that I had caught the essence of the image. I stopped working. I ate fruit . . . I drank coffee . . . I smoked . . . I sipped wine . . . I enjoyed.
>
> It was a magnificent day.

But all this work came to nought when Sandoz decided to withdraw its patronage, leaving the FDA and the NIMH as principal arbiters of what constituted proper research. As far as the health bureaucracies were concerned, lack of creativity was not a disease. Consequently to use LSD in that manner verged on abuse. Al Hubbard flew to Washington to argue the point—he carried with him a letter pointing out that numerous industries, as well as NASA, had used psychedelics to solve specific problems—but he got nowhere.

The simple fact was that priorities had changed; the political breezes were blowing cold; research congruent with that view was funded, while the rest was left to die a benign bureaucratic death; when the IND's (official government permission to experiment with an Investigational New Drug) of this latter group came up for renewal, they were rejected. This was what happened to Hubbard and Stolaroff and dozens of others. Even Jean Houston and Robert Masters, who were about to publish *The Varieties of Psychedelic Experience*, which was unquestionably the best scientific account of what happened beyond the Door, even they lost the right to do LSD research.

But if anyone exemplified the dilemma of the LSD research community, it was Sidney Cohen. Since the publication of *The Beyond Within* in 1964, Cohen had been the most visible champion of sensible research—a clear-eyed "LSD expert" who was capable of articulately demolishing the propaganda of Leary while refraining from the sort of offbeat speculations that had apparently disqualified Humphrey Osmond from being invited to the Congressional hearings. The man who had coined the word *psychedelic,* who had given Aldous Huxley mescaline, was perhaps too eccentric to qualify as an expert; Cohen, who preferred the term *unsanity* when talking about the psychedelic state, was far more acceptable.

Cohen was popular on the lecture circuit, appearing often with Richard Alpert, who played the psychedelic radical (328 personal LSD experiences) to Cohen's scientific moderate (seven carefully controlled ingestions). By appearing on the same stage with Alpert, Cohen risked the ire of his colleagues, who accused him of adding to Alpert's—and by extension Leary's—legitimacy. "True he broadcasts a point of view with which you and I disagree," Cohen replied. "What should we do about this? Should he be ignored, insulted or ostracized? None of these will be effective; in fact they would help him. He must be engaged, and his views effectively answered."

Alpert, on the other hand, tended to see Cohen as a hypocrite. It was okay for him to turn on Henry and Clare Booth Luce, but let anyone else try that and Cohen would start lecturing about strict medical use. But Alpert liked Cohen nevertheless; he was a nice guy "who is using the cards he's got in his hands to play what he can. Playing in the middle, all the way through."

What Alpert didn't appreciate, though, was just how difficult a balancing act staying in the middle had become. To refute the public statements of enthusiasts like Leary, moderates like Cohen were forced to paint increasingly bleak pictures of what would happen should the spread of psychedelics continue unchecked. Unfortunately, the very negativity of their rhetoric was creating a climate in which it was difficult to justify even basic research: if LSD was that volatile, how could anyone be safe . . . !

A variation of Gresham's law occurred, as sensationalized rhetoric replaced rational debate. By the autumn of 1966, opponents were hinting that LSD probably caused long-term brain damage. Their evidence? The fact that so many kids, post-LSD, showed little desire to adjust to the corporate-suburban lifestyle embraced by their parents. Without a blink, the ethic of adjustment had been elevated to an organic process of the brain.

Leary, not to be outclassed, countered with an equally outrageous gambit. Interviewed by *Playboy*, he announced that LSD was the most powerful aphrodisiac ever discovered. "Let me put it this way," he said, "compared with sex under LSD, the way you've been making love—no matter how ecstatic the pleasure you think you get from it—is like making love to a department-store-window dummy." And as a coup de grâce, he added: "The three inevitable goals of the LSD session are to discover and make love with God, to discover and make love with yourself, and to discover and make love with a woman."

Was it any wonder that moderates like Sidney Cohen concluded things were out of control?

Pondering LSD's strange career, Cohen thought he could detect three distinct phases. The first phase was a scientific one. In LSD researchers had chanced upon a tool capable of unlocking the Dark Room of the Unconscious. But just as they were digesting and arguing over the rather astonishing things they had found in there, a parallel plot had appeared: the science story had turned into a religion story. Shepherded by Aldous Huxley and Gerald Heard, LSD had become a way to accelerate evolution, creating the possibility that for the first time Man would truly merit the title *Homo sapiens.* But then the religion story had become a cultural revolt of the lowest possible character—"a mindless sensory whingding" was Cohen's description.

Instead of *Homo sapiens,* LSD had created *Homo hippie!*

BOOK THREE

THE PURE VOID

"These powders and pills threaten our nation's health, vitality and self-respect."

—President Lyndon Johnson—State of the Union address, January 1968.

22

THE COUNTERCULTURE

On October 7, 1966, the day after the California bill criminalizing LSD took effect, a delegation of hippies arrived at San Francisco's City Hall. They carried an offering of morning glory seeds and store-bought mushrooms, which they hoped to use, they told a bemused press corp, to expand the consciousness of Mayor Shelly. They were in the midst of this presentation, which was half loony theatre, half polemic, when a group of antiwar activists, led by Jerry Rubin, arrived to hold their own press conference.

It was a Sixties Rohrschach: on one side of the Hall stood the activists, in work boots and jeans, while across from them were these golden-robed hippies. And in between . . . in between the antagonism was palpable.

There is no simple way to explain what went on in the Sixties, no easily identifiable event, like the assassination at Sarajevo, which one can point to and say, "there, tensions might have been growing for decades, but that's the spark that touched off the explosion." Indeed, the more thoroughly you study the Sixties, the more comforting becomes a concept like the *zeitgeist*. Strip away the decade's thick impasto of sex, drugs, rebellion, politics, music, and art, and what you find is a restless imperative to change, a "will to change," if you will, and one that could be as explanatory for the latter half of this century as Nietzsche's "will to power" was for the first.

Change jobs, spouses, hairstyles, clothes; change religion, politics, values, even the personality; try everything, experiment constantly, accept nothing as given. It was as though the country as a whole was undergoing a late adolescence, and not just the 20 million Baby Boomers whose leading edge began turning eighteen in 1964. Either that or the Boomers, the largest generation ever, possessed enough mass of their own to alter the normal spin of things.

But alter it in what direction? Somehow the satire of *Mad* magazine and the kinetic electricity of Elvis, the surreal dailyness of Beaver Cleaver and the fear of the Bomb; somehow the awful drabness of Dad in his official corporate uniform, the gray flannel suit, and the awful sameness of the suburbs, those theme parks of the good safe life; somehow all these had combined into a combustible outrage. It was an almost obscene irony, but the kids who had enjoyed the richest, most pampered adolescence in the history of the world had now decided that it was all crap. "We've got so many things we could puke," they said. "We live in the most manipulated society ever created by man."

Since infancy (or so it seemed to the Boomers) their minds had been measured, their psyches sculpted, their emotions straitjacketed, and for what? Why, to preserve the good old Corporate American Way of Life!

The corporations, so omnipotent during the Fifties, were vilified as the source of most of what was wrong with America, whether it was the imperialism that had brought on the Vietnam War or the subtler neurosis that caused people to measure their self-worth in terms of the number and quality of the consumer items they were able to surround themselves with. The same throwaway culture that the parents found convenient and liberating was dismissed by the children as ugly, trashy, and stupid when measured against the ecological cost of living in such a manner.

But the kids also realized that the corporations were only the visible tip of the iceberg, that the real menace was less tangible, although by the late Fifties it already had a number of provocative names: *the military-industrial complex, the power elite, the Garrison Society,* and—the ultimate winner in terms of usage—*the Establishment.*

What these terms attempted to describe was a conspiracy of money and power whose tentacles stretched into every nook and cranny of daily life. Corporations were members of the Establishment. But so were labor unions. Politicians were valued players, of course, but so were teachers, reporters and generals. Republicans and Democrats were merely different frequencies in the Establishment spectrum, while liberalism was nothing more than a clever way of allowing the illusion of change while maintaining the perquisites of power. Uniting these disparate elements was an overt commitment to anticommunism and American hegemony abroad, together with a domestic brand of democracy that sounded more like a well-run corporation than the noble experiment of the Founding Fathers. Instead of "the people," Establishmentarians talked about the managed and the managers, a formula that was not too dissimilar to the one followed in the Establishment's archenemy, the USSR.

Reflecting upon this woeful state of affairs, the Baby Boomers decided that not only didn't they want to be managed, but they could do without the occupation of manager as well. Norman Mailer caught their mood exactly when he wrote that "the authority had operated on their brain with commercials, and washed their brain with packaged education, packaged politics. The authority had presented itself as honorable, and it was corrupt, corrupt as payola on television, and scandals concerning the leasing of aviation contracts—the real scandals as everyone was beginning to sense were more intimate and could be found in all the products in all the suburban homes which did not work so well as they should have worked, and broke down too soon for mysterious reasons. The shoddiness was buried deep . . ."

Of course not every Sixties kid accepted this critique. For each one who wanted to seize power, dismantle the Establishment, and redistribute the wealth, there were at least ten others who just wanted to get through school, get laid, get a job, and get out of going to Vietnam; for every kid who grew his hair long, smoked dope, listened to rock music, and proclaimed an urgent longing to make a clean break with American society, there was a corresponding kid who drank beer, worshiped the local football team, and measured his personal worth by the car he drove. The differential between silent majority and noisy minority probably varied little for the kids of the Sixties from that of their parents. But it didn't seem that way, if only because the silent majority is never news. And they are even less so when the *zeitgeist* is changing rapidly.

Compared to the quiescent teens of the Fifties, the Baby Boomers seemed a generation of Jacobins, a rude, unwashed, overeducated mob who, if not precisely endangering the State, certainly threatened one's peace of mind.

One of the difficulties in writing about the Sixties is deciding when the story began. Was it the day President Kennedy was assassinated in Dallas, a day imprinted on every Baby Boomer the way Pearl Harbor was for their parents? Kennedy was the Establishment's best salesman; with programs like the Peace Corp he almost managed to sell liberalism to the Baby Boom. But his death left a vacuum that was soon filled with anger and cynicism.

Or was it during the first freedom marches in Mississippi, when the kids learned just how loath the Establishment was to extend basic rights to the Blacks? Reflecting on what had happened to the consciousness of those kids who went South in the summer of 1964, Michael Novak later wrote: "Enough young people have been beaten, jailed and even killed while trying to bring about simple constitutional rights to American Negroes to have altered the inner life of a generation. The young do not think of law enforcement as the enforcement of justice; they have experienced it as the enforcement of injustice."

Or did it begin in the fall of 1964, when a group of Berkeley students staged a spontaneous sit-in that quickly grew into the Free Speech Movement?

The seeds of the FSM were sown in early September, when Berkeley Chancellor Clark Kerr, perhaps acting upon the liberal assumption that politics in the old sense was dead, banned all politicking outside Berkeley's main gate on Bancroft Way. For years Bancroft Way had been an ideological flea market, with groups of every persuasion soliciting funds and dispersing literature. Although Kerr's decision drew protests from nearly every student group, from the fledgling Students for a Democratic Society to Youth for Goldwater, Kerr refused to relent and in late September suspended eight students for political activities.

Then, on October 1, a young mathematics graduate student named Jack Weinberg was arrested for refusing to abandon the table he was manning for CORE—the Committee on Racial Equality. A campus squad car was dispatched and when it arrived Weinberg went limp, a technique he had acquired the previous summer during the freedom marches in Mississippi. As the security guards dragged him to the car, an outraged crowd began to form, effectively blocking the exit. For the next thirty-two hours, speaker after speaker climbed atop the car's hood, exhorting the students to seize the moment and strike. It was as though somebody had touched a match to a mood that had been building for years, not just a few weeks.

I felt "torn open, everything boiling in me," wrote Michael Rossman in *The Wedding Within the War,* his memoir of the Sixties. A colleague of Weinberg's in the Berkeley mathematics department, and a fellow radical, Rossman described the aftermath of the cop car siege as "the Tearing Loose—the active beginning of the end of my life within the old institutions."

On December 2, 1964, four hundred members of the Free Speech Movement seized Sproul Hall and held it until they were dragged out singing by hundreds of helmeted riot police. Five days later, an audience of eighteen thousand gathered at Berkeley's Greek Theatre to listen as Clark Kerr poured forth his vision of the true academic community as a "knowledge factory" whose purpose lay in creating socially productive individuals. Now this was the wrong tack to take with students who increasingly resented the factory analogy, but the real mistake came after the speech. As the meeting ended, Mario Savio, a young philosophy major who had become one of the leaders of the FSM, stepped to the rostrum. He intended to invite everyone to a mass rally where Kerr's speech could be debated, but before he could open his mouth to speak he was grabbed by two policemen and wrestled to the floor. A wave of anger swept the crowd. As Godfrey Hodgson later wrote, "one minute Clark Kerr, the champion of liberalism, had been talking about the powers of persuasion against the use of force, and the next moment armed agents of the University were choking his opponent, the symbolic representative of free speech."

The next afternoon the faculty voted 824–115 to accede to the FSM's demands. The Baby Boom had received its first taste of political power.

Not surprisingly, the facts attending the birth of the FSM were drowned in an ocean of learned speculation, as journalists and political scientists rushed to explain this momentary aberration. Although few of the commentators could see beyond their own ideological categories—Lewis Fuer, a reputed expert in left-wing political phenomena, dismissed the FSM as "intellectual lumpen-proletariats, lumpen beatniks, and lumpen agitators" who espoused a "melange of narcotics, sexual perversion, collegiate Castroism and campus Maoism"—most divined the central theme of the protest, which was a hearty dislike of the liberal ideal of a rationally managed society. It was a revolt against the depersonalization implied by the factory analogy that Kerr was so fond of, which was why the IBM card, with its ubiquitous warning "do not fold, spindle or mutilate," became the symbol of all they despised. Rossman described the target of the FSM as the Big Daddy Complex, which was his name for the species of liberal paternalism that had banished political diversity not only from Bancroft Way, but from the University curriculum as well. The motto of the Big Daddy Complex, he wrote, was the phrase "for your own good," and its "effect is to inhibit autonomous adulthood."

This last was a crucial point: instead of adopting the definition of psychological maturity that the mental health movement had proposed in the Fifties, with its emphasis on conformity and responsibility to the larger ideals of society, the Baby Boomers were moving in the opposite direction. The ability to let go, to explore the depths of one's own psyche, to conform to individual rather than social imperatives—these were the new benchmarks of psychological maturity.

Another element that the commentators completely ignored was the exhilaration that came from collective action. During the fifteen-hour occupation of Sproul Hall, life had been lived in a wholly new key. It was, to bend Maslow's term, a collective peak experience whose import lay not so much in the demands that had brought them together, as in the fact that they *were* together. The protestors had turned Sproul Hall into a carnival, with Chaplin movies on the walls and folksingers in the stairwells. "We ate terrible baloney sandwiches and then established the first Free University, conducting some dozen classes cross-legged atop the Civil Defense disaster drums stored in the basement," remembered Rossman. "People smoked grass in the corners . . . and at least two women had their first full sexual experiences under blankets on the roof, where walkie-talkies were broadcasting news to the outside."

In the months following the seizure of Sproul Hall, the Free Speech Movement evolved into a whole series of Grand Causes, beginning with the Dirty Speech Movement (free speech obviously meant the right to say fuck you) and ending with the first protests against the Vietnam War. Dozens of earnest young politicos flocked to Berkeley to make common cause with the revolution. Typical of the new arrivals was a moustachioed young Marxist named Jerry Rubin. Although not the first, Rubin was certainly one of the earliest to realize that political organizing—what the establishment always called "outside agita-tion"—could furnish the basis for an interesting and varied career.

Like Kesey, Jerry Rubin was another of those Fifties teens who had wanted more. "Young kids want to be heroes," he once told *New York Times* reporter Anthony Lukas. "They have an incredible energy and they want to live creative, exciting lives. That's what America tells you to do, you know. The history you learn is hero-oriented: Columbus, George Washington, Paul Revere, the pioneers, the cowboys. America's promise has been 'Live a heroic life.' But then, when it comes time to make good on its promise, it can't. It turns around and says, 'Oh, you can get good grades, and then get a degree, then get a job in a corpora-tion, and buy a ranch house and be a good consumer.' But kids aren't satisfied with that. They want to be heroes. And if America denies them an opportunity for heroism, they're going to create their own."

Rubin was twenty-six when the FSM provided him with his first taste of heroic action. Having spent the summer in Cuba, Rubin was primed, when the FSM erupted that fall, to see visions of Fidel in Mario Savio. "Like I'd gone to Cuba," he marveled, "and here it was right here." With his fellow organizers, beginning in the spring of 1965 he worked long and hard at building a classic leftist political movement. And by the fall of 1965 their efforts were beginning to pay off. In October they attracted thousands for a proposed march on the Oakland Army Terminal, where an attempt would be made to prevent shipments of war material bound for Vietnam from leaving the port.

But even as it gathered strength, the political protest movement was beginning to fragment. Signs of this appeared at the rallies, where, instead of picket signs and revolutionary slogans, more and more demonstrators carried flowers and balloons, harmonizing on Beatles songs instead of "We Shall Overcome." There was a growing hedonism that didn't jibe with the militant discipline required by previous political vanguards. As Lewis Fuer had observed, there was altogether too much sexual perversion and too many narcotics. To Rossman, it seemed that the energy unleashed at Berkeley was beginning to turn, not right or left, "but into . . . something else, without a name."

An illustration of the forces that were dividing the Baby Boom came during the big October protest. Before setting out for the Oakland harbor, the crowd had been addressed by a number of prominent speakers, Ken Kesey among others. Kesey apparently had been invited on the assumption that the author of *Cuckoos Nest* had to believe that the Vietnam War was folly. What the organizers of the march hadn't foreseen, however, was that Kesey also thought that marches and speeches about seizing power were equally fallacious.

A few weeks before the march, quite by chance, Kesey had received an insight into the negative side of *Homo gestalt.* It happened during a Beatles concert at San Francisco's Cow Palace. Not only were the Pranksters in attendance, but they were spreading the word that after the concert the Beatles were coming down to La Honda for a "freaking good rout." This wasn't true, of course, but given the Pranksters' record in bending events to their advantage, it wasn't completely untrue either. Who could say whether the psychedelic superheroes could pull the Fab Four into their movie or not; in any case, it was a worthy test of Prankster power.

But then a strange and terrifying thing had occurred. Even before the Beatles appeared on the stage, thousands of teenyboppers had opened their mouths and started to scream, rocking the Cow Palace with a kind of insane animal energy. To Kesey there was nothing mind-expanding about this group mind: in fact the thought that forced its way into his consciousness was cancer! This was *Homo gestalt* about to devour itself. Thoroughly spooked, he had quickly rounded up the Pranksters and had fled back to La Honda.

Standing by the speaker's platform, listening to the yammer of the crowd and the booming oratory of the speakers, Kesey was reminded of his Cow Palace epiphany. When his turn came at the microphone, he bounded onto the stage flanked by a bevy of Day-Glo, guitar-wielding Pranksters. Whipping out a harmonica, he began honking his way through "Home on the Range."

"You're playing their game," he drawled into the microphone. "We've all heard all this and seen all this before, but we keep doing it . . . I went to see the Beatles last month . . . And I heard twenty thousand girls screaming together at the Beatles . . . and I couldn't hear what they were screaming either . . . But you don't have to . . . They're screaming Me! Me! Me! Me! . . . I'm Me! . . . That's the cry of the ego, and that's the cry of this rally! . . . Me! Me! Me! And that's why wars get fought . . . ego . . . because enough people want to scream Pay attention to Me . . . Yep, you're playing their game."

And then he offered the marchers some advice. "There's only one thing to do," he said between draws on the harmonica. "There's only one thing gonna do any good at all, and that's everybody just look at it, look at the war, and turn your backs and say . . . Fuck it!"

Which is exactly what a lot of kids began doing. And in the process, they also began turning their backs on the political agenda of activists like Rubin and the Students for a Democratic Society (SDS), which was emerging as the most astute and rambunctious of the youth political organizations.

There were quite a few names for these new rebels. They themselves preferred *head* or *freak,* words illustrative of their belief that they represented a new evolutionary branch in the *Homo sapiens* line; Leslie Fiedler, the literary critic, lobbied for new mutant. But the label that stuck was hippie.

By the end of 1965, the youth protest movement had two symbolic capitals: one was in the Berkeley coffeehouses that lined Telegraph Avenue; the other was across the Bay, in Haight-Ashbury, the birthplace of the hippies.

The word *hippie,* indeed the whole phenomenon of the Haight-Ashbury, first came to light in September 1965, in the course of a San Francisco *Examiner* article about a coffeehouse called the Blue Unicorn.

The Unicorn, which advertised the cheapest food in the city, was a little hole in the wall on Hayes Street, near Golden Gate Park, in the midst of a twenty-five-block district that derived its name from two intersecting streets—Haight Street, which ran in a flat line toward the Pacific Ocean; and Ashbury, a much shorter thoroughfare which climbed up Mt. Sutro and stopped. Like the Unicorn, the Haight-Ashbury was something of a hole-in-the-wall district, full of ornate but shabby Victorian houses dating back to the Teens, when so many politicians had built themselves mansions above Haight Street that the area had been nicknamed "politicians' row."

But in the intervening years the Haight-Ashbury had tumbled so far down the socioeconomic ladder that during World War II it had been considered an appropriate spot for worker housing. After the war refugees from Eastern Europe and a small population of Orientals had tried to resuscitate its former splendor, but when Blacks began moving into the district—encouraged by urban renewal, which was razing their traditional ghetto to the west—these homesteaders had packed up, leaving the Haight in the curious position of offering lavish living for dirt cheap prices. For a few hundred dollars it was possible to rent a whole house, complete with leaded windows and ballroom.

Now it happened that this abandonment coincided with the disintegration of the North Beach Beat scene, due to a combination of rising rents, police harassment, and obnoxious tourists who flocked to see the beatnik in his native habitat. The Haight was an obvious solution, and by the time the *Examiner* tumbled to what was happening, it supported a thriving bohemian community, of which the Unicorn was the heart and soul.

This, then, was the gist of what journalist Michael Fallon had to report to his readers: the Beat movement, far from being dead, was alive and flourishing in what had once been one of San Francisco's tonier neighborhoods. But if the Haight was where the Beat movement had fled to, then something had happened in the passage. Compared to the moody, nihilistic beatniks of old, those clichéd cave creatures in their black turtlenecks, the patrons of the Unicorn were like vivid butterflies in their pink striped pants and Edwardian greatcoats. They were sunny and cheery, and the word *love* punctuated their conversation with alarming frequency: all kinds of love, elevated ethereal love and plain old physical love. And on nights when LEMAR—the acronym for the legalize marijuana movement—wasn't meeting at the Unicorn, the Sexual Freedom League was.

Like any scientist fortunate enough to discover a new class of fauna, Fallon's first instinct was to give it a name, which he did by borrowing Norman Mailer's hipster and contracting it into hippie, a word that caught some of the Unicorn's buoyancy, but one the hippies themselves were never fond of. From their perspective, hippie was just another example of the subtle derogation practiced by the mainstream media whenever it was confronted by something outside its usual ken. Hadn't Fallon's fellow journalist, Herb Caen, done something similar when he tagged Ginsberg & Co. with the diminutive beatnik?

But whether they liked it or not, hippie it was and would be.

Oddly, Fallon's inventiveness later served to obscure the fact that in many respects the hippies were second-generation Beats. This was clearer in the early days, when it was still easy to trace the connection between the old Beat fantasy of creating an alternative culture— the word "counterculture" was still years off—and what was aborning in the Haight. "We have a private revolution going on," wrote Bob Stubbs, the owner of the Unicorn, in one of the policy statements he used to distribute to his customers. "A revolution of individuality and diversity that can only be private. Upon becoming a group movement, such a revolution ends up with imitators rather than participants."

A very private revolution: at the time of Fallon's article, there were probably only a dozen houses scattered throughout the Haight that could have been characterized as hippie. And yet the district pulsed with energy. "Even if you lived elsewhere, your forays to the neighborhood were always important," wrote one frequent visitor. "The Haight-Ashbury had four or five grapevines cooking at all times . . . and the two words that went down the wire most often in those days were *dope* and *revolution.* Our secret formula was grass, LSD, meditation, hot music, consolidation, and a joyous sexuality."

Had you lived in any of those houses in the autumn of 1965, it would have been immediately clear that the key ingredient in that formula, the reason why the Haight was not the North Beach six years later, was LSD. LSD was the Haight's secret weapon, with emphasis on secret. "Taking it was like being in a secret society," remembers one pioneer. "Hardly anything was being said about it publicly . . . [although] not an illegal drug, people acted as if it were; it seemed illegal."

It also seemed intensely serious. In the compelling phrase of one hippie, LSD was hard kicks: "hard kicks is a way of looking at your existence, not like mistreating your body or throwing your mind to the crows. It's a way of extending yourself [so that] something spectacular and beautiful can be available to you."

It was axiomatic, in the beginning, that hard kicks were dangerous. They were not a game for the timid or insecure. But insofar as they offered a way out of the white suburban world that so many of the early hippies had been born into, they were worth the risk.

At first the hippies used LSD as a deconditioning agent. This, you may recall, had been William Burroughs's great project, one he had bequeathed to Ginsberg and Kerouac, and one that had become, by the mid-Sixties, part of the Baby Boom's emotional baggage. That American society was manipulative was one of the Haight's basic tenets. LSD put this into perspective, and by doing so (as Leary tirelessly pointed out) it opened up the possibility of reprogramming oneself; using LSD the games could be examined, the defenses leveled, and better strategies adopted.

The word on Haight Street was that a few good acid trips were the equivalent of three years of analysis. But that didn't mean that a few more were the same as six years. You plateaued after a certain number of excursions to the Other World, and at that point the "bad trip" became important. Bad trips, provided they came after an appropriate level of expertise had been obtained, were vital if you were to progress to still higher levels.

According to the hippies, LSD was "one of the best and healthiest tools available" for the examination of consciousness. "Acid opens your door, opens the windows, opens your senses. Opens your beam to the vast possibilities of life, to the glorious indescribable beauty of life." You could "drop down into your unconscious to see the pillars and the roots of the tree which is your personality. . . . You see what your hangups are; you might not even overcome them but you cope with them, and that's an amazing advance."

The Haight then, in its earliest incarnation, was a kind of sanitarium, an indigenous Baden Baden that offered a therapeutic regime of good vibes and drugs, rather than mountain air and mineral springs.

Which was why the population of the district exploded in early 1966. The catalyst, to the extent that there was just one, was Kesey and the Acid Tests, particularly the Trips Festival, which had been like throwing a switch that sent a surge of energy through the isolated pockets of hipness surrounding the Bay Area. In the course of several impetuous months, Kesey and his Merry Pranksters managed to introduce more people to LSD than all the researchers, the CIA, Sandoz, and Tim Leary combined. Most were college students or ex-students temporarily on the bum until they settled down to a profession. They came to the Trips Festival with their ontological categories intact . . . by the time they left all that remained was a haunting glimpse of the ineffable—the one Leary had given up Harvard to pursue, and Kesey literature. Lacking a Millbrook or a La Honda to flee to, they found their way to the Haight.

By June 1966, an estimated fifteen thousand hippies were living in the Haight, an increase that baffled the hippies about as much as it did everyone else. "God has fingered that little block system between Baker and Stanyon Street," they told the curious. "And we spend all our time, verbally and nonverbally, trying to discover why." Helen Perry, one of the first of the social scientists to arrive on the scene, likened the Haight to "the delta of a river," where all the unrooted sediment of America was washing ashore. But even Perry was unclear as to why the undercurrents of American life should be sweeping so many into this odd backwater . . . asked why they had chosen the Haight, the hippies murmured vague things like, "I fell in with some vibrational energies and ended up here."

Entrepreneurs began refurbishing the abandoned storefronts along Haight Street, opening businesses whose character was apparent in their names: the I-Thou Coffee Shop, the Weed Patch, the Psychedelic Shop. This last, the inspiration of two brothers, Ron and Jay Thelin, was conceived as an information center for the private revolution. The primary focus of the Psychedelic Shop was books—books by Leary and Alpert, by Watts, Huxley, and Hesse, plus a decent selection of Eastern texts. "We went out and asked different friends of ours to compile books that they thought we should have," the Thelins recalled. "It was supposed to be information on dope. It was pro-LSD."

The Thelins, although atypical in that they were natives of San Francisco, were in most other respects fairly representative of the early hippies: they were children of the middle class, Presbyterians, paperboys, eagle scouts. "I read *Time* magazine when I was in the Army, and I voted for Richard Nixon. I watched TV, and I believed that we were going to legislate equality." For Ron the turning point had come with his discovery of Ginsberg and Kerouac, followed by Thoreau and Alan Watts and, eventually, LSD. For Jay Thelin the transforming event had been a talk by Richard Alpert, during which Alpert had stressed the need for solid information to guide the increasing number of adventurers who were exploring the Other World. After the lecture Jay had persuaded his brother to sell the boat and umbrella business they had been operating in Lake Tahoe, and invest in the Haight.

The Psych Shop had been open only a few days when someone slipped a note under the door: "You're selling out the revolution. You're commercializing it. You're putting it on the market." But the place was an immediate success, socially as well as financially. It rivaled the Unicorn as a hangout and profits were sufficiently high that the Thelins soon expanded, adding a darkened meditation room that became a favorite spot for sexual trysts.

Had you spent a few hours there, eavesdropping upon the conversations, basking in what the sociologists would soon call "the hippie modality," you could have plumbed most of the depths of this odd community. Plumbed them, that is, once you had learned the language.

It is usually forgotten that the psychedelic movement inaugurated one of the great epochs of American slang. Within months a complex argot had developed, most of which had to do with drugs and drug taking, activities for which a private code seemed natural. LSD was acid; a frequent user was an acidhead; a single dose was a hit or a tab. Marijuana was known variously as pot, hemp, hay, grass, reefer, or simply good shit . . . in any case the point was to get high. Getting high at the Fillmore was a groovy (pleasurable) experience, though depending on any number of ancillary factors, it might also turn into a heavy (emotionally fraught) experience, or possibly even a far out one—far out, and its semantic sibling, out of sight, were Edge City words: in those realms things either verged on the cosmic (the very best) or turned into a bummer (the very worst). In any case, it was all Karma (fate) and there was no sense hassling over what was inevitable. That was a game the straights (everyone who wasn't hip) played, all those uptight nine-to-fivers with no appreciation of the Here and Now, so caught up were they in the materialism gig. Ironically, the hippie argot was the one thing the straight world found useful. It wasn't long before Madison Avenue was featuring advertisements for cars and soft drinks with modifiers like "mindblowing" and "far out."

Another thought that would have struck a visitor to the Psych Shop in early 1966 was how esoteric most of the reading was. Among the fiction, Herman Hesse was the obvious best-seller—sales of *A Journey to the East, Steppenwolf,* and *Siddhartha* would make Hesse the largest-selling German author in America by the end of the Sixties—closely followed by the science fiction novels (*Stranger in a Strange Land, Childhood's End,* etc.) that the Pranksters had found so illuminating. Balancing the fiction was a section of technical works on the psychedelic experience, Leary, Huxley, Watts, plus a variety of Eastern and occult texts, ranging from the *Tibetan Book of the Dead* to the *Zohar*.

Aldous Huxley would have been overjoyed at this intermingling of East and West, but he might have been a trifle disturbed at the amount of occult chaff that was getting mixed in with the grains of perennial philosophy. Although Huxley had predicted that LSD would awaken the Baby Boom's slumbering appetite for spiritual meaning, he hadn't anticipated what would happen once this hunger began searching for something to feed upon . . . in the Haight, the perennial philosophy came heavily spiced with astrology, numerology, alchemy, black magic, voodoo; a crazy quilt of arcane practice and contemporary jargon that affronted the trained Western intellect's need to formalize, to abstract out a workable map from anarchic reality.

Which was entirely appropriate given the hippie's preference for direct experience. Go with the flow, they said, do your own thing. What Neal Cassady had such an abundance of—that ability to be perfectly attuned to the moment—was one of the highest states of grace a hippie could attain. Cassady hadn't written great novels or poems, he wasn't a professor or a scientist; in the normal scheme of things he was a failure; but in the Haight he was respected as a symbol of the balanced man. He was treading the inner path with style and wit, which was all anyone could hope for.

Not that the hippies saw a lot of Cassady; Ginsberg was a much more tangible presence. Rather they absorbed his essential style through the medium of the Pranksters and the Trips Festival. Just as they absorbed Leary and Huxley and Alan Watts, picking up those parts that struck a responsive chord, and dispensing with the rest. When a hippie claimed that "I'm from another race, not black, not white, maybe I'm of a race that's not here yet, a race without a name," what you heard were echoes of Huxley's evolutionary romanticism filtered through the dog-eared science fiction epics that graced every hippie pad. When they talked about life being a series of games and the individual a collection of masks, defenses, and often self-deceptive strategies, the intelligent observer cross-referenced that statement with Tim Leary's transactional psychology; while a descriptive like "hard kicks" was unquestionably a daredevil child of Kesey's can-you-pass-the-Acid-Test perspective.

A diligent dissector could find a bit of all of the above in the hippie habit of replacing baptismal names with newer, psychedelicized handles; like Frodo, Chocolate George, the Hun, Coyote. As one hippie explained his own name change: "the Teddybear you see is only a facade. There's another me whose name is Harold. Right now Harold is a very tiny person inside of me, but he's still there. When you come to the Haight, everybody chooses a name and builds a personality to fit it. I built Teddybear; but now I'm starting to lose Teddybear—thank God!—and some day Teddybear will be dead. You come here to change, and I think the ultimate change you come here to find is the 'you' that you imagine and the real 'you' merging into one."

If, for some reason, the Berkeley activists had chosen one symbol to represent their struggle, they probably would have picked the ubiquitous clenched fist, with its message of angry resistance.

The hippies, on the other hand, dreamed of erecting a statue of St. Francis on the edge of the Haight, an immense figure, carved from a giant redwood, whose outstretched arms would welcome pilgrims to the capital of the New Age.

There was something appropriately medieval about this fantasy—appropriate because to arrive in the Haight-Ashbury during the Summer of Love was not too different from arriving in twelfth-century Paris. There was the same quality of exotic commotion—"That one big street, Haight Street, was just packed with every kind of freak you could imagine . . . guys with mohawk haircuts, people walking around in commodore uniforms"—overlaid by the same overpowering interest in the mystical. "There are at least fifteen hundred saints in the Haight," opined one hippie. "Saints and holymen. I mean they're of all ages and sexes. Some of them are in their seventies and some of them are in their fifteens and some of them are in their cradles." In the local vernacular, these saints were known as "heavy cats."

Daily life in the Haight had a quality of animation that was difficult to describe, although Leonard Wolf, an English professor at San Francisco State and one of the earliest hippie watchers, came close when he compared it to "an anthill where all the ants are drunk but busy and somehow, when all the tumult has died down, successful." It took a while for the neophyte to understand why the situation was so charged, but eventually it dawned upon them: on any given day roughly half the people in the Haight were either tripping, or had been tripping, or were about to trip.

Everyone, in other words, was living in cosmic time, which was fine if you happened to belong to an ashram or a monastic order. But if you didn't there were certain practical drawbacks to spending several days a week pushing the envelope with LSD. Little things like the problem of holding down a job in order to earn enough money to buy food and pay the rent. Because it was difficult, after an evening of acid, to motivate oneself to rise with the sun and hustle down to the local Food Mart to unpack crates and stick little price tags on cans, the hippies tended toward part-time jobs like delivery boy and messenger. Thus they had to accomplish in two days what most people did in five.

A burst of concentrated activity followed by long stretches of chemical contemplation—that was the hippie ideal. Whenever anyone chided them for their dissolute lifestyle, they would laugh and claim they were a laboratory for what life would be like in the future, once computers and machines had replaced the need to labor.

Everything was pooled—money, food, drugs, living arrangements. The underlying ethic was that the hippies were all members of an extended family, although the preferred word was *tribe,* a sign of their deep admiration for the Native Americans, whom they revered as an example of how the free live.

Your first night in the Haight was usually spent in one of the many communal crashpads, sandwiched together with a dozen friendly strangers. Your inhibitions and frequently your virginity were the first things to go, followed by your clothes and your old values—a progressive shedding that was hastened along by your first acid trip. Within days your past life in Des Moines or Dallas or wherever was as remote as the school outings you took as an adolescent.

When not working or tripping, which was seen as a kind of work, you could probably be found sunbathing in Golden Gate Park or strolling along Haight Street, stopping at the Drugstore for coffee and the Psychedelic Shop for the latest gossip. Every week there were a couple of new stores to investigate, places like the Weed Patch (drug paraphernalia), the Laughing Raccoon Gallery (crafts), the Blushing Peony (funky clothes), the Print Mint (psychedelic posters), and Quasar's Ice Cream (food). And there was always a new band playing at the Fillmore or the Avalon Ballroom. The Fillmore was the inspiration of Bill Graham, the man who had produced Kesey's Trips Festival. Impressed by the amount of money Kesey had generated with little more than a rock band, some slides, and a drug, Graham had rented an abandoned auditorium in the Black Fillmore district and had begun holding rock dances with local bands, many of whom were living in the Haight.

The Charlatans, who were famous for actually having gotten a summer-long gig, occupied a house at 1090 Page, while the Grateful Dead, Kesey's Acid Test band, were householding a few streets away. In time they would be joined by Big Brother and the Holding Company, the Jefferson Airplane, Quicksilver Messenger Service, and numerous other groupings whose musical half life was too brief to register on the historical consciousness, but whose economic contributions to the Haight were invaluable. With their retinue of hangers-on and their ability to generate sizable sums of cash, the rock bands were one of the linchpins of the Haight-Ashbury economy.

But the bands played another, subtler, role in shaping the hippie ethic. It was thought that rock music was the perfect complement to the psychedelic experience. "It engages the entire sensorium, appealing to the intelligence with no interference from the intellect," wrote former Beat novelist turned hippie philosopher, Chester Anderson. "Rock is a tribal phenomenon, immune to definition and other typographical operations, and constitutes what might be called a 20th-century magic."

Dancing to rock music was a perfect illustration of how two people could do their own thing together.

The outside world rarely impinged. And when it did, it only brought further confirmation of the Establishment's Big Daddy Complex, of which the crusade against LSD was a classic example. Judging from the 123 million prescriptions written for tranquilizers and sedatives in 1965, and the 24 million for amphetamines, America loved its mind drugs. It couldn't live without them. And frequently—three thousand overdoses per year—it couldn't live with them. But tranquilizers and sedatives were ruled okay because they damped down the fires of life; they stupefied the mind rather than opening up its glorious, ecstatic (and sometimes dangerous) depths.

Or consider what happened when a group of hippie entrepreneurs tried to join the local business group, the Haight Street Merchants' Association: they were shown the door. Apparently there was no place for a Psychedelic Shop or a Weed Patch within the parameters of conventional capitalism. Undeterred, the hippies quickly formed a rival business group, the Haight Independent Proprietors, a name that owed much of its existence to the fact that it abbreviated into HIP.

But these were just two entries in an enormous ledger of misunderstanding and suspicion. It seemed to the kids that the parents were always saying NO! That everything about them, their hair, their music, their clothes, the way they talked, their heroes, their dreams, all were considered illegitimate by a generation who couldn't stop patting itself on the back over how democratic and liberal it was.

On the other hand, it seemed to the parents that the kids were always saying "fuck you!" That everything about them, their hair, their relationships, the clothes they wore, the cars they drove, etc.

This internecine squabble soon became dignified as the Generation Gap, and while the sociologists and psychologists labored mightily to explain its genesis, the kids couldn't have cared less: they wanted to let the chasm widen until there was sufficient space to create their own alternative culture. This, as the Pranksters would have put it, was the ruling fantasy; the only debate was over which direction this emancipation would take. Would the flow favor the activists or the hippies? Or was there a third alternative?

That this was even a matter for debate testifies to how quickly the hippie ethic was spreading. In March 1966, while its medical section was announcing an LSD epidemic, *Time*'s cultural pages were reporting on the proliferation of "oddball cult groups"—the word *hippie* having not yet gained currency. Almost overnight, in every major city, a small community of "acidheads" (*Time*'s word) had appeared. And while none of these communities equaled the Haight in terms of cohesion or size, all were remarkably similar, filled with colorfully garbed, college-educated contemplatives who talked about LSD with the kind of worshipful fervor last heard in the West during the high Middle Ages.

The activists, at first, were contemptuous. But as the private revolution gathered strength, they became alarmed and began to view the hippie as a dangerous usurper, more concerned with "vibes" than Vietnam. "You've got to straighten out your own heads first," went a famous editorial in the hippies' premier newspaper, the San Francisco *Oracle:* "How can we have a groovy, happy society unless everyone has reached his own nirvana?" This was a worthy point certainly, but it was also one of those endlessly debatable chicken and egg propositions. Can a society of individuals heal its own social ills without first addressing its internal flaws? A century of psychological thinking suggested otherwise. As Leary put it: "If all the Negroes and left wing college students in the world had Cadillacs and full control of society, they would still be involved in an anthill social system unless they opened themselves up first."

The activists were unmoved by this line of reasoning. It was too wimpy, too individual, too whimsically religious (groovy nirvana?). "What about India?" was a stock rejoinder, and one that usually silenced the proponents of the karmic path to social healing. In essence this was a disagreement over materialism. The activists wanted to redistribute the wealth until everyone enjoyed a middle-class standard of living; they wanted to hold the liberal ideal's feet to the fire until it came across. But the hippies wanted none of that. They found the rampant materialism of the middle class repugnant. And although they were hazy on what they preferred instead, it certainly had nothing to do with a rising GNP.

So that was the choice—hippie or activist: a contemplative life predicated on the tenuous possibility of enlightenment, or a worthy struggle that would cleanse America of its racist, imperialistic tendencies, and lead to what seemed to be (in the few rare theoretical formulations) a benign socialism. It seemed impossible, to the activists at least, that any educated person could opt for the first course. Yet they were. And in increasing numbers.

What the activists overlooked, what skewed their expectations, was a misunderstanding of the role LSD was playing in redefining the counterculture's thrust. With LSD, exulted Ginsberg, "technology has produced a chemical which catalyzes a consciousness which finds the entire civilization leading up to that pill absurd." If this was true, then the suggestibility of the psychedelic state, which Leary had studied so intently, made it one of the most potent revolutionary tools of all time, far more powerful than the manifestoes and slogans of the political radicals.

And contrary to all expectations, there was more LSD around than ever before. The days when one had to cultivate a source in the medical community were long past, thanks to a handful of enterprising chemists whose underground labs were flooding the market with remarkably potent product. These chemists were shadowy characters for the most part, with one notable exception, Augustus Owsley Stanley, the Third.

23

THE ALCHEMIST

Owsley enters our story on the night Kesey flees from the Beatles concert, only to find La Honda besieged by hundreds of celebrity-hungry teenyboppers, a consequence of the Prankster rumor that, postconcert, the Beatles were coming to Kesey's for "a freaking good rout." The Pranksters were in the process of herding this grumbling mob back across the bridge, when this guy materialized in front of Kesey and announced, in the confident tones of a somebody, "I'm Owsley."

Sizing him up—"a cocky little guy, short, with dark hair, dressed like an acid head, the usual boho gear"—the Pranksters' initial impulse was to laugh. Who could have guessed that within months this cocky little guy's fame would rival that of the Chief himself? Or, listening to his "strange wound-up nasal voice," that Tim Leary would say of him: "I've studied with the wisest sages of our times: Huxley, Heard, Lama Govinda, Sri Krishna Prem, Alan Watts—and I have to say that AOS3, college flunkout, who never wrote anything better (or worse) than a few rubber checks, has the best up to date perspective on the divine design than anyone I've ever listened to."

Or that *Newsweek* would compare him to Henry Ford. Or that within months, every underground chemist would be marketing their wares as his, for by then Owsley acid would be the true coin of the realm.

Of all the acts of self-transformation in this book, none was as remarkable as that of Augustus Owsley Stanley the Third.

Had he been born a century earlier, Owsley would have been a classic bounder, the sort of well-born cad who added contradictory dashes of spice and morality to the novels of the Victorian era. But

Owsley arrived in the same year as Kesey, 1935, although there were no dirt farmers or western migrations in his ancestry: Owsley was pure Southern gentry. His grandfather, the first Augustus Owsley Stanley, had been a U.S. senator from Kentucky; his father was a Washington lawyer. Owsley grew up in Alexandria, Virginia, across the Potomac from the capital, where early on he exhibited the symptoms of what guidance counselors call underachievement. His intelligence was beyond question—the headmaster of Alexandria's Charlotte Hall School considered him "almost like a brainchild, a *Wunderkinder,* tremendously interested in science"—but he was willful and wild. He was expelled from Charlotte Hall in the ninth grade for intoxication. When he was eighteen he dropped out of school altogether, severing all ties with his family.

Owsley's scientific aptitude gained him admittance to the University of Virginia's School of Engineering. He lasted a year. By 1956 he was in the Air Force. He spent eighteen months at Edwards Air Force Base, in the high desert plateau east of Los Angeles, specializing in electronics and radar. After his discharge, he moved to Los Angeles, where the electronics boom was just beginning, and spent the next few years drifting from job to job, never making more than eight thousand dollars a year, and never really exercising the intellect he knew he possessed.

During these years Owsley married, divorced, and remarried in a Tijuana ceremony that was later invalidated. He fathered a child, moved back with his first wife and then out again—"just a little boy afraid to grow up, a Peter Pan," one of his wives later told a reporter. In 1963 he was arrested for writing $645 dollars worth of bad checks, for which he received a suspended sentence and three years' probation.

After his trial ended, Owsley decided to take another crack at college, this time at Berkeley. He rented a room in a cheap boardinghouse that catered to students and ex-students and began "moving in boxes full of such stuff as ballet shoes, a complete beekeeper's outfit and a painting in progress that showed the arm of Christ on the cross, portrayed more or less from a Christ's-eye view." Whatever competition he had as "house eccentric" was soon routed.

Owsley wrote poetry, studied Russian, drew strange but technically acceptable pictures, was a ballet enthusiast and an electronics nut. He was a sharp but eccentric dresser, a bit of a dandy, and he preferred to be known by his nickname, Bear. He reminded housemate Charles Perry of a character in William Burroughs's *Naked Lunch,* the one who "has a theory on everything, like what kind of underwear is healthy." Some of his theories were truly brilliant, others merely weird, but he defended them all with a tenacity that was wearing on those who thought the whole thing was about becoming mellow, hanging out, absorbing and contemplating. But if Owsley was hyperopinionated, he wasn't a bully about it. "There was something disinterested and nobly intentioned in his relentless enthusiasms. And his ideas were never boring," remembered Perry.

> Owsley never ate dinner with us because he was antivegetarian. He argued that since the human race is descended from carnivorous apes, our digestive system is designed for meat alone, and vegetables are slow poison. Once when we smoked some hashish and developed a case of the munchies, he accused me of trying to poison him with apple pie. "I haven't had any plant food in my system for years," he groused between mouthfuls. "My digestion will be fucked up for a month."

He lasted a semester at Berkeley before quitting to take a technical job at KGO-TV. On the surface it seemed he was settling back into his habitual rut, and indeed he might have but for two additional factors. The first was his discovery of LSD. What happened to Owsley in the Other World we can only surmise from the reports of others. Tim Leary, in his incomparable style, wrote how Owsley had "taken the full LSD trip, hurled down through his cellular reincarnations, disintegrated beyond life into pulsing electronic grids, whirled down beyond atomic forms to that unitary center that is one, pure, radiant, humming vibration." And when he whirled back up he was no longer the dilettante artist, the brilliant fuck-up. Owsley returned with a mission: he was going to save the world by making the purest and cheapest and most abundant LSD possible.

And this was where the second factor became important. By the purest chance, Owsley had just begun a romance with a chemistry graduate student at Berkeley named Melissa.

Owsley's first lab was in the bathroom of a house near the Berkeley campus. There is some evidence that in addition to LSD, he was also making methedrine. At least this was what the police thought when they raided the house in February 1965, and confiscated a chemical that may or may not have been an intermediate step toward LSD. It wasn't methedrine, in any case, although that is what the police decided to charge him with.

Owsley's reaction to the bust became the foundation of his legend. Instead of panicking, he hired Arthur Harris, the deputy mayor of Berkeley, as his lawyer, and Harris quickly got the case thrown out on the grounds that no methedrine had been found. But Owsley wasn't content with simple vindication. Once the charges were dropped, Owsley turned around and successfully sued the police for the return of all his confiscated laboratory equipment. Then he disappeared.

He surfaced briefly in Alexandria, Virginia, where he contacted his family. "He was only four miles away but we spoke on the phone," his father later told a reporter. "He got mad at me, tried to tell me booze is worse [than drugs]. I told him to wash his hands and come back and talk to me about it . . . We haven't had a pleasant relationship. We're not in accord with what he's doing. His life is divorced from ours. He's had two wives and a child by each and lives with another woman. When he came here with that floozy I wouldn't let him in." As a parting shot, AOS 2 described his son as "emotionally unbalanced, but has a brilliant mind."

Los Angeles became Owsley's new base of operations. He formed a company called Bear Research Group and began ordering the necessary chemicals for synthesizing LSD. Using the Bear Research cover, he purchased substantial quantities of lysergic monohydrate, the essential ingredient in the LSD synthesis. All told he accumulated 800 grams— 500 from Cyclo Chemical and 300 from International Chemical and Nuclear Corp—signing, in both instances, affidavits to the effect that the chemicals would be used for research purposes only. He paid cash— twenty thousand dollars in hundred-dollar bills to Cyclo alone, which suggested that the Berkeley factory, despite its short lifespan, had been more lucrative than anyone supposed.

Owsley received his first shipment of lysergic monohydrate on March 30, 1965. By May he had turned it into LSD. His method of distribution was largely word of mouth, which may be why the police once again learned of his clandestine lab. Unbeknownst to Owsley, Captain Alfred Tremblay, commander of the Los Angeles narcotics division, was emptying his garbage cans at regular intervals. Among the items Tremblay retrieved were several order forms, one of which came from Portland, Oregon, with a request for forty capsules and a postscript: "love to Melissa."

A year later Owsley's garbage would be prominently displayed during Tremblay's Congressional testimony. But by then Owsley had vanished from Tremblay's turf. As soon as his first run was complete he returned to San Francisco, where he amazed his old housemates with the fact that he had actually made his own LSD. According to Charles Perry, Owsley's first product was "devastatingly strong in an almost heavy-handed way that recalled Owsley's own insistent manner." Like the Pranksters, Owsley's psychedelic perspective contained a lot of machismo; he was always taunting his friends to "take two and really cut loose into the cosmos."

Owsley learned of Kesey sometime in the summer of 1965, setting the stage for their fateful meeting in the early morning hours after the aborted Beatles party. Fateful because without Owsley the Acid Tests probably would never have taken place, for the simple reason that LSD was too difficult to obtain. The dream of handing out thousands of doses was just that, a fantasy, or had been until that cocky little boho materialized out of the crowd of teenyboppers and said, "I'm Owsley."

This was the second bar in the Owsley legend: he was the Pranksters' chemist.

Flush with money, Owsley became the counterculture's most benevolent patron, buying sound equipment for indigent bands like the Grateful Dead and bankrolling the Haight's first newspaper, the San Francisco *Oracle*. According to his old housemate, Charles Perry, Owsley's Berkeley hideout frequently resembled a medieval court, with "a regular retinue of petitioners . . . present[ing] themselves like serfs pleading for boons from the King. I can still see Owsley listening warily but regally to their requests, enthroned in the nude on a huge fur-covered chair, drying his hair with a hair dryer." Owsley's personal enthusiasms, always exotic, became even grander. He collected oriental rugs and state-of-the-art electronics. He kept an owl, which he fed live mice. He made personalized perfumes, mixing the essences to suit his interpretation of the recipient's personality. If Owsley didn't invent the hippie dealer look, he certainly perfected it, with his elaborate turquoise belts and hand-tooled boots. Food was another of his passions, and he enjoyed entertaining his entourage at various fine restaurants. The price of the meal was usually an Owsley soliloquy, either on the subject of antivegetarianism or else his famous LSD rap, a marathon romp through Einsteinian physics and Buddhist philosophy, which added up to one large aperçu: the Divine Force had given mankind LSD to counteract the discovery of nuclear fission.

This wasn't a perspective unique to Owsley. Aldous Huxley and Gerald Heard had also been bemused by the coincidence that Albert Hofmann had begun having his famous premonitions about the twenty-fifth synthesis only a few weeks after Enrico Fermi achieved fission on that Chicago tennis court; indeed Heard used to say that LSD was simply God's way of saving man from the Bomb. According to Ralph Metzner, "Owsley's theory was that the higher intelligences controlling and supervising the progress of the planet could not let the atomic fission experiments go too far: the danger to all forms of life from nuclear radiation was too great. So a minute change in the LSD molecule, a slight rotation on the side chain perhaps, was engineered, to make this a drug that could open men's minds . . ."

Thus Owsley's career as an underground chemist was graced by divine approval.

It would be wrong, however, to give the impression that Owsley was at the mercy of his own flamboyance; there was a counterbalancing side to his nature that was secretive, suspicious, and paranoid. And as his notoriety increased, it was this side of Owsley's character that came to the fore. He loved thinking up James Bond stratagems to fool the Captain Tremblays of the world. Like any good spy, he varied his routine, never arriving anywhere when he said he would. At the last Acid Test, which took place a few weeks after Kesey's bogus suicide, Owsley passed himself off as a technical advisor for the Grateful Dead.

This was in Los Angeles. The Pranksters had rented a warehouse on the fringe of the Watts ghetto and were spreading the word through the LA underground that an Acid Test was about to occur. Owsley was there with a new aide, a young electronics wizard named Tim Scully. Scully had spent the last several months building audio equipment to Owsley's specifications. In Prankster slang, Owsley had a thing about the kind of music the Dead were beginning to play. Although he couldn't articulate it very well—or at least he never managed to explain to Scully what he meant—he believed that rock had a role to play in the cosmic scenario second only to that of LSD.

But Owsley's newfound interest in the Grateful Dead didn't mean that he had abandoned his old role as chief alchemist for the Pranksters. When the two garbage pails full of Kool-aid were placed in the center of the warehouse, he liberally dosed one with his latest product.

But something was missing. Kesey's absence had torn a hole in the Unspoken Thing. A lot of the blame for this later fell on Babbs, who had inherited Kesey's mantle. It was felt that Babbs gave too many orders, that he tried to impose an army mentality. Certainly he lacked the Chief's talent for providing guidance while appearing disinterested, the "non-navigator." But whether he can be blamed for what happened at Watts is highly questionable. What happened at Watts was something Kesey might have foreseen had he pondered the message of the Cow Palace concert. Ten people might experiment with the group mind and *Homo gestalt* and the result be altogether marvelous. Even a hundred or a thousand might spend a pleasant afternoon provided skilled people were in charge of the setting. But as the numbers increased, so did the possibility of the animal suddenly running amuck, and devouring itself. As the Acid Tests increased in size, the ideal of opening up new vistas of consciousness began to brush against an almost demonic urge to erase all limits.

This was painfully evident at Watts. Whenever somebody began freaking out, the Pranksters would rush over with a camera and microphone to record the moment. The mike was hooked into a reverb system that created a disturbing echo effect, particularly if the victim was babbling or sobbing, which was usually the case. When the Grateful Dead objected that this was cruel and uncharacteristically fascistic, a bitter argument broke out between the band and the Pranksters. By morning everyone was in a sour mood.

Everyone, that is, with the possible exception of Tim Scully. For Scully, journeying to Los Angeles with the Pranksters was comparable to what running away to join a circus had been for an earlier generation.

Ever since the eighth grade, when his entry in the Bay Area Science Fair (he took second place) attracted the interest of some scientists at Berkeley's Lawrence Livermore Lab, Tim Scully had been a science prodigy. Growing up in suburban Pleasant Hills, which was across the Bay from San Francisco, he was the classic teenage science nerd: brilliant, shy, friendless, weird, and completely at sea in the loafer and letter-sweater ambiance that still dominated teenage life. While his peers spent summer vacations at the beach or on the tennis courts, Scully could be found at Lawrence Livermore, working on arcane physics problems. During his junior year he decided to see whether he could change mercury into gold by bombarding it with a flow of neutrons, and began building a linear accelerator in the school science lab. But fears that he might accidentally irradiate the school prompted the principal to suggest that college would be a much better place for someone of his talents, and at the end of his junior year Scully entered Berkeley, intending to major in mathematical physics. In this he was faithfully following the family script, which saw him obtaining his Ph.D. in some suitably hard science, prior to becoming a high-paid government scientist. But then he discovered LSD.

Tim Scully took his first LSD on April 15, 1965, a few hours after mailing in his tax return. Financially, 1964 had been a good year for the twenty-year-old Scully. His services, as a designer of electronic prototypes, had been in such demand that he had been forced to take a leave of absence from Berkeley; but he had also made enough money to buy a house.

Scully experienced the by now classic psychedelic epiphany: this drug can save the world! But it also seemed obvious to him that "the government would be terrified of this stuff" and would move quickly to suppress it. Therefore someone had better stockpile as much raw material as possible. A few hours in the Berkeley library, perusing the technical literature, impressed upon Scully the necessity of obtaining a large quantity of the key ingredient in the LSD synthesis, a compound called lysergic acid monohydrate. This proved more difficult than he had supposed. Lysergic acid monohydrate was rare and very expensive, or so the salesman at the local chemical company claimed; the likelihood of his being able to obtain any was slim. Scully was puzzling over his next move when he learned that a guy named Owsley possessed most of the lysergic monohydrate in the Bay Area.

The two finally met in the fall of 1965, around the time the Trips Festival was beginning to jell. Owsley didn't bestow his trust immediately. He vetted Scully for weeks, dropping by at odd hours to discuss electronics and philosophy, and recounting wild stories about the Acid Tests and the Pranksters. Owsley took Scully to hear the Grateful Dead practice, hoping that Tim would see what he meant when he talked about the role music would play in the coming revolution. Scully failed that particular test, but overall he made a favorable impression upon Owsley, who proposed that they spend the winter building electronic equipment for the Grateful Dead, and then in the spring, if all went well, they'd make some LSD together.

Scully worked with the Grateful Dead until late spring 1966, which was when Owsley decided it was time to go back into production. He rented a house in Point Richmond, down the coast from San Francisco, and set up his lab in the basement.

One of the misapprehensions that gained a foothold during the debate over LSD was that any bright teenager could whip up a batch in his high school chem lab. This was nonsense. Making LSD was a process fraught with complications, particularly if all you had at your disposal was a makeshift lab in the basement of a suburban tract house. The first batch Scully was involved in had a screw-up at the very beginning. Owsley was using sulfur trioxide as a reagent, and sulfur trioxide was very scary stuff. Spill a drop on your skin, and there would be a quick, neat hole. Let any escape into the air, and all the moisture in the immediate vicinity turned into sulfuric acid.

So the three of them, Scully, Owsley, and Melissa, were kneeling on the concrete floor fiddling with the ampule, which they had placed inside a clear plastic laundry bag that Owsley had filled with dry nitrogen. The idea, perfected by Owsley, was that they would slip a file inside the bag, sever the neck of the ampule, pour a specified amount of the sulfur trioxide into what was called an addition funnel, and then seal the ampule with an acetylene torch. Only this time, as soon as they severed the neck of the ampule, a droplet of sulfur trioxide came flying out and *poof*—the air turned into sulfuric acid. Choking and gagging, they filled the addition funnel and sealed the ampule and then threw open the garage doors and raced outside, followed by a cloud of noxious gas that rolled down the highway and out across the lawns of Point Richmond. Luckily, public consciousness of the drug problem had not yet reached the level where the sight of three eccentrically dressed bohemians exiting a garage followed by a cloud of gas would excite suspicion.

But in general things went smoothly, in twenty-four-hour shifts, with the three of them hurrying back and forth beneath the yellow bug lights, to the omnipresent *whuuump* of the vacuum pump. According to Scully, "Owsley felt that the state of mind he was in at the time when the reaction was run was a crucial influence on people's experience when they took LSD. He had a friend who was a disk jockey at one of the local radio stations and he'd call up and say, 'Okay, I'm about to do a batch now, play the following record,' so he could get in the right mood for it. He'd sit there making arcane passes around the flask as he was concentrating on it."

Being an acid chemist was an intoxicating experience. Scully remembers it as "incredibly addictive. It's certainly got to be one of the most exciting things going. Here you are, you think you are doing something that could be pivotal in the history of the world. That this may be the thing that saves the world from destruction. And of course its real neat being a cultural hero."

The early batches were small, seldom larger than 10 or 20 grams, with a gram containing anywhere from three to four thousand individual doses. Fractioning the LSD into those doses was an interesting technical challenge. In the early days the liquid LSD had been titrated directly onto a sugar cube or a vitamin C tablet, although occasionally it was sealed into an ampule. Then crude tableting machines were obtained. These were worked by hand and they created a kind of dusty penumbra, with the result that whoever was doing the tableting was soon off in the corner, tripping madly. To own a state of the art tableting machine became the underground chemist's grail, and much time was spent mulling over the problem of how to obtain one without alerting the watchdogs at the BDAC and the FDA.

Considerable time was also devoted to the problem of how to mass-market the psychedelic movement. Scully believed that time was of the essence, that a government crackdown was imminent. "I was more of that opinion than almost anyone I knew," he says. "I felt real strongly about it and was pushing everybody else. Because the other folks felt that it would mostly just go along at a natural evolutionary pace and what's the hurry? There's something that Owsley used to say that was really apt and that is that LSD is a lot like a virus—viruses can't reproduce themselves. What they do is infiltrate into a healthy cell and cause that cell to generate more of the virus."

Scully had numerous fantasies about how to speed up the scenario. One of the wildest involved *Life* magazine, which allowed you to insert little postcards that could be mailed off for whatever product you were advertising. Why not print up a batch of postcards with a little dot of acid on every one of them, Scully wondered. Then, after all the issues were mailed, announce that anyone who was interested in LSD should cut out the lower right-hand corner of the postcard. "We would get about 10 or 11 million doses into peoples hands that way—an efficient distribution system, worldwide."

Actually, an efficient distribution system was already forming. Because of Owsley and the several other chemists who were working in the Bay Area, the Haight-Ashbury was becoming the LSD capital of the world. People arrived daily to buy LSD, and then flew back to Boston or Cleveland or a dozen other major distribution points.

In fact, Owsley acid had such good word of mouth that some of the other chemists began advertising their products as his. To fool them, Owsley injected his batches with various dyes, a fairly straightforward marketing decision that soon took a surprising and unanticipated turn. All sorts of extrachemical effects were attributed to the different colored chemicals: this one was mellow, that one intensely visual. Bemused and a little disturbed by this phenomenon, Scully and Owsley concocted a little experiment. Taking 50 grams of recently produced LSD, they divided it into five piles and dyed each a different color. Then they waited for the street notices. The word was that the red stuff was righteously mellow, but the green was awfully speedy. And it was rumored that one of the other colors had been cut with strychnine.

Owsley and Scully were working at Point Richmond when the California law making LSD illegal went into effect. With jail a real possibility, the nature of the game changed. This was particularly true for Owsley, who had the highest profile of any of the underground chemists. It did not take much insight to realize that of the hundred or so agents that BDAC was training at Berkeley, a sizable proportion would be delegated to Owsley. So he decided to process another 200 grams and then close up shop. He wanted to hang out, travel with the Dead, absorb the burgeoning hippie scene.

But Scully discovered he couldn't stop. He was addicted to the process, to the excitement, and he pressed Owsley to let him invest some of the profits in a new lab, preferably outside California. Owsley agreed and as a parting gesture took him around to the local chemical supply companies, where he introduced Scully as a close personal friend who deserved first rate service. Now the chemical supply companies were in a difficult position in late 1966. BDAC was pressuring them to report any irregular customers who wandered in off the street and walked out again with fifteen thousand dollars worth of esoteric lab equipment. But fifteen thousand dollars was fifteen thousand dollars, and the companies were reluctant to turn in an old and valued customer like Owsley. They had, however, no such loyalty to Scully. So they turned him in.

Scully didn't realize what was happening until he had finished loading his equipment into the used Sunshine cookie truck he had bought especially for the move: "There was a very helpful, new stock clerk who helped load the truck, who wanted to gossip with me, and who then got in his car and started to drive away behind me. He was as clumsy at the whole thing as I was, so I immediately recognized he was a cop. I didn't recognize it until he got in his car. I wasn't sensitive enough, but he wasn't at all subtle about how he tried to follow me."

Scully had a friend along, an Oriental philosophy student who had been the first person to give Tim marijuana, back in the uncomplicated days when being shadowed by a federal agent was something that happened on TV, not in real life. Both were aghast until it dawned on them: we haven't done anything illegal. Yet. There was no law against driving around in a Sunshine cookie truck full of legal chemicals. But unless they shook off the surveillance—which was not the easiest thing to accomplish in a big yellow truck—they could kiss their fifteen thousand dollars goodbye.

Scully pulled off the road and began studying road maps of the Bay Area: "We decided San Jose was the place to lose them because that was the town that had the most roads going in and out of it. We figured they only had a limited number of cars, so if we could lose them for just a few minutes, then we could pick up one of the roads going out of town and get away." They sailed into San Jose as rush hour began, beat a light just as it turned red, made a few quick turns and motored on without mishap to Denver, where Scully rented a house with a basement and attached garage, just off the park, across from the zoo.

When the lab was operational, he went to Owsley to get the promised lysergic monohydrate. But Owsley put him off, saying the time wasn't right. In fact what had happened was this: fearing that they might be busted, Melissa had stashed the precious lysergic monohydrate in a safe deposit box in Arizona under a phony name, and now she couldn't remember what the name was. They had tried everything, including hypnosis, to no avail.

But Owsley didn't tell Scully that. Instead he handed him a 3 × 5 card with several lines of notes. This was the next step, he assured Scully, the superdrug they had been waiting for. All Tim had to do was figure out how to synthesize it.

In time, the next step would acquire a name, STP, and a reputation: "Like being shot out of a gun. There's no slowing down or backing up. You feel like your brakes have given out . . ."

But the appearance of STP properly belongs to a part of our story known as the Summer of Love, which was what the fog-bound summer of 1967 was called, when one hundred thousand kids descended on the Haight. And for an instant it seemed the psychedelic wave would sweep the continent, from sea to shining sea. But then the waters receded, leaving behind the usual debris, plus a bitter aftertaste for what had almost been.

By the time the Summer of Love was over, so was the psychedelic dream.

24

THE NEXT STEP

Although the Summer of Love officially began on June 21, the summer solstice, its actual beginning occurred the previous fall, specifically on October 6, 1966, the day the California law making possession of LSD a misdemeanor went into effect.

Declaring that the long arm of the State was reaching into their psyches, the hippies welcomed the new law with a sort of Boston tea party—plenty of drugs, free food, and music—which took place in a narrow strip of park paralleling Haight Street known as the Panhandle. The get-together had a name, the Love Pageant Rally, and to everyone's surprise and delight, several thousand extravagantly garbed hippies turned out, prompting one middle-aged tourist to remark to a local journalist: "Why, you don't see anything like this in Philadelphia."

Nor, discounting the Trips Festival, which already seemed ancient history, had anything like it been seen in San Francisco before. For the first time, surrounded by fellow freaks, it dawned on the hippies that their ruling fantasy might really be correct, that the evolutionary tides might really be flowing in their direction. Perhaps it was a consequence of all the LSD, but from the Love Pageant on, a naive optimism permeated the Haight, combined with a mystical faith that whatever was needed would be provided. Almost overnight the Haight found itself with its own newspaper, the San Francisco *Oracle,* its own police force, the Hells Angels, and its own radio station, KMPX, whose lobby usually included a hippie or two in full lotus; its own Chamber of Commerce in the HIP merchants and its own social workers in the Diggers. And there was talk of a hip employment agency, a hip hotel, and a hip cafeteria that would serve food grown on communal farms run by hippies tired of the urban grind.

Everyone was on the lookout for portents. One night Allen Cohen, a man of considerable stature due to the fact that he was one of Owsley's dealers, dreamed of a newspaper with rainbows all over it. Cohen described his vision to the Thelin brothers, who ran the Psychedelic Shop, and they agreed, to the tune of several thousand dollars, that it would be nice to have a rainbow-colored newspaper that concerned itself with the true inside story, meaning the true inner story, as opposed to an objective recitation of who did what, when and where. And thus was the *Oracle* born.

At its peak the *Oracle* enjoyed press runs of one hundred thousand, came sprayed with jasmine, contained informative columnists like the Gossipping Guru and the Babbling Bodhisattva, and was read in such far-flung capitals as Moscow, where the *Liberary Gazette* was a subscriber. "The text floats up the page in bubbles," wrote a reviewer in *Editor & Publisher.* "Or it pours in fountains. Colors blush over the page." And those little bubbles were not what one normally associated with journalism. Under Cohen's editorship, the *Oracle* specialized in an idiosyncratic form of philosophical commentary. For example: when one of the local drug dealers was murdered, Cohen didn't bother with the usual police blotter angle. Instead he offered "a poetic invocation of some of the forces that were involved in the crime."

Had Cohen ever offered a poetic invocation of some of the forces at work in the Haight, he might have divided the subject into various scenes, meaning various milieus: there was the music scene circling around the various bands; the sacramental scene involving the acid chemists like Owsley; the mercantile scene of the HIP merchants; the pedagogical scene that happened whenever two hippies got together, although it had more formal venues like the Free University and Happening House; the hang loose scene that took place every sunny day on Hippie Hill near the Golden Gate's tennis courts. And holding all these scenes together was a curious kind of meta-scene, the ritual scene. If the Love Pageant Rally imparted any lesson, it was that the private revolution needed some regular form of community ritual in order to progress. What forms these rituals assumed varied according to what group was running them. Chet Helms and the Family Dog, for instance, specialized in large-scale dance happenings. The Love Conspiracy Commune preferred festivals—filter the local strawberry festival through a hippie sensibility and you will get some idea what these were like. And then there were the Diggers, who didn't specialize in any one type. The purpose of the Digger rituals was to keep the revolution on track, to prevent it from being co-opted. The Diggers, you could say, were the conscience of the Haight.

The first Diggers—the name originally belonged to a group of seventeenth-century religious communists who made the mistake of demanding access to the uncultivated land in Cromwellian England, and were exterminated—were actors. They belonged to a theatrical enterprise known as the San Francisco Mime Troupe, which performed a kind of political *commedia del' larte* wherever there was space for stage and audience. The Mime Troupe specialized in street theater, which was perhaps why a few of the company began to see the Haight as a wonderful context for a perpetual theater of the absurd.

The Diggers announced their presence in a series of anonymous broadsides that mocked the smell-the-flower fatuousness of so many of the hippies. Cosmic was fine, LSD was fine, they said, but when you came back down you still had to cope with outrageous rents and bad food and all the temptations of the established culture, particularly money. "Money lust is sickness," the broadsides said. "It kills perception . . . almost all of us were exposed to this disease in childhood, but dope and love are curing us." Not surprisingly, the HIP merchants were a frequent target of Digger critiques. "How long will you tolerate people [straight or hip] transforming your trip into cash?" And they even went so far as to picket one festival, the First Annual Love Circus, because admission was a steep $3.50.

From broadsides the Diggers progressed to street theater: the Birth and Death ritual, the New Year's Wail, the Invisible Circus, the Death of Money parade. This last, consisting of six pallbearers wearing enormous papier-mâché animal heads and carrying a black-draped coffin down Haight Street, was a spectacle worthy of the surrealists. Gradually, however, the Diggers began talking less and doing more. They set up shop in an old garage known as the Free Frame of Reference, which was a reference to the huge yellow frame that they lugged around, largely so they could make the pointed joke of inviting onlookers to "step into our frame of reference now." They opened a Free Store that was full of cast-off clothes and housewares scrounged in daily forays around San Francisco. And the goods really were free. More than one Samaritan watched in astonishment as the Diggers, after ceremoniously accepting a contribution, proceeded to light their cigarettes with it. And if anyone demanded to see the person in charge, the Diggers always replied, "You are!"

The Diggers made their most substantial contribution, however, with the food feeds. Every afternoon at 4 P.M. their Dodge truck arrived in the Panhandle loaded with big aluminum garbage cans of soup, the fruits of the sort of artful hustling that the Beats had perfected back in the Fifties.

Guaranteed at least one square meal a day, with clothes on their back and dope in their pockets, the hippies were ready for . . . the next step.

That's how it was usually referred to, just an oblique reference to the next step. Remember the feeling of giddy anticipation that had swept over Millbrook leading the Castalians to believe they were increments away from finding the formula for Enlightenment, recall the frissons of imminent breakthrough that had permeated La Honda just before the Acid Test jelled—the same thing was now loose in the Haight.

And it was at this instant that Ken Kesey chose to reappear, back from the dead, or at least from Mexico, where he had spent the last seven months hiding out from the FBI at various coastal resort towns. He had snuck back across the border in Texas dressed as a cowboy. And then it was straight to San Francisco for a few public appearances that Kesey hoped would act as "salt in J. Edgar Hoover's wounds." One day he turned up at his old alma mater, the Stanford Writing Program, and delivered an impromptu lecture to an astonished class of would-be writers, before slipping away a few minutes ahead of the police. Another time he invited a reporter to a Prankster policy session and conducted an impromptu news conference, during which he made it clear that he had come back to deliver a message to the psychedelic movement. And this message was: it's time to go beyond LSD, time to take the next step.

According to Kesey, he had been throwing the *I-Ching* one night in Manzanilla, a resort town north of Guadalajara, when a sudden electrical storm had blown in from the Pacific. "What's next?" was the question Kesey had asked the *Ching*. "I can't spend the rest of my life eating frijoles and dodging *federales*. What should I do?" And before he could even consult the answering hexagram, "there was lightning everywhere and I pointed to the sky and lightning flashed and all of a sudden I had a second skin, of lightning, electricity, like a suit of electricity, and I knew it was in us to be superheroes and that we could become superheroes or nothing."

And from this epiphany, which, like all LSD illuminations was a little difficult to explain in real time, had come Kesey's latest fantasy, the Acid Test Graduation. A symbolic ritual that would prepare the way for the next step. The Pranksters would rent a space and put on an actual graduation ceremony, with valedictory orations from Cassady and Babbs, and authentic sheepskins, and when it was all over "the graduating acid heads will take off their caps and gowns and display next year's superhero costumes." Hopefully there would be six, maybe even seven thousand graduating acid heads, costumed from head to toe, and in the confusion Kesey would slip in, accept his diploma, and then slip away without attracting the notice of his pursuers, who were sure to be out in force.

It was a grand fantasy, and it might have come off if only Kesey had managed to elude capture for another two weeks. But on October

19 he was spotted and arrested after a short chase down the San Francisco freeway. For a time it looked like the judge might deny bail; he sat on the motion for five days before setting it at thirty thousand dollars, and then only after Kesey's lawyers had argued that their client had returned to America expressly to warn his young followers against using LSD. That was what the Acid Test Graduation was all about. Ken wants "to warn his young followers against drug use," his lawyers said. "He wants to tell the kids there is no purpose in taking drugs, and that it is dangerous until science finds out more about it." No mention was made of next year's superhero costumes.

This put Kesey in a delicate position, which was made even more delicate by his sudden love affair with the media. Everyone wanted a piece of the Kesey story. Camera crews came out to shoot him posed in front of his feverish bus; he did the talk shows, both TV and radio; he met with feature writers, among them a New York dandy named Tom Wolfe, who saw the Kesey story as a ribald cautionary tale of one artist's unique solution to Fitzgerald's classic puzzler: why aren't there any second acts in American literary careers. But then the mysto steam began hissing in Wolfe's head, and he realized that this was no common artist flirts with criminality story: it was a religious parable. It was "Tsong-Isha-pa and the *sangha* communion, Mani and the wan persecuted at the Gate . . . Gautama and the brethren in the wilderness leaving the blood-and-kin families of their pasts for the one true family of the *sangha* inner circle—in short, true mystic brotherhood—only in poor old Formica polyethelene 1960s America . . ."

At least Wolfe heard the mysto steam. Most of the reporters were completely at sea when Kesey began talking, in his soft country drawl, about waiting for a sign, waiting for the next step to be revealed. "I don't know what this is going to be in any way I could just spell out, but I know we've reached a certain point but we're not moving anymore, we're not creating anymore, and that's why we've got to move on to the next step," he told the press in one of his more candid moments.

Presumably Leary had a piece of it, and Kesey, and the hippies, and maybe some of the rock bands . . . the rumor was that the Beatles, the biggest mass marketing phenomenon of all time, were into LSD . . . all of them possessed a piece of the puzzle, and when the time came all the disparate players would be drawn together and . . . the next step.

The hippies wanted to believe this desperately. But what was Kesey doing putting down LSD in the pages of the *Chronicle?* And what did he mean when he talked about going beyond acid? Give it up altogether? That was the Establishment's line and the Establishment had Kesey by the proverbial testicles, what with three felony counts. The Haight hummed with speculation, much of it paranoid. According to the leading paranoiacs, Kesey's public statements were just a smokescreen. What he was planning was a monster Acid Test, the biggest and most powerful one ever, the group mind pushed to its omega point. And either the State would shatter or. . . . There was always a long pause as the implications of that sank in. Everyone had heard rumors that the Acid Test had turned fascistic down in LA. And hadn't Kesey actually said on TV, when asked what his main message for the graduating acidheads would be, hadn't he quipped: "Never trust a Prankster!" What kind of a valedictory was that?

The feeling grew that it was immaterial whether Kesey was correct or not about going beyond acid to the next step; the point was that the Acid Graduation might wreck the Haight, the Psychedelic movement, the private revolution, everything. And for the first time, the Pranksters began to lose control of their movie. The Graduation was scheduled to take place October 31, Halloween, in Bill Graham's Winterland, but at the last moment Graham, who had produced the Trips Festival, reneged: Kesey was another Elmer Gantry, he said. The Pranksters raced around looking for another venue, but finally had to settle for an old abandoned pie factory down on Harriet Street. Few hippies turned up and most of those melted away before the finale, having come largely so that they could tell any future friends that, yeah, they made the Prankster scene once or twice. Kesey was there in ballet tights and at the end he pulled everyone in close, huddled them together, Faye, the kids, the Pranksters, some of the old Perry Lane crowd, and for one last time they synched up and tried to . . . *Homo gestalt!*

And then, to the strains of "Pomp and Circumstance," they graduated. But whether it was to the next step or not, no one knew.

The hippies, at the last moment, rejected Kesey and his superhero fantasy. And while part of this denial was certainly a legitimate wariness of the Pranksters' infatuation with control, part of it was also selfishness. Despite the rhetoric of "no leaders," the Haight was not without its status quo, its hierarchies of prestige, as one writer put it, and it was these elements who were most alarmed by the sudden reappearance of the Pranksters. Although they were as committed as anyone to the concept of the next step, they were understandably reluctant to ruin what was becoming a very comfortable and, in some cases, a very lucrative scene.

All this made the Prankster Graduation one of those pivotal moments that you find in myths, when the hero fails a crucial test because he lacks faith; when, to put it psychologically, his old conditioning reasserts itself and he turns away from the one thing he must do. And it is problematic whether the opportunity will ever arise again.

It was something Tim Leary would have understood had he been on the West Coast. Had he been there, he might have told the story of the time in India when he had met the holy man on the bank of the Ganges and had fled, only to realize later he had met the Buddha and had run away. There were times, Leary might have counseled, when you just had to go with the flow, and trust the great god of synchronicities to make sure everything worked out.

Certainly that's the course Leary was following. Instead of lowering his profile while his legal appeals worked their way through the judicial system, Tim was actually more visible than ever. He had shaken off his beleaguered prophet pose—it wasn't a respectable way to play the ancient game—and he had come to the realization that if jail was an inevitability, then one might as well play the final scenes with zest and cunning.

The time for playing the science game was over. The psychedelic movement was now in a legal and political phase, which meant that the sly man countered with the religion game.

In late September 1966 Leary announced that he was forming a psychedelic religion, henceforth known as the League for Spiritual Discovery. Never one to flub a media opportunity, he made this announcement at a formal press conference at the New York Advertising Club. "Like every great religion of the past we seek to find the divinity within and to express this revelation in a life of glorification and the worship of God," he told the hastily scribbling journalists. "These ancient goals we define in the metaphor of the present—turn on, tune in, drop out."

Turn on, tune in, drop out. Within months every hippie and most of their parents were familiar with that little enigmatic jingle, which had come to Leary one morning in the shower, a gift of his unconscious. But what did it mean, particularly that last, drop out? Ralph Metzner urged Tim to amend it to "turn on, tune in, drop out, and come back." But Tim had just laughed at that. "Oh that's your trip," he'd said, a gibe at Metzner's recent rapprochement with the mainstream psychology. No, ToTiDo meant exactly what Leary said it did at the New York Advertising Club: "Turn on means to go beyond your secular tribal mind to contact the many levels of divine energy which lie within your consciousness; tune in means to express and to communicate your new revelations in visible acts of glorification, gratitude and beauty; drop out means to detach yourself harmoniously, tenderly and gracefully from worldly commitments until your entire life is dedicated to worship and search."

At the close of the press conference, Leary announced that the League's first "public worship service" would be held that very night at the Village Theater, in New York's East Village. Instead of prayer meetings or sermons or Acid Tests, Tim had come up with a psychedelic mystery play loosely based on Herman Hesse's *Steppenwolf*. Its official title was *Death of the Mind* and it starred Ralph Metzner as Harry, a typically neurotic New Yorker. For most of the play Harry lay, writhed and danced behind a scrim, lost in the metaphorical depths of an LSD trip. A booming bass drum symbolized his heartbeat, while above the scrim images of what he was experiencing flashed upon a screen. Leary sat stage front, dressed all in white, patiently intoning the classic words of the psychedelic guide: "Relax, float downstream, trust your divinity, trust your energy processes."

Eight hundred people caught opening night, netting the League a swift twenty-four hundred dollars. That sort of profitability aroused the Hollywood agents, and there was talk of a movie deal.

Reactions to *Death of the Mind* varied. *Time* printed a review in its Show Business section that described it as "religioso gimmicks, weirdo music, sexo fantasy, all boffo." Abbie Hoffman, the future founder of the Yippies who at the time was a New York street politician of fairly Marxist persuasion, caught the show at the Village Gate and was impressed with Leary's "karmic salesmanship" but not his message. "Leary and I had many a run-in," Hoffman later wrote. "I would argue that he was creating a group of blissed out pansies ripe for annihilation and Leary would just flash a big grin and laugh a lot." Naturally Hoffman tried LSD, and while he didn't agree with Tim that it was going to wipe out injustice, he had to acknowledge its power as an organizing tool: "Taking acid created a feeling of definite separation from those who had not. To this day, on some level, I still don't trust people who have not opened themselves up enough for the experience."

Robert Anton Wilson, who had interviewed Tim during those first balmy months at Millbrook, caught the show in Chicago and was appalled. "It seemed that a brilliant scientist had turned himself into a second rate Messiah." But then Anton Wilson, who was an editor at *Playboy*, lunched with Tim and was forced to revise his assessment: "Tim was more turned-on, vibrant, joyous and grandiose than ever, but he also had even more sense of humor than previously and kept poking fun at his guru act. Neither of us said it aloud, but it was understood that much of Tim's current persona was just agitprop for the one cause he really believed in: the possibility that LSD, wisely used by professionals, could reprogram enough nervous systems to accelerate consciousness and intelligence before we laid ourselves and our planet to waste."

Anton Wilson, at one point during the lunch, raised the spectre of Wilhelm Reich, who had started out as one of Freud's most brilliant and iconoclastic pupils, and who had ended up dead in a Maine prison hospital, for running afoul of the FDA. Leary was unimpressed with the parallel. "I fully expect to live past the hysteria and persecution," he told Wilson, "till everything I've claimed is confirmed and accepted, till it becomes dull truism. But then I'll be espousing some new heresy I hope, and be in hot water again."

Perhaps the toughest critic to catch *Death of the Mind* was Diana

Trilling, who attended with husband Lionel. They were spotted by a celebrity-conscious reporter from the New York *Times,* who compared them to "atheists attending a religious ritual out of sociological interest . . . (their) expressions faintly tinged with boredom and distaste." But Trilling's distaste did not obscure her critical talents, and her published account of the evening caught a number of nuances that the others missed. In particular, she saw through Leary's bumptious exterior to his fatigue. He was "a weary impresario, a weary pedagogue, a weary Messiah" who wore "the pale but indelible marks of doom."

Events, Trilling sensed, were spinning out of control, despite Tim's optimistic claims of "having a blueprint for change." Leary the intellectual had been absorbed by Leary the performer. "When he takes the microphone in his hand, one feels it is a natural extension of his infatuate ego and that it will more and more become his staff and his role, his auxiliary drug, his surrogate selfhood."

But what really bothered Trilling, even more than the speciousness of Leary's monologue—"it creates the illusion of coherence, it seems to proceed reasonably enough; it is only when one applies oneself to it that it eludes the grasp"—was the quality of follower he was attracting:

> Young, village, but middle-class, good contemporary faces of the kind one wants to trust, the faces of people to whom intellectual leadership might be thought appropriate, except that they had made another choice and the signal of it was in their eyes. The four of us appeal to each other: Is it only the gifted who go in for this sort of thing? Are these the best, the brightest, of their generation?

It was a troubling thought. Was Leary skimming the cream of a generation? Was that why he could confidently predict that in ten years America would be a totally psychedelic society, and why he dismissed so cavalierly the growing evidence that LSD was causing some psychotic breakdowns? Were these kids, wondered Trilling, "simply casualties of the new dispensation, eggs that had to be broken to make Dr. Leary's omelette"?

That was the serious interpretation. The cynical interpretation had it that Leary had thought up the League in order to generate some quick cash for his legal expenses. And there was some truth to this. But the League was also a shrewd move given the recent criminalization of LSD. In 1964 the Supreme Court of California had affirmed that members of the Native American Church could use peyote in their religious ceremonies, thus establishing a slim precedent for other psychedelic-based religions.

But was the League for Spiritual Discovery the next step? The hippies thought not. They found the Leary roadshow, which didn't arrive in San Francisco until January 1967, entirely boring. *Float down-stream? Turn off the mind?* How tame. At least Kesey had understood the need to . . . explode! Tim Leary was just a middle-aged publicity seeker who hadn't come to terms with his own conditioning. He was a Harvard professor who had taken LSD. He was a drag. (He was also the victim of the same jealous paranoia that had sunk Kesey and the Acid Gradua-tion.) The private revolution did not need any self-appointed guru telling it what to do. They would find the next step on their own, thank you.

And, surprisingly, they did. They called it the Gathering of the Tribes for the First Human Be-In, and whatever else it might have been, it was first and foremost a party of magnificent proportions. Three thousand were expected, over twenty thousand came, approximately one-fortieth of the greater San Francisco area, jammed into a section of the Golden Gate known as the Polo Field. Weekend hipsters. Teeny-boppers in tight jeans and Mexican blouses. Berkeley radicals looking slightly uncomfortable in their politically correct workshirts and boots. Even a few aging beatniks with their bongos. But mostly there were hippies, looking as though they had ransacked the prop room of a particularly cheesy summer theater, wandering around in serapes and desert robes and Victorian petticoats and paisly bodystockings, be-decked with bells and flowers, young boys with nasturtiums wagging from their ears and at least one gray-haired grandmother with a rose tied to her cane.

Helen Perry came to the Be-In wearing a silver bell. A middle-aged sociologist best known for her biography of American psychiatrist Harry Stack Sullivan, Perry had been living in the Haight for several months, studying its peculiar rituals. Later she came to see the Be-In as the moment when she ceased being an impartial observer and became "an initiate into this new society, this new religion . . . Sounds and sights turned me on, so that I had the sensation of dreaming. The air seemed heady and mystical. Dogs and children pranced around in blissful aban-don, and I became aware of a phenomenon that still piques my curiosity: the dogs did not get into fights and the children did not cry."

It was the Love Pageant Rally writ large, which was appropriate since the Be-In, like so many things in the Haight, had its origin in the exuberance that had followed the banning of LSD. Allen Cohen had been standing with Michael Bowen, artist and agent for a curious militia known as the Psychedelic Rangers, and both had been marveling at the size of the crowd. "We should hold another of these real soon," Cohen had said. "Yeah but next time I'll bet we could get ten times the people," predicted Bowen. But a better name was needed. Love Pageant Rally didn't capture the essential quality. They were pondering this dilemma when Richard Alpert wandered up. What should we call these things, Cohen had asked. And Alpert, after a moment of sage reflection, had observed that it was a gathering of Human Beings being together. To which Bowen had replied, "a Human Be-In."

That had been in early October. By late December the Be-In had acquired an irresistible momentum. And its governing concept had changed. It was no longer simply human beings being together, but a gathering of the tribes, a hip pow wow that would attempt, once and for all, to unite the activists and the hippies and anyone else who wanted to join the future. At least that's what the official Be-In press release proclaimed. "The night of bruited fear of the American eagle-breast-body is over," it said. "Hang your fear at the door and join the future. If you do not believe please wipe your eyes and see."

Although future Be-Ins would be occasions for considerable media pontification—comparisons to medieval carnivals and Hitler Youth Rallies were popular—the coverage that first afternoon was thin. The man from the *Examiner,* perhaps irritated at having to work on such an exquisite Saturday, described what took place as "a living fever dream." "All the high priests turned out in their costumes to be stared at," he wrote. "Many of those staring were dogs." Although dismissive, at least the *Examiner* appreciated the novelty of the Be-In, something that could not be said for his colleague from the *Chronicle.* HIPPIES RUN WILD, read that paper's morning-after headline.

But they hadn't, really. They sat and listened to the poetry, they danced to the Grateful Dead, they craned their necks to get a better look at Timothy Leary, they jeered when someone cut the trunk cord from the main generator, silencing the stage, and they cheered when the power was restored and the MC, a local character optimistically named Buddha, announced that "this generator is now protected by the Hells Angels." Perhaps it was all the pot and LSD that gave the day its mystical bouquet, but for a few hours everyone felt at peace, even the activists; for a few hours the constituencies of Jerry Rubin, Allen Ginsberg, Timothy Leary, the Grateful Dead, Dick Gregory, even the *roshi* from the local Zendo, were one. Robed figures moved through the crowd with paper bags of Owsley acid, while a contingent of students from San Francisco State manned a booth marked LSD RESCUE, ready to guide any unfortunate bad tripper through his misery. The Diggers handed out free turkey sandwiches, while mountainous Hells Angels strode through the crowd, walkie-talkies dangling from their studded belts. The Angels were handling security, which meant they spent most of their time entertaining children who had wandered away from their parents and were now panicking. What a sight: the hardest outlaw bikers in the free world clowning around on the ground like old Day

Care pros, while over the PA boomed messages like: "The Hells Angels have a little girl here next to the platform and she has curly hair. She says her name is Mary. She wants to see her mother."

Perhaps because the speakers were alotted only seven minutes, no rhetorical heights were scaled. A poet named Robert Baker received gusts of applause when he recited a parody of "The Night Before Christmas," with each line referring to either marijuana or LSD. Ginsberg contributed a short rhyme—"Peace in your heart dear, peace in the park here"—and McClure recited a long alliterative play on the line, "this is it, and it is all perfect." Even Tim Leary, despite fears that he might be a tad too professorial, kept it short. "We want to get western man out of the cities and back into the tribes and villages," he had said, speaking tentatively into the microphone. And then he had paused to absorb the spectacle, those twenty thousand tripping human beings, *Homo gestalt,* citizens of *Island,* apostolic vanguard of a process that might actually be encoded in the genes, written into the DNA. What could he possibly tell them that they hadn't already intuited in their first flash of LSD clairvoyance. So he had abandoned his prepared speech and after leading the crowd in "tune in, turn on, drop out," had sat down and spent the rest of the afternoon playing pattycake with a little girl.

At one point Ginsberg, not quite trusting the aroma of inevitability wafting up from the field, turned to Ferlinghetti and whispered, "What if we're all wrong."

But it didn't feel that way. It felt as if they were riding a high and beautiful wave. As one of the *Oracle* columnists said, they were the Lovebeast slouching toward Bethlehem. "In seven or eight years," Richard Alpert confidently predicted to a reporter for the LA *Free Press,* "the psychedelic population of the U.S. will be able to vote anybody into office they want to. Allen Ginsberg? Sure. Allen is a very smart guy and Allen is a master politician . . . imagine what it would be like to have anybody in high political office with our understanding of the universe. I mean, let's just imagine that Bobby Kennedy had a fully expanded consciousness. Just imagine him, in his position, what he would be able to do."

The Be-In produced a glow that infected everyone. But it also left them puzzled. If the Be-In was the next step, then what did it mean?

To explore this dilemma, the *Oracle* convened a council of elders— Tim Leary, Allen Ginsberg, Gary Snyder, Alan Watts—on Alan Watts's houseboat in Sausalito Bay. The proposition under consideration was whether the counterculture should "drop out," as Leary urged, or "take over," as Ginsberg and Snyder believed. Ginsberg in particular hoped that a further rapprochement could be brought about between the hippies and the activists. He based this on his recent experiences on the college campuses of the Midwest; for he had sensed an extraordinary latency in the students who turned out to hear him by the thousands. Even in the Midwest the kids were restless, dissatisfied, waiting for something—the next step?—something that the leaders of this Unspoken Thing might turn to their advantage, with a little LSD and the right set and setting.

Gary Snyder agreed with Ginsberg, provided the activists could be "brought around to a more profound vision of themselves and society." But Leary couldn't have been more scornful. Why waste time with the activists, he argued, they're obsolete. "They are repeating the same dreary quarrels and conflicts for power of the thirties and the forties, of the trade union movement, of Trotskyism and so forth. I think they should be sanctified, drop out, find their own center, turn on, and above all avoid mass movements, mass leadership, mass followers."

But what does drop out really mean, Ginsberg wanted to know. To the activists it meant "a lot of freak-out hippies goofing around and throwing bottles through windows when they flip out on LSD." But what did Tim mean when he said, as he had at the Be-In, tune in, turn on, drop out?

What did Tim think the next step was?

Leary didn't have to think about it. For months he had had a vision of thousands of small tribal communities spread across the globe, patterned after Millbrook, taking no part in "the plastic robot Establishment. . . . I can envision ten MIT scientists, with their families, they've taken LSD . . . They've wondered about the insane-robot-television show of MIT. They drop out. They may get a little farm out in Lexington, near Boston. They may use their creativity to make some new kinds of machines that will turn people on instead of bomb them."

That might be fine for MIT scientists, said Snyder. But what about the others, the kids who had no idea how to build a house or grow a vegetable garden. You couldn't just go out and do these things; you had to learn how first. "Like we've gotta learn to do a lot of things we've forgotten to do," Snyder said. Even Tim agreed with that. Academies would have to be set up. Or perhaps they already existed. Wasn't the Haight like a big school anyway? What if they made it even more so? It would be like a big launching pad. Kids would drop out, come to the Haight for a few months, and then fan out to one of the rural communes that were already starting to appear. . . .

In a few years we'll be two species, Leary declared. One was the anthill. "It's run like a beehive with queens—or kings—and it'll all be television . . . and sexuality will become very promiscuous and almost impersonal. Because in an anthill it always turns out that way. But you're gonna have another species who inevitably will survive, and that will be the tribal people, who won't have to worry about leisure because when you drop out then the real playwork begins. Because then you have to, as Gary says, learn how to take care of yourself."

But Snyder disagreed, this time laughingly. Mankind wasn't splitting into two species; it was becoming one. "The children of the ants are all going to be tribal people," he said. "That's why it's going to work. We're going to get the kids, and it's going to take about three generations." The psychedelic movement was merely accelerating a change that was already under way. You saw it in automation and cybernation, in the advent of the affluent leisure society, in the widespread interest in spirituality and the contemplative technologies of the Orient. People were going to simplify their lives, predicted Snyder. The consumer society was going to fade away. And when that happened all the energy that had gone into acquiring things would be redirected. Instead of playing with his adult toys, the new man would play with his mind, with states of consciousness, levels of sensitivity.

What a vision! An evolution not a revolution. Three generations. And it was all starting now. Or at least this was the crucial moment, the pivot upon which the fate of the smart monkey hinged, forward to paradise, backward to the nuclear abyss. That's the way it felt. A mixture of exhilaration and exhaustion. Could they pull it off?

"Hey Leary," Ginsberg asked after they had basked for a few minutes in the Be-In glow, "what're you going to do when this is all over?" Leary laughed. "Live on a beach somewhere, take LSD once a week, and have babies," he said. "What about you Watts?" "I'm going to continue as a pontifex. A bridge-builder between two worlds: the world of the people who are anxious and concerned and square and think that they can use their will to put things right . . . and the world of the dropout. I'm going to stay bang in the middle and I'm going to learn the languages of both tribes." "And you Ginsberg?" "Oh, buy some land with a congenial group of friends—my tribe—and just fiddle around with manuscripts and go walking in the woods and then rush off and take a plane to India."

To the readers of that issue of the *Oracle,* the next step was clear: invite the world to the Haight-Ashbury for a Summer of Love.

25

IT CAME FROM INNER SPACE

When an idea struck the hippies as being implacably right, it had a way of spreading like brushfire, which is only to say that whenever true inspiration hit, it was quickly fed out along the synapses of the group mind, making the atmosphere even more cosmic than usual.

Portents . . . visions . . . fifty thousand, maybe even a hundred thousand true brothers (and sisters, of course) all grokking together for the summer, then returning home to the Poughkeepsies and Oshkoshes of America with word that a new vision had been glimpsed, out in California, the first since Emerson, the next step!

Snyder had predicted it would take three generations; the hippies planned on doing it in three months.

An organizing committee sprang up, the Council for the Summer of Love, to coordinate logistics. With an estimated fifty thousand kids coming to the party, some serious planning was required. One group began working on future Be-Ins, which were scheduled for the vernal equinox and the summer solstice, and others tackled the problems of part-time work (the Hip Job Coop) and free legal counsel (HALO—the Haight Ashbury Legal Organization). The Diggers, perhaps because they had the weightiest reputation when it came to getting things done, were delegated the problems of food and housing. They announced that by summer they would have at least one free restaurant in operation, and possibly even a free hotel, if karma smiled on their negotiations for the Reno, a five hundred-room transient hotel in San Francisco's skid row. They were also scouting ghost towns out in the eastern California desert ("hippie Hoovervilles"), and needed "tools, lumber, tarpaper and cement" for the free farm they had just acquired in Sonoma, on Lou Gottlieb's Morningstar ranch.

It was an impressive and very American display of energy—you could almost imagine Mickey Rooney as a Digger. The hippies had that same "let's put on a show" naive idealism, only in real time, not movie time, which meant that they encountered certain problems that were usually finessed in the Hollywood versions of the American dream. Mainly money. The only people in the Haight who had excess cash were the rock bands, the acid chemists, and the HIP merchants, and while the first two tithed generously (as well as providing the twin sacraments of LSD and rock music) it was felt that the HIP merchants were foot dragging in their commitment to the next step. It was bad enough that they were commercializing the private revolution, selling boutique beads and patched blue jeans at Fifth Avenue prices, but now they were exhibiting all the symptoms of money sickness. The Diggers began a campaign to nationalize the HIP merchants. In February they issued a broadside urging them to lower their prices and become nonprofit, profit-sharing collectives. The unamused owners of Wild Colors, a hippie craftstore, hung the following letter in their front window:

> Dear Diggers: This store grosses about $2000 a month. Of that about $1500 goes to the nearly 100 local artists and craftsmen who sell their work here.
> Of the remaining $500, about $250 goes for rent, utilities, advertising and many other business expenses.
> Of the remaining $250, at least $50 goes to pay for shoplifted merchandise. The remaining $200 is what my partner and I live on. That works out to about 45¢ an hour.
> Why do we do it? Because love is more important to us than money.

But others, notably the Psychedelic Shop, agreed with the Diggers and announced they were going public, shares would be available for any hippie who wanted to invest. Now the Thelins were absolutely sincere in their belief that this was the appropriate direction for hip capitalism to take, but most cynics couldn't help but register the fact that the Psych Shop was also $6000 in debt—since opening the calm center in the back, they'd been forced to curtail store hours, and that was easing them toward bankruptcy. But their gesture was warmly received. "Instead of sickly exploiting the hip community, they're healthily living in it," congratulated a Communications Company broadside. (ComCo, the inspiration of former beat novelist, Chester Anderson, functioned as a sort of instant newspaper, filling the leisurely gaps between one issue of the *Oracle* and the next.) "Be advised."

It was only two words, that "be advised," but it added a new element to the Haight, a certain frisson of *conform or else*; as the private revolution hardened into the hippie personality, it was losing some of its graceful tolerance.

One reason this was happening was because the Haight-Ashbury was about to undergo an ambiguous fifteen minutes of fame as the most notorious streetcorner in the world. Every national magazine and major newspaper in the country would send a reporter to do a standard "I Was a Hippie for a Day" story. Some, like the *Chronicle*'s man, stayed undercover for a couple of weeks, and Washington *Post* reporter Nicholas Von Hoffman took in the whole three-act play that summer. But most donned blue jeans and a paisley shirt and spent a day or two standing around outside the Drugstore, trying not to sound like a narcotics agent, asking things like, "Why do you wear your hair so long?" *Because I think I'm beautiful.* "Why are your clothes so colorful?" *Because I have self-respect. Say, have you ever stopped to think that writing STOP on a sign is a pretty silly way to communicate that concept? It'd be much better if stop signs had God's eyes on them, don't you think. People would stop for God's eyes.* And so on, until you asked how he knew what God's eyes looked like, and he'd wink and say, "cause I looked into them, baby."

There was something about the psychedelic temperament that couldn't resist baiting the straights. They were so nervous about life; all you had to do was walk up to them on the street and hand them a flower and they'd freak, as though you'd just given them a joke flower that was about to spray them with *eau de deviant.* Perhaps the best put-on, the grandest, was the Great Banana Conspiracy, which first broke in the Berkeley *Barb* that March. A new psychedelic had been discovered, the *Barb* reported, one anyone could obtain, since the only ingredient was dried banana peel. Dry the peel, scrape off the inner portion, and smoke it. The high, according to cognoscenti quoted in the *Barb,* was comparable to opium, with some nice psilocybin shadings.

From the *Barb* the banana hoax bounced to the wire services and thence across the country. Students held banana smoke-ins and grocery stores experienced a repeat of the run on morning glory seeds a few years earlier, as scraggly young kids began appearing at the checkout counters with carts full of bananas. Was America going to have to ban the banana? Or require licenses before people could buy them? A congressman from New Jersey jokingly introduced two new acts to Congress: the Banana Labeling Act of 1967 and the Banana and Other Odd Fruit Disclosure and Reporting Act of 1967. But not everyone was laughing. United Fruit was more than a little alarmed. They asked Sidney Cohen to find out whether bananas really were hallucinogenic, a question that the FDA also was taking very seriously. And after a lengthy and sober evaluation, it was announced that bananas were good sources of potassium and fiber, and definitely not hallucinogenic.

When it came to the hippies, the country alternated between "we are amused" and "we are not amused." A hippie is someone who "dresses like Tarzan, has hair like Jane, and smells like Cheetah," quipped the newly elected governor of California, Ronald Reagan, while in another speech he described the Bay Area as a hotbed of evil that he intended to stamp out. *Look* described the archetypical hippie pad as "a filthy litter strewn swarming dope fortress that was a great deal less savory and sanitary than a sewer," while *Time* praised its occupants as leading "considerably more virtuous lives than the great majority of their fellow citizens. This, despite their blatant disregard for most of society's accepted mores and many of its laws—most notably those prohibiting the use of drugs." But others detected, in their talk of pushing evolution and creating a new Man, the aroma of fascism. The hippies are a "fascistic reservoir" because "they are a rootless community that makes a fetish of having no leaders [and thus] may easily be mobilized by an unscrupulous leader." On the surface this appeared to be a contradiction, but it did touch upon something that the private revolution hadn't considered: so far the Haight had lacked leaders precisely because people like Kesey, Ginsberg, and Snyder refused to play that role; the real test would come when leaders who were eager to play that role emerged. Would they be rejected, or would the hippies, their internal compasses skewed by the drugs, follow like a slavish mob? Writing in the *Nation,* poet Karl Shapiro described the hippies as the "perfect cultural broth for fascism. The Beat people had a marginal politick and a sense of community; their drug was weed. The new generation has no need of politick or community or poetry. They have acid."

But how much acid they had no one knew. The Los Angeles *Times,* a week after the Be-In, estimated that one hundred thousand doses were sold each week in the Haight, most to out-of-town buyers. FDA director Goddard, pressed by Congress to get to the bottom of the illicit LSD trade, wrote that there was still no reliable information as to how much LSD was actually being consumed, but between May 1, 1966, and April 30, 1967, the Bureau of Drug Abuse Control had seized approximately 1.6 million doses, had arrested ninety-four people, and had an additional 460 investigations under way. To illustrate the magnitude of the problem facing the country, Goddard related the following anecdote: On March 31, a 1958 International Harvester truck with cab and insulated van had been stopped by the Colorado Highway Patrol near the Utah border. The truck matched the description of a truck that had been observed in Craig, Colorado, in the vicinity of a drugstore that was burglarized. A search warrant was obtained and in the cab the police found a plastic bag containing 800 milligrams of LSD. Further poking uncovered additional vials of LSD and DMT. But the real surprise came when they opened the back doors and looked inside: the trailer was full of lab equipment. It was a mobile LSD lab.

There were the usual fulminations against LSD as a dry rot in the American soul and the usual symposiums of experts asking themselves why the kids of America were rejecting the time-honored stimulants of their parents. Sociologist Kenneth Kenniston attributed it to "psychological numbing." Part of the price of living in an advanced industrial society, he explained, was a deadening of the senses. "Our experiences lack vividness, three dimensionality and intensity. Above all, we feel trapped or shut in our own subjectivity." The hippies were using LSD as "a chemical sledgehammer for breaking out of [their] shell," Kenniston wrote, and while he deplored the means, he couldn't help but acknowledge the legitimacy of the search.

But that didn't console the San Francisco city fathers. Drug abuse was costing the city an estimated thirty-five thousand dollars a month; since the beginning of the year San Francisco General had been seeing an average of four bad LSD trips a day, many of them runaway adolescents barely out of puberty; and in two years the city-wide venereal disease rate had risen by a factor of six. The Haight was an open sore, and now these misguided deviants had the chutzpah to invite the youth of America to join them in a summer-long orgy of drugtaking and loitering. Mayor Shelley, in March, issued a statement that said, in effect, not in my city, you don't. "I am strongly opposed to any encouragement of a summer influx of indigent young people who are apparently being led to believe by a certain element of society that their vagrant presence will be tolerated in this city," said the mayor.

A few days later a platoon of health inspectors descended on the Haight, accompanied by a full complement of reporters. No doubt they were expecting a confirmation of filth and degradation thesis, since the adjective *dirty* had attached itself to the hippies like a birthmark. However, as public health director, Dr. Ellis D. ("LSD") Sox was forced to admit, "The situation is not as bad as we had thought." Of the fourteen hundred buildings examined, only sixty-four had violations, and only sixteen of those housed hippies.

But the raid presaged an increasingly active policy of official harassment. Police began daily raids in the Haight, sweeping the streets, demanding proof of age, arresting runaways, busting careless hippies for possession of pot and LSD, and in general wreaking havoc with the private revolution.

Paranoia, which was the shadow side of the kind of ecstatic energy that seemed to accompany prolonged LSD experimentation, began to build. A fascist putsch was being planned, went the whispers, every hippie in prison by July. "All spring the Haight shook with premonition," remembers Michael Rossman, "the airways of gossip were incessant with flashes of apocalypse . . . deep fear throbbed in the Haight."

As the Summer of Love approached, the Haight quivered in a contagion of first-night jitters.

* * *

Charles Perry, in his history of the Haight-Ashbury, describes the Haight in the summer of 1967 as "part old Calcutta with beggars squatting on the sidewalk, part football stadium crush, with people selling programs—the *Oracle,* the *Barb* and two new papers, the Haight-Ashbury *Tribune* and the Haight-Ashbury *Maverick."* The street scene was a visual equivalent to the posters Bill Graham was commissioning to advertise the Fillmore, a swirling, colorful anarchy whose bizarre calligraphy, indecipherable at first, soon became second nature. So it was with the Haight. What to outsiders appeared demented madness was perfectly clear to anyone who was *attuned.*

Take clothes. An astute observer could date the various hippie fauna just by the cut of their clothes. The earliest residents were dandies, partial to cowboy outfits and Edwardian rigs, complete with bowlers and canes. Then came the Day-Glo superhero collages that the Pranksters had pioneered, followed by the ethnic borrowings, the serapes and desert robes, the peasant blouses, the Tibetan prayer costumes. Standing on Haight Street during the Summer of Love, an astute observer could pick out the older hippies, moving like peacocks through a monotonous sea of gray sludge: faded denim was the dominant hue that summer, blending into the fog that came rolling up Haight Street, mingling with the garbage smell and the dirt, accentuating the loneliness and despair—by midsummer it was clear that the yin had arrived to balance out the yang of the Be-In glow.

Haight Street, said the *Oracle,* had become the "abstract vortex for an indefinable pilgrimmage . . . walking barefoot with hair askew, hand-made robes over torn blue jeans, the young people wander from noon until nearly two. Wandering aimlessly up Haight St., over to the free store at Carl and Cole, then back to Masonic for a cream pie and coke or to the Panhandle for Digger stew." And these wanderers weren't the true brothers of the post Be-In visions; rather they were the imitators that Bob Stubbs had warned about. They weren't beautiful, they had bad teeth and acne scars and it was easy to see they hadn't been voted homecoming king or queen back in Oshkosh or Biloxi, or wherever they'd come from. These kids were rejects; they'd come here because they were losers, and while that had a certain Christian appropriateness, it was not what the Council for the Summer of Love had expected. And along with the sheep came the usual complement of wolves, the hustlers and petty criminals. For the first time crimes other than shoplifting became a problem. One day Jerry Garcia was strolling down Haight Street when he came across a chilling ComCo bulletin:

> Pretty little 16-year-old-middle-class chick comes to the Haight to see what it's all about & gets picked up by a 17-year-old street dealer who spends all day shooting her full of speed again & again, then feeds her 3000 mikes & raffles off her temporarily unemployed

body for the biggest Haight Street gang bang since the night before last.

Garcia was amazed. Why would anyone print such a depressing piece of news? "That was the point," he recalls, "where I thought, this scene cannot survive with that in there. It just goes all wrong."

Complicating the problem were the tourists, who crawled down Haight Street, bumper to bumper, windows shut, doors locked, as though passing through one of those zoos where the animals roam free and it is the humans who're encaged. In March the Gray Line, a bus company that had operated a similar tour during the heyday of the beatniks, began advertising the Hippie Hop: for six dollars it would take ordinary Americans beyond the "bearded curtain," on the "only foreign tour within the continental limits of the United States. . . . Among the favorite pasttimes of the hippies, besides taking drugs, are parading and demonstrating, seminars and group discussions about what's wrong with the status quo; malingering; plus the ever-present preoccupation with the soul . . ."

The hippies devised various strategies to deflect this boorish scrutiny. At first they loped into the traffic and distributed mocking handbills which read, "Middle Class Brothers! Loosen Up, let God flow through you. Remember we are with you as you drive through the valley of the shadow of death." Then they discovered the mirror game. In one of their scrounges the Diggers came across a bin of broken mirrors. The next time the Gray Line buses arrived, the hippies ran alongside holding up mirrors to the windows so the tourists could take a good look at themselves. But then the Diggers thought up the walk-ins, which involved hundreds of people walking across the street in geometric patterns, snarling traffic for miles, and generally ending with the arrival of a vanload of police.

Then in early July a small riot broke out, as a group of frustrated hippies began jumping up and down on car bumpers, banging on hoods, terrifying the tourists. The police arrived, twenty carloads of them, and a fight broke out amid cries of "fascist bastards" and "police brutality." Although numerous bones were broken, the only fatality was a dog, clubbed to death by an overexcited policeman.

Malnutrition, overcrowding, a few bad apples, paranoia, bad drugs, big egos, the absence of any leaders who were willing to call themselves leaders, the constant police harassment—there were dozens of reasons why it was going bad. Meetings were called to try to puzzle out a strategy. The usual people attended, the Thelins, the Diggers, Leonard Wolf of Happening House, Allen Cohen from the *Oracle*. There was no dearth of suggestions, things like: "We have to say the Ommm sound. Every day there should be a procession down Haight Street to bring the good vibes back." Or: "I think it would be a good idea to open a cathouse because there's lots of straight guys on the street who're always asking where they can get laid. And when they can't get laid their energy gets very negative." Everyone knew the vibes were turning sour, could sense it with that awakened third eye. Whenever they took LSD it was all black apocalypse and visions of the bloody crucified Christ flying across the immense nothingness of the universe.

Bad trips became the most frequent trips (San Francisco General was treating an average of 750 panic reactions a month), and for the first time the LSD psychotic became something more than a media favorite. William Irwin Thompson, a historian who was teaching at MIT, ran into the dark side of the hippie dream one night at Esalen: "His hair was very short, and it was clear from his looks that he had not been with the movement very long. Zen and the *I Ching* meant nothing to him, but the weeks of grass, speed and acid seemed to be taking him into a hell that increased his contempt and resentment for the hippies who surrounded him with talk of love." As Thompson watched, appalled, the kid began to chant to himself, "Blood, Blood, Blood, Hate, Hate, Hate." It was one thing, Thompson realized, to celebrate, a la Leary, the death of the mind. But it was something quite different "to stare unperturbed into the violent eyes of a person who has gone out of his mind."

Ralph Metzner, who had moved to California and was working up the coast from San Francisco at Mendocino State Hospital, had some equally grim visitations, as casualties from the Haight-Ashbury began arriving at the hospital. One told him, "It's coming so fast I can't function at that speed." Another said, "You, Leary and Alpert started this whole mess. That's why I took acid. Now I'm going straight to hell. I can't stop it."

Three days later he slit his wrists and bled to death.

Instead of coming together as one beautiful tribe, the Haight was getting zooier. Those who could, got out of town, like hosts abandoning their own party; others, like the Diggers, began carrying guns.

A miscalculation had been made, perhaps as far back as the gray November day when Leary, over hot milk, had rejected Huxley's elitist perspective in favor of Ginsberg's *pro bono publico* perspective. And this, with a generous nod to Kesey and the Pranksters, was the result: kids gobbling LSD wherever and whenever they could, completely ignorant of set and setting, without the least bit of interest in the Unspoken Thing. As Nicholas Von Hoffman, who was perhaps the most astute journalist to visit the Haight that summer, observed, "Their own genius for manipulating the mass media and dominating the youth culture undid them. The taste and demand for acid increased exponentially; the programming diminished. People didn't prepare themselves for dropping it; they didn't take it within the bounds of the little millennarian communities of the Haight . . . they just swallowed pills anywhere because they wanted to get stoned and see colors."

LSD wasn't a trip to the Other World for these kids: it was mind-blowing fun, better than a fast car or a quick orgasm. When there wasn't any acid around, they were equally willing to shoot up methedrine (which had the added byproduct of decreasing hunger) or heroin. The cliché that nobody who grokked the meaning of LSD could poison their body with speed or heroin turned out to be just that, a cliché. The older hippies ran around putting up signs saying "Speed Kills" but it didn't do any good. Instead of creating a taste for enlightenment, LSD was promoting a love of sensation, the more intense the better, and it began to dawn on the hippie leadership that there were a lot of kids in the Haight that summer who were going to keep sledgehammering at their shells until there was nothing left but the ubiquitous dust.

There were small private deaths and large public ones, the most chilling being the murder of Superspade, one of Owsley's dealers. Superspade had been a fixture on Haight Street, wearing a button that said: Superspade, Faster than a Speeding Mind. Now he was dead, shot in the back of the head, stuffed into a sleeping bag and dumped over a cliff in Marin.

It was rumored that the Mafia was moving in on the psychedelic trade, circulating bad acid so that the hippies would turn to more lucrative habits, like heroin and speed. Signs appeared saying "Boycott Syndicate Acid," but how could you tell?

It was a classic case of projection. The problems were not out there—they were at the heart of the Haight itself, and perhaps even at the heart of the psychedelic experience. There was a point, during every LSD user's career, when the trips to the Other World became negative. In a therapeutic sense, this was good. It meant that the subject was finally confronting the various repressions and neurotic clusters that were inhibiting the smooth evolution of the self. And provided the therapist or guide was skilled, the subject could usually pass through this personal Dark Wood and continue the journey. But what happened with individuals also happened with groups. There was a period when the group mind also passed through the shadow, as it were, and it was here, as the Pranksters learned during the Watts Acid Test, when the urge to erase all limits, to annihilate everything was overwhelming.

The Haight had reached this point in its collective journey, and one of the reasons it was unable to summon the wisdom to guide itself past this darkness was STP.

People took STP and went on three-day trips, many of them terrifying. "I saw myself on fire and then I began to feel the pain of fire . . . I was in hell." It was the ultimate macho trip and descriptions of it sounded like war stories, people exploding through the envelope and burning, or filled with a cold wind that wouldn't stop blowing through the hollows of their mind. STP didn't stay a secret for long. The authorities knew about the new superpsychedelic ("the next step," enthused the chemists, the first of many new combinations) almost immediately because as soon as STP hit the street the emergency rooms filled with nervous, flipped-out kids who quickly became screaming, sobbing kids when the thorazine (the traditional antidote for a bad LSD trip) took effect. Apparently thorazine acted as a booster to the STP, pushing the horror up a few more notches.

That wasn't the whole story, by any means, although it was the one that the average citizen received. What happened to most STP users was subtler, and perhaps even more profound. When Dick Alpert took it, he generally liked it and predicted a useful future. But he also made a curious remark: "I felt I had lost something human. I felt that I had lost my humanity." Alpert wasn't particularly bothered by this (for reasons that will become clear) but it really worried Ken Kesey. Kesey took STP and "forgot something. I lost a thing we take for granted, something that's been forged over I don't know how many thousands of years of human effort, and it's now in us. All I knew when this high was over was that I'd forgotten it, and it was the most important thing I'd ever known and I'd known it since I was a kid." Kesey had a hard time articulating exactly what this was ("a way of relating that, when it's gone, leaves you mighty bleak") but finally he settled for "the tiller." STP had burned away his tiller.

For the first time people were examining the fine print of the psychedelic contract, and one of the clauses they found most troubling was the possibility that besides burning away their "tillers," psychedelics were also altering their chromosomes. In March *Science* had reported that LSD, introduced to a test tube of chromosomes, caused significant breaks. And follow-up studies seemed to confirm that the white blood cells of people who had used LSD frequently showed a high percentage of breaks. The *New England Journal of Medicine* suggested that the effects of psychedelics might be similar to those of radiation, which was a sobering thought to the hippies, particularly since they were so fond of saying that God had given them LSD to counteract the Bomb. Although most scientists were quick to question the validity of the chromosome research (aspirin, thorazine, and the common cold affected chromosomes) and the underground newspapers published long (and ultimately valid) critiques of the work, it didn't diminish the anxiety that clutched at every hippie's heart: hadn't Leary always talked about LSD releasing cellular energies? What if it did? What if they really were becoming mutants? Or was it just another fusillade in the propaganda battle, an ingenious reply to Leary's thousand-orgasm gambit?

These were subtle psychological currents whose movements became clear only months later. At the time it was much simpler and much more satisfying to blame the government (the fascist putsch rumors had yet to abate) and the press. "This wasn't a Summer of Love" the hippie called Teddybear told one reporter. "This was a summer of bull and you, the press, did it. The so-called flower children came here to find something because you told 'em to, and there was nothing to find."

For the first time the next step was obvious. The Haight-Ashbury should die, so the rest of the country could be reborn. "I think it might be a good idea for us to get a pocketful of acid and go to Topeka, Kansas, and begin the work of turning people on," said Allen Cohen at one of the final strategy meetings. "There's a lot of turned-on people in New York and here, but in between is a tribal wasteland."

In a few days it would be a year since the California law criminalizing LSD had taken effect; a year since the Love Pageant Rally. It was a good time to say goodbye, so thousands of black-bordered notices were printed up:

> Hippie in the Haight-Ashbury District of this city
> Hippie, devoted son of Mass Media
> Friends are invited to attend services beginning
> at sunrise, October 6, 1967, at Buena Vista Park.

At noon on the sixth, a fifteen-foot coffin was solemnly paraded down Haight Street followed by some two hundred mourners in elaborate costumes shaking tambourines. Ten sweating pallbearers carried the giant box once around the entire Haight-Ashbury, ending in the Panhandle, where it was ceremoniously set alight. But someone had called the fire department and within minutes a couple of engines came screaming up. "The remains," someone yelled. "Don't let them put it out."

But they did, their giant hoses turning the coffin into a charred soggy mass. All that was left of hippie was a hissing cloud of steam that drifted off toward the center of the country, where the radio stations were still playing Scott McKenzie's song:

> *If you're going to San Francisco*
> *Be sure to wear some flowers in your hair.*
> *If you're going to San Francisco*
> *You're going to meet some gentle people there.*

The song had entered the charts in May; by the end of the summer it had climbed all the way to number 4, which made it perhaps the most conspicuous beneficiary of the Summer of Love.

26

TOO MANY GURUS

It is ironic, but here, at the climax of our story, all the major players are offstage.

Ken Kesey was in prison, having been sentenced at the end of June to six months in the San Mateo County Sheriff's honor camp, which was forty-five miles south and east of the Haight, smack in the middle of a redwood forest. He'd installed a stereo next to the camp swimming pool and was introducing his fellow model inmates to the psychedelic sound. At first he'd been assigned to the camp tailor shop, but after redecorating it with psychedelic murals, he'd been transferred to a road gang. Prison, he wrote in his notebook, was even crazier than the nuthouse . . .

Equally scarce that summer was news of Augustus Owsley Stanley the Third, although his product, particularly Scully's STP, was everywhere. The hippies joked that Owsley had gotten so far out he'd gone into another dimension, which was why the Feds couldn't catch him. He was working on the next superpsychedelic, they whispered, which he was going to call FDA, in honor of the agency.

Then there was Leary, rumored to be in India, although actually he was back at Millbrook, living in a teepee on Ecstasy Hill. Tim had gone tribal that summer, wearing buckskins and a beaded headband, and waxing lyrical over the communal joys of teepee living. It was his first idle stretch since India, and he spent it getting high and listening to the new Beatles album, *Sergeant Pepper's Lonely Hearts Club Band,* on a portable stereo. "I've dropped out completely myself," he told a *Look* magazine writer. "I'm already an anachronism in the LSD movement anyway. The Beatles have taken my place. That latest album—a complete celebration of LSD." He called them "the four evangelists."

For visitors, Tim exuded a relaxed harmoniousness, as though the solitude of the Hitchcock estate was all he could ever desire. But in actual fact he was there because he had no where else to go. He was flat broke and left the reservation only for lectures (his fee had risen to one thousand dollars) and "bread quests." A few months earlier he had been confidently predicting that the psychedelic mystery celebration would "become the most popular form of drama in the western world during the next decade." But now it was apparent that he, like so many impresarios, had misjudged the popular mood. *Death of the Mind* and its successor, the *Illumination of the Buddha* ("Each of you is the Buddha. Did you forget that? When they say he's the prince, they mean he's a well brought up boy who went to UCLA. He had a thousand dancing girls or a television set. They kept him from the discovery that there was a way of turning on—of solving the riddle of sickness . . . age . . . death. So the Buddha dropped out of school and quit his job and set out on the internal voyage.") had only driven him deeper into debt, adding an additional ten thousand dollars to his already staggering legal bills.

But Tim didn't let his financial and legal problems undermine his optimism. America "will be an LSD country within fifteen years," he cheerfully informed a BBC interviewer. "Our Supreme Court will be smoking marijuana within fifteen years. It's inevitable, because the students in our best universities are doing it now." Was he serious? How was one to interpret that flashing grin? "Beauty is dandy, but humor is quicker," wrote the writer from *Look*, "and any nonintoxicated visitor to Millbrook soon gets the sense that he is being put on or—in a more durable vernacular—joshed." *Look*'s assessment of Tim was that he wasn't a bad man, just not a very good wizard.

But others, even some former friends and supporters, were beginning to have doubts. Alan Watts thought Tim was suffering from what Jung called inflation, which was a sort of messianic neurosis that came from misreading the mystical experience. Tim had become a storefront messiah, a Socrates intent on corrupting the young, the P. T. Barnum of the Other World . . . having shed his old ego, he was now in the process of growing a giant new one. "He may mislead a whole generation with his paranoid self-importance," said a writer who had been a frequent visitor to Millbrook in the past.

However, even broke and living in a teepee, Leary still personified the psychedelic *zeitgeist:* the problem wasn't that Tim Leary thought he was a guru: the problem was that every third Tom, Dick, and Harry either thought they were a guru, or had a guru who thought, etc., etc. In fact, Leary wasn't even the chief guru at Millbrook anymore: he was only one of three. Visitors to the estate could now choose between playing the inner game with Art Kleps and his Neo-American Church, who were headquartered in the Gate House, or they could go the psychedelic Hindu route and join the Shri Rama Ashram, which occupied the Big House and was under the guidance of an itinerant guru named Bill Haines, or they could opt for the League of Spiritual Discovery, in which case they needed to get a teepee and pitch it with the others on Ecstasy Hill.

Consumer choice, in the grand American tradition, had come to the private revolution. Following the Summer of Love, the hippie ethic—the San Francisco *Chronicle,* no doubt trying to get the lexical jump on its rival, the *Examiner,* coined the word *freebie* to describe the new nonhippies, but that died a quick merciful death—fractionated into a dozen different sects and cults, each with its own techniques for accessing the Other World. The deeper hippies, the ones who hadn't come to the Haight for a lark, began chanting and meditating; they sat down and finally read all those arcane Tibetan texts they'd bought at the Psychedelic Shop. A surprising number joined the Hare Krishnas, one of the most ascetic and dogmatic sects around. Others gravitated to various gurus (the Maharishi and Meher Baba were popular) or followed charismatic hippies, either good ones like Steve Gaskin, or tragic ones like Charlie Manson, whose little family would become a mocking paradigm of Leary's tribal vision.

Michael Murphy, one of the co-founders of the Esalen Institute (whose human potential experiments would fill the media void left by the death of hippie) described what was happening this way: "I've always thought of the Beats as the first wave on the beach. The hippies were the second and now maybe we're getting a third, the sadhaks, who will be more experienced meditators. A lot of people have been done in by drugs, I think. Now that has passed its peak. The interest is here to stay but wisdom is coming."

The heavy meditators—Murphy's sadhaks—claimed their highs were superior to those of drugs because they were free of all the physiological "noise" that accompanied a psychedelic trip to the Other World. There was no overwhelming surge of panic from the reptilian brain; no fight or flight anxiety from the midbrain, no straying into a replay of your birth. LSD had been a necessary tool, but now it was time to move on. Psychedelics were "like a boat one uses to cross a river," Alan Watts wrote, but once on the opposite bank the journey continues on foot.

This new direction was sanctified in the fall of 1967, when Leary's "four evangelists," the Beatles, publicly announced that they were giving up psychedelics for transcendental meditation, and were becoming disciples of the Maharishi at his ashram in Rishikesh, on the banks of the Ganges. The Beatles were by no means the only celebrities attracted by the diminutive rolypoly yogi with the squeaky voice. Mia Farrow, the Hollywood actress, was also learning how to meditate in Rishikesh, as was Donovan, the psychedelic troubador, whose "Sunshine Superman" and "Mellow Yellow" were routinely condemned as being "pro-drug" by the people who worry about such things. For a few months the Maharishi and his ashram were as familiar as Jackie Kennedy or the White House, as paparazzi competed for the shots of JohnPaulRingoGeorge walking obediently beside their perfect master. Fleet Street covered their meditational progress as though it were Derby Day: Paul held the record with four hours, while John and George were minutes behind, and Ringo wasn't even in the game. Indeed, Ringo only lasted ten days at Rishikesh, before sneaking away, telling the press that the food hadn't agreed with his stomach. Paul McCartney held out for nine weeks before leaving, then John went, finally George. "We thought there was more to him than there was," McCartney later told the press. "He's human, we thought at first he wasn't."

The Maharishi ultimately survived the Beatles' defection, but the calls from the Johnny Carson show and the *Today* show stopped coming.

But not everyone who went to India came home disillusioned or discomposed. At the same time that the Beatles were practicing emptying their minds at Rishikish, another character in our story, Richard Alpert, was achieving the state of grace that he'd been seeking since watching himself vanish on Tim's couch in the Newton house. Alpert had finally looked into the eyes of someone who knew!

It had happened like this. By June 1967 Alpert was again at loose ends, unable to resume his career as a mainstream psychologist, yet bored with the psychedelic lecture circuit. His mother had just died, and he could feel the black mood that had troubled him since Zihuatanejo beginning to build. So when a friend invited him along on a search for Indian holymen, he had eagerly agreed, particularly since they planned to travel in style, picking up a new landrover in Teheran and staying in the best hotels. Most of the time they partied, smoking Afghani hash and dipping regularly into Alpert's bottle of Owsley acid. Alpert gave LSD to every holy man who would try it: some said "I don't feel anything," others compared it to meditation, and a few asked, "Where can I get some more?" For three months they puttered across Iran, Afghanistan, and India, before fetching up in Nepal.

They were sitting in the Blue Tibetan in Katmandu, discussing their plans, when it happened. Alpert's friend wanted to continue on to Japan to visit the Zendos; Alpert was considering a return to the U.S. Maybe he'd become a chauffeur, he mused, murmuring his mantras while his employer shopped in Bergdorf Goodman's. It was a vision right out of Somerset Maugham's *The Razor's Edge*, and it was momentarily interrupted when a 6-foot 7-inch Westerner with long blonde hippie hair and wearing a traditional *dhoti* pushed his way into the Blue Tibetan. Alpert glanced up, their eyes connected, and with a little electric shiver he realized: *this guy knew.*

His name was Bhagwan Dass, and he seemed to take it for granted that Alpert was going to follow him on a temple pilgrimage to India. Alpert wasn't so sure. He kept telling himself that he hadn't come halfway around the world to end up scurrying after a twenty-three-year-old surfer from Laguna Beach, California. But when Bhagwan Dass left Katmandu, Alpert was with him, barefoot, wearing a *dhoti*, ready to beg his way across India, to put his health and welfare in the hands of the uncommunicative Bhagwan Dass. Whenever Alpert tried to gossip about his days with Tim or tell funny stories about Harvard, Bhagwan Dass would shush him and say, "Be here now." It was hard not to be. Those first few weeks were painful in the extreme. Alpert's feet turned into gigantic blisters and he contracted dysentery, which led to a physical breakdown. He became like a little boy, totally dependent on Bhagwan Dass, who insisted on stopping in every little village to play his stringed instrument (Alpert was given a drum and commanded to beat) and receive the homage that the Indians freely give to those on the ancient path. All that remained of the old Alpert was his passport, his return airplane ticket, a couple of travelers checks, and his bottle of LSD.

One day Bhagwan Dass announced that it was time to visit his guru. They borrowed a car and drove one hundred miles to a little temple in the Himalayan foothills where, as soon as the vehicle came to a stop, Bhagwan Dass leapt out, tears streaming down his face, and disappeared up a mountain path, running swiftly. Alpert followed, as he had been doing for months, but reluctantly. He was beginning to have second thoughts: whatever magic this giant surfer had acquired, it wasn't rubbing off. And the sight of Bhagwan's guru, a tiny little man sitting on an ordinary blanket contemplating the enormous blonde American who was prostrate at his feet, did nothing to reassure him. The first question the man on the blanket asked Alpert was whether he was a rich American, and when Alpert replied that he did okay, the man immediately asked for a car. Alpert was taken aback—"I had come from a family of fundraisers for the United Jewish Appeal, Brandeis and the Einstein Medical School and I had never seen hustling like this." The meeting was shaping up as grist for one of his comic monologues, a great story if and when he played the Village Gate again, but then the guru started talking about Alpert's mother, dead not quite a year, and he correctly diagnosed that her death had been caused by complications of the spleen. Alpert had been in control up to this point, but now his head began to swim, he felt a violent pain in his chest and he began to cry: "I wasn't happy and I wasn't sad. The only thing I felt like was that I was home. The journey was finished."

Or almost finished. The psychologist in Alpert required one more proof. The next morning he gave the little man three of Owsley's best, 900 micrograms, and sat down to wait ("The little scientist in me says, 'this is going to be very interesting.' "). But Bhagwan's guru just twin-kled at him as though nothing out of the ordinary was taking place. No Doors opening in my mind, thank you, because they're already wide open. The guy was permanently high, Alpert realized, and that's exactly how he wanted to be.

Alpert stayed in that little Himalayan ashram until the middle of 1968. Every morning he would rise and bathe in the river, do his yoga, meditate, and wait for his teacher to arrive, a terse little man who would come in with a chalkboard and write something like: "If a pickpocket meets a saint, he sees only his pockets." Alpert shed sixty pounds plus his name: he was now Ram Dass. And if he wasn't there yet, he did feel light and beautiful and terrifically high.

But Alpert is the exception in this finale. At roughly the same time that he was giving his guru three of Owsley's best, Owsley was being arrested in upstate California, the culmination of a pursuit that had cost the government (according to John Finlator, BDAC's director) several million dollars and several dozen cars. The Feds had chased Owsley all over the west, embarrassed by his high media profile as a psychedelic Robin Hood. One story, in the Los Angeles *Times,* had a leather-jacketed Owsley speeding up to a Sunset Boulevard bank on a red motorcycle, like Brando in *The Wild One.* Owsley had walked up to the teller and from his pockets, his helmet, his boots had come wads of small bills, twenty-five thousand dollars worth of small bills. Changing them into 250 crisp new hundred-dollar bills, he had climbed back onto his red motorcycle and sped away. It was the beginning of his public fame: the LSD millionaire, thirty-one years old and all that money.

Owsley made a brief blip on the police screens in April 1967, when he was arrested in upstate New York after a visit to Millbrook. The police stopped him for speeding and driving with a broken taillight, but they later released him on his own recognizance. They retained, how-ever, some of his belongings, among which was a key to a safety deposit box at Manufacturer's Hanover Trust Company. And inside that box was $225,000. Owsley's girlfriend had a duplicate key, so that was no problem; and although the possibility of police surveillance worried them, a more important consideration was finding a permanent haven for Owsley's LSD profits. Billy Hitchcock was called in as someone who knew about high finance, and within hours a courier was on his way from the Bahamas. A few weeks later the psychedelic movement had its first Swiss bank account under the code name Robin Goodfellow.

It was useful having a European source of cash, since Europe was about the last place where you could obtain large quantities of lysergic monohydrate and ergotomine tartrate, the key ingredients for making LSD. And that wasn't going to be the case for too many more months:

already the U.S. was pressuring its allies to pass anti-LSD legislation similar to its own. Tim Scully was particularly passionate in his belief that they should stockpile as much raw material as possible, and he also became involved in Billy Hitchcock's fantasy of buying an island, ideally somewhere in the Caribbean, and establishing an offshore drug lab. This was known as the Dr. No fantasy, after the James Bond movie of the same name. Hitchcock was also advising the acid chemists to link up in a kind of cartel, so they could pool resources, control production and set price, and in general function like a normal business.

Owsley knew about these schemes, but he wasn't too interested. Although he enjoyed being "the Mr. Big of the S.F. scene," as one of his new assistants, a young head named Teenie Weenie Deanie described him, and was "quite fond of himself and his position in the emerging acid world of 1967," Owsley was rapidly tiring of the heat that went along with the status of Mr. Big. The constant pursuit was wearing him down; his paranoia, never a small thing, was beginning to eat away at his belief that he was divinely protected from the bumbling efforts of the Feds.

They caught him (thirteen federal and state narcotics agents) a few days before Christmas, 1967, in the California town of Orinda, where he was tableting the latest product from Scully's Denver lab. They caught him with 217 grams of product, about three-quarters of a million doses, which his lawyer, when the case came to trial two years later, argued were for personal consumption. Throughout the trial Owsley would refuse to talk to the press, claiming he was just an illusion the media had created. "You mean to say you're just a figment of my imagination?" one reporter asked. "That's right," he snapped. If he had it to do over again, Owsley would've chosen to be the Shadow instead of Robin Hood. When the trial ended, the judge sentenced him to three years in prison and fined him three thousand dollars.

But while Owsley's arrest certainly removed a major personality from the psychedelic scene, it didn't dent the flow of LSD. There was more product than ever, and a lot of it came from the new LSD cartel, which never really had a name, although it has come down to us as "The Brotherhood of Eternal Love." The name came from a bunch of former Laguna Beach surfers and juvenile delinquents who'd dropped acid, grokked the true vision, and incorporated themselves with the State of California as the Brotherhood of Eternal Love. They ran a head shop/crafts store called the Mystic Arts in Laguna Beach, and had a communal ranch out in the desert. But their primary occupation was smuggling: the Brotherhood were probably the best dope smugglers in America. They were almost as well known among the cognoscenti as Owsley: when Leary was fighting his Texas conviction, the Brotherhood gave his defense fund ten thousand dollars. Tim, who became quite close to the Brotherhood and particularly to its house guru, an ethereal hippie named John Griggs, used to refer to them as "reincarnations of a roving band of Portuguese pirates."

The Brotherhood's primary focus was marijuana and hashish; they never took a profit on LSD, since they saw that part of their operation as a charitable spreading of the sacrament. They got most of their LSD from the cartel that Tim Scully had formed with several other chemists, notably Nick Sand, who was the young man whose panel truck, nabbed at the Colorado border, had so alarmed FDA director Goddard.

But if the Brotherhood had replaced Owsley as the best-known distributor of LSD, it had also inherited his status as BDAC's number-one target. Sometimes, working in the lab, Tim Scully would have these sudden flashes of himself on trial. Just a quick sharp feeling of impending confinement. And had he pursued these precognitive visions, he might have heard the Judge, Samuel Conti, saying, "put a fancy name on it, call it a psychedelic movement, call it the Brotherhood of Eternal Love, call it the wonderful Hells Angel movement—whatever you wanted to call it, they all ended up in one thing. They all ended up in the degradation of mankind, the degradation of society."

Which brings us finally to Tim Leary. For the next two years Leary played an inspired but ultimately futile end game with the authorities. He was arrested, by one count, ten more times, although the figure may be higher. When he was evicted by the Hitchcock Cattle Company from Millbrook in February 1968, he told a reporter from the Associated Press that he was going underground to avoid police harassment, adding, with his usual mocking grin, that one day he would be recognized as the wisest man of the twentieth century. But it was not in Leary's nature to play the underground game; he loved the limelight and was never happier than when he had an audience; but he also realized that there was no profit in hiding out, nor any dignity: you couldn't get this far into the ancient game and then hair out, as the surfers said.

In the spring of 1968 he turned up in San Francisco, with his old Harvard buddy Charles Slack in tow. Slack, his career as a psychologist temporarily on hold, was working as a journalist for a New York magazine. He'd run into Leary at the Village Gate, where a few of Tim's friends had held a public farewell party for him. Slack had attended largely to satisfy his curiosity over whether his old colleague had really (as his secretary claimed) become God. He found the same old Tim, or almost the same old Tim. The charmingly persuasive Leary who had insisted that Slack drop everything he was doing and accompany them to California was a familiar fellow. And Slack had read enough of Tim's public statements so that the Grand Vision didn't faze him—"first come the children. They are already turned on. Then will come the ordinary working adults, regular nine-to-five people, who will soon turn on. The professions will be next—doctor-lawyer power roles. It is impossible to remain tied to a profession during or after an LSD session." But he was unprepared for the adoration that Leary evoked in the gullible young. As soon as he set foot in the San Francisco airport he'd been surrounded by a corona of eager young faces, for whom he wove a bit of Irish blarney:

"I am going to start my own country," he told the kids. "I am going to interest an investor in the purchase of large amounts of land to the south. After we buy our land, we will set up our own government, declare ourselves independent of the U.S.A. and set up our own country with our own laws or lack thereof, as the case may be. Our laws will stress complete freedom of the mind and body: freedom to ingest any substance which will lead toward spiritual enlightenment or interpersonal understanding, freedom of the mind, internal freedom."

It was Slack's first brush with psychedelic reality, as opposed to the consensual version accepted by most Americans. Start your own country? How credible was that coming from a man who didn't even have the cash to rent a car from the airport? Leary's finances had never been worse. Yet his fame had never been greater. There was a popular button that said, simply, "Leary is God."

Soon after arriving in San Francisco, Leary took Slack on a pub-crawl of the Haight, ducking into coffee shops and ashrams. "I love this world," he confided. "I have everything I need here. It's all very together. I have beauty, laughter, art, companionship, sex, style, gorgeous chicks around every turn. And most important of all, I have spirituality. After all, I am a religious leader and I must behave like one."

"I'll bet you're on personal terms with every stoned kooky religious nut in town," Slack said.

"Every one," replied Tim.

It was sometime after this that Slack asked Tim what the secret of his success was and Leary replied with one word: Faust.

> "You're joking," I said when it sank in.
> "No," he replied, "but it often begins as a joke."
> "You mean you . . . you don't mean it. You didn't."
> "Yes I did," he said. "Didn't I, Ed?"
> "He sure did," said Ed in a steady voice.
> "Oh my God," I said.
> "But that's exactly what I said, too, at the time."

Typical Tim. Yet it did send a shiver up the spine. There was no guarantee, after all, that the powers you contacted in the Other World were holy as opposed to infernal. One look at the Haight-Ashbury made that clear. It was full of burn-outs with those peculiarly dead eyes that were one of the most unsettling legacies of the private revolution.

Crime, which had fallen in the early years of the Haight, had climbed sharply in the final months of 1967, ending the year with seventeen murders, one hundred rapes, and not quite three thousand burglaries. And there was no sign of any slacking off. The old guard was long gone, many to communes or to farms in Marin or the foothills east of the City. Most of the original shops were closed—the *Oracle* was gone, the Psychedelic Shop; about the only survivor from the Summer of Love was the Haight-Ashbury Free Medical Clinic, which was treating a growing population of heroin and speed addicts.

Anger was the dominant mood. In February a tourist ran over a dog and the Haight went wild, although it was nothing compared to the July riot that went on for three nights, with kids tearing up clumps of pavement and tossing Molotov cocktails off the rooftops. Of course the Haight wasn't unique in this: 1968 was the year the top blew off the pressure cooker, particularly at the Democratic National Convention, where the kids and the Chicago police raged at each other for five days.

Instead of love, the Sixties were ending with hate.

But this didn't seem to bother Tim. "This is my world," he told Slack as he guided him through the ruins of the Haight. "This is my scene. I made it and it made me." And the symbiosis wasn't over. Ralph Metzner spent Christmas of 1968 with Tim at the Brotherhood of Eternal Love's desert ranch, and he was distressed by the changes in his friend's character:

> It did indeed sadden my heart to see Tim, whom I had loved deeply as a friend, being pulled increasingly downward into more and more separated and darkened states of consciousness, to the point where he could talk of the "white light of the Buddha being the fire from the gun of a revolutionary," or speak casually of "offing a pig," or advocate the use of cocaine or heroin to reach particular "states of consciousness." I was also dismayed by the increasingly chaotic and meaningless ramblings which came from his pen and were published in his name.

Tim invited Metzner to drive back to Laguna with him, but due to the illness of a friend Metzner demurred. He was lucky. When Tim reached Laguna Beach his car was stopped by the police and two pounds of marijuana were found in the trunk.

It was added to the conga line of Leary legal briefs that was winding its way through the judicial system. In 1969 his appeal of his Texas conviction finally reached the Supreme Court. And on May 20, the Supreme Court threw out his conviction on the grounds that the marijuana stamp tax was an improper and confusing law: you couldn't force somebody to declare and pay a tax on a substance that was illegal.

Although Texas immediately announced that they would retry Mr. Leary on different grounds, the Supreme Court decision filled Leary's sails. The next day he announced that he was running for governor of California, the candidate of a new party whose name was FERVOR, an acronym of Free Enterprise, Reward, Virtue and Order. Among other things, FERVOR proposed selling marijuana in state stores. (When asked about nonsmokers, Leary said, "They can buy brownies.") But its most radical proposal had to do with its philosophy of government. Leary had a distinctly Platonic model in mind: if elected he would lease the government to either Ronald Reagan, the Republican incumbent, or Jesse Unruh, the democratic challenger; they would handle the tedious details like appointing judges, while he and Rosemary would live in a teepee on the lawn of the governor's mansion, and function as philosopher-kings.

His election posters depicted a byronic Tim gazing into the cosmic distance, while below him frolicked a village of mushroom people.

It was his last public gesture. In February 1970, a Texas court resentenced him to ten years in prison. Leary quickly appealed. But a few weeks later, on March 21, a California jury convicted him on the Laguna Beach bust. Calling him an "insidious menace" and a "pleasure-seeking, irresponsible Madison Avenue advocate of the free use of drugs," Superior Court Judge Byron McMillan refused to set bail. If he wanted to appeal his one- to ten-year conviction, he could do it from a jail cell. On April 23, the California Supreme Court denied his petition for bail, without comment. And on May 18 he was remanded to the California Men's Colony West, a minimum security prison in San Luis Obispo, midway up the coast between Los Angeles and San Francisco. He looked terrible. Rosemary commented he was "forty-nine going on five thousand." Combined with the Texas sentence, he faced a possible twenty years in jail, and that wasn't counting his upcoming Dutchess County trial on an eleven-count indictment stemming from some raids on the Big House in late 1967.

And so the psychedelic movement ground to a close. The drugs were still available, more so than ever, but it was a rare person who took them to push the envelope. For the kids, a trip to the Other World was like a trip to Disneyland, lots of scary rides and laughs, but no wisdom.

Kesey, Owsley, IFIF, the Acid Tests, Castalia, the Trips Festival, the Harvard Psilocybin Project, the Be-In—it had receded into memory so fast it was almost as if it had happened to an older brother, or an uncle, or maybe they'd read about it in some book or magazine—it didn't seem real. Had they really thought they could transform Uncle Sam into the Buddha? The fact was, the good times were too painful to talk about because they always led to the bad times, to all the people who had been left behind, either burned out or in prison or on the run or irrevocably lost, like Neal Cassady, dead on a railroad track outside the Mexican town of San Miguel Allende; or Jack Kerouac, dead of a hemorrhage; or John Griggs, the leader of the Brotherhood, dead from bad psilocybin. Or Sharon Tate, dead from a malignancy that had been growing all the while in the Haight-Ashbury, unnoticed, but that was no excuse.

The game was over, almost. On the night of September 12, 1970, Tim Leary was crawling along the roof of cellblock number 324, his trademark tennis sneakers covered with black paint. Up ahead was the telephone cable that led to a pole outside the twelve-foot chain-link fence. And beyond that was his getaway car, paid for by a twenty-five thousand-dollar grant from the Brotherhood of Eternal Love. The car, if it was out there, was driven by a member of the Weather Underground, which was the militant residue of the now defunct SDS.

All Leary had to do was wrap himself around the cable and pull himself to freedom. But by the time he was a third of the way across his muscles were screaming and he knew he would fail. *"Would they poke me down like a wild raccoon with sticks? I should have quit smoking. I should have pumped more iron. Forty-nine years and 325 days of my life built up to this ordeal. There was no fear—only a nagging embarrassment. Such an undignified way to die, nailed like a sloth to a branch."*

But then he felt it, that old surge of cellular energy, the lifeforce. He was going to make it. No one was going to shoot him. The car would be waiting. And Rosemary. And beyond that, freedom. Once again he was heading into the wind.

Like the wild geese.

EPILOGUE: AN AFTERNOON IN THE EIGHTIES

I first heard about venus in the summer of 1983 in Los Angeles. Five of us were sitting around a marble table in a stucco ranch near Malibu, eating lunch and chatting about asteroid mining and the fifth generation of computers, when the host inquired whether any of us had tried venus yet.

"Lois and I took it the other night and got sick to our stomachs," he said.

The man on my right, a movie producer, wrinkled his brow and asked, "Venus? Is that the new space-time one?"

Our host nodded. "Technically it's called something like 2CB."

"Well Edgar mentioned that there was some problem when he took it, but he thought eventually it'd prove useful."

"Oh Lois and I had a great time. We just spent half the night in the toilet, that's all."

This was shoptalk, impenetrable to an outsider like myself. My perplexity must have been obvious because at one point the host, an amiable raconteur who dabbled in computer software and philosophy, leaned over and whispered, "This must be your first trip to the neuro-consciousness frontier."

In retrospect, I should have expected something like that to happen in California, the Athens of postwar consciousness. A small library could be filled with books written to explain what Walt Whitman called "the flashing and golden pageant of California." Most of these volumes spin a familiar tale—how for the last century and a half California has operated like a huge national sinkhole, swallowing first the 49ers, then the Okies, with a steady trickle of those bored with prairie life and prairie towns in between; how California became the final resting place for everyone who expected the *dolce vita* to be just beyond the next ridge; how thirty years ago all this social energy began to transform itself into pop culture; how every few months the media was heralding some new California fad: the Beats, the surfers, the Free Speech Movement, the topless craze, the hippies, Esalen, EST, ET, and now the neuro-consciousness frontier, which is simply the old Psychedelic Movement retooled for the technological eighties.

California didn't invent LSD, of course, but it certainly played a major role in defining its use. Is it possible to imagine Ken Kesey and his Merry Pranksters in any other setting? The Haight-Ashbury hippies comporting themselves in Philadelphia, say, or Akron? By the end of the Seventies even tertiary members of what Tim Leary once called "the game between the Establishment and the utopian visionaries," were living in California, ensconced on university campuses or in places like Esalen, the think tanks of the consciousness movement.

Which is why, when I began researching this book, I bought a plane ticket and went west. The story I planned to write was a little bit of a native guignol, a black comedy about what happens when the most materially advanced country in the world suddenly stumbles upon a drug, LSD-25, that seems to promote the most fundamental and embarrassing sort of religious ecstasy. It seemed a straightforward project, commencing in 1943 with Albert Hofmann's inadvertent discovery and then proceeding along various plotlines until it reached its denouement in the early Seventies. I didn't see any story beyond that point—most of the leaders were in jail, most of the drugs were illegal, and a fierce publicity campaign had convinced most of us that psychedelics, besides scrambling your perceptual categories, scrambled your chromosomes as well.

There was—as the hippie newspapers had predicted—no scientific truth to these charges. *Science,* summarizing the National Institute of Mental Health's first sixty-eight studies of possible LSD-related genetic damage, concluded that "Pure LSD ingested in moderate doses does not damage chromosomes, *in vivo,* does not cause detectable genetic damage, and is not a teratogen or carcinogen in man." But by that time the fledgling psychedelic movement had fragmented into the dozens of consciousness crazes—EST, TM, Arica, Scientology, transpersonal psychology, yoga—that gave the Me Decade much of its zest.

I was wrong, of course, as I discovered near the end of my third interview. I was sitting in the plush offices of a San Francisco psychiatrist and we were reminiscing about his sojourn at Leary's psychedelic resort in Zihuatanejo, Mexico, in the summer of 1963. Leary, you may recall, had erected a wooden lifeguard tower out on the Pacific littoral with the idea that someone should be sitting up there at all times, tripping, a symbol of Zihuatanejo's higher purpose. And the good doctor had spent his share of time in the tower, trying to tune into the cosmic plentitude. It was a comic picture, and we were chuckling about it when the doctor suddenly asked if I was going to discuss any of the new drugs in my book.

New drugs?

"Well I don't know," I said after a long pause. "Do you think any of them are worth pursuing?"

"Certainly you should consider Ecstasy. It's becoming very popular. Adam is similar, you know. A colleague of mine is using it in therapy with the state's permission. And I think you should take a good look at Vitamin K. That's what all the serious players are using."

LSD, while still available as a street drug, was considered somewhat antiquated by the professional explorers of inner space. It has been superseded by a new generation of psychedelics with names like Ecstasy, Adam, Intellex, 2CB, Vitamin K, and a handful of others, most synthesized from various methoamphetamines and tryptomines.

"Thanks to the Sixties," the doctor continued, "there are people in this country who are extremely skilled in handling altered states. I guess you could call them a circle of adepts."

A few days later I jotted down a similar description while interviewing Tim Leary's old friend and colleague, psychologist Frank Barron. "I think the whole thing is going to be coming back in a much more sophisticated form," Barron told me as we sat in his UC-Santa Cruz office. "There are drugs now that will make people very extroverted, and some that will increase intuition and some that will increase sensation. I think the process of developing chemical analogs is going to proceed independently, maybe without much regard even for any of the theory. But it's a question of getting them used by the people who are able to observe, in a discriminating way, their effects. So the existence of a community of adepts, as it were, is a valuable resource for testing out such drugs. That's what's happening. That's the scientific underground."

Two weeks later I found myself sitting around a marble table in a stucco ranch near Malibu, talking about venus, a drug which may or may not give access to new dimensions, on the edge of the neuro-consciousness frontier.

That was the beginning of my association with as curious and fascinating a bunch of characters as I will probably ever meet. Some were loathe to talk to a writer. Others requested anonymity. And a few were understandably paranoid, leading to some Kafkaesque interludes. One worried therapist insisted that I stare into his eyes for a full minute. "Since I was a little boy I've been able to look someone in the eyes and tell if they're lying," he explained. Did I pass? Flunk? He didn't say. Instead he pulled out a sheet of paper and asked me to make a statement to the effect that I was not now a government agent, nor had I been one in the past. "Handwriting analysis is another of my specialities," he said, scanning my illegible scrawl.

But in the end almost all of them talked, if you can use so pedestrian a word for conversations that were a Baedaker of the intellectual avant-garde, skipping from mind drugs to the theory of implicate order to the Gaia hypothesis. Twenty, sometimes even thirty years after their first entanglement with the Other World, they were still entranced, still excited by the implications, still convinced they were embarked upon a great adventure whose import would one day be acknowledged. Their enthusiasm was infectious, and the interviews usually ended with address books and words to the effect of: "Well, if you're serious about this you'd better talk to so and so."

Which is how I came to spend an afternoon with an octogenarian former professor who lived in one of those scholarly retirement bungalows, full of books and cats. After the initial pleasantries we retired to his study and spent the next few hours discussing psychedelic history and examining—there can be no other word for that small box filled with pharmaceutical envelopes—his stash.

"What's this one say?" the professor asked me, squinting blindly at the tiny script on one of the envelopes.

"It says Adam."

"Oh that's a very intriguing drug. It's different from LSD and psilocybin, of course, but it's extremely useful."

He passed me two more envelopes, which bore the neatly printed labels MDA and LSD. I opened the latter. Inside were six saccharine-sized pellets. According to the envelope, each contained 250 micrograms, the classic Sixties dose.

More envelopes followed, and with them came stories of Tim Leary. "Tim was the most creative member of the Harvard faculty that I ever met," he said. "A charming man. Very Irish. He gave me LSD and I had the most beautiful mystical visions."

It was Leary who launched the professor on the long-term psychedelic research project that has been his obsession for these last twenty years. He was reticent about its thrust, like most writers, but he did hint that one day it might end up in the pile of manuscripts next to Jeremy Tarcher's couch.

Which led me to Jeremy Tarcher, a Los Angeles publisher who specialized in the New Age market and a cautious supporter of the new psychochemicals. "I've spoken with hundreds of people who've used these substances," Tarcher told me as we sat on his leather couch, in an office that overlooked the billboards along Sunset Strip. "Men who are prominent in psychology, in the sciences. Men who will testify to the benefits of these drugs, but who would never speak out publicly for fear of ruining their careers.

"I have an absolute conviction, from personal experience, that these drugs hold a potential for evolution and education. Some of these new drugs are so extraordinary, so useful, that there is no question that they will convince people of their essentially benign quality beyond the ability of the media and the government to tell them otherwise."

Because he is a sympathetic publisher, Tarcher operates as a clearinghouse for neuro-consciousness theory. Next to the couch was a pile of manuscripts at least a foot high. Rummaging through them, Tarcher extracted a wrinkled sheet of paper. It was a letter from Terrence McKenna, who wrote that his brother, Dennis, was preparing a book whose thesis was that psychopharmacological plants represented the missing link in our evolution from primate to human.

"I can't wait to read it," Tarcher said.

Which brought me to Terrence McKenna, who jokes that he represents the lunatic fringe of what is already a pretty anomolous undertaking. A product of the Sixties, with a degree in Shamanic Studies from Berkeley and a mesmerizing nasal voice, McKenna preferred to characterize himself as an explorer rather than a scientist. A few years ago Terrence and Dennis spent thirty-seven days in the upper Amazon Basin, investigating a local mushroom. They wrote about their experiences in *"The Invisible Landscape,"* a book that mixes equal doses of psychedelics, shamanism, schizophrenic theory, molecular biology, and the holographic theory of the brain. Terrence makes part of his living by conducting seminars into the epistemological implications of the neuro-consciousness frontier. I possess several tape recordings of Terrence waxing eloquent, and whenever anyone asks about the current state of psychedelic thinking, I let his taped voice overwhelm them.

Although everyone in the neuro-consciousness game knew everyone else, and most attended the annual symposiums at Esalen, this by no means implied a consensus concerning these new psychedelics. Far from it. With the possible exception of certain leftist sects, it was difficult to imagine a group quite as riven with disagreements and doctrinal squabbles. Take the problem of names. Depending on who was doing the classifying, these substances were liable to be called any of a half dozen names. The die-hards still clung to *hallucinogens,* which is still the medically appropriate term. Those who researched the drugs in the Fifties and were worried by Huxley and later appalled by Leary, generally preferred *psychotomimetic.* A few used Osmond's *psychedelic,* but in general this was reserved for those who had made their first trips to the Other World during the Sixties. Although still the most popular name, lately there has been a lobbying effort to discard psychedelic as irreversibly tainted by Leary, Kesey, the hippies, et al., and replace it with entheogen, a bit of philology best translated as "the god within."

Or consider the question of which drugs were the best, the most useful, the *premier cru* of psychedelic technology. Tarcher was a staunch supporter of Ecstasy: "Vitamin K gives a wild and imaginative trip, but it is of no transcendental meaning. Ecstasy, on the other hand, is an exquisitely useful, heart-opening, defense-destroying, insight-provoking drug, which is bound to give a help in any psychotherapeutic process."

"There is no question, in my mind at least," I was assured by a booster of K, "that vitamin K offers the most profound experience."

And Terrence McKenna dismissed most of the new drugs as irrelevant. "The relevant drugs are DMT, LSD, and mescaline and psilocybin, particularly the latter," he said.

And on, and on. Within this welter of opinion it was possible to distinguish two philosophic camps, the scientists and the humanists: those who believed the investigation of inner space constituted a new natural science and those who still subscribed to the argument that psychedelics, if properly used, would create a better person. For the latter, the important drug was Ecstasy, while the former placed their hopes on Vitamin K.

Some comments, culled from my notes, concerning Ecstasy, aka 3,4-methylenedioxymethamphetamine, aka MDMA:

"They wanted to create a more spiritual substance. So they worked on it, shaving off molecules, polishing it for about fifteen years and when it finally came out, people said, 'this is it.'"

"It's an empathy drug. What I've noticed about this stuff is that it eliminates the affect of the past, like fear. It's the perfect domestic psychedelic."

"It kind of melts defenses. I have found it to be very healing and helpful. It's a very transformative experience. What happens is not painful, though some people think about painful emotions. There is a lot of empathy, an ability to see something negative and understand it in a more compassionate way, basically to become more loving."

Empathy was a word I heard whenever the subject of Ecstasy arose. It was an empathogen, one therapist stressed. Not a psychedelic.

I was told to take Ecstasy with someone I loved and that's what I did one autumn afternoon, sitting outside in the afternoon sun. I live in the middle of farm country, so the road was full of farm trucks bringing in the fall silage. For the first twenty minutes we felt nothing, then a slight amphetimal rush that grew in strength until it suddenly evaporated. What followed was a six-hour conversation that dipped and soared from the trivial to the personally profound.

My impression was that Ecstasy didn't create insights so much as remove barriers and eliminate the native fear of appearing emotionally clumsy and foolish. You were high, but you weren't high. There was none of LSD's powerful rush into the unconscious, no hallucinations or cosmic *apercus;* just a pleasant but emotionally draining communion. For weeks afterward, whenever I encountered people who were locked into an emotional bind, I had to resist the urge to butt in and say, "Well, there's this drug . . ."

Having taken the drug, I could understand why some psychotherapists (blissfully unaware that the hippies had made similar claims regarding LSD) were comparing a good Ecstasy session to two years of traditional therapy. But one thing I was never clear about, despite repeated surveys, was exactly how many therapists were using Ecstasy. I was quoted figures ranging from two hundred to two thousand. "There are probably 150 in the Bay Area alone," I was told.

Certainly Ecstasy had made sufficient inroads into the progressive wing of the therapeutic community so that in 1984 the Association of Humanistic Psychology saw fit to include a panel on the new psychedelics at its annual conference. Most of the data presented were anecdotal: this psychiatrist had found Ecstasy fruitful for couples work; that one was using it to accelerate traditional talk-therapy. It was, in certain respects, a replay of the LSD conferences of the Fifties, with several notable differences. The first was the creation of a stable language in which to discuss these matters: thirty years of haggling has pruned the psychedelic lexicon into an acceptable shape, so that one no longer has to waste half one's time defining terms. That was a positive difference. On the negative side was a disturbing absence of any basic research. Dozens of therapists were using Ecstasy in their practice, but no one was bothering to draw up protocols and conduct a formal research project. As of the '84 Congress, only one therapist, psychiatrist George Greer, had bothered to sit down and write up his data.

After surveying MDMA's effect on twenty-nine different patients, Greer concluded that it facilitated a shedding of emotional defenses, thus leading to new levels of insight. Roughly half his sample also reported a decreased interest in other drugs and intoxicants: "These substances seemed less appealing after experiencing MDMA," he wrote. And aside from post-session headaches and fatigue, only one experienced complications, in this case a disabling anxiety attack that was a repeat of previous, predrug episodes.

"The single best use of MDMA," Greer wrote in a privately printed monograph, "is to facilitate more direct communication between people involved in a significant emotional relationship."

In a way the Ecstasy story was a reverse of the LSD story: it had gone from the street, or rather the living rooms of the adepts, to the therapist's couch. Indeed it was Ecstasy's ability to promote a kind of gentle psychological clarity that first attracted the adepts; it was a little like first gear when you were learning to drive a car.

With its curious ability for melting defenses and deflating the bogies of the Freudian unconscious, Ecstasy minimized the number of bad trips. It didn't send you rocketing around a corner and into a clammy dark room full of horrifying noises and monstrous shadows, the way LSD did; it wafted you there in the gentlest possible manner and nine times out of ten you realized, with a shock, that those monstrous shadows had rather common and amusing causes. And those horrifying noises were only the beating of your heart, the rasping of your breath.

Using Ecstasy, you could bump around in the biographic realm, ironing out various neuroses and familiarizing yourself with those existential terrors, like being alive without a clear purpose other than the fact that one day you will die; terrors that become a little less terrifying the more you get to know them.

And Ecstasy also hinted at how powerful the mind could be, that once first gear was mastered, there was a second gear, and a third.

Compared to MDMA, Vitamin K was tenth gear.

Where everyone who favored Ecstasy spoke of its mildness, the K people always led off by talking about its power. It was wild and strong—five thousand times stronger than LSD, one user told me after I pressed him for a comparison, although we both knew that in these realms numerical comparisons were meaningless.

"You need to apprentice through other mind drugs," said a doctor who came recommended as a veteran of altered states. "I would be reluctant to see this drug get out on the street. I'd even be reluctant to see it in the hands of many therapists."

The doctor credits K's anaesthetic properties with the unusual profundity of the experience. Other psychedelics create a certain amount of anxiety. One might say, borrowing Tim Leary's old image of a multicircuited brain, that regardless of how blissed out the consciousness is in circuit #7, circuit #1, the bio-survival circuit, is probably sending out flight or fight responses, which gets translated into anxiety and thence into a bad trip. "But K puts one in a parasympathetic, vegetative mode. The muscles are relaxed. There is no anxiety. No body screaming hunger. So it opens a different lock to the universe.

"From what I've learned during the first experience you find the key to that door and you have that 'oh my God' experience, 'I'm home.' This is a one-time only experience, everything after that is just a reminder."

One of the most diligent investigators of Vitamin K is neuroscientist John Lilly, who once took the drug every day for a hundred days. "On K I can look across the border into other realities," Lilly claims. "I can open my eyes in this reality and dimly see the alternate reality . . . I can experience the quantum reality. I can see John Wheeler's hyperspace from within."

Stan Grof, who is probably the most respected psychedelic researcher in America, calls K "an absolutely incredible substance. In some sense [it is] much more mysterious than LSD," he says. "Far out unbelievable things happen that have incredible implications for the understanding of reality, what is behind the scenes, and so on. It seems to be totally unpredictable. You can't judge from your previous experience what your next one will be. It can take you to subatomic reality, or astrophysical, to other galaxies. It can make you live the life of a tadpole. The mythology of a certain culture can come to life for you, or you can experience what you feel is the consciousness of inanimate objects. There doesn't seem to be an order that I can detect. There are a couple of papers, published in Persia, about its therapeutic potential, which were quite favorable. But I'm not quite convinced of its therapeutic power. I do, however, think it has incredible potential for coping with the problems of death. If you have a full-blown experience with K, you can never believe there is death, or that death can possibly influence who you are."

Perhaps the most mysterious thing that can happen during a K experience is summed up in the following passage, taken from a user's report that was published in *High Times:* "I'm moving through some kind of train tunnel. There are all sorts of lights and colors, mostly in the center, far, far away . . . and little people and stuff running around the walls of the tube, like little cartoon nebbishes."

Those little cartoon nebbishes sound rather comical, yet they are one of the hottest topics on the neuro-consciousness frontier. Because when you talk to these little nebbishes—and you can—they are full of information about things like the history of the universe and the future of earth. "On vitamin K," Lilly reports, "I have experienced states in which I can contact the creators of the universe, as well as the local creative controllers."

What are these little nebbishes—most adepts prefer to call them entities—doing in there? Where do they come from? Can you believe anything they say? "It is no great accomplishment to hear a voice in the head," maintains Terrence McKenna. "The accomplishment is to make sure it is telling you the truth." All I know is that one of the oddest evenings of my life was spent with a group of adepts at the Humanistic Psychology convention, gossiping about what so and so's entity had said about this metaphysical conundrum (do we really die?) and that one (is human evolution directed toward an omega point?). To borrow Tom Wolfe's useful image, the mysto steam was hissing in my head.

Although they are perhaps the most interesting and visible of the new psychedelics, MDMA and Vitamin K are really just the tip of the iceberg. It seemed that every time I talked to one of the adepts on the phone, they'd say something like, "Have you heard about the latest tryptamine combination? We're calling it the Mayan Brothers." After a while I began wondering where all these drugs were coming from. What I discovered was that the neuro-consciousness game, as currently constituted, wouldn't exist if it weren't for a small number of neurochemists who have dedicated their spare time to exploring the molecular implications of the psychedelic family of drugs.

"I have sort of a team and we work together," was the way one of these chemists explained it to me. "We'll sit down and maybe someone will suggest matching this molecule with that one. Out come the paper and pencils and we scratch away for a few hours until we figure out how to put it together. Then it's into the lab to synthesize it, which can take about a week. Then we try it on ourselves, starting at very low dosages and working up."

In the course of a year they may design a dozen different mind drugs this way, the bulk of which are duds. But one or two usually prove interesting enough to warrant further research. Should any of these substances be especially interesting, they are passed along to the adepts, and the slow process of accumulating data regarding set, setting, and effects begins. And eventually the mimeos appear, short, often anonymous monographs ("Though it is important that this information be known to those who are following this path of internal work," states one that I have in my possession, "it is not important to know the identities of those who bring this information to you. In the end, it all comes from the same source.") that summarize what is known and make suggestions for fruitful areas of inquiry.

II

Maybe it was just my closeness to the book I was writing, but the neuro-consciousness frontier, circa 1983, reminded me a lot of the psychedelic movement, circa 1962: there was the same quality of excitement, the same mix of therapeutic and metaphysical interests, the same cautious optimism. All that was lacking—providentially, the adepts would say—was a Tim Leary. So I decided to pay him a visit.

The ghost of psychedelic movements past was living in the Hollywood Hills, a few miles from Jeremy Tarcher's office, the publisher of Leary's latest and best autobiography, *Flashbacks.* It was oppressively hot on the day we met, but Tim insisted on sitting outside. "I don't mind this kind of heat at all," he told me, and indeed he didn't. As the day sweltered on, Leary's energy level soared. Every few minutes, it seemed, he was either on the phone arranging future interviews for me, or he was dashing off to his office to locate a paragraph in a book he had recently read that would footnote something he had just been saying. It was my first exposure, outside of my research, to the Leary charm.

It was almost twenty years to the day since Leary had cut himself loose from the Academy, choosing to live by his wits. In the interim he had plumbed most of the depths of pop celebrity: drug guru, youth politician, exile, prison inmate, talk-show host, stand-up comic, best-selling author, and, most recently, a star attraction on the collegiate lecture circuit, touring in tandem with G. Gordon Liddy, the Watergate burglar who first attracted headlines when he arrested Leary at Mill-brook in 1966. Together they had produced Return Engagement, an odd little film that opens with a deadpan version of "America, the Beautiful," vocals by Liddy, tinkling piano courtesy of Leary.

Two questions people always asked me about Leary were (1) was he still sane and (2) did he feel any shame for what he had done? The answers are yes and no. For a man who had spent part of his late fifties in prison, Leary was remarkably articulate and sensible. And he exhibited no shame or guilt over the hundreds of kids who had not come back from the Other World. In fact he felt that it was he who had been the responsible one, while the government, in its usual blindness, had only exacerbated the problem. When it became clear that the kids were going to use these drugs regardless of what the Establishment said, it was Leary who had attempted to provide a safety net in the form of guides and the various booklets that emerged from Millbrook. Had the government wisely taken his advice and established clinics around the country where people could have taken LSD in carefully controlled settings, then the psychedelic movement would have been nipped in the bud.

But they didn't and it wasn't and in the longer evolutionary game, Leary feels he has won. He feels he has been instrumental in turning on the largest generation America ever produced, of subtly altering its values away from materialism and destruction and toward . . . toward what, only time will tell. Certainly the variety of interests that groups itself under the rubric "the New Age" is largely an outgrowth of the psychedelic movement, although just as an oak is much more than the seed it springs from, the New Age is far more complex and impressive than anyone could have guessed back in 1967, when the hippies thought they were creating a new world with nothing more than love and LSD. Yes, sitting in the hot Hollywood sun, Tim Leary exudes an air of paternal accomplishment. By 1988, he told me, the Baby Boomers will have Washington in the palms of their hands, and they won't accept shoddy government just as they won't settle for "bad sex, bad dope or anything less than Gloria Vanderbilt's signature on their jeans."

It is only when you meet Leary that you finally understand just how persuasive a combination his intelligence, charm, and enthusiasm can be. There is something in the man's personality that shortcircuits skepticism. Perhaps it was loss of fluids due to the LA sun, but I found myself cheerily assenting to his image of an enlightened Baby Boom saving first the Republic and then the world.

In my sober moods, I didn't believe this for a second. In fact I found it equally possible that history would prove Sidney Cohen correct. Cohen had warned that Tim was skimming the cream of a generation and leading them down a blind alley. While the Best and the Brightest were grooving on the cosmic, the second-rate and the venal were appropriating the traditional slots of power.

Cohen was certainly correct to the extent that many who took the LSD trip never returned. By which I don't mean they died. The total number of people who died due to LSD during the Sixties is much less than what alcohol brings us in one week. Nevertheless the shroud of death hangs over the psychedelic era, due partly to a small number of overpublicized deaths, but largely, I think, to the fact that something did die, something that was subtler than the organic body, something that the burned-out hippie with his glazed eyes and dated slang exemplified in the extreme.

Perhaps what I am talking about is simply what happened when the old conditioning was wiped away before a really good replacement had been found. The hippies, the acidheads, were left dangling in limbo, conscious for the first time that for every inch of territory gained, every iota of consciousness expanded, an equal amount had been lost.

One couldn't, for example, after a serious immersion in LSD, go back to the 9-to-5 world of sales managers and upward mobility. Better to work for yourself, doing something simple and useful, which was why so many hippies became entrepreneurs, farmers, craftspeople. For most, the psychedelic experience dealt a serious blow to their desire for power, and all those buttresses to the power urge that go by the name ambition. Suddenly they had nothing to motivate them, particularly when they backed away from the rigors of the ancient pursuit of Mammon. They lacked an alternative structure. Indeed it is from this void, this need to find a way of life apart from the either/or of rampant materialism or secluded mysticism, that the New Age movement has derived much of its vigor.

Another way to get at what I'm talking about is to consider LSD's effect on the imagination. What at first was a stimulus, a supercharging, became over time a dulling: the visions caused by these drugs were so wondrous that they rendered everything else petty and slight. For a novelist, whole novels would happen in rippling, instant, fantastic, mind-whacking fictions. Yet when you tried to capture them, they evaporated. This, it seems to me, is what happened to Kesey. Writing became too pedestrian, too slow—it could never approach the dazzle of his LSD visions. And although he thought he saw a way out of this impasse through the creation of a new psychedelicized art form, Kesey's grasp fell tantalizingly short of this reach. And when he came back to earth he realized that in reaching for the heights, he had sacrificed his desire (if not his talent) to be a novelist. Never again could he write the smooth marketable fictions that fill the bookshelves every fall and spring. Instead he retired to Oregon, purchased a farm, and set out to build a life that would balance what he had learned beyond the Door with what he had to do to stay healthy and sane in the second half of the twentieth century.

No, the outcome of Leary's evolutionary game is still in the balance. As is LSD's ultimate legacy among those who embraced its message. The conventional wisdom these days is that LSD was an important transformational technology—"It is impossible to overestimate the importance of psychedelics as an entry point drawing people into other transformational technologies," writes Marilyn Ferguson in *The Aquarian Conspiracy,* her survey of the New Age. "For tens of thousands of left-brained engineers, chemists, psychologists and medical students the drugs were a pass to Xanadu, especially in the 1960s"—but one that has now been superseded by safer and more responsible techniques.

Of course Leary no longer sees himself as a drug guru either—that was just a role he played, at first for his own amusement, and then because his fans and detractors expected it of him. Aware that many of the adepts blame him for LSD's loss as a legitimate scientific tool, he has even gone so far as to admit that perhaps the "Huxley-Heard-Barron elitist position was ethologically correct and that the Ginsberg-Leary activism was naively democratic . . ." These days he characterizes himself as a "humanist scientist of the 21st Century" and is resolutely elitist where the new psychedelics are concerned.

Science is something few people think of when they hear Leary's name, although that is how he began, and perhaps how he will end. We forget that at those moments when he wasn't stirring the cauldron of cultural ferment, Tim could be found in his study, trying to balance what he had experienced using LSD with what he knew about the brain.

The model he finally came up with divided the brain into eight circuits, or minibrains, four in the left hemisphere and four in the right. Each circuit imposed its own paradigm on the kind of information it filtered out of mind-at-large. Thus the first circuit, that of bio-survival, saw the world totally in terms of life and death, trust and suspicion. The second circuit was the emotional circuit, followed by the dexterity-symbolism circuit and the socio-sexual circuit. With the exception of alcohol, drugs played no part in the first four circuits, but this changed when you crossed to the right brain. According to Leary, marijuana activated the sixth circuit, the neurosomatic circuit; mescaline and psilocybin accessed the neuroelectric circuit; LSD was the specific door into the neurogenetic circuit; and the eighth, the neuro-atomic circuit, was reached by Vitamin K.

Of course Leary wasn't the only model builder to come out of that short-lived period of open psychedelic research; he was just the most audacious and frequently the most difficult to understand. It was fundamental to Leary's temperament that his Big Picture enthusiasms tended to overshadow his command of Little Picture details; his model of the unconscious was freighted with borrowings from the cutting edge of genetics and quantum physics, gray areas that were barely understood by their own pioneers. The result was less model than metaphor.

A contrasting picture of what the unconscious looked like was put forth by Robert Masters and Jean Houston in their exhaustive examination of 206 LSD subjects, *The Varieties of Psychedelic Experience.* Sifting their data, Masters and Houston arrived at a four-tiered model of the unconscious: (1) the sensory; (2) the recollective-analytic; (3) the symbolic; (4) the integral.

The first layer, the sensory, was described as a storehouse of "vivid eidetic images brilliantly colored and intricately detailed . . . the images are most often of persons, animals, architecture, and landscapes. Strange creatures from legend, folklore, myth . . ."

Immediately beneath the sensory level was another storehouse, the recollective-analytic, which was the familiar domain of psychotherapy. Using LSD, Masters and Houston had no problem guiding almost all of their 206 subjects into these top two realms. But after that, progress was difficult. Only a fifth of their sample was able to descend to level three, the symbolic. Here things resembled Jung's archetypes—"the symbolic images," wrote Masters and Houston, "are predominantly historical, legendary, mythical, ritualistic and 'archetypal.' The subject may experience a profound . . . sense of continuity with evolutionary and historic process. He may act out myths and legends and pass through initiations and ritual observances often seemingly structured precisely in terms of his own most urgent needs . . . Where the symbolic dramas unfold, the individual finds facets of his own existence revealed in the person of Prometheus or Parsifal, Lucifer or Oedipus . . ."

But of the forty who penetrated to the symbolic level, only eleven were able to go still further, attaining the integral, which Masters and Houston described as "a confrontation with the Ground of Being, God . . . Essence or Fundamental Reality."

It is difficult to understand how the work of Masters and Houston, of Myron Stolaroff and Oscar Janiger, of the dozens of other legitimate researchers, could have been ignored by the therapeutic community, but it was. In fact, it was more than ignored: when the backlash against psychedelics began in the media and on Capitol Hill, the therapeutic community fell all over itself in its eagerness to denounce the LSD work as bad science, and the researchers who had been involved in it as charlatans. A curious, almost Kafkaesque situation arose whereby those who knew the most about psychedelics were relegated to the sidelines of the debate, while those who knew the least were elevated to the status of "expert." And what followed was truly bad science, with politics and the laboratory reinforcing the worst sides of each.

The professional careers of a lot of adepts were damaged, if not destroyed, during this period, and it is difficult for them not to feel bitterness either toward Leary, or the hippies, or toward their colleagues who made sure they were henceforth excluded from the funding cycle that feeds Big Science. But what really galls them is that when the government took away their tools, it left them in a state of suspended curiosity. None of the hundreds of questions raised by psychedelics, many of them fundamental to the way the mind processes information, have been answered. Rather, the powers that be have performed a holding action comparable to the one the Papal Curia tried with Galileo, when they confined him to a house in Arcetri and forbade him the right to continue his research.

But if the history of science teaches us anything, it is that uncomfortable data cannot be swept under the rug indefinitely. Galileo, we know, was not silenced; his manuscripts were smuggled out and published after his death, laying the groundwork not just for the science of astronomy, but for experimental physics in general. Similarly, since the death of the psychedelic movement, the "bad science" of the LSD researchers has been resurrected in the guise of a new branch of psychology, transpersonal psychology.

If anyone personifies this transition, it is the Czechoslovakian emigré Stanislav Grof, who, besides being one of the founders of transpersonal psychology, was also one of the leading psychedelic researchers during the sixties. Grof began working with LSD in 1954 in Prague. He came to the U.S. in 1967 for what he thought was a one-year sabbatical to work with the psychedelic therapy team assembled by Albert Kurland at Spring Grove Hospital, in Catonsville, Maryland (*As of this writing, Kurland is the only researcher with an active IND for LSD research, although his proposals are routinely denied funding), but when the Russians invaded Czechoslovakia, he decided to seek asylum.

"There was no problem with LSD in Prague," Grof told me during my visit to Esalen, where he is now a resident scholar. "The problem was how to report the states that were happening. For example, Freud was on the proscribed list, so you had to be careful not to make it appear that it had something to do with psychoanalysis. And you had to be careful not to mention any mystical states—Marxism and religion, that would have been the end."

Ironically, Grof found the Western sciences to be just as culture-bound. When LSD was removed from the therapeutic armamentarium, Grof was left with a wealth of often contradictory and confusing data— some five thousand sessions' worth—from which he has constructed a model of inner space similar to that of Masters and Houston, but with several notable differences.

Like Masters and Houston, Grof found that his LSD subjects passed through four layers of experience. The first was the fairly trivial display of images and colors that Masters and Houston had called the sensory and Grof the aesthetic, followed by the traditional domain of psychotherapy, which Grof refers to as the psychodynamic as opposed to Masters and Houston's recollective-analytic. But at this point the two models diverge. Grof believes that the brain stores biographical information in what he calls COEX (condensed experience) systems, which are linked by single themes such as humiliation, violence, or love. Using LSD as a "mental amplifier," it is possible to examine these COEX systems, until, after a few dozen excursions, the next level is reached, the one Grof calls the perinatal.

The perinatal is the most unusual and potentially revolutionary feature of Grof's model. Although it contains all of the symbolic features described by Masters and Houston, Grof ascribes an unusual source to these symbols: the physical experience of birth. What Grof suggests, to borrow a bit of Tim Leary's vocabulary, is that the actual physical voyage from the comfort of the womb through the constricting uterus and up into the light forms a primary imprint that operates as an organizing principle for much of the unconscious. Grof believes he has identified four different constructs—he refers to these as basic perinatal matrices (BPM)—which correspond to various stages in the physical birth process, but whose reach extends far beyond the actual biological moment. Besides "having specific emotional and psychosomatic content of their own," he writes in the recently published *Beyond the Brain,* "these matrices also function as organizing principles for material from other levels of the unconscious. From the biographical level, elements of important COEX systems dealing with physical abuse and violation, threat, separation, pain, or suffocation are closely related to specific aspects of BPM. The perinatal unfolding is also associated with various transpersonal elements, such as archetypal visions of the Great Mother or the Terrible Mother Goddess, Hell, Purgatory, Paradise or Heaven, mythological or historical scenes, identification with animals, and past incarnation experiences."

Grof describes the perinatal as an intersection between the individual self and the collective unconscious. On one side of this divide traditional psychology pertains, while on the other a new grammar is needed, one that unites the mystical tradition with the scientific insights of analysts like Jung, Reich, and Rank. Grof calls this new grammar transpersonal psychology, and although he regrets the loss of LSD as an exploratory probe, he has devised a number of nondrug techniques that seem to work about as well.

LSD was simply ahead of its time, Grof told me as we watched the surf crashing against the rocks below Esalen. It had arrived on the scene before science had any theoretical framework capable of reconciling mystical and perinatal experiences. And in the process of creating that framework, it had been lost.

Did Grof see any chance that it could be recovered?

"I'm not sure it's wise at this point in time to bring psychedelics back," he said. "The factor of who is using them is so big. People tend to do really crazy things. A tool like psychedelics is going to be tricky, it's going to be dangerous. And I don't see how you educate people."

But a few minutes later he was hopefully speculating that learner drugs like Ecstasy might point the way toward the development of a safe and comprehensive inner technology. Certainly something along that line had to occur if we were to find the solution to one of our species' central paradoxes—to wit, that while the smart monkey was capable of harnessing nuclear energy and voyaging to the stars, he was still enslaved by certain primitive emotions and instinctual drives that had run his life, and frequently ruined it, since the Stone Age.

III

My epilogue, up until this point, has occurred in a vacuum. There has been no notice of the larger world beyond the tiny subculture of the adepts, no hint that there are those who would be less than pleased by a new generation of psychedelic drugs.

But that world exists, and on May 31, 1985, the Drug Enforcement Agency announced that it was placing Ecstasy on Schedule 1, which meant that manufacturing or selling the drug would now be punishable by a possible fine of $125,000 and fifteen years in prison. In placing Ecstasy in Schedule 1, the DEA exercised its brand new emergency banning power, which allows the agency to temporarily bypass the normal round of hearings required by law when a drug is scheduled.

But those hearings still had to take place, and in anticipation the adepts began preparing a defense, gathering testimonials from therapists who had used the drug in their practice and soliciting funds to perform their own toxicity studies. This last was a crucial move, as the DEA justified its action on the grounds of a study done with MDA, a cousin of MDMA, which suggested the drug promoted some neuronal damage in test rats. The adepts even hired a law firm. The DEA was a bit nonplussed by the response. "It's the first clandestinely manufactured designer drug who got itself a lawyer and gathered so-called experts on the subject," marveled one DEA official.

As *Storming Heaven* goes to press, the MDMA hearings are still dragging on, but there is an even greater cloud on the horizon: the Designer Drug Enforcement Act. The DEA would make it illegal to manufacture any substance with a molecular similarity to any of the currently scheduled drugs. It would also require that researchers conducting private research in this area clear their activities with the Food and Drug Administration first. Should this bill pass, it would effectively criminalize the neuro-consciousness frontier.

But I sincerely doubt whether it will be the end of our story. Something Herman Hesse wrote in *The Journey to the East* comes to mind, a few paragraphs that could easily serve this book as an epigraph:

"I scorned all evasion. I told him frankly that I was a participant in that great enterprise of which he must also have heard, in the so-called 'Journey to the East' or the League expedition, or whatever it was then described as by the public. Oh yes, he smiled ironically, he certainly remembered it. In his circle of friends, this singular episode was mostly called, perhaps somewhat disrespectfully, 'the Children's Crusade.' This movement was not taken quite seriously in his circle. It had indeed been compared with some kind of theosophical movement or brotherhood. Just the same, they had been very surprised at the periodic successes of the undertaking. . . . Then, to be sure, the matter apparently petered out. Several of the former leaders left the movement; indeed, in some way they seemed to be ashamed of it and no longer wished to remember it. News about it came through very sparingly and it was always strangely contradictory, and so the whole matter was just placed aside *ad acta* and forgotten like so many eccentric political, religious or artistic movements of those postwar years. At that time so many prophets sprang up, so many secret societies with Messianic hopes appeared and then disappeared again leaving no trace.

"His point of view was clear. It was that of a well-meaning skeptic. All others who had heard its story, but had not themselves taken part in it, probably thought the same about the League and the Journey to the East. It was not for me to convert Lukas, but I gave him some correct information; for instance, that our League was in no way an off-shoot of the postwar years, but that it had extended throughout the whole of world history, sometimes, to be sure, under the surface, but in an unbroken line, that even certain phases of the World War were nothing else but stages in the history of our League; further, that Zoroaster, Lao Tse, Plato, Xenophon, Pythagoras, Albertus Magnus, Don Quixote, Tristram Shandy, Novalis and Baudelaire were cofounders and brothers of our League.

"He smiled in exactly the way that I expected."

ACKNOWLEDGMENTS

There is usually, hidden behind the scrims of any literary project, a small army of individuals without whom the production would be much less polished, if not nonexistent. This is very much the case with *Storming Heaven*. If Oscar Janiger hadn't given freely of his time and his rather astonishing archives, if Myron Stolaroff had been too busy to spend a night and a day reliving some emotionally fraught memories, if Ralph Metzner hadn't graciously mailed off his uncompleted autobiography to someone he knew only as a voice on the phone, if Tim Leary had been as difficult to reach (both physically and intellectually) as certain others who shall remain nameless—well, as I say elsewhere, you could play the what-if game forever.

It is a difficult thing (for me at least) to go poking around in the old campfires of people I've never met, and I was continually amazed at the graciousness and hospitality with which I was received. So without any further ado, and in no particular order, I would like to extend heartfelt thanks to Tim Scully, Stan Krippner, Frank Barron, Jack Downing, Nina Graboi, Gunther Weil, Michael Kahn, Jean Millay, Anne and Sasha Shulgin, Jean Stolaroff, Terrence and Kat McKenna, Stan Grof, Jeremy Tarcher, Peter Stafford, Allen Ginsberg, Walter Houston Clark, Albert Kurland, Gordon Wasson, Lisa Sleeman, the library staffs at Columbia University, UCLA, and the University of Oregon, and of course John Browner, whose contribution to this book is so complex, that even after an hour of heavy thought I still can't pin it down to a sentence or two.

Finally, a couple of bouquets to the business side of this book: first to my agent, Scott Hudson, and next to my editor, Upton Brady, who stood by this book, and stood by, and thank God was still standing by the time the manuscript finally arrived in New York.

NOTES

Prologue: An Afternoon in the Sixties

"Allen Ginsberg and Jack Weinberg . . ." San Francisco *Oracle*, Vol. 1, No. 5, np. "When the Berkeley political activists . . ." Berkeley *Barb*, Jan. 13, 1967. "the triumph of the West . . ." Godfrey Hodgson, America In Our Time, p. 293. "almost everywhere boys dress . . ." Landon Jones, *Great Expectations*, p. 69. "The centre cannot hold. . . . slouches towards Bethlehem . . ." Yeats, *Selected Poems*. "Tim Leary's a professor . . ." Jane Kramer, *Allen Ginsberg in America*, pp. 5–6. "that one big street . . ." Peter Joseph, *Good Times*, p. 133. "the madness of the place, the shouts . . ." Nicholas Von Hoffman, *We Are the People Our Parents Warned Us Against*, p. 30. "we are now entering the largest hippie colony . . ." *Saturday Review*, August 1967, p. 52. "a fantastic universal sense . . ." Hunter S. Thompson, *Fear and Loathing in Las Vegas*, p. 68. "change and elevate the consciousness of every American . . ." *New Yorker*, Oct. 1, 1966. "that everybody who hears my voice . . ." Jesse Kornbluth, ed., *Notes from the New Underground*, p. 69.

A Bike Ride in Basle

"a peculiar presentiment . . ." Albert Hofmann, *LSD: My Problem Child*, p. 14. "an uninterrupted stream of fantastic images . . ." Albert Hofmann, *Ibid.*, p. 15. "malevolent insidious witch . . ." Hofmann, *op. cit.*, p. 17. "such a silent and sudden illumination. . . ." Havelock Ellis, *Contemporary Review*, Jan. 1898, "it seems as if a series. . . ." Havelock Ellis, *Ibid.*, p. 139. "while admiring the ripe descriptive powers . . ." *British Medical Journal*, Feb. 5, 1898, p. 390. "Raymond went out and found a green branch. . . ." Harvey Wasserman, *Harvey Wasserman's History of the United States*, p. 204. "henceforth I'll take the visions on trust . . ." "all existing drugs . . ." Aldous Huxley, *Moksha*, p. 4–5. "are you certain you made no mistake . . ." Hofmann, *op. cit.*, p. 21. "mescaline intoxication is indeed a true schizophrenia . . ." Robert S. De Ropp, *Drugs and the Mind*, pp. 177–79. Delysid. Sandoz LTD. Basle, Switzerland.

The Cinderella Science

"literate America and much of illiterate America . . ." Grace Adams, *Atlantic Monthly*, 1936, p. 82. "we went together to Kurt Goldstein's seminar . . ." Jerome Bruner, *In Search of Mind*, p. 33. "so overjoyed at having a psychoneurotic tool . . ." Martin Gross, *The Brain Watchers*, p. 22. "neither a crackpot nor a foreigner . . ." *Time*, October 25, 1948, p. 69. "is there any hope . . ." *Time*, June 2, 1947, p. 74. "no anxieties, no fears . . ." *Time*, June 9, 1947. "fertile soil into which all kinds of mind twists. . . ." *Newsweek*, Jan. 20, 1947. "quiet and retiring, anxiously over conscientious . . ." *Newsweek*, Jan. 20, 1947. "alcoholism and drug addiction . . ." Eric Goldman, *The Crucial Decade*, p. 107. "contributions from all disciplines . . ." Roy Grinker, *Fifty Years in Psychiatry*, p. 30. "we are obviously very close to reproducing . . ." Aldous Huxley, *Moksha*, p. 112. "the man who discovers . . ." Oscar Janiger, personal interview. "the audience almost jumped on their chairs . . ." William Sargant, *The Unquiet Mind*, p. 70. "they felt so insulted . . ." Sargant, *Ibid.*, p. 71. "one doesn't have to know the cause of a fire. . . ." *Time*, October 25, 1948. "a vitalizing transaction . . ." Frank Barron, *Creativity and Psychological Health*, p. 72. "a rubbish heap as well as a treasure house . . ." *White Crows*, p. 150. "terrible power . . . a power that fathered . . ." *Psychology Today*, March 1973, p. 55. "the Id, which makes up most of the unconscious. . . . if they aren't pulling together . . ." *Time*, October 25, 1948, pp. 65–66.

Laboratory Madness

"we noticed predominantly. . . ." *Journal of Psychiatry*, February 1952, p. 556. "in the LSD test situation. . . ." *American Journal of Psychiatry*, June 1955, p. 884. "if I were to give you . . ." Art Kleps, Congressional Hearings, 1966. "this is serious business . . ." *The Journal of Nervous and Mental Disease*, September, 1955, p. 217. "well you know she has schizophrenia . . ." Humphrey Osmond interview. "not much less bright . . ." Osmond interview. "the chaps who had done . . . penicillin," Osmond interview. "quite the most interesting thing around . . ." Osmond interview. "no one is really competent . . ." *Hibbert Journal*, January 1953.

Intuition and Intellect

"the most intelligent writer . . ." Aldous Huxley, *A Memorial Volume*, p. 62. "far less than Aldous had learnt in a few weeks . . ." Aldous Huxley, *A Memorial Volume*, p. 17. "went on for hours relating . . ." Sybille Bedford, *Aldous Huxley* Vol II., p. 174. "without interruption until he had turnend . . ." Aldous Huxley, *A Memorial Volume*, p. 36. "nobody since Chesterton . . ." Cyril Connolly, *Enemies of Promise*, p. 53. "an astonishing reversal of thought . . ." Aldous Huxley, *A Memorial Volume*, p. 64. "my primary occupation . . ." Huxley, *Letters*, p. 784. "clear cold logic engines . . ." T. H. Huxley, *A Liberal Education and Where to Find It*,

p. 32. "Aldous possessed the key to an inviolable inner fortress . . ." Aldous Huxley, *A Memorial Volume*, p. 57. "There is, apart from the sheer grief of the loss . . ." Bedford, *Aldous Huxley* p. 47. "knowing nothing, she understands everything . . ." Sybille Bedford, *Aldous Huxley*, p. 101. "I have done an admirable short story . . ." Sybille Bedford, *Aldous Huxley*, p. 122. "a kind of freedom which might be described . . ." Aldous Huxley, *A Memorial Volume*, p. 19. "a kind of amphibious creature . . ." Aldous Huxley, *A Memorial Volume*, p. 65. "the many toned wit . . . the learning . . ." *The Times Literary Supplement*, Jan. 22, 1925; quoted book jacket, *Those Barren Leaves*, Perennial Classic. "strange and terrible. . . ." *Saturday Review*, March 15, 1947, p. 14. "knowing more than anyone I know. . . ." Oscar Janiger interview. "like a river over a vast area of knowledge . . ." Christopher Isherwood, *My Guru and His Disciple*, p. 9. "practically unreadable. . . ." Huxley, *Letters*, p. 322. "the style is formed, the specific frame . . ." *Kenyon Review*, Summer 1965. "a machine for the production of gods . . ." "mere vitality without consciousness . . ." Richard Bucke, *Cosmic Consciousness*, p. 16. "wrapped in a flame-coloured cloud . . ." Richard Bucke, *Ibid.*, p. 23. "no account of the universe . . ." William James, *Varieties of Religious Experience*, p. 288. "nature develops him to a certain point . . ." P. D. Ouspensky, *The Psychology of Man's Possible Evolution*, p. 5. "too much nirvana and strawberry jam . . ." Robert S. DeRopp, *Warrior's Way*, p. 115. "too fond of their own opinions . . ." Robert S. DeRopp, *Ibid.*, p. 115. "endow a band of research chemists. . . ." Aldous Huxley, *Moksha*, p. 9. "I am some kind of essayist . . ." *Atlantic Monthly*, July 1970, p. 104.

The Door in the Wall

"but Aldous what if we don't like him. . . . we can always be out . . ." Huxley, *Moksha*, p. 33. "You can always arrange to stay late . . ." Huxley, *op. cit.*, p. 33. "I knew you'd get along . . ." Osmond interview. "is it too much to hope . . ." Huxley, *Moksha*, p. 30. "what Adam had seen . . . eternity in a flower . . . this is how one ought to see . . ." Huxley, *op. cit.*, 17, p. 34. "If you started the wrong way. . . . so you think you know where madness. . . . No I couldn't control it . . ." Huxley, *op. cit.*, p. 57.

Out in the Noonday Sun

"the most extraordinary and significant . . ." Huxley, *Moksha*, p. 42. "shutting out most of what we should otherwise . . ." Huxley, *Doors of Perception*, p. 23. "as Mind at Large seeps . . ." Huxley, *Ibid.*, p. 26. "we can easily become the victims . . ." Huxley, *Ibid.*, p. 73. "cross a dividing ocean, and find ourselves . . ." Huxley, *Moksha*, p. 62. "an experience of estimable value . . ." *The Reporter*, March 2, 1954, p. 46. "how odd it is that writers like Belloc . . ." Huxley, *Selected Letters*, p. 701. "it took two days of intense work . . ." Huxley, *Selected Letters*, p. 704. "do work of fundamental importance . . ." Huxley, *Ibid.*, p. 718. "melt like an iceberg . . . the little man, meeting Pan . . ." Heard and Huxley talk, Oscar Janiger collection. "negative emotions, the fear which is the absence of confidence . . ." Huxley, *Heaven and Hell*, p. 110. "with tears streaming down his face . . . go toward the light . . ." Huxley, *Selected Letters*, p. 737. "those last three hours . . ." Sybille Bedford, *Aldous Huxley*, p. 187. "things keep cropping up . . ." Huxley, *Selected Letters*, p. 742. "the electroshock boys, the chloropromiziners . . ." Huxley, *Moksha*, p. 61. "conspicuously friendly way . . . Narodney, the cockroach man . . ." Huxley, *Selected Letters*, p. 761. "the mezazoic reptiles of the Ford Foundation . . ." Huxley, *Selected Letters*, p. 684. "lodging quietly at a medium-priced hotel . . ." Seattle *Post Intelligencer*, January 31, 1920. "what babes in the wood. . . ." Huxley, *Moksha*, p. 70. "some new developments might be taking place . . ." Huxley, *Letters*, p. 729. "certainly if future experiments . . ." Huxley, *Letters*, p. 780. "what came through the closed door was the realization . . ." Huxley, *Moksha*, p. 81. "temptations to escape from the central reality . . . false nirvanas . . ." Huxley, *Moksha*, p. 81. "my own view is that it would be important to break experimentation . . ." Huxley, *Ibid.*, p. 84. "about a name for these drugs . . ." Huxley, *Ibid.*, p. 107.

The Other World

"and suddenly I found myself giving birth to myself . . ." Proceedings, Josiah Macy Foundation Symposium, p. 78. "when you make contact . . ." Oscar Janiger intv. "the room is breathing . . . why don't you climb down from there . . ." Janiger intv. "without being a mathematician . . ." Anaïs Nin, *Diary*, vol. 5, p. 257. "I was taken by surprise. This was no confused. . . . . though we have been using the available research materials," Macy Symposisum, p. 11. "it is as though everything that bothered them . . ." Macy Symposium, p. 12. "the integrative experience . . . are all fused into a very meaningful episode . . ." Eisner and Cohen, *Psychotherapy with Lysergic Acid*, p. 533. "he was the sparkplug . . ." Janiger intv. "I have been born again . . . I found I was hiding behind all kinds of defenses . . ." Geoffrey Wansell, *Haunted Idol*. "we met two Beverly Hills psychiatrists . . ." Huxley, *Selected Letters*, p. 881. "our parties were meaningful and special . . ." Nin, *Diary*, Vol. 6, p. 333. "you're fortunate enough to have a natural access . . ." Nin, *op. cit.*, p. 131. "conform or else has become something of an eleventh commandment . . ." Robert Lindner, *Must You Conform*, p. 167. 'we may be very grateful that our opponents . . ." Gerald Heard Collection, UCLA. "the man who comes back through the Door . . ." Huxley, *Doors of Perception*, p. 79. "to see if God was there . . ." Christopher Isherwood, *My Guru and His Disciple*, p. 219. "every occult and far out subject under the sun . . ." Alan Watts, *In My Own Way*, p. 123. "highly improbable that a true spiritual experience . . ." Watts, *Ibid.*, p. 342. "pervasive pure light . . . when are you coming back. . . . oops I'm off again . . ." David Ebin, *The Drug Experience*, pp. 296–97. "I thought you went to all these places . . ." Myron Stolaroff interview. "radiating an enormous energy field . . ." Stolaroff interview. "was the greatest discovery . . ." Stolaroff interview. "in the relative privacy of learned journals . . ." Huxley, *Selected Letters*, p. 801. "would it not be best to let Hubbard go on his way . . ." Huxley, *Letters*, p. 843. "please ignore what I wrote . . ." Huxley, *Letters*, p. 844. "we are aware of man's fallibility . . ." Janiger collection. "if the psychologists and sociologists . . ." Huxley, *Doors*, p. 67. "a dangerously stupid idiotic thing . . ." Janiger interview. "Alan, Alan, please say something. . . . this isn't a gift . . ." Janiger interview.

NOTES

Noises Offstage

"bent in poses of adoration . . ." Marks, *The Search for the Manchurian Candidate* p. 111. "prophesy wildly, engage in feats of prodigious physical exertion . . ." Sahagun, *Historia General de las cosas de Nueva Espana.* "some saw in a vision that they would die . . ." Sahagun, Ibid. "when evening and darkness come . . ." Furst, *Flesh of the Gods,* p. 191. "pilgrims seeking the grail . . . yet never learn that he is your curandero. . . ." Furst, *Ibid.,* p. 192. "partake in the agape . . . very archetypes of beautiful form . . . mere perfect adumbrations . . ." *Life,* May 27, 1957. "I wanted to assign . . ." Hofmann, *LSD, My Problem Child,* p. 111. "mushroom man is elated . . ." Martin Seymour-Smith, *Robert Graves,* p. 476. "likes to think that his mushrooms . . . I tried to disabuse him . . ." Huxley, *Letters,* p. 825. "we have now found . . ." Wasson, *Mushrooms, Russia & History.* "I had a terribly bad cold . . . he was like a landlubber at sea . . ." John Marks, *The Search for the Manchurian Candidate,* p. 114. "eliminate the will of the person . . ." Technical Report No 331–45, U.S. Naval Technical Mission in Europe, p. 239. "biological and chemical materials . . ." CIA documents, Janiger archives. "operationally pertinent materials only . . ." Marks, p. 62. "terrible monsters with fantastic eyes . . ." Marks, p. 71. "quite possible. . . . remain secret . . ." Marks, p. 116. "research in the manipulation of human behavior . . ." CIA documents, Janiger archives. "it is pharmacologically safe . . . patients usually like the experience . . ." Proceedings, Josiah Macy Conference, April 22, 23, 24, 1959, p. 12. "obviously the language is bad, I am floundering . . . psychedelic . . . I think Dr. Osmond coined it . . ." Macy, p. 53. "they come in one day. They know they are going to take a treatment . . ." Macy, p. 59. "those who have not had the transcendental . . ." Macy, p. 61. "sound and music, visual stimuli . . ." Macy, p. 174. "I start the patient with small doses . . . 75% of the patients will get to the point . . ." Macy, pp. 114–115. "to change something in the totality of the person . . ." Macy, pp. 112.

Slouching Toward Bethlehem

"the grand inquisitor . . ." Alfred Kazin, *New York Jew.* "the Eisenhower siesta . . ." William Manchester, *The Glory and the Dream,* p. 772. "the old innate optimism . . ." John Brooks, *The Great Leap,* p. 49. "imperfect, but always improving . . ." Frederick Lewis Allen, *The Big Change,* p. 284. "what's good for our country . . ." Manchester, p. 648. "big, lush, uniform . . ." Landon Jones, *Great Expectations,* p. 39. "the suburbanites like doctors . . ." Jones, p. 41. "your future is great . . ." Jones, p. 37. "leadership came from the group . . ." Manchester, p. 578. "the psychological theory . . ." Martin Gross, *The Brain Watchers.* p. 13. "the square American, the nonneurotic . . ." Gross pp. 21–22. "any fledgling Luther . . ." Manchester, pp. 783–4. "brought into the malt shops . . ." Theodore Roszak, *The Making of the Counterculture,* p. 24. "phony and fake . . ." Jones, p. 64. "forced from without . . ." Robert Lindner, *Must You Conform,* p. 191. "The only people for me are the mad ones . . ." Jack Kerouac, *On the Road,* p. 12.

NOTES

Starving, Hysterical, Naked

"oh let's have some more . . ." Dennis McNally, *Desolation Angels,* p. 63. "I tell you that I repudiate . . ." McNally, p. 66. "his feet are flat . . ." Victor Bockris, *With William Burroughs,* p. xvii. "as a child . . ." Bockris, p. xiii. "low evil decadence . . ." McNally, p. 74. "I knew [Burroughs] was capable . . ." Gerald Nicosia, *Memory Babe,* p. 62. "the poisons of a dying culture . . ." McNally, p. 72. "a sideburned hero of the snowy west . . ." McNally, p. 89. "a slim hipped hedonist . . ." William Plummer, *Holy Goof,* pp. 39–40. "he lived right now . . ." *Memory Babe,* p. 91. "to consume anything and everything . . . that's the girl I'm going to marry . . ." *Memory Babe,* pp. 99, 103. "he had no sneer in him . . ." *Memory Babe,* p. 127. "why Jack fastened on this . . ." *MB,* pp. 127–8. "mad to live . . ." Kerouac, p. 12. "clickety pop word bursts . . ." McNally, p. 133. "the writing is dewlike . . ." McNally, p. 134. "nakedness of mind . . ." McNally, p. 167. "skid row winos . . ." *MB,* p. 213. "harking back to the hobo . . ." *MB,* p. 213 "Jack'd sit and write . . ." *MB,* p. 190. "at the lowest, beatest ebb . . ." McNally, p. 191. "no trek through virgin jungle . . ." *Yage Letters,* pp. 28–29. "he shook a little broom . . ." *Yage,* pp. 28–29. "Yage is space-time travel . . ." *Yage,* p. 47. "outwardness . . . confidence . . ." John Tytell, *Naked Angels.* "Doctor I don't think . . ." Lewis Hyde, *On the Poetry of Allen Ginsberg,* pp. 405. "ah sunflower . . ." *Paris Review* interview, Spring 1966. "I suddenly realized. . . . I've seen God . . ." *Paris Review,* Spring 1966. "the whole notion of being smarter, more psychotic . . ." Peter Manso, *Mailer,* p. 258. "fake intellectual hipster . . . name dropping bits of zen and jazz jargon . . ." Alan Watts, *Chicago Review,* Summer 1958. "even had he been able to . . ." Rick Fields, *How The Swans Came to the Lake,* p. 214. "a psychological impasse . . ." Fields, *Chicago Review,* Summer 1958. "six poets and the Six Gallery . . ." McNally, p. 203. "I saw the best minds . . ." Allen Ginsberg, *Howl.* "bringing two ends of an electric wire together. . . . Howl was the trigger . . ." *MB,* p. 261. "hold back the edges of your gowns . . ." *Howl.* "there are several poetry readings each week . . ." *New York Times Book Review,* Sept. 2, 1956. "the most powerful poem . . . it is a howl against everything . . ." *Times Book Review.* "the danger of turning into a popular entertainer. . . ." *Nation,* Feb. 23, 1957. "historic occasion . . . principal avatar . . ." McNally, p. 240. "proof of illness rather than a creation of art . . . series of Neanderthal grunts . . ." McNally, pp. 240–1. "the bulk off it is comprised . . ." *Life* magazine, November 30, 1959. "all right, all right . . ." Lenny Lipton, *The Holy Barbarians.* "I'm surprised the room didn't smell worse . . ." *Partisan Review,* Spring 1959. "undisciplined and slovenly amateurs . . ." *Partisan Review,* Spring 1959. "what they have in common is the conviction . . ." *New Republic,* Sept. 16, 1957. "were so psychotic or so crippled . . ." *Life,* Nov. 30, 1959. "all your vehement, vaporous . . ." Hyde, p. 410. "one is hip or one is square . . ." Norman Mailer, *The White Negro.* "to divorce . . . to exist without roots . . . the psychopath murders . . ." Mailer. "public officials will do well to disregard . . ." *JAMA* 127:1129, 1945. "when Yeats looked into the future . . ." Herb Gold, *Playboy,* Feb. 1958. "a great rucksack revolution . . ." Jack Kerouac, *The Dharma Bums,* p. 78. "we'd already had, by '48 . . ." Glen Burns, *Great Poets Howl,* p. 404. "that year on the literary scene . . ." Manso, p. 309.

NOTES

Wild Geese

"I had run through and beyond . . ." Tim Leary, *High Priest*, p. 283. "vacationing on research grants . . ." *HP*, p. 12. "the most beautiful woman . . ." Tim Leary, *Flashbacks*, p. 9. "who dashed in and out . . . making scenes . . ." *FB*, p. 25. "one moment of wild merriment . . ." *FB*, p. 26. "a timid, fantastically religious . . ." *FB*, p. 25. "believed the wonderful myth . . ." *FB*, p. 39. "I have always felt . . ." *FB*, p. 40. "all things joyous, frivolous . . ." *FB*, p. 26. "a figure out of Scott Fitzgerald . . ." sigh no more ladies . . . Tim Leary leaves a mashed up mashie . . ." Boston *Globe Magazine*, Nov. 29, 1970. "a wise old New Englander . . . supreme court . . ." *FB*, p. 72. "I am ill adapted to a military career . . ." *Esquire*, Oct. 1967. "an arrogant disdainer of fear-directed bourgeois conformity . . ." *High Priest*, p. 283. "one can make tape recordings . . ." Frank Barron, *Creativity and Psychological Health*. "the therapy patients . . ." *Journal of Consulting Psychology*, 19, 1955. "destroyed, his hair turned gray . . ." Barron interview. "thousands of test scores . . ." *HP*, p. 4. "I walked around Harvard square . . ." Jerome Bruner, pp. 32–33. "existential means you study . . ." *HP*, p. 13. "when he talked they would look . . ." *Psychology Today*, September 1968. "and those who heard him . . ." Art Kleps, *Millbrook*, p. 19. "when Timothy arrived . . ." Michael Kahn intv. "escape the middle class . . ." Charles Slack, *Tim Leary, the Madness of the Sixties, and Me*, p. 55. "make hybrids . . ." Slack, p. 56. "every poor Roxbury kid who ever stole . . ." Slack, pp. 53–55. "Wow! I learned more in six hours . . ." Koestler, *Sunday Telegraph*, December 3, 1961. "rush back and tell everyone . . ." *HP*, p. 8. "western literature had almost no guides . . ." *FB*, p. 42.

The Harvard Psilocybin Project

"a new scientific truth . . ." Stan Grof, *Beyond the Brain*, p. 13. "Tim was in a converted closet . . ." Weil intv. "this is no field for the faint of heart . . ." *HP*. "delighted to see that my skin . . . I felt as though . . . cosmically alive . . . the only reasonable way to live . . ." *Journal of Nervous & Mental Diseases*, 137, 1963. "taking the drug is such an overwhelming . . ." *The Reporter*, August 15, 1963. "extremely unusual in the austere and cynical . . ." Metzner mss. "too academic, too dainty British . . ." *FB*, p. 84. "crashing disagreement over the conduct of the sessions . . ." Metzner mss. "It's a bit embarrassing . . ." *Psychedelic Review* #3, 1964. "it may be that the job is one . . ." Huxley, *Letters*, p. 875. "for a while . . . the moksha medicine . . ." Aldous Huxley, *Island*, p. 173. "that's how everything of culture and beauty . . ." *FB*, p. 44. "a pretty good cover . . ." Barron intv. "our project was being contacted . . ." FB p. 46. "they are mines . . ." Gerald Heard collection, UCLA. "Timothy, you are the key figure . . ." *HP*, p. 112. "you may be right . . ." Janiger collection. "from the detached and scholarly . . ." Watts, pp. 402–403. "the secretary general . . ." *Esquire*, July 1968, p. 84. "a very mild a simple seeming cat . . . that single mysterious Thing which was our fate . . ." *Yage Letters*, pp. 56–58. "I'm the messiah . . ." *Esquire*, July 1968. "Allen, the quintessential egalitarian . . ." *FB*, p. 50. "it was at this moment . . ." *FB*, p. 50. "like he had no idea . . ." Jane Kramer, *Allen Ginsberg in America*, pp. 187–88. "something big is happening . . ." Ossmann, *Sullen Art*, p. 92. "people are beginning to see . . ." Ossmann, p. 94. "I spoke to Willem de Kooning . . ." *Esquire*, July 1968. "walking on water . . ." *FB*, p. 67. "amor vincit omnia . . ." "my work and understanding . . ." *HP*, p. 215. "big time sexual magazine . . . salaries will be vast . . . I am looking for French connection . . ." *Esquire*, July 1968. "I'm the king of the Beatniks . . ." *FB*, p. 65. "he left silently without farewell . . ." *HP*, pp. 228–29. "absolutely dazzled . . ." Michael Kahn intv. "I strongly urge you . . ." *FB*, p. 114. "I could arrange experiments . . ." *FB*, p. 112. "hedonic consciousness . . ." *FB*, p. 112. "Dave McClelland had been . . ." Michael Kahn. "a weakened ego . . ." Barron, p. 75. "I have always based my life . . ." *FB*, p. 64. "Come to bed you idiot . . ." Alpert, *Be Here Now* (unpaged). "until you know a Jewish middle-class . . ." *New Times*, Sept. 4, 1978. "charming, intelligent, witty . . . unusually sensitive. . . . it gave him great pleasure . . ." David McClelland, *Power: The Inner Experience*, p. 207. "in Palo Alto I had a job buying coffee . . ." "I wasn't a genuine scholar . . ." *BHN*. "you're too sick to leave . . ." *BHN*. "I'm just back from Europe . . ." *BHN*. "an ambitious academic politician . . ." *FB*, pp. 21, 77. "I worked hard to get that status . . ." *BHN*. "who's minding the store . . . when I could finally focus . . ." *BHN*. "we made a straight out deal . . ." Leary intv. "was easily bored . . ." *FB*, p. 126. "let's see if we can turn . . ." Metzner mss. "big cats in a zoo . . ." Metzner mss. "the loosening of thought . . . because you're a fucking mad scientist . . ." *FB*, p. 86. "a bit of pagan magic had occurred . . ." *FB*, p. 87. "the most efficient way to cut through the game structure . . ." *How to Change Behavior*, Xerox of address.

What Happened at Harvard

"I began to realize . . ." "the history of the project . . ." Xerox of McClelland memo. "it is probably no accident . . ." Xerox of memo. "Timothy is like a great director . . ." Kahn intv. "pleasurable experiences. . . . I think religions will neglect these experiences . . ." *Newsletter* #1. "the directors of the center envision . . ." Harvard *Crimson*, February 20, 1962. "I wish I could treat this as a scholarly disagreement . . ." Harvard *Crimson*, March 15, 1962. "nothing can be done to save Tim . . ." Leary intv. "the meeting ended on a note of civilized calm . . ." *FB*, p. 122. "from the date of this session . . ." *HP*, pp. 256–57. "divine rascal . . . witty multi-reality tales . . ." *FB*, p. 116. "getting involved with Hollingshead . . ." Krippner intv. "considering what he was pouring . . ." Metzner mss. "you gotta try this . . ." *FB*, p. 117. "we've lost Timothy . . ." Metzner mss. "we got snotty, we got put downy . . ." Kahn intv. "such a guileless, humorous . . ." Metzner mss. "laugh and laugh . . . he never for a moment . . ." Kahn intv. "I know that inwardly, starting at an early age . . ." Metzner mss. "we began to see ourselves as unwitting agents . . ." *Esquire*, July 1968. "the Tim Leary game . . . ontological confrontation . . . I have never recovered . . ." *FB*, p. 119. "that's antediluvian stuff . . ." Krippner intv. "the ashram itself . . ." *HP*, pp. 297–300. "on the one hand I am a shameless . . ." Alan Watts, *In My Own Way*, p. 55. "it seemed to Tim . . ." Watts, p. 406. "fresh faced gee whiz . . ." *FB*, p. 102. "weird exciting chords . . ." *HP*, p. 311. "pursuing the religious life today . . ." Tim Leary, *Politics of Ecstasy*, p. 38. "he began to turn into a mystic . . ." Walter

Houston Clark, *Chemical Ecstasy,* "wanted out of science . . ." Michael Kahn intv.

The Politics of Consciousness

"the whole damn climate changed . . ." Janiger intv. "if you want to know . . ." Janiger intv. "truth and lies and absurdity . . ." Thelma Moss, *The Body Electric,* p. 19. "you are the astronauts of inner . . ." Adam Smith, *Powers of Mind,* p. 27. "the basic molecules of the universe . . ." Smith, p. 29. "one turns in all directions . . ." Peter Mathiessen, *The Snow Leopard,* p. 44. "most were magic shows . . ." Mathiessen, p. 47. "she started to laugh . . ." Mathiessen, p. 46. "considering the enormous scope of the psychic response . . ." *Journal of Nervous and Mental Disease,* 130, 1960. "a 3-D film tape . . ." *Archives of General Psychiatry,* March 1960. "as I plummeted down . . ." Thelma Moss (Constance Newland), *Myself and I,* p. 96. "all this repressed material. . . . I must be insane . . . flakes of multi-colored snow . . ." *The Province,* Sept. 2, 1959. "did I die . . ." *The Province* Sept. 2, 1959. "one of my ex patients . . ." Stolaroff intv. "partly medical, partly scientific . . ." San Mateo *Call Bulletin,* Jan. 5, 1963. "a higher power or ultimate reality . . ." *Journal of Neuropsychiatry,* Nov–Dec, 1962. "having lost the battle . . ." *Journal of Neuropsychiatry.* "the central perception . . ." *Journal of Neuropsychiatry.* "imperishable self rather than a destructible ego . . ." *Journal of Neuropsychiatry.* "latent psychotics are disintegrating . . ." *Archives of General Psychiatry,* August, 1963. "mental and emotional equilibrium . . ." *JAMA* 185, 1963. "useful adjunct to psychotherapy . . ." *Saturday Evening Post,* September 1963. "restricted to investigators . . ." *Archives of General Psychiatry,* May 1963. "the most lasting value. . . ." Jane Dunlap (Adelle Davis), *Exploring Inner Space,* p. 206. "I traveled deep . . ." Thelma Moss, bookflap. "the best statement on the subject . . ." Alan Watts, *The Joyous Cosmology,* p. xiv. "back through the tunnels . . ." Watts, *JC,* pp. 65–67.

The Fifth Freedom

"we were swimming . . ." Gunther Weil intv. "the personal, the role . . ." IFIF literature. "the most vivid descriptions . . ." Richard Alpert, *The Only Dance There Is,* p. 114. "Oh nobly born . . ." *Saturday Evening Post,* September 1963. "this was the most exciting thing . . ." *Reporter,* August 15, 1963. "I'll help him with pleasure . . ." McClelland, *Power,* p. 209. "powerful, nonverbal, meta-intellectual . . ." Solomon, *LSD,* p. 84. "I think we're pushing the edge . . ." Stafford, *The Magic Gram.* "an anthill civilization . . . mere puppets . . ." Harvard *Crimson,* April 23, 1962. "a medical degree doesn't equip . . . control tower at La Guardia . . ." *Politics of Ecstasy* p. 72. "we're through playing the science game . . ." *Reporter,* August 15, 1963. "very tricky social and cultural dilemmas . . ." Harvard *Crimson,* October 25, 1963. "it tears my heart out . . ." Cashman, *LSD,* p. 58. "may result in serious hazard . . ." Harvard *Crimson,* November 26, 1962. "fairly persistent campaign to interest . . ." Solomon, *LSD: The Consciousness-Changing Drug,* p. 86. "a major civil liberties issue . . ." Harvard *Crimson,* Dec. 13, 1962. "an interest shown by Aldous Huxley . . ." *New York Times,* Dec. 11, 1962. "talked such nonsense . . ." Huxley, *Letters,* p. 945. "an opportunity of working . . ." Huxley, *Letters,* p. 946. "wreak havoc . . .

Tim, I am convinced . . . I suppose there is little hope . . ." Stolaroff archives. "rich people, aficionados of psychoanalysis . . ." Solomon, p. 88. "would never be without . . . abstracted look . . . quick and kindly young man . . ." Solomon, p. 88. "in my opinion . . ." Solomon, p. 78. "unspoiled by commercial civilization . . ." IFIF literature. "in 1961 we estimated . . ." *HP*, p.132. "even in the hands of Tim, the eternal juggler . . ." Michael Hollingshead, *The Man Who Turned on the World*, p. 77. "influenced by the ideas elaborated . . ." IFIF literature. "they all wear a beatnik uniform . . ." *Reporter*, August 15, 1963. "on certain days the tension . . ." Metzner mss. "they were all standing around . . ." Barron intv. "absolute allegiance to the two psychologists . . ." *Crimson*, May 28, 1963. "he was being brave about it . . ." Barron intv. Not because we're dirty boys . . ." *Reporter*, August 15, 1963. "I turned down over two hundred guys . . ." *Reporter*, August 15, 1963. "the game is about to be changed . . ." Leary, *Politics of Ecstasy*, p. 57.

Horse Latitudes

"the aim of the transpersonative . . ." IFIF lit. "all I'm saying is our consciousness linked up . . ." private interview. "tremendous heat . . ." Metzner mss. "I felt Leary had done no original work . . ." *Saturday Evening Post*, Sept. 2, 1963. "loomed Transylvanian . . ." *FB*, p. 189. "you are witnessing a good old-fashioned . . ." Leary, *P of E*, p. 48. "rivals for the title of world's worst bores . . ." *Esquire*, Sept. 1963. "licensing will be necessary . . ." *Harvard Review*, Summer 1963. "might be harmful . . ." *Harvard Review*, Summer 1963. "the siren song of expanded consciousness . . ." *JAMA*, 185, 1963. "rhapsodic talk . . . powerful and often . . ." *JAMA*, 185, 1963. "the day came when I sat . . ." *Saturday Review*, June 1, 1963. "a lady psychiatrist . . ." *Saturday Review*. "keep the children away . . ." *Saturday Review*. "we read the entire manual . . ." Laura Huxley, *This Timeless Moment*, pp. 278–79. "if I go . . . you know very well . . ." Laura Huxley, pp. 282, 284. "light and free you let go . . . like a piece of music . . ." Laura Huxley, 286–87. "rarest of alloys . . . it will be clear to all of us . . . under what heading . . ." *Psychedelic Review*, Vol. 1, #3, 1964. "to a number of his readers . . ." Bedford, *Aldous Huxley*, p. 330. "which is better . . ." David Solomon, *LSD*, p. 47. "explosive population increase . . ." Solomon, p. 47. "on the verbal level . . ." Solomon, p. 47. "the last thing I want . . ." Laura Huxley, p. 124.

Pushing the Envelope

"Jesus Christ, do I have to fuck . . ." Art Kleps, *Millbrook*, p. 19. "a golden year . . . on this space colony . . ." *FB*, pp. 190. "unparalleled ugliness . . ." *Reporter*, May 19, 1966. "strange mutation of Thoreau's Walden . . ." *Newsweek*, May 19, 1966. "anthropologists from the 21st century . . ." *FB*, p. 190. "it became apparent . . ." *Psychedelic Review* #4. "we did a lot of sitting . . ." Metzner mss. "in the evolutionary sense . . ." IFIF newsletter. "it was my destiny to join . . ." Hesse, *Journey to the East*. "a group of perfectly respectable . . ." Kleps, p. 16. "making your own bed . . . better, more lively . . ." Kleps, pp. 23, 33. "like a ghost . . . scare the living piss . . ." Kleps, pp. 27. "Frank Merriwhether type . . . how can I make more . . ." Kelps, p. 51. "jazz musicians, avant garde . . ." Metzner mss. "Christ it's crazy up there . . ." "Tim is anything more important than anything . . ." Kleps, pp. 25–26. "you realize this is a very reckless conversation . . ." Leary, *P of E,* p. 165. "now, after fighting their way . . ." *Newsweek,* July 27, 1964. "girls in bikinis . . ." *Newsweek,* July 27, 1964. "the straights . . ." Hollingshead, p. 88. "I had seen perhaps twenty of them . . ." Kleps, p. 71. "we are very much affected . . ." Metzner mss. "LSD takes you out . . ." Robert Anton Wilson, *Cosmic Trigger,* p. 21. "the most important rule . . ." Wilson, p. 27. "we are shocked . . ." *FB,* p. 197. "our days pass . . ." Stolaroff archives. "an avid concert and ballet goer . . ." Slack, p. 27. "in my ways I was like . . ." *FB,* p. 206. "treating the ceremony as high camp . . ." *FB,* p. 206. "this morning I sat . . ." Metzner mss. "the incredible complexities . . . like whispering in your lover's ear . . ." Metzner mss.

The Boy Most Likely to Succeed

"hard shell baptists . . . root hungry . . ." "big rebellious cowboy . . ." *Genesis West* 3, nos. 1–2, p. 40. "a boy has to know he can . . ." *Genesis West,* p. 27. "one of the prettiest . . ." Tom Wolfe, *Electric Kool-Aid Acid Test,* p. 23. "in every high school . . ." *Saturday Review,* May–June, 1983. "a single Batman comic book . . ." *Genesis West,* p. 20. "I want to find out which side of me . . ." *Genesis West,* p. 27. "He had Jack London . . ." Wolfe, p. 31. "that old Zorba the Greek . . ." Wolfe, p. 31. "a thousand years from now . . ." *Genesis West.* "like a young Viennese analyst . . ." Wolfe, p. 36. "bad scene stuff . . . intended to demonstrate. . . ." *Genesis West.* "suddenly I was shifted over . . ." Peter Joseph, *Good Times,* p. 384. "managed the night mopping . . ." *Garage Sale,* p. 12. "came more easily to my hand . . ." *Garage Sale,* p. 7. "when you start fooling around with dope. . . ." Joseph, p. 385. "the man whom the other young rebels . . ." Stephen Tanner, *Ken Kesey,* p. 12. "it's the oldest living thing . . ." San Francisco *Chronicle,* July 21, 1963. "it was there that I first felt . . ." *The Free You,* no. 15, October 1968. "just when you're starting . . ." Wolfe, p. 54. "worldly failure was along Cassady's . . ." Plummer, pp. 110–11. "started to recapitulate . . ." Plummer, p. 129. "one of the quickest. . . ." Plummer, p. 129. "was to be as afraid . . ." Plummer, p. 132. "careening, corner-squealing . . ." Plummer, p. 129. "we got so we could be right there . . ." "like a great hearted. . . ." Wolfe, p. 56. "it was as though somebody . . ." Wolfe, p. 12. "New Orleans was a relief . . ." Wolfe, p. 79. "they were all deep into . . ." Wolfe, p. 111. "a towering redwood . . . tiresome literary disaster . . ." Wolfe, p. 91.

Turn and Face the Strange

"Cassady doesn't have to think . . ." Jonathan Eisner, *Unknown California,* p. 123. "there was the tantalizing idea . . ." Scully intv. "after two successful novels . . ." "Michael Strelow, *Ken Kesey,* p. 96. "there were no ground rules . . ." Wolfe, p. 146. "this steam, I can actually . . ." Wolfe, p. 16. "there was a feeling in the air . . ." Hunter Thompson, *Hells Angels,* p. 230. "a bad effect on the neighbors . . ." Thompson, p. 232. "that must have tortured . . ." Thompson, p. 233. "in the land of Oz . . . the real Hells Angels . . ." Freewheeling Frank, *Freewheeling Frank,* pp. 73–74. "contrary to all expectation . . ." Thompson, p. 238. "that goddamned Ginsberg . . ." Thompson, p. 250. "on behalf of myself . . ." Thompson, p. 257. "vague haphazard slow death . . ." Lewis Hyde, *On the Poetry of Allen Ginsberg,* p. 238. "no more mental universe arguments . . ." Hyde, p. 238. "a large black-bird . . ." Hyde, p. 241. "it seems that everybody . . . these things which must be condemned . . ." Hyde, pp. 244–45. "the central casting office . . ." Kramer, p. 16. "marchers should bring Crosses . . ." Berkeley *Barb,* Nov. 19, 1965. "in the huge wooden house . . ." Ken Kesey, *Garage Sale,* p. 213. "sunny disposition . . ." LA *Free Press,* September 17, 1965. "these were peaceful, beautiful people . . ." LA *Free Press,* September 17, 1965. "we thought we had a few more years . . ." Stafford, *The Magic Gram.* "with all the senses open . . ." Wolfe, p. 8. "they had film and endless . . ." *Rolling Stone,* Jan. 20, 1972. "you can freak out in there . . ." *Rolling Stone,* Jan. 20, 1972. "thousands of people . . ." "once the music stops it becomes . . ." Robert Sam Anson, *Gone Crazy and Back Again,* p. 52. "wasted four years . . ." "anything I know about organization . . ." *Rolling Stone,* Dec. 13, 1969. "look at it go right into the sun . . ." San Francisco *Chronicle,* Jan. 21, 1966. "a bust, a bore, a fake . . ." San Francisco *Chronicle,* January 24, 1966. "the place was jammed . . ." *Chronicle,* Jan. 24. "it was like we were all born . . ." Leonard Wolf, *Voices of the Love Generation,* p. 228. "we'll let him . . ." San Francisco *Chronicle,* January 27, 1966. "if it weren't that your record until now . . ." San Francisco *Chronicle,* Jan. 18, 1966.

In the Zone

"when two dogs fight . . ." *The Reporter,* May 19, 1966. "fifty years old have lost . . ." *P of E,* p. 103. "I saw mattresses on the floor . . ." *The Reporter,* May 19, 1966. "sleeping or waking . . ." *The Reporter.* "what's death but the end . . ." *FB,* p. 209. "suddenly I understood . . ." *FB,* p. 211. "in recent years . . ." *FB,* p. 214. "you are the predictable . . ." *FB,* p. 215. "one day that made . . ." Metzner mss. "act as a sort of amplifier . . ." Metzner mss. "was probably as close . . ." Metzner mss. "it is time that I tell . . ." *FB,* p. 221. "the key to personal evolution . . ." *FB,* p. 213. "limped back to Millbrook . . ." *FB,* p. 224. "a playground for rowdy . . ." *FB,* p. 224. "lying naked and freaked . . ." Slack, p. 28. "reincarnated in Scottish kilts . . ." Metzner mss. "ridiculous waste of LSD . . ." Metzner mss. "people were constantly looking . . ." *Be Here Now.* "you are a natural born comedian . . ." Hollingshead, p. 115. "could jeopardize an enviable . . ." Hollingshead, p. 115. "the height of folly . . . how I reacted . . ." *FB,* pp. 225–26. "the first step . . . the second step . . . the third step . . . welcome to an experiential weekend . . . please do not engage . . ." Hollingshead, pp. 130–34. "they think they've fallen . . ." Hollingshead, p. 136. "contemplate the wonders . . ." Hollingshead, p. 138. "I'd wake up to see Tim . . ." Nina Graboi memoirs. "Tim said nothing at all . . ." Hollingshead, p. 117. "in the dream . . ." Metzner mss. "there are 3000 Americans . . ." *P of E,* p. 121. "a blue ribbon panel . . ." Cashman, *LSD,* p. 74. "I'm going to jail . . ." Barron intv. "I've charted my . . ." *P of E,* p. 116. "wondered idly if she was . . ." *FB,* p. 229. "find a house with a white . . ." *FB,* p. 234. "that were to change my legal . . ." *FB,* p. 236. "Timothy is the most . . ." Alpert letter. "lysergic acid hits the spot . . ." *FB,* p. 251. "the First

Amendment . . ." *New York Times,* March 18, 1966. "outwardly he still . . ." Metzner mss. "creative energies were being subverted . . ." Martin Garbus, *Ready for the Defense,* p. 288. "I'll do anything to drive . . ." Garbus, p. 279. "studded with natural . . . ecstatic sessions . . . unless the voyager . . ." Castalia brochure. "the aim is to make Millbrook . . ." Castalia brochure. "it ain't no dirty movie . . ." G. Gordon Liddy, *Will,* p. 109. "Oh they're busting . . . I'm afraid the closest you'll come . . ." Liddy, pp. 113–15.

Psychotic Reaction

"in spite of lurid statements . . . long hair beatnik . . ." White House Conference on Narcotics, 1963. "the disease is striking . . ." *Time,* March 11, 1966. "tone of the most common . . ." Congressional Hearings, May 1966. "already psychologically deranged . . ." Congressional Hearings, May, 1966. "cases of attempted rape . . ." LA *Times,* July 12, 1966. "only when you sensationalize a subject . . ." Rufus King, *The Drug Hangup,* p. 294. "the sprawled body of a young girl . . . it was an unprovoked crime . . ." Harry Ainslinger, *Marijuana: Assassin of Youth.* "man I've been flying for three days . . ." *Time,* April 22, 1966. "both students and members of the faculty . . ." Young and Hixon, *LSD on Campus,* p. 17. "middle-aged underachievers, stale artists . . ." LA *Times,* May 4, 1966. "they are life's losers . . ." *Time,* March 11, 1966. "I'm sure you'll agree that this young lad . . ." Congressional Hearings. "we have seen something which in a way . . ." Congressional Hearings, Senate Subcommittee of Organization and Coordination, 1966, p. 147. "how should one evaluate the outcome . . ." *JAMA,* 187:758, 1964. "there is no published evidence . . ." *New England Journal of Medicine,* Dec. 2, 1965. "for Sandoz to be so timorous . . ." *Science,* July 8, 1966. "summer of one-way correspondence . . ." *Science,* Nov. 18, 1966. "in the hope that it will tell . . ." Young and Hixson, p. 99. "just as hypnosis . . ." LA *Times,* June 19, 1966. "everything you hear about LSD is nonsense . . ." LA *Times,* June 19, 1966. "radiating light in white chinos . . ." *Newsweek,* June 27, 1966. "the most carefully prepared . . ." Stolaroff letter. "are you really called a boo hoo . . . on the day the prison doors close . . ." Kleps, pp. 122, 125. "I believe that the criteria . . ." Congressional Hearings. "and what is going to happen . . . are we going to have high school courses . . . I would let research . . ." Congressional Hearings. "I do not say we should stop . . ." "our social duty now . . ." San Francisco *Chronicle,* June 17, 1966. "I don't know what more we could want . . ." Stolaroff letter. "I looked at the paper I was to draw on . . ." Stolaroff archive. "who's using the cards he's got . . ." Stafford. "let me put it this way . . ." *P of E,* pp. 106–107.

The Counterculture

"the authority has operated . . ." Norman Mailer, *Armies of the Night,* p. 103. "enough young people have been beaten . . ." *Commonweal,* July 14, 1967. "torn open, everything boiling . . ." Michael Rossman, *The Wedding Within the War,* p. 93. "one minute Clark Kerr . . ." Godfrey Hodgson, *America in Our Time,* p. 295. "intellectual lumpen proletariats . . ." Rossman, p. 127. "the effect is to inhibit . . ." Rossman, p. 155. "we ate terrible . . ." Rossman, p. 122. "young kids want to be heroes . . ." J. Anthony Lukas, *Don't Shoot-We Are Your Children,* p. 362. "like I'd gone to Cuba . . ." Lukas, p. 357. "but into . . . something else . . ." Rossman, p. 76. "you're playing their game . . ." Wolfe, pp. 197–98. "we have a private revolution going on . . ." Charles Perry, *The Haight Ashbury,* p. 20. "even if you lived elsewhere . . ." Hank Harrison, *The Dead,* p. 45. "taking it was like being in a secret . . ." C. Perry, p. 7. "hard kicks is a way of looking . . ." Leonard Wolf, *Voices of the Love Generation,* p. 260. "acid opens your door, opens the window . . ." Wolfe, p. 221. "drop down into your unconscious . . ." Wolfe, p. 46. "God has fingered that little block . . ." Wolf, p. 11. "I fell in with some vibrational . . ." Wolf, p. 5. "we went out and asked . . ." Wolf, p. 225. "I read *Time* magazine . . ." Wolf p. 216. "I'm from another race . . ." Nicholas Von Hoffman, *We Are the People . . .,* p. 132. "the Teddybear you see . . ." Von Hoffman, p. 52. "that one big street . . ." Peter Joseph, *Good Times,* p. 133. "an anthill, where all the ants . . ." Wolf, p. xlvi. "it engages the entire sensorium . . ." Jesse Kornbluth, *Notes from the New Underground,* pp. 77–79. "oddball cult groups . . . acidheads . . ." *Time,* March 11, 1966. "you've got to straighten out your own . . ." San Francisco *Oracle,* January 13, 1967. "if all the negroes . . ." *P of E,* p. 117. "technology had produced . . ." Kornbluth, p. 67.

The Alchemist

"a cocky little guy . . . strange wound-up nasal voice . . ." Wolfe, p. 186. "I've studied with . . ." *P of E,* p. 231 "almost like a brainchild . . ." *High Times,* February 1979. "just a little boy . . ." LA *Times,* October 3, 1966. "moving in boxes . . ." *Rolling Stone,* November 25, 1982. "has a theory . . ." *Rolling Stone,* November 25, 1982. "there was something disinterested . . ." *Rolling Stone,* November 25, 1982. "taken the full LSD trip . . ." *P of E,* p. 231. "he was only four miles . . ." LA *Times,* October 3, 1966. "love to Melissa . . ." Narcotic Rehabilitation Act of 1966, Alfred Tremblay testimony, May, 1966. "devastatingly strong . . ." *Rolling Stone,* Nov. 25, 1982. "a regular retinue . . ." *Rolling Stone,* Nov. 25, 1982. "Owsley's theory was that . . ." Metzner mss. "the government would be terrified . . ." Tim Scully intv. "Owsley felt that . . ." Scully intv. "incredibly addictive . . ." Scully intv. "I felt real strongly . . ." Scully intv. "we would get about 10 . . ." Scully intv. "there was a very helpful . . ." Scully intv. "we decided San Jose . . ." Scully intv.

The Next Step

"the text floats up the page . . ." *Editor and Publisher,* Nov. 11, 1967. "a poetic invocation . . ." Gene Anthony, *The Summer of Love,* p. 59. "money lust is sickness . . ." ComCo bulletin. "how long will you tolerate . . ." Digger handout. "salt in J. Edgar Hoover's wounds . . ." Wolfe, p. 327. "to warn his young followers . . . he wants to tell them . . ." San Francisco *Chronicle,* October 22, 1966. "Tsong-Isha-pa . . ." Wolfe, pp. 27–28. "I don't know what this is going to be . . ." Wolfe, p. 339. "never trust a prankster . . ." Wolfe, p. 340. "like every great religion . . ." *New York Times,* Sept. 20, 1960. "oh that's your trip . . ." Metzner mss. "turn on means . . ." *New York Times,* Sept. 20, 1966. "religioso gimmicks . . ." *Time,* Sept. 30, 1966. "Leary and I had many a run-in . . . taking acid . . ." Abbie Hoffman, *Soon to Be a Major Motion Picture,* pp. 90–91. "It seemed that a brilliant . . . Tim was . . ." Anton Wilson, p. 41. "I fully expect . . ." Anton Wilson, p. 41. "atheists attending . . ." *New York Times,* Sept. 21, 1966. "a weary impresario . . . having a blueprint for change . . . when he takes the microphone . . . it creates the illusion . . . young, Village, but middle-class." *Encounter,* June 1967. "simply casualties of the new . . ." *Encounter,* June, 1967. "an initiate into this new society . . ." Helen Perry, *The Human Be-In,* pp. 85, 86. "Yeah but next time . . ." Anthony, p. 135. "the night of bruited fear . . ." Anthony, p. 155. "a living fever dream . . . all the high priests . . ." San Francisco *Chronicle,* Jan. 14, 1967. "this generator is now protected . . ." Berkeley *Barb,* Jan. 20, 1967. "the Hells Angels have . . ." Helen Perry, p. 87. "peace in your heart . . . this is it . . ." *Barb,* Jan. 20, 1967. "we want to get Western man . . ." *Barb,* Jan. 20, 1967. "what if we're all wrong . . ." "In 7 or 8 years . . ." LA *Free Press,* Jan. 1967. "brought around to a more profound . . ." Kornbluth, p. 143. "they are repeating . . ." Kornbluth, p. 141. "a lot of freak-out hippies . . ." Kornbluth, p. 144. "the plastic robot establishment . . . I can envision . . ." Kornbluth, pp. 148, 150 "like we gotta learn to do a lot of things . . ." Kornbluth, p. 150. "it's run like a beehive . . ." Kornbluth, p. 156. "the children of the ants . . ." Kornbluth, p. 158. "I'm going to continue . . ." Kornbluth, pp. 184–85. "fiddle around with . . ." Kornbluth, p. 185.

It Came From Inner Space

"Dear Diggers . . ." Berkeley *Barb,* Feb. 10, 1967. "instead of sickly exploiting . . ." ComCo bulletin. "dresses like Tarzan . . ." Don McNeil, *Moving Through Here,* p. 154. "a filthy litter-strewn . . ." *Look,* August 22, 1967. "considerably more virtuous . . ." *Time,* July 7, 1967 "they are a rootless community . . ." *Christian Century,* August 16, 1967. "perfect cultural broth . . ." *Nation,* June 10, 1967. "psychological numbing . . . our experiences . . ." *Drug Awareness,* pp. 116, 123. "I am strongly opposed . . ." San Francisco *Chronicle,* March 24, 1967. "the situation is not as bad . . ." *Chronicle,* March 24, 1967. "all spring the Haight . . ." Rossman, p. 209. "part old Calcutta . . ." C. Perry, p. 173. "abstract vortex . . ." Wolf, p. x1. "pretty little 16 . . ." Wolf, p. x1i. "that was the point . . ." *Rolling Stone,* Jan. 20, 1972. "only foreign tour . . ." *Saturday Review,* August 19, 1967. "middle-class brothers . . ." Von Hoffman, p. 130. "his hair was very short . . ." W.I. Thompson, *At the Edge of History,* p. 46–47. "it's coming so fast . . ." Metzner mss. "their own genius . . ." Von Hoffman, pp. 40–41. "I saw myself on fire . . ." *New York Times,* July 2, 1967. "I felt I had lost . . ." Don McNeil, *Moving Through Here,* p. 74. "forgot something . . ." Stephen Tanner, *Ken Kesey,* p. 100. "This wasn't a summer of love . . ." Washington *Post,* October 21, 1967. "I think it might be a good idea . . ." Von Hoffman, pp. 97–98. "Hippie in the Haight . . ." McNeil p. 147. "the remains . . ." McNeil, p. 148. "if you're going to San Francisco . . ." Words & music by John Phillips.

Too Many Gurus

"I've dropped out completely . . ." *Look,* August 8, 1967. "become the most popular . . ." LA *Times,* Feb. 5, 1967. "each of you is the Buddha . . ." LA *Times,* Feb. 5, 1967. "will be an LSD country . . ." Roszak, p. 168. "beauty is dandy . . ." *Look,* August 8, 1967. "he may mislead . . ." *Look,* August 8, 1967. "I've always thought . . ." Gustaitis, *Turning On,* p. 95. "like a boat one uses . . ." Rick Fields, p. 252. "we thought there was more . . ." Norman, *Shout,* p. 404. "I had come from . . ." *BHN.* "I wasn't happy and I wasn't sad . . ." *BHN.* "the little scientist . . ." *BHN.* "if a pickpocket meets . . ." *BHN.* "the Mr. Big . . ." *Rolling Stones's The Sixties,* p. 182. "put a fancy name on it . . ." Brotherhood of Eternal Love trial. "first come the children . . ." Slack, p. 46. "I am going to start . . ." Slack, p. 69. "I love this world . . . I'll bet you're on personal terms . . . every one . . ." Slack, p. 143. "you're joking . . ." Slack, p. 144. "this is my world . . ." Slack, p. 143. "it did indeed sadden . . ." Metzner mss. "insidious menace . . . pleasure seeking . . ." *New York Times,* March 22, 1970. "49 going on . . ." *New York Times,* March 22, 1970. "would they poke me down . . ." *FB,* p. 295.

Epilogue: An Afternoon in the Eighties

Note: due to the tenuous legality of the activities described in this chapter, many of my conversations were private, and will remain so. "pure LSD ingested in moderate doses . . ." *Science* 172:1971. "on K I can look across. . . ." John Lilly intv., *Omni,* Jan. 1983. "vivid eidetic images . . . the symbolic images . . . a confrontation with the ground of being . . ." Masters and Houston, *The Psychedelic Experience,* pp. 143, 156; 147, 214. "having specific emotional . . ." Stan Grof, *Beyond the Brain,* p. 101. "I scorned all evasion . . ." Herman Hesse, *A Journey to the East,* pp. 53–54

BIBLIOGRAPHY

Abramson, Harold A. (editor). *The Use of LSD in Psychotherapy.* New York: Josiah Macy, Jr., Foundation Publications, 1960.

Abramson, Harold A. (editor). *The Use of LSD in Psychotherapy and Alcoholism.* New York: Bobbs-Merrill, 1967.

Allen, Frederick Lewis. The Big Change. New York: Harper & Brothers, 1952.

Alpert, Richard (Ram Dass). *Be Here Now.* San Cristobal, New Mexico: Lama Foundation, 1971.

Alpert, Richard, Cohen, Sidney, and Schiller, Lawrence. *LSD.* New York, New American Library, 1966.

Alpert, Richard (Ram Dass). *The Only Dance There Is.* Garden City, New York: Anchor Books, 1974.

Anson, Robert Sam. *Gone Crazy and Back Again.* New York: Doubleday, 1981.

Anthony, Gene. *The Summer of Love.* Millbrae, California: Celestial Arts, 1980.

Bedford, Sybille. *Aldous Huxley, A Biography.* New York: Alfred A. Knopf, 1975.

Blum & Associates. *Utopiates.* New York: Atherton Press, 1964.

Bockris, Victor. *With William Burroughs.* New York: Seaver Books.

Boisen, Anton. *The Exploration of the Inner World.* New York: Harper Torchbook, 1962.

Braden, William. *The Private Sea: LSD and the Search For God.* New York: Bantam, 1968.

Bruner, Jerome. *In Search of Mind.* New York: Harper Colophon, 1983.

Burns, Glen. *Great Poets Howl: A Study of Allen Ginsberg's Poetry, 1943–1955.* New York: Peter Lang, 1983.

Burroughs, William S. *The Job.* New York: Grove Press, 1974.

Caldwell, W. V. *LSD Psychotherapy.* New York: Grove, 1968.

BIBLIOGRAPHY

Carey, James T. *The College Drug Scene.* Englewood Cliffs, New Jersey: Prentice-Hall, 1968.

Clark, Walter Houston. *Chemical Ecstasy.* New York, Sheed and Ward, 1969.

Clarke, Arthur C. *Childhood's End.* New York: Ballantine Books, 1971.

Cohen, Sidney. *The Beyond Within.* New York: Atheneum, 1965.

Connolly, Cyril. *Enemies of Promise.* New York: Persea Books, 1983.

Cook, Bruce. *The Beat Generation.* New York: Charles Scribner's Sons, 1971.

DeBold, Richard, and Leaf, Russell. *LSD, Man & Society.* Watertown, Connecticut: Wesleyan University Press, 1967.

De Ropp, Robert S. *Drugs and the Mind.* New York: Grove Press, 1961.

De Ropp, Robert S. *Warrior's Way.* New York: Dell, 1979.

Dickstein, Morris. *Gates of Eden.* New York: Basic Books, 1977.

Didion, Joan. *Slouching Toward Bethlehem.* New York: Simon and Schuster, 1979.

Ebin, David. *The Drug Experience.* New York: Grove Press, 1961.

Eszterhas, Joe. *Nark.* San Francisco: Straight Arrow Books, 1974.

Farber, Thomas. *Tales for the Son of My Unborn Child.* New York: E.P. Dutton & Co., 1971.

Finlator, John. *The Drugged Nation.* New York: Simon and Schuster, 1973.

Furst, Peter. *Flesh of the Gods.* New York: Praeger, 1972.

Ginsberg, Allen. *Allen Verbatim.* New York: McGraw-Hill, 1975.

————. *Howl and Other Poems.* San Francisco: City Lights, 1956.

————, and Burroughs, William, *The Yage Letters,* San Francisco: City Lights, 1956.

Grinspoon, Lester. *Psychedelic Drugs Revisited.* New York: Basic Books, 1979.

Grinspoon, Lester. *Psychedelic Reflections.* New York: Human Sciences Press, 1983.

Grof, Stanislav. *Beyond the Brain.* Albany, New York: State University of New York, 1985.

Grogan, Emmett. *Ringolevio.* New York: Avon, 1972.

Gross, Martin L. *The Brain Watchers.* New York: New American Library, 1963.

Gustaitis, Rasa. *Turning On.* New York: Macmillan, 1962.

Harrison, Hank. *The Dead.* Millbrae, California: Celestial Arts, 1980.

Heinlein, Robert A. *Stranger in a Strange Land.* New York: Avon, 1967.

Hersh, Burton. *The Mellon Family: A Fortune in History.* New York: William Morrow, 1978.

Hesse, Herman. *The Journey to the East.* New York: Noonday, 1965.

Hodgson, Godfrey. *America in Our Time.* New York: Vintage, 1978.

Hoffman, Abbie. *Soon to Be a Major Motion Picture.* New York: Perigee Books, 1980.

Hofmann, Albert. *LSD: My Problem Child.* Los Angeles: Tarcher 1983.

BIBLIOGRAPHY

Hollingshead, Michael. *The Man Who Turned on the World.* London: Blond & Briggs, 1973.

Horman, Richard E., and Fox, Allen M. *Drug Awareness.* New York: Avon, 1970.

Huxley, Aldous. *The Doors of Perception and Heaven and Hell.* London: Penguin, 1961.

———. *The Doors of Perception.* New York: Perennial Library, 1970.

———. *Island.* New York: Perennial Classic, 1972.

———. *Letters of Aldous Huxley* (ed. Grover Smith). New York: Harper & Row, 1969.

———. *Moksha.* Los Angeles: Tarcher, 1982.

———. *Perennial Philosophy.* New York: Harper Colophon, 1970.

———. *Tomorrow and Tomorrow and Tomorrow.* New York: Signet, 1964.

Julian Huxley (ed.). *Aldous Huxley—A Memorial Volume.* New York: Harper & Row, 1965.

Huxley, Laura. *This Timeless Moment.* New York: Ballantine, 1971.

Hyde, Lewis. *On the Poetry of Allen Ginsberg.* Ann Arbor: University of Michigan Press, ND.

Isherwood, Christopher. *My Guru and His Disciple.* New York: Penguin, 1981.

James, William. *The Varieties of Religious Experience.* New York: New American Library.

Jones, Landon. *Great Expectations.* New York: Coward, McCann & Geohegan, 1980.

Joseph, Peter. *Good Times.* New York: William Morrow, 1974.

Kazin, Alfred. *New York Jew.* New York: Vintage, 1979.

Kesey, Ken. *Ken Kesey's Garage Sale.* New York: Viking, 1973.

———. *One Flew Over the Cuckoos Nest.* New York: Viking, 1962.

Kleps, Art. *Millbrook.* Oakland: The Bench Press, 1975.

Kramer, Jane. *Allen Ginsberg in America.* New York: Random House, 1969.

Laski, Margharita. *Ecstasy.* New York: Greenwood Press, 1968.

Leary, Timothy. *Changing My Mind, Among Others.* New Jersey, Prentice-Hall, 1982.

———. *Flashbacks.* Los Angeles: Tarcher, 1983.

———. *High Priest.* Cleveland: World Publishing Company, 1968.

———. *The Politics of Ecstasy.* England, Granada Publishing, 1973.

Lee, Martin A., and Shlain, Bruce. *Acid Dreams.* New York: Grove Press, 1986.

Lindner, Robert. *Must You Conform.* New York: Grove Press, 1961.

Louria, Donald. *The Drug Scene.* New York: Bantam, 1970.

Lukas, J. Anthony. *Don't Shoot—We Are Your Children!* New York: Random House, 1971.

Mairowitz, David Zane. *The Radical Soap Opera.* New York: Avon.

Manchester, William. *The Glory and the Dream.* Boston: Little, Brown, 1974.

Manso, Peter. *Mailer: His Life and Times.* New York: Simon and Schuster, 1984.

Marks, John. *The Search for the Manchurian Candidate.* New York: Times Books, 1979.

Masters, R. E. L., and Houston, Jean. *The Varieties of Psychedelic Experience.* New York: Holt, Rinehart & Winston, 1966.

Matthiessen, Peter. *The Snow Leopard.* New York: Viking, 1978.

McClelland, David. *Power.* New York: Irvington, 1975.

McNally, Dennis. *Desolate Angel.* New York: McGraw-Hill, 1980.

McNeil, Don. *Moving Through Here.* New York: Lancer Books, 1970.

Metzner, Ralph. *The Ecstatic Adventure.* New York: Macmillan, 1968.

Metzner, Ralph. *Opening to Inner Light.* Los Angeles: Tarcher, 1986.

Moss, Thelma. *The Body Electric.* Los Angeles: Tarcher, 1982.

Newland, Constance. *Myself and I.* New York: New American Library, 1962.

Nicosia, Gerald. *Memory Babe.* New York: Grove Press, 1983.

Nin, Anaïs, *The Diary of Anais Nin.* New York: Harcourt Brace Jovanovich, 1966.

Norman, Philip. *Shout.* New York: Warner Books, 1982.

Nuttall, Jeff. *Bomb Culture.* New York: Dell, 1968.

Ossman, David. *The Sullen Art.* New York: Corinth Books, 1963.

Ouspensky, P. D. *The Psychology of Man's Possible Evolution.* New York: Bantam, 1968.

Perry, Charles. *The Haight-Ashbury.* New York: Rolling Stone Press, 1984.

Perry, Helen Swick. *The Human Be-In.* New York: Basic Books, 1970.

Plummer, William. *The Holy Goof.* Englewood Cliffs, New Jersey: Prentice-Hall, 1981.

Pope, Harrison, Jr.. *Voices from the Drug Culture.* Boston: Beacon Press, 1974.

Reynolds, Frank. *Freewheelin' Frank.* New York: Grove, 1968.

Rossman, Michael. *Wedding Within the War.* New York, Doubleday, 1971.

Roszak, Theodore. *The Making of a Counter Culture.* New York: Anchor Books, 1970.

Sale, Kirkpatrick. *SDS.* New York: Vintage, 1973.

Sargant, William. *The Unquiet Mind.* Boston: Atlantic-Little, Brown, 1967.

Schrag, Peter. *Mind Control.* New York: Pantheon, 1978.

Seymour-Smith, Martin. *Robert Graves.* New York: Holt, 1983.

Slack, Charles W. *Timothy Leary, The Madness of the Sixties, and Me.* New York: Peter H. Wyden, 1974.

Smith, Adam. *Powers of Mind.* New York: Random House, 1975.

Smith, David, Luce, John, *Love Needs Care.* Boston, Little, Brown, 1970.

Solomon, David, LSD: *The Consciousness-Expanding Drug*, New York, Berkeley Medallion, 1966.

Stafford, P.G., and Golightly, B. H. *LSD: The Problem-Solving Psychedelic.* New York: Award Books, 1967.

Stafford, Peter. *Psychedelics Encyclopedia.* Los Angeles: Tarcher, 1983.

Stern, Jess. *The Seekers.* New York: Bantam, 1970.

Strelow, Michael. *Ken Kesey.* Eugene, Oregon: Northwest Review Books, 1977.

Sturgeon, Theodore. *More Than Human.* New York: Ballantine Books, 1983.

Thompson, Hunter. *Fear and Loathing in Las Vegas.* New York: Random House, 1971.

———. *Hells Angels.* New York: Ballantine, 1966.

Von Hoffman, Nicholas. *We Are the People Our Parents Warned Us Against.* New York: Quadrangle, 1968.

Watts, Alan. *In My Own Way.* New York: Vintage, 1973.

———. *The Joyous Cosmology.* New York: Vintage, 1962.

Weil, Andrew. *The Natural Mind.* Boston: Houghton Mifflin, 1972.

Wiener, Jon. *Come Together: John Lennon in His Time.* New York: Random House, 1984.

White, John. *Frontiers of Consciousness.* New York: Avon, 1974.

Wilson, Robert Anton. *Cosmic Trigger.* New York: Pocket Books, 1977.

Wolf, Leonard. *Voices from the Love Generation.* Boston: Little, Brown, 1968.

Wolfe, Tom. *The Electric Kool-Aid Acid Test.* New York: Bantam, 1981.

Yablonsky, Lewis. *The Hippie Trip.* New York: Pegasus, 1968.

Young, Warren and Hixon, Joseph, *LSD on Campus.* New York: Dell, 1966.

U.S. Government Reports:

Drug Safety. Hearings before a Subcommittee of the Committee on Government Operations, House of Representatives, March 9, 10; May 25, 26; June 7, 8, 9, 1966.

The Narcotic Rehabilitation Act of 1966. Hearings before a Special Subcommittee of the Committee on the Judiciary, United States Senate, January 25–27; May 12, 13, 19, 23, and 25; June 14–15; July 19, 1966.

Organization and Coordination of Federal Drug Research and Regulatory Programs: LSD. Hearings before the Subcommittee on Executive Reorganization of the Committee on Government Operations, United States Senate, May 24–26, 1966.